Airport Planning & Management

2nd Edition

Alexander T. Wells, ED.D

TAB Books
Division of McGraw-Hill, Inc.
Blue Ridge Summit, PA 17294-0850

Portions of this text were drawn from a special report entitled Airport System Development prepared by the Office of Technology Assessment in August, 1984.

SECOND EDITION
THIRD PRINTING

© 1992 by **TAB Books**.
First edition © 1986 by **TAB Books**.
TAB Books is a division of McGraw-Hill, Inc.

Library of Congress Cataloging-in-Publication Data

Wells, Alexander T.
    Airport planning & management / by Alexander T. Wells.—2nd ed.
        p.   cm.
    Includes bibliographical references and index.
    ISBN 0-8306-3086-4
        1. Airports—Planning. 2. Airports—Management. I. Title.
    II. Title: Airport planning and management.
    TL725.3.P5W45   1992
    387.7'36—dc20   92-783
                                                           CIP

Acquisitions Editor: Jeff Worsinger
Book Editor: Norval G. Kennedy
Director of Production: Katherine G. Brown
Series Design: Jaclyn J. Boone
Cover: Holberg Design, York, Pa.
Cover Photo: Artist's rendering of the Pittsburgh International Airport
                Midfield Terminal by Tasso Katselas Associates, Inc. Project
                Architect and General Consultant

Photo credits:
Smithsonian Institution, 3
Federal Aviation Administration, 35, 215, 271
Miami International Airport, 61
Reynolds, Smith & Hill, 79, 107, 249
Pascoe Building Systems, 173
Port of Seattle, 189, 293, 349
Delta Air Lines, 317

Contents

Acknowledgments vi

Preface vii

PART 1. INTRODUCTION

1
CHAPTER

The airport-airway system   3
The formative period   5
The national airport plan   8
Postwar federal aid to airports   12
Airport and Airway Development Act of 1970   16
Airport development in the 1980s   23
Concluding remarks: Assessment of Federal Airport Policy   25

2
CHAPTER

The airport system   35
Introduction   36
Classification of airports   40
The economic role of airports   44
Current issues in airport system development   47
Airport information sources   54

3
CHAPTER

Airport system planning   61
Introduction   62
The planning process   64
Need for integration among plans   74

PART 2. PLANNING AND FUNDING THE AIRPORT

4
CHAPTER

Airport requirements and site selection   79
Introduction   80
Inventories   81
Forecasting   86
Demand/capacity analysis   94

Environmental impact study   96
Site selection   99

5
CHAPTER
Airport layout and land use plans   107
Introduction: Phase three of the master plan   108
Airport layout plan   109
Approach and clear zone report   130
Land use plan   132

6
CHAPTER
Terminal area and airport access plans   139
Introduction: Continuation of phase three   140
Terminal area plans   142
Airport access plans   167

7
CHAPTER
Financial planning   173
Financial plan   174
Airports in the municipal bond market   181

PART 3. MANAGING GROWTH

8
CHAPTER
Airport capacity and delay   189
Introduction   190
Capacity, demand, and delay   191
Factors affecting capacity and delay   194
Measuring delay   196
Approaches to reducing delay   198

9
CHAPTER
Airside technological improvements   215
Introduction   216
Airport and airspace technology   218
Guidance, surveillance, and control   220
Airspace use procedures   227
Weather and atmospheric effects   233
Noise control and abatement   236
Airport surface utilization   240

10
CHAPTER
Landside technological improvements   249
Introduction   250
Terminal facilities and services   251

Landside access 259
Applications of technology to airport problems 264

PART 4. THE MANAGEMENT PROCESS

11
CHAPTER

Financial management 271
Airport accounting 272
Planning and budgeting 276
Approaches to financial management at commercial airports 278
Pricing of airport facilities and services 283
Trends in airport financial management since deregulation 289

12
CHAPTER

Organization and administration 293
Airport ownership and operation 294
The airport organization chart 296
Airport management as a career 306
The airport manager and public relations 309

13
CHAPTER

Airport operations 317
Pavement maintenance 318
Snow removal 324
Safety inspection program 329
Bird hazards 332
Crash, fire, and rescue 333
Security 338
Ground support equipment 341

14
CHAPTER

Airport relations with tenants and the public 349
The airport as landlord 350
Liability insurance 356
Aircraft noise 358

Glossary 367

Abbreviations 397

Study guide 401

Index 493

To my wife Mary

———

The wind beneath my wings
for 30 years.

———

Out of respect and love.

Acknowledgments

I am sincerely appreciative of the many public and private institutions that have provided resource material from which I was able to shape this text. In this regard, I am particularly indebted to the Federal Aviation Administration for their numerous publications.

To the many students at Broward Community College and Embry-Riddle Aeronautical University who reacted to material in *Airport Planning & Management*, I owe a special thanks, because they represent the true constituency of any textbook author.

My appreciation is extended to the fine people at TAB Books, including Jeff Worsinger, Lisa Black, Steve Bolt, Kimberly Martin, Sherry Hill, and the late Bill Worsinger, whose encouragement got me started on the first edition back in 1984.

Special thanks to Joni and Julie Williams for fast and accurate typing with numerous revisions and deadline dates.

Preface

The second edition of *Airport Planning and Management* retains the objectives of original text: First, to provide a solid treatment of the major elements in the process of planning and managing airports; and second, to demonstrate how this process is being applied to the dynamic post-deregulation era. I believe that professors want students not only to describe what is, but also to know why things are and how they are applied. This text is sufficient to achieve those results.

Recognizing that a course in airport planning and management is normally a student's first exposure to the field, the book is introductory, not exhaustive. In this regard, I have been influenced considerably by my experience of 20 years in teaching aviation management courses. The text has been designed to introduce the student to the subject including the major elements in the planning process and managerial and operations functions carried on at an airport. An appropriate balance of depth and breadth of subject matter is considered based upon my judgment of the needs of the average college student taking this course.

Students are encouraged to explore and keep abreast of current periodicals such as *Airline Executive, Airport, Airport Services Management, Air Transport World, Aviation Week & Space Technology*, and *Commuter Air*. It is hoped that the ability to reason accurately and objectively about problems facing airports and the development of a lasting interest in airport management and operations will be two valuable by-products of the text's basic objectives.

The text has been critically reviewed, updated, and revised where appropriate. Clear and interesting communication has been a priority, as it was in the first edition. Smooth structure and flow of the material coupled with careful explanations and a focus on the principles continue to be my major writing objective. It is anticipated that professors will supplement the basic material covered with current applications drawn from their own experiences and timely articles and reports.

Several key revisions have been incorporated in the second edition. All statistics, charts, and tables have been updated. I have revised the first three chapters, updating the historical perspective through the 1980s and the airport system planning process in light of the new FAA National Plan of Integrated Airport Systems (NPIAS). Other areas in the text have been revised to bring the discussion up-to-date. A student study guide with more than 750 objective questions has been added as a separate appendix to the second edition.

Characteristics of this text

This text employs a number of features that are designed to facilitate student learning:

△ *Chapter Outlines*. Each chapter opens with an outline of the major topics to be covered.

△ *Chapter Objectives*. After the outline, each chapter includes the broad objectives that the student should be able to accomplish upon completing the chapter.

△ *Relevance*. Most of the examples, applications, and extensions of the basic material are drawn from and apply to the environment of airport planning and management of the 1980s and early 1990s.

△ *Staying Power*. The text is designed to have staying power over the years. It emphasizes the basic functions and practices that will not change appreciably over time.

△ *Figures, Tables, and Exhibits*. Important points in each chapter are illustrated with strong visual materials.

△ *Logical Organization and Frequent Headings*. The material covered here has been put in a systematic framework so that students know where they have been, where they are, and where they are going in the text. Part 1 of the text introduces the student to the airport-airway system including its structure and historical perspective. Part 2 includes the major elements in the master planning process. Part 3 provides alternatives to expanding existing and building new airports through better utilization. Part 4 focuses in on the organization and management of airports. Frequent headings and subheadings aid organization and readability.

△ *Key Terms*. Each chapter concludes with a list of key terms used in the text.

△ *Review Questions*. Review questions at the end of each chapter cover all of the important points.

△ *Suggested Readings*. A list of suggested readings is included after all chapters for students who wish to pursue the material covered in greater depth.

△ *Glossary of Airport Terms*. All key terms appearing at the end of each chapter, as well as many other terms used in the text and others of significance in airport planning and management, are included in the glossary.

△ *Study Guide*. A guide including more than 750 multiple choice, true/false, and fill-in questions.

△ *Complete Index*. The book includes a complete index to help the student find needed information.

Organization of the text

The following is an outline of *Airport Planning and Management*.

Part 1   Introduction

1. The *airport-airway system: A historical perspective* provides a historical sketch of the airport-airway system including the federal legislation that has affected its growth and development. The chapter concludes with an assessment of federal airport policy.

2. *The airport system* provides a review of the structure of the system including the type and number of airports in the United States. The economic importance of airports is covered along with a discussion of current issues and factors affecting the airport system.

3. *Airport system planning* concludes the introductory part with a review of the planning process from the national, regional, state, and local levels. The objectives of the local airport master plan are covered and coordination at all levels of planning is stressed.

Part 2   Planning and funding the airport

4. *Airport requirements and site selection* covers the first two phases of the airport master planning process. The first phase includes an inventory of existing facilities, socioeconomic factors, and community values. This is followed by a discussion of forecasts needed and methods of forecasting. Demand/capacity analysis and the environmental impact study round out the first phase. The second phase concentrates on the factors affecting site selection.

5. *Airport layout and land use plans* includes the third phase of the airport master plan. The airport layout plan is thoroughly explored followed by a complete discussion of all airside facilities. The remainder of the chapter covers the approach layout plan including FAR Part 77 and land use planning on and around the airport.

6. *Terminal area and airport access plans* is a continuation of the third phase, with a focus on landside facilities. Terminal area plans are analyzed in depth including design concepts and passenger handling systems. Facility requirements for the air carriers, concessionaires, and others are examined, along with the planning steps involved in determining space requirements. The critical subject of airport access plans rounds out the discussion under this chapter.

7. *Financial planning* is the last chapter under part 2 and completes the fourth and final phase of the airport master plan. The financial plan includes an economic evaluation of the entire plan of development. A comprehensive review of financing methods is included followed by a discussion of airports in the municipal bond market.

Part 3   Managing growth

8. *Airport capacity and delay* is the first of three chapters dealing with the problem of how to cope with growth in air travel by utilizing the existing system more efficiently. Part 3 presents an alternative to expanding and/or building new airports. This chapter defines the growing problem of capacity and delay and discusses the causal factors. Various approaches to reducing delay are completely examined, including diversion of traffic, restriction of access by aircraft type, quotas, differential pricing, and slot allocations.

9. *Airside technological improvements* introduces the student to a number of approaches designed to improve airside efficiency. All of the new technological advances either planned or presently being installed are thoroughly covered.

10. *Landside technological improvements* concludes the discussion on managing growth by focusing in on the landside technological improvements designed to improve capacity and reduce delay.

Part 4   The management process

11. *Financial management* is unquestionably one of the most important functions of management. This chapter examines the revenue and expense areas in a typical airport. The residual-cost approach and the compensatory approach to financial management are covered in depth. Other areas

covered include pricing of airport facilities and services and trends in financial management since deregulation.

12. *Organization and administration* introduces the student to the various types of airport ownership and operation including governmental, multi-purpose port authority, and airport authority. This is followed by a comprehensive review of the organizational structure of a typical commercial airport including a description of the job responsibilities for key management personnel. The chapter concludes with a discussion of career opportunities in airport management and the important role that the airport manager plays in public relations.

13. *Airport operations* consists of the day-to-day operational concerns of management. Major areas of discussion in this chapter include pavement maintenance, snow removal, safety inspection, bird hazards, crash, fire and rescue (CFR), security, and ground support equipment. Many excellent articles appearing in the trade magazines can be used to supplement and complement the subjects in this chapter.

14. *Airport relations with tenants and the public.* One of the important functions of airport management is that of serving as a landlord. The primary responsibilities of management in their relations with the air carriers, concessionaires, and members of the general aviation community are covered in this chapter. The airports' liability exposure is reviewed, including coverages afforded under the basic airport premises liability policy. Chapter 14 concludes with a thorough discussion of one of the major problem areas facing management, that of noise. This discussion includes federal responsibilities, measurement of noise, noise and land use, and local noise abatement programs.

Part 1
Introduction

The airport-airway system: a historical perspective

Outline

The formative period
The National Airport Plan
Postwar federal aid to airports
Airport and Airway Development Act of 1970
Airport development in the 1980s
Concluding remarks: Assessment of federal airport policy

Objectives

When you have completed this chapter you should be able to:

△ Recognize the importance of the Post Office Department in establishing the early airmail routes.

△ Discuss the significance of the Kelly Act of 1925; the Air Commerce Act of 1926.

△ Explain how the Bureau of Air Commerce was established.

△ Describe the purpose of the Civil Aeronautics Act of 1938.

△ Explain how the Civil Aeronautics Administration was established.

△ Summarize the role of the federal government in providing airport aid during World War II.

△ Highlight several of the important recommendations made by a select committee in 1944 that led to the Federal Airport Act of 1946.

△ Discuss the purpose and major features of the Federal Airport Act of 1946.

△ Describe the events leading up to passage of the Federal Aviation Act of 1958.

△ Explain the role of the Department of Transportation.

△ Distinguish between the Airport and Airway Development Act of 1970 and the Airport and Airway Revenue Act of 1970.

△ Discuss some of the important amendments under the Airport and Airway Development Act of 1976.

△ Give an assessment of Federal Airport Policy from pre-World War I days through the early 1990s.

The formative period

When the Wright brothers succeeded at Kitty Hawk on December 17, 1903, in man's first flight, the place from which they took off could hardly be called an airport. It was, however, ideally suited for the requirements of the Wright Flyer. With the invention of the airplane, it naturally followed that such a machine had to have a place to take off, land, be repaired, and eventually fueled: an airport.

Historically, the development of civil airports has been an intricate meshing of military, commercial, and private activity. Construction and maintenance of airports was, in general, considered a local responsibility, in contrast to the development of the airway system, which the federal government regulated from the start. Although records indicate that there were operational airports as far back as 1909, for the most part they were indistinguishable from local athletic fields, parks, and golf courses.

By 1912, there were 20 recognized airports in the country, all of which were privately owned and operated. With the outbreak of World War I, civil airport development ceased and all new airports were military. Sixty-seven additional airports were built during the war, but only 25 remained operational following the war.

Early airmail service

The first regular airmail route in the United States was established on May 15, 1918, between New York City and Washington, D.C. The service was conducted jointly by the United States War Department and the Post Office Department. The War Department furnished the planes and pilots and performed the operation and maintenance, and the Post Office Department attended to the sorting of the mail and its transportation to and from the airport and the loading and discharge of the planes at the airports. This joint arrangement of the War and Post Office Department was continued until August 12, 1918, when the Post Office Department took exclusive responsibility for the development of the mail service on a larger scale of operations.

Communities suddenly became aware of the importance of having an aerial connection to the rest of the country. By 1920, there were 145 municipally owned airports and the nationwide airport system was beginning to form. Domestic airmail service grew considerably during the period between 1918 and 1925. Facilities for air transportation had been established, and the desirability of continued direct government operation or private operation under contract with the government was widely discussed. The policy of the United States government in the intercity transportation of mail had traditionally been to arrange with railroads, steamship lines, and other means for its long-distance transportation.

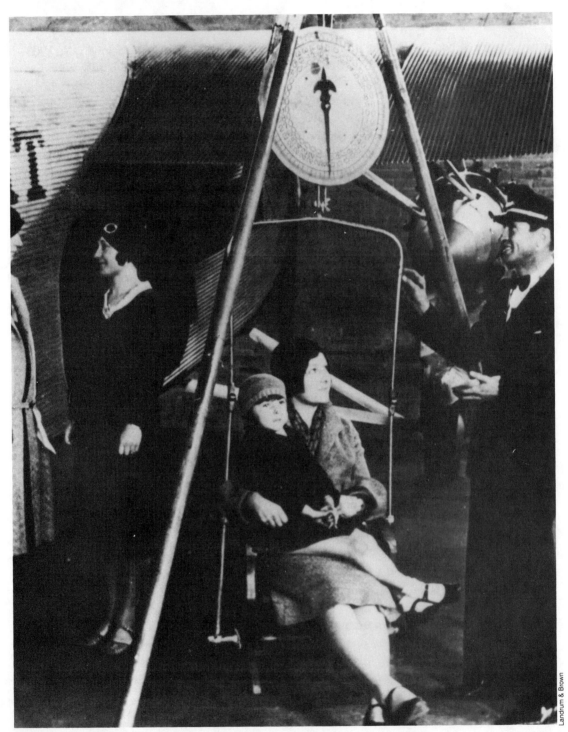

Passengers weigh in prior to departure from Chicago Midway Airport in 1927.

The next stage in the development of the service was ushered in by the Contract Air Mail Act of 1925, the so-called *Kelly Act*, which authorized the postmaster general to enter into contracts with private persons or companies for the transportation of the mail by air. Contracts were let for a number of feeder and auxiliary main lines during 1925 and 1926, and for the portions of the transcontinental airmail route during 1927.

Development of the airway system

On May 20, 1926, President Coolidge signed the *Air Commerce Act of 1926* into law. The object of the Air Commerce Act was to promote the development and stability of commercial aviation in order to attract adequate capital into the business and to provide the fledgling industry with the assistance and legal basis necessary for its growth. The act made it the duty of the secretary of commerce to encourage air commerce by establishing civil airways and other navigational facilities to aid aerial navigation and air commerce.

The regulation of aviation provided for in the act included the licensing, inspection, operation of aircraft; the marking of licensed and unlicensed aircraft; the licensing of pilots and of mechanics engaged in aircraft work; and the regulation of the use of airways.

Pilots for National Air Transport, one of the companies that would later become United Airlines, preparing for departure from Chicago Midway Airport in 1927.

In July 1927, a director of aeronautics was appointed, who, under the general direction of the assistant secretary of commerce for aeronautics, was in charge of the work of the Department of Commerce in the administration of the Air Commerce Act. By November 1929, because of the increasing volume of work incident to the rapid development of aviation, it was necessary to decentralize the organization. Three assistants and the staffs of employees of the divisions under their respective jurisdictions were assigned to the assistant secretary of commerce for aeronautics. These included a director of air regulation, a chief engineer of the airways division, and a director of aeronautics development to assist in aeronautical regulation and promotion. The organization was known as the Aeronautics Branch of the Department of Commerce.

The work was further reassigned by executive order of the president in 1933 so as to place the promotion and regulation of aeronautics in a separately constituted bureau of the Department of Commerce. An administrative order of the secretary of commerce provided for the establishment of the *Bureau of Air Commerce* in 1934. The bureau consisted of two divisions, the division of air navigation and the division of air regulation.

A revised plan of organization for the Bureau of Air Commerce, adopted in April 1937, placed all the activities of the bureau under a director, aided by an assistant director, with supervision over seven principal divisions: airway engineering, airway operation, safety and planning, administration and statistics, certification and inspection, and regulation.

From 1926 until 1938, the federal government was prohibited by the Air Commerce Act of 1926 from participating directly in the establishment, operation, and maintenance of airports; however, in response to the Great Depression, the Civil Works Administration—from the fall of 1933 up until it was superseded by the Federal Emergency Relief Administration (FERA) in April of 1934—spent about $11.5 million establishing 585 new airports, mostly in smaller communities. The FERA spent its appropriation on 943 airport projects, mostly in smaller cities, with 55 new airports receiving aid.

In July 1935, the Works Progress Administration (WPA) took over the federal airport development work. Under the WPA, there was an emphasis upon spending on the larger airports and projects were of a more permanent nature. Under the WPA, about half of the expenses for material and equipment was borne by the sponsors; the remainder, including labor, was supplied by the federal government.

The National Airport Plan

On June 23, 1938, the *Civil Aeronautics Act of 1938* was approved by President Roosevelt. This act substituted a single federal statute for the several general and airmail statutes that had up to this time provided for the regulation of the aviation industry. It placed all the functions of air and regulation of aviation and air transportation in one authority. The new act created an administrative agency consisting of three partly autonomous bodies. The five-man Civil Aeronautics Authority was principally concerned with economic regulation of air carriers; the Air Safety Board was an independent body for the investigation of accidents; and the administrator concerned himself with construction, operation, and maintenance of the airway system.

The personnel, property, and unexpended balances of appropriations of the Bureau of Air Commerce of the Department of Commerce was transferred to the new Civil Aeronautics Authority. The transfer of the responsibilities of the Bureau of Air Commerce to the CAA, effected in August 1938, under the provisions of the act, brought to a close a 12-year period during which the development and regulation of civil aeronautics were under the jurisdiction of the Department of Commerce.

Reorganization of the CAA in 1940

During the first year and a half of its existence, a number of organizational difficulties arose within the Civil Aeronautics Authority. As a result, President Roosevelt, acting within the authority granted to him in the Reorganization Act of 1939, reorganized the Civil Aeronautics Authority and created two separate entities, the *Civil Aeronautics Board* (CAB) and the *Civil Aeronautics Administration* (CAA). The five-man authority remained as an independent operation and became known as the Civil Aeronautics Board; the Air Safety Board was abolished and its functions given to the Civil Aeronautics Board; and the administrator became the head of an office within the Department of Commerce known as the Civil Aeronautics Administration. The duties of the original five-man authority were unchanged, except that certain responsibilities, such as accident investigation, were added because of the abolishment of the Air Safety Board. The administrator, in addition to retaining his functions of supervising construction, maintenance, and operation of the airways, was required to undertake the administration and enforcement of safety regulations, and the administration of the laws with regard to aircraft operation. Subsequently, the administrator became directly responsible to the secretary of commerce. The term *CAA*, which originally meant Civil Aeronautics Authority, became the Civil Aeronautics Administration.

Early federal aid to airports—the war years

Section 303 of the Civil Aeronautics Act of 1938 authorized the expenditure of federal funds for construction of landing areas provided the administrator certified "that such landing area was reasonably necessary for use in air commerce or in the interests of national defense." War broke out in Europe in September 1939, which prompted Congress in 1940 to appropriate $40 million for *Development of Landing Areas for National Defense* (DLAND).

Under DLAND, the monies were spent by the Civil Aeronautics Administration, with the approval of the secretaries of war, commerce, and the Navy, for not more than 250 airports necessary for the national defense. Actually, in 1941, work was started on some 200 airports, and an additional 149 were added to the program later in the year. Under this program, government subdivisions furnished the land and agreed to operate and maintain the improved field, and the essential landing facilities were developed by federal funds. This program was coordinated with the work and funds of the other federal programs engaged in airport construction and improvement.

In 1940, the Army Air Corps started expansion, with the result that the previously mentioned program for the improvement of 399 civil airports soon became inadequate to provide the proper dispersion of fields and interceptor bases. The program expanded to comprise 504, then 668, and then a total of 986 airports that received aid under the war emergency.

During the war years the federal government, through the CAA, spent $353 million for the repair and construction of military landing areas in the continental United States. This does not include funds spent by the military agencies. During the same period, the CAA spent $9.5 million for the development of landing areas in the United States solely for civil purposes.

Many of the new airports constructed were planned so as to be useful to civil aviation in the postwar period. As a result, more than 500 airports constructed for the military by the CAA were declared surplus and were turned over to cities, counties, and states for civil aviation purposes. An understanding was reached between the federal government and the sponsor that the facilities would be available to the public without discrimination and to the government in the event of a national emergency.

Section 302(c) of the Civil Aeronautics Act of 1938 directed the civil aeronautics administrator to make a field survey of the existing system of airports and to report to congress with recommendations as to future federal participation in airport construction, improvement, development, operation, or maintenance.

An advisory committee was appointed, composed of representatives of interested federal agencies, both military and civil, state aviation officials, airport managers, airline representatives, and others. The first survey and report, made in 1939, did not result in congressional action, but a revised plan and recommendations submitted in November 1944 were influential in calling attention to the private airport deficiencies of inadequate distribution and inadequate facilities. This 1944 revision of the National Airport Plan was the basis, in part, upon which the Federal Airport Act of 1946 was enacted, so it will be helpful to review its principal recommendations:

1. That Congress authorize an appropriation to the office of the administrator of civil aeronautics not to exceed $100 million annually to be used in a program of federal aid to public agencies for the

development of a nationwide system of public airports adequate to meet the present and immediate future needs of civil aeronautics.

The administrator should be authorized to allocate such funds for any construction work involved in constructing, improving, or repairing (as distinguished from day-to-day maintenance of) an airport, including the construction, alteration, and repair of airport buildings other than hangars, and the removal, lowering, marking, and lighting of airport obstructions; for the acquisition of any lands or property interest necessary either for any such construction or to protect airport approaches; for making field surveys, preparing plans and specifications; supervising and inspecting construction work, and for any necessary federal expenses in the administration of the program.

2. That such a program be conducted in cooperation with the state and other nonfederal public agencies on a basis to be determined by the Congress. That the federal contribution be determined by the Congress in passing the necessary enabling legislation. A good precedent for the proportionate sharing of costs exists in the public roads program which has operated satisfactorily for many years on a 50/50 basis.

3. That any project for which federal aid is requested must meet with approval of the administrator of civil aeronautics as to scope of development and cost, conform to Civil Aeronautics Administration standards for location, layout, grading, drainage, paving, and lighting, and all work thereon be subject to the inspection and approval of the Civil Aeronautics Administration.

4. In order to participate in the federal aid program, a state shall:
   a. Establish and empower an official body equipped to conduct its share of the program.
   b. Have legislation adequate for the clearing and protection of airport approaches, and such other legislation as may be necessary to vest in its political subdivisions all powers necessary to enable them to participate through the state as sponsors of airport projects.
   c. Have no special tax on aviation facilities, fuel, operations, or businesses, the proceeds of which are not used entirely for aviation.
   d. Ensure the operation of all public airports within its jurisdiction in the public interest, without unjust discrimination or unreasonable charges.
   e. Ensure the proper operation and maintenance of all public airports within its jurisdiction.
   f. Make airports developed with federal aid available for unrestricted use by United States government aircraft without charge other than an amount sufficient to cover the cost of repairing damage done by such aircraft.

   g. Require the installation at all airports for which federal funds have
      been provided, a standard accounting and fiscal reporting system
      satisfactory to the administrator.

5. That sponsors of projects be required to enter into contracts with the
   Civil Aeronautics Administration ensuring the proper maintenance and
   protection of airports developed with federal aid and their operation in
   the public interest.

Postwar federal aid to airports

After the war, Congress turned its attention back to civil aviation with the passage
of the *Federal Airport Act of 1946*, which was signed by President Truman on May
13, 1946. It was the purpose of the Federal Airport Act to give the United States a
comprehensive system of airports, administered by the Civil Aeronautics Administration. Small communities that needed airports to help develop their social and
economic structure were theoretically supposed to benefit from this program.

The Congress appropriated $500 million for airport aid over a seven year
period beginning July 1, 1946. The maximum yearly expenditure was set at $100
million. Of the total amount, 25 percent was placed in a discretionary fund to be
used by the civil aeronautics administrator as he saw fit for airport construction.
Half of the remaining 75 percent was apportioned to the states, based on population, and the other half, based on land areas. The discretionary fund allowed the
administrator to choose the projects regardless of their location. The money had
to be spent on operational facilities such as runways and taxiways.

This federal aid program provided that the federal government would pay as
much as 50 percent of the cost and that the airport sponsor would pay the balance,
or at least 50 percent of the cost. As far as the large cities were concerned, this
was excellent because they could issue and sell bonds to pay for their share of the
cost; however, for the small cities, even 50 percent of the cost of development was
too much of a burden.

For an airport or governmental unit to be available for such aid, it was necessary that the airport be in the National Airport Plan. Under the Federal Airport
Act, the administrator was directed to prepare such a plan. In formulating the
plan, the administrator had to take into account the needs of both air commerce
and private flying, technological development, probable growth, and any other
considerations he found appropriate.

As a condition to his approval of a project, the administrator had to receive in
writing a guarantee that the following provisions would be adhered to:

1. The airport would be available for public use without unjust
   discrimination.

2. The airport would be suitably operated and maintained.

3. The aerial approaches would be cleared and protected and future hazards would be prevented.

4. Proper zoning would be provided to restrict the use of land adjacent to the airport.

5. All facilities developed from federal aid would be made available to the military.

6. All project accounts would be kept in accordance with a standard system.

7. All airport records would be available for inspection by an agent of the administrator upon reasonable request.

The Federal Airport Program progressed from the paper to the construction stage during 1947, and by February of the following year the Civil Aeronautics Administration had made 133 grant offers to local sponsors totaling $13.3 million. This marked the beginning of the federal government's present participation in construction of airport facilities.

On August 3, 1955, President Eisenhower signed Public Law 211, making major changes in the federal-aid-to-airports program and removed the 1958 time limit prescribed by the original act, as amended in 1950. In the main, these changes established a four-year program with authorizations amounting to $63 million for each fiscal year 1957-1959, made all types and sizes of airports eligible for aid, included airport buildings as eligible items of development, and provided that funds apportioned yearly to states continue on the area-population formula.

Federal Aviation Act of 1958

Recognizing that the demands on the federal government in the years ahead would be substantial, the director of the Bureau of the Budget requested a review of aviation facilities problems in 1955. William B. Harding was appointed as a consultant to the director. Harding, in turn, solicited the help of a number of prominent individuals in aviation to form his committee. In later December 1955, Harding submitted his report. Reporting that the need to improve air traffic management had already reached critical proportions, the group recommended that an individual of national reputation, responsible directly to the president, be appointed to provide full-time, high-level leadership in developing a program for solving the complex technical and organizational problems facing the government and the aviation industry.

Following approval of the Harding Committee recommendations, President Eisenhower appointed Edward P. Curtis his special assistant for aviation facilities planning. His assignment was to direct and coordinate "a long-range study of the nation's requirements," to develop "a comprehensive plan for meeting in the most effective and economical manner the needs disclosed by the study," and "to formulate legislative, organizational, administrative, and budgetary recommendations to implement the comprehensive plan."

In 1956, an event occurred that defied all odds: A TWA Super Constellation and a United DC-7 collided over the Grand Canyon, killing 128 people. Suddenly it was a crowded sky, and the outcry for reform became louder and clearer. If a pair of conceptually obsolete piston airliners could have a midair collision, what would happen with jets?

On May 10, 1957, Curtis submitted his report, "*Aviation Facilities Planning*," to the president. The report warned of "a crisis in the making" as a result of the inability of our airspace management system to cope with the complex patterns of civil and military traffic that filled the sky. The growing congestion of airspace was inhibiting defense and retarding the progress of air commerce. Concluding that many excellent plans for improving the nation's aviation facilities had failed in the past to mature because of the inability of our governmental organization to keep pace with aviation's dynamic growth, Curtis recommended the establishment of an independent Federal Aviation Agency "into which are consolidated all the essential management functions necessary to support the common needs of the military and civil aviation of the United States." Until such a permanent organization could be created, Curtis recommended the creation of an Airways Modernization Board as an independent office responsible for developing and consolidating the requirements for future systems of communications, navigation, and traffic control needed to accommodate United States air traffic.

Congress was receptive to this recommendation and passed the *Airways Modernization Act of 1957* on August 14, 1957. The purpose of the act was "to provide for the development and modernization of the national system of navigation and traffic control facilities to serve present and future needs of civil and military aviation." The act further provided for its own expiration on June 30, 1960. Appointment of Elwood R. Quesada as chairman was confirmed by the Senate on August 16, 1957.

On May 20, 1958, a military jet trainer and a civilian transport plane collided over Brunswick, Maryland, killing 12 and becoming the third major air disaster within a period of three and a half months. This tragedy spurred governmental action already underway to establish a comprehensive Federal Aviation Agency. Instead of taking two or three years to create a single aviation agency as was predicted, there was a virtual stampede in congress to enact legislation. The *Federal Aviation Act of 1958* was signed by the president on August 23, 1958. Treating comprehensively the federal government's role in fostering and regulating civil aeronautics and air commerce, the new statute repealed the Air Commerce Act of 1926, the Civil Aeronautics Act of 1938, the Airways Modernization Act of 1957, and those portions of the various presidential reorganization plans dealing with civil aviation.

The law provided for the retention of the Civil Aeronautics Board as an independent office including all its functions except the safety-rule-making powers, which were transferred to the Federal Aviation Agency. The *Federal Aviation Agency* was created with an administrator responsible to the president. The agency incorporated the functions of the Civil Aeronautics Administration and the Airways Modernization Board.

Section 103 of the act concisely stated the administrator's major powers and responsibilities:

1. The regulation of air commerce in such manner as to best promote its development and safety and fulfill the requirements of national defense.
2. The promotion, encouragement, and development of civil aeronautics.
3. The control of the use of the navigable airspace of the United States and the regulation of both civil and military operations in such airspace in the interest of the safety and efficiency of both.
4. The consolidation of research and development with respect to air navigation facilities, as well as the installation and operation thereof.
5. The development and operation of a common system of air traffic control and navigation for both military and civil aircraft.

On November 1, 1958, Elwood R. Quesada, special assistant to the president for aviation matters and chairman of the airways modernization board, became the first administrator of the Federal Aviation Agency.

The Department of Transportation

For many years it was argued that there had been a proliferation of federal activities with regard to transportation. In 1966, President Johnson chose to deliver a special transportation message to Congress. He focused in on the need for coordination of the national transportation system, reorganization of transportation planning activities, and active promotion of safety. In his address President Johnson contended that the U.S. transportation system lacked true coordination and that this resulted in inefficiency. He advocated creation of a federal Department of Transportation (DOT) to promote coordination of existing federal programs and to act as a focal point for future research and development efforts in transportation.

Congressional hearings were held on several bills involving most of President Johnson's recommendations. Although some opposition was expressed to specific proposals, there was general support for creation of the *Department of Transportation*. The legislation creating the DOT was approved on October 15, 1966. DOT commenced operations on April 1, 1967, and Alan S. Boyd was appointed the first secretary of transportation.

The agencies and functions transferred to the DOT related to air transportation included the Federal Aviation Agency in its entirety and the safety functions of the Civil Aeronautics Board, including the responsibility for investigating and determining the probable cause of aircraft accidents and safety functions involving review on appeal of the suspension, modification, or denial of certificates or licenses. The Federal Aviation Agency was downgraded to the *Federal Aviation Administration* (FAA). The administrator of the FAA was still appointed by the president but from then on reported directly to the secretary of transportation.

The act also created within the new department a five-member *National Transportation Safety Board* (NTSB). The act charged the NTSB with (1) determining the cause or probable cause of transportation accidents and reporting the facts, conditions, and circumstances relating to such accidents, and (2) reviewing on appeal the suspension, amendment, modification, revocation, or denial of any certificate or license issued by the secretary or by an administrator.

Conclusion

During its 24-year lifetime (1946-1969), the Federal Aid for Airports Program generated $1.2 billion in federal aid to airports, all of it drawn from the general treasury. Most of the money—close to $1 billion—was used to build runways and roadways, while the rest was spent on land, terminal buildings, and lighting systems. For all of its success, however, FAAP failed to anticipate the travel boom of the 1960s, which overloaded the country's commercial air routes and prompted carriers to expand their fleets.

Airport and Airway Development Act of 1970

The tremendous growth in all segments of aviation during the late 1960s put a strain on the existing airway system. Air delays getting into and out of major airports began to develop rapidly. Along with the delays in the air, congestion was taking place in parking areas and terminal buildings. Public indignation at the failure of the system to keep pace with the demand for air transportation reached a peak in 1969. It was undoubtedly hastened by the widely-publicized touchdown of the first of the new family of wide-bodied jets, the Boeing 747. President Nixon told Congress in 1969 that stacks of airplanes over the nation's airports were ample evidence that something needed to be done.

It was evident that to reduce congestion, substantial amounts of money would have to be invested in airway and airport improvements. For airports alone it was estimated that $11 billion in new capital improvements would be required for public airports in the 10-year period 1970-1980. The amount of money authorized by the Federal Airport Act of 1946 was insufficient to assist in financing such a vast program. The normal and anticipated sources of revenue available to public airports were also not sufficient to acquire the required funds for capital expenditures.

Congress responded with an idea it borrowed from the interstate highway program: a trust fund supported by taxes on people who used the national aviation system. Such a mechanism, according to its proponents, would shift the cost of increasing the system's capacity from taxpayers to those groups who benefited most directly: passengers, shippers, and aircraft owners.

On May 21, 1970, President Nixon signed a two-title law that was to run for 10 years. Title I was the *Airport and Airway Development Act of 1970*, and Title II was the *Airport and Airway Revenue Act of 1970*. The new legislation assured a fund estimated at the time to generate more than $11 billion in funds for airport and airway modernization during the decade. By establishing an Airport and Airway Trust Fund modeled on the Highway Trust Fund, it freed airport and airway development from having to compete for General Treasury funds, the basic reason for the funding uncertainties and inadequacies of the past. Into the trust would go new revenues from aviation user taxes levied by the Airport and Airway Revenue Act, and other funds that Congress might choose to appropriate to meet authorized expenditures.

Revenues would be raised by levies on aviation users:

1. An 8-percent tax on domestic passenger fares.
2. A $3 surcharge on passenger tickets for international flights originating in the United States.
3. A tax of 7 cents a gallon on both gasoline and jet fuel used by aircraft in noncommercial aviation.
4. A 5-percent tax on airfreight waybills.
5. An annual registration fee of $25 on all civil aircraft, plus (1) in the case of piston-powered aircraft weighing more than 2,500 pounds, 2 cents a pound for each pound of maximum certificated takeoff weight, or (2) in the case of turbine-powered aircraft, 3.5 cents a pound for each pound of maximum certificated takeoff weight.

Advantages of the user charge/trust-fund approach

The principal advantages of the user-charge/trust-fund approach to revenue raising and funding were that it (1) provided a predictable and increasing source of income, more commensurate with need; (2) permitted more effective and longer range planning; and (3) assured that the tax revenues generated by aviation would not be diverted to nonaviation uses.

First five years under the act

Two grant-in-aid programs were provided for under the 10-year 1970 Airport and Airway Development Act: the *Planning Grant Program* (PGP), and the *Airport*

Development Aid Program (ADAP). The grant programs were fund matching assistance programs in which the federal government paid a predetermined share of approved airport planning and development project costs, and the airport owners at the various state and local levels, who were eligible to participate in the program, paid the rest. The 1970 act also provided that the funding authority of the grant-in-aid programs would expire on June 30, 1975, at the end of the act's first five years of operation. The object ws to see what, if any, changes needed to be made before further funds were authorized for the act's remaining five years.

The major weaknesses of the Federal Airport Act, which was repealed by the new legislation, were the inadequacy of the resources provided under it and the nature of the formula for distributing those resources. The annual authorization under the old act totaled only $75 million and of this total, the distribution of $66.5 million was fixed by a formula apportioning 75 percent of it by population and area among the states: half in the ratio of each state's population to the total population of all the states, and half in the ratio of each state's area to the total area of all the states. Though the remaining 25 percent of $66.5 million, plus any state's apportionment under the population-area formula if unclaimed for two fiscal years, went into a discretionary fund with certain other funds, this discretionary fund was too small to make significant impact on critical, high-priority areas.

By contrast, the new airport and airway act increased the total annual authorization by nearly four times for each of the first five years—to $280 million—and it provided a distribution formula improved in the light of the experience under the Federal Airport Act. Of the $280 million, $250 million would be available each year for modernization and improvement programs at air carrier and reliever airports and $30 million annually for general aviation airports.

In its provisions concerning planning, the new legislation reflected not only certain lessons of experience but also the emergence of certain new planning factors. For example, experience under the Federal Airport Act with the National Airport Plan, which covered a period of five years and was revised annually, led to the requirement in the new law for a National Airport System Plan (NASP) covering at least 10 years and revised only as necessary. Notable among factors explicitly mentioned for the secretary's consideration in preparing the NASP, but not mentioned in relation to the NASP, were, among others, (1) the relationship of each airport to the local transportation system, to forecasted technological developments in aeronautics, and to developments forecasted in other modes of intercity transport; (2) factors affecting the quality of the natural environment.

The provision for planning grants also marked a significant difference between the new legislation and the old. The new law authorized the secretary to make grants of funds to planning agencies for airports' system planning, and to public agencies for airport master planning. At the same time, it authorized a total of $75 million for such grants. Planning grants, however, could not exceed $15 million in any one fiscal year, nor could any such grant exceed two-thirds of an airport project's cost.

Airway modernization also benefited from the increased funding authorized by the Airport and Airway Development Act. Throughout the decade of the 1960s, appropriations for airway facilities and equipment averaged $93 million a year. The new legislation authorized "not less than" $250 million a year for the first five fiscal years for acquiring, establishing, and improving air navigation facilities. A principal beneficiary of this more generous authorization would be the FAA's efforts to automate the air traffic control system of the National Airspace System.

ADAP funding under the act, for which the federal share for large and medium air carrier hubs had been 50 percent, and for the smaller air carrier, general aviation, and reliever airports, 75 percent had initially been $280 million per year. In 1973, under the amendments to the act of that year, the funding level was set at $310 million (TABLE 1-1).

Table 1-1. ADAP spending (millions) 1971-1975. Source: FAA

FY	Amount permitted under 1970 act (authorizations)	Amount approved by Congress each year (appropriations)	Amount actually spent by FAA (obligations)
1971	$ 280	$ 170	$ 170
1972	280	280	280
1973	280	280	207
1974	310	300	300
1975	310	335	335
Total	$1,460	$1,365	$1,292

Total ADAP funds obligated under the act over the five-year period totaled close to $1.3 billion, a figure that exceeded by $100 million the $1.2 billion airport development aid funds disbursed by the federal government in the entire 24-year history of the earlier Federal Aid Airport Program. The $1.3 billion had made it possible for the FAA to provide and fund a total of 2,434 ADAP projects during the five-year period. Of this number, 1,528 had been completed at air carrier locations, 757 at general aviation airport locations, and 149 at reliever airport locations. The beneficiaries included 520 air carrier airports, 624 general aviation airports, and 81 reliever airports. For the air carrier airports, the federal funds expended came to $1.09 billion; for general aviation airports, to $212.8 million; and for reliever airports, to $61.6 million.

With this infusion of additional federal money, 85 new airports were built and more than 1,000 others significantly improved. The improvements included 178 new runways, 520 new taxiways, 201 runway extensions, hundreds of miles of security fencing, and fleets of crash, firefighting, and rescue (CFR) equipment. They also comprised some of the most advanced approach-aid equipment available, including 28 instrument landing systems (ILS), 141 runway end identifying lighting systems (REILS) and 471 visual approach slope indicators (VASI).

The act had served its purpose well during the first five years. Nevertheless, as its obligational authority began drawing to a close, it was clear that the required review was fortunate in its timing. With a sharp increase in air carrier and general aviation operations, mounting environmental and terminal access problems, along with increasing inflation, there was no time to be lost in getting it underway.

Airport and Airway
Development Act Amendments of 1976

On July 12, 1976, President Ford signed into law the *Airport and Airway Development Act Amendments of 1976*. ADAP funding levels for the remaining five years under the 1970 act were sharply increased as shown in TABLE 1-2.

Table 1-2. ADAP funding (millions) 1976-1980. Source: FAA

FY	Air carrier airports	General aviation airports	Total
1976	$ 435	$ 65	$ 500
1977	440	70	510
1978	465	75	540
1979	495	80	575
1980	525	85	610
Total	$2,360	$375	$2,735

Some of the important amendments included under the 1976 Act were as follows:

1. Expanded the types of airport development projects eligible for ADAP funding. These now included: (1) snow removal equipment; (2) noise suppressing equipment; (3) physical barriers and landscaping to diminish the effects of aircraft noise; and (4) the acquisition of land to ensure environmental compatibility. Nonrevenue producing public use terminal area facilities for the movement of passengers and baggage at airports serving CAB certificated air carriers also became eligible for

ADAP funding, except that in such cases the federal share would be 50 percent.

2. Established the "Commuter Service Airport," a new air carrier airport category comprising about 130 airports that served noncertificated air carriers, and enplaned at least 2,500 passengers annually. This new airport category was created in recognition of the substantial growth of commercial commuter services during the previous five-year period, their potential for future growth, and the resulting need to assure airports serving them proper development funding.

3. Directed that the reliever airports in the National Airport System, previously grouped for funding purposes with the air carrier airports, be included instead with the general aviation airport category because, aside from their usefulness as relievers, they were basically general aviation airports.

4. Increased the federal share for ADAP grants. For small air carrier hubs, general aviation airports, reliever airports, and commuter service airports, the federal share would be 90 percent for FY 1976 through FY 1978, and 80 percent for FY 1979 through FY 1980. For the 67 large and medium hubs in the National Airport System, it went from the previous 50 percent to 75 percent and remained there throughout the entire five year period.

5. Increased the federal share for PGP grants from 66.7 to 75.0 percent.

6. Ordered the preparation and publication by January 1, 1978, of a major revision of the National Airport System Plan (NASP). Last submitted to Congress in 1973, and kept updated since, the NASP comprised more than 4,000 locations, including 649 served by the certificated air carriers.

7. Directed by the initiation of a series of studies having to do with the following: (1) the feasibility of landbank-banking as an expedient in airport development; (2) the case for soundproofing public institutions located near airports; (3) the identification of places in the United States where major new airports would be needed, and alternative approaches to their financing; and (4) the identification of needed airports across the nation, which for economic reasons were threatened with closure, with an analysis in the individual case of what could best be done to keep them open.

8. Authorized the appropriation from the Airport and Airway Trust Fund for the five-year period FY 1976 through FY 1980 for disbursement in annual increments of the following sums: (1) up to $1.15 billion to cover the costs of flight checking and maintaining the air navigation

facilities of the federal airway system; (2) $1.275 million to assist the
states in developing their own general aviation airport standards; and (3)
$1.3 billion for the purpose of acquiring, establishing, and improving
federal air navigation facilities.

These were the major provisions of the 1976 act as it further amended the
Airport and Airway Development Act of 1970. In signing the new legislation,
President Ford stated, "The Airport and Airway Development Act of 1976 will
make possible the continuing modernization of our airways, airports, and related
facilities in communities throughout our fifty states."

Airline deregulation

Passage of the Air Cargo Deregulation Act of 1976, and, more importantly, the *Airline Deregulation Act of 1978*, signaled an end to the 40-year history of economic
regulation of the airline industry. The deregulation of airlines was part of a general
trend gaining momentum in the 1970s to reduce government regulation of private
industry. By this time, many observers in Congress and elsewhere had begun to
doubt that federal regulation was encouraging orderly competition and had come to
suspect that the regulatory process was imposing unnecessary costs and creating
distortions in the marketplace. Even before Congress passed the deregulation acts,
the CAB itself had conducted a number of experimental reductions of certain types
of regulation in order to encourage competition. With the 1978 act, the market was
opened to new firms, and carriers gained much greater freedom to enter or leave
markets, to change routes, and to compete on the basis of price. The 1978 act also
called for the "sunset" of the CAB by the end of 1984, with transfer of its few
remaining essential functions to the DOT and other departments.

Deregulation has had a profound effect on the airport system. Once air carriers were permitted to change routes without CAB approval, they dropped many
unprofitable points, confirming the fears of some opponents of deregulation that
air service to small communities would suffer. Service to some smaller cities continued under the *Essential Air Service* provisions of the deregulation act, which
provides subsidies (through 1998) to the last carrier in a market so as to prevent
selected cities from losing service altogether. In many cases, small commuter carriers entered the markets abandoned by larger carriers. In addition, the airlines'
new freedom has greatly changed their relationships with airport operators, who
can no longer depend on the stability of the carriers serving the airport and who
must accommodate new entrants.

Aircraft noise

One of the major issues affecting airport development, especially since the beginning of the jet age, has been aircraft noise. The FAA has responsibility for regulating aircraft noise—in the Federal Aviation Regulations Part 36 (1969) and Part

91 (1976)—and for establishing procedures for airspace use; however, the federal government has not taken on the task of directly regulating the noise level at a given airport, which is considered the province of the airport operator. *The Aviation Safety and Noise Abatement Act*, passed by Congress in 1979, was intended to "provide assistance to airport operators to prepare and carry out noise compatibility programs." It authorizes the FAA to help airport operators develop noise abatement programs and makes them eligible for grants under ADAP.

Airport development in the 1980s

Between 1971 and 1980 the trust fund received approximately $13.8 billion, of which $4.1 billion was invested in the airport system through ADAP grants. The Airport and Airway Development Act expired in 1980 and Congress did not agree on reauthorizing legislation until passage of the Airport and Airway Improvement Act of 1982. During fiscal years 1981 and 1982 the taxing provisions of the trust fund were reduced, and revenues were deposited in the General Fund and the Highway Trust Fund. However, Congress continued to appropriate airport aid, $450 million for each of the two years. At least part of the delay in passing new legislation was due to the debate over "defederalization," an action which would have made the nation's largest airports ineligible for federal aid on the grounds that they were capable of supporting themselves financially. Defederalization was dropped from the final version of the legislation, but Congress directed the Department of Transportation to study the matter and to report at a later date.

Airport and Airway Improvement Act of 1982

The *Airport and Airway Improvement Act of 1982* re-established the operation of the Airport and Airway Trust Fund with a slightly revised schedule of user taxes. Operators of piston aircraft were required to pay 12 cents per gallon for avgas, an increase of 5 cents over the 1970 tax rate. Turbine aircraft operators paid 14 cents per gallon for jet fuel, an increase of 7 cents.

The act authorized a new capital grant program, called the *Airport Improvement Program* (AIP). In basic philosophy, AIP was similar to the previous ADAP. It was intended to support a national system of integrated airports which recognizes the role of large and small airports together in a national air transportation system. Maximized joint use of underutilized, nonstrategic U.S. military fields was also encouraged.

The 1982 act also contained a provision to make funds available for noise compatibility planning and to carry out noise compatibility programs as authorized by the Aviation Safety and Noise Abatement Act of 1979.

The Airport and Airway Improvement Act has been amended several times. For example, the Continuing Appropriations Act, passed in October 1982, added a section providing authority to issue discretionary grants in lieu of unused apportioned funds under certain circumstances, and the Surface Transportation Assistance Act, passed in January 1983, increased the annual authorizations for the AIP for fiscal years 1983 to 1985. Overall, the Airport and Airway Improvement Act of 1982 authorized a total of $4.8 billion in airport aid for fiscal years 1983 through 1987.

A 1987 amendment, the *Airport and Airway Safety and Capacity Expansion Act of 1987*, extended the authority for the AIP for five years. It authorized $1.7 billion each fiscal year through 1990 and $1.8 billion each year for fiscal years 1991 and 1992. This amendment also authorized a new procedure in which a sponsor is advised of federal intentions to fund long-term high priority capacity projects as appropriations allow and to reimburse sponsors for certain specified work performed before a grant is received. This procedure is implemented through a letter of intent issued to sponsors. Another provision of the 1987 amendment established a requirement that 10 percent of the funds made available under the AIP be given to small business concerns owned and controlled by socially and economically disadvantaged individuals, known as the Disadvantaged Business Enterprise Program.

The Airport and Airway Improvement Act also required the secretary of transportation to publish a report on the status of the *National Plan of Integrated Airport Systems (NPIAS)*. The NPIAS emphasizes system planning and development to meet current and future needs; it includes development considered necessary to provide a safe, efficient, and integrated airport system meeting the needs of civil aviation, national defense, and the postal service. An airport must be included in this plan in order to be eligible to receive a grant under the AIP. The NPIAS edition covering 1990 through 1999 identified 3,285 existing and 407 proposed airports. These airports account for an estimated 88 percent of general aviation and virtually all operations by scheduled air carriers. The NPIAS includes estimates of the type and cost of development that will be required at each airport through 1999. The development recommendations are drawn primarily from plans prepared by state and local agencies responsible for airport planning and development.

The NPIAS only includes development that is eligible for federal aid under the Airport Improvement Program; it does not include hangars, nonpublic areas of terminal buildings, automobile parking facilities, and ground access facilities beyond the airport boundary. Neither does the NPIAS include the effects of inflation on cost estimates that were prepared in 1989. While all of the development in the NPIAS is eligible for federal aid, it is expected that about two-thirds will be accomplished with local and state funds, derived primarily from airport income and user fees.

The estimated cost of NPIAS development is $40.5 billion over the ten-year period, 1990 through 1999. This corresponds to an annual capital investment of $4.05 billion for development that is eligible for federal aid. Actual capital spending in 1989 was estimated to be $4.49 billion for all development, including items not eligible for federal aid.

The largest portion of the proposed development (81 percent) is for airports that receive scheduled air carrier service. Reliever airports account for 6 percent and general aviation airports 13 percent of the total development.

Concluding remarks:
Assessment of federal airport policy

In large measure, the system of airports that we have in the United States today owes its existence to federal policy, whose express purpose has been to foster the development of civil aviation. In the earliest years of civil aviation, the government's actions were confined to subsidy of aircraft manufacturers through military purchases and indirect support of aircraft operators by airmail contracts. Because airports were regarded as essentially local enterprises, they did not receive federal aid. But from the beginning, civil aviation was perceived as an adjunct to military aviation in providing national defense, and in the World War II era this became the rationale for direct federal government assistance to civil airports.

In the years after 1945, the federal government took an even more important step in supporting the civil airport system when it turned over to local authorities hundreds of airports that had been built and operated as military installations but were then deemed surplus. This infusion of capital facilities not only expanded the airport network serving commercial aviation, it also encouraged the purchase and use of general aviation aircraft by assuring ample landing facilities within reach of nearly everyone in the country.

By 1960, this divestiture of military holdings had largely run its course, and the emphasis of federal policy shifted to upgrading and expansion of major airports to accommodate jet aircraft and to alleviate problems of congestion and delay in airline traffic that were beginning to emerge. Smaller airports were not neglected; between 1960 and 1970, $510 million—about 20 percent of all federal expenditures for airport capital improvements—were directed to small communities and to improving the quality of general aviation facilities. In addition to construction and improvement of runways and airfield facilities, the federal government aided general aviation in other ways. The network of flight service stations was expanded, and the number of airports with FAA-operated control towers grew substantially, with nearly all of the additions coming at smaller airports. Safety of civil aviation was an important motivating factor, but so too was the desire to establish and maintain an extensive system of well-equipped airports serving all classes of civil aviation, providing readily available commercial air transportation and operating bases for aircraft used for business purposes and private flying.

The passage of the Airport and Airway Development Act of 1970 institutionalized federal airport aid by establishing the Airport and Airway Trust Fund, supported by user fees, which provided a dedicated source of revenue for capital improvement. This act not only committed federal support to the airport system, it also gave the federal government a strong—perhaps dominant—voice in how that system would develop. By identifying the kinds of airports eligible for capital grants, by specifying the types of projects that would be supported, and by establishing formulas for federal, state, and local funding, the Airport Development Aid Program effectively set the pattern of airport development for the 1970s. After a brief period of uncertainty in 1980-82, when Congress allowed the legislative authorization of ADAP to lapse, previous federal policy on airport development was reaffirmed in September 1982 with passage of the Airport and Airway Improvement Act of 1982, which established the Airport Improvement Program.

AIP preserved the general approach to airport aid established under ADAP, with certain revisions to correct what were perceived as imbalances in the allocation of funds and to adjust the shares paid into the trust fund by various classes of airport and airspace users through ticket and fuel taxes. The principal differences between ADAP and the new AIP are in the proportion of federal aid to be allocated to air carrier, reliever, and general aviation airports, the earmarking of 8 percent for noise projects, and extension of federal aid for the first time to privately owned general aviation airports.

Investment of $4.1 billion in federal monies for airport capital projects under ADAP between 1971 and 1980 and $7.9 billion more in state and local funds enabled the airport system to keep abreast of construction needs, but not to eliminate the chronic delay problems at a dozen or so major metropolitan airports. The capacity gains achieved at major airports were largely offset by growth in passenger traffic, which rose by about 75 percent during the decade.

Between 1980 and 1989, domestic air travel demand, measured in revenue passenger miles (RPM) increased from 254 billion RPM to 423 billion RPM per year. The FAA forecasted 577 billion RPM annually by 2000. If this level is attained, air travel demand will have grown by 127 percent over the span of 20 years.

Aircraft operations, a better measure of the load on the airport and airway system, have also increased sharply. Since 1980, aircraft operations by major air carrier and regional airlines have increased by 50 percent, reaching 21 million takeoffs and landings in 1989. FAA forecasted almost 30 million operations in 2000, more than double the 1980 total. Other indicators of aviation activity (passenger enplanements, fleet size, and hours flown) exhibit similar historical and projected growth rates.

The boom in air travel during the last decade has been spurred by several factors: airline deregulation, a robust economy, reduced fares, and an increasing propensity of the public to rely on aviation for trips more than 200 miles. During the 1980s, more people flew more often than ever before, and the indications are that the trend will continue.

Cargo destined for Europe, Asia and points all over the world begins its journey at Los Angeles International Airport. This key U.S. air link to the vital Pacific Rim is one of the three top air cargo centers in the world. The airport handles more than 1 million tons of cargo annually.

In accommodating the burgeoning demand, the nation's airports and airways have been severely strained. Congestion and delay have mounted in the airspace, on runways, and in airport terminals. In 1987, 21 major airports experienced more than 20,000 hours of flight delays in air carrier operations. If some way is not found to accommodate growing demand, 39 U.S. airports could be so affected by the end of this century. At the largest airports, those that collectively handle almost half of all airline passengers, air carrier delays could reach 50,000 to 100,000 hours annually by 2000 according to an FAA forecast.

Passenger travel is not the only element of civil aviation that has grown. Air cargo operations and general aviation (private and business flying) also have placed increasing demand on the airport and airway system. The movement of freight and express mail by all-cargo aircraft has expanded rapidly in the past 20 years and is projected to increase at a higher rate than the overall growth of passenger traffic for the next two decades. This growth, however, is from a very small base. In 1970, air cargo accounted for less than 1 percent of all commercial aircraft movements. Today, the air cargo share is about 3 percent. By 2010, it might reach 5 percent. At the top 10 hub airports, general aviation (GA) makes up a small part of the traffic, typically less than 8 percent. At other commercial service airports, the GA share is larger; but the overall pattern is that, as air carrier operations increase at an airport, GA traffic declines. Most GA aircraft avoid large airports, and those that do use them are often professionally piloted business or executive-transport aircraft with performance characteristics comparable to large jets.

Accommodating cargo and GA operations at airports and on the airways is an important concern, but it is separable from the problem of providing capacity for commercial passenger transport. In many cases, GA and cargo aircraft can, and do, make use of alternatives, such as reliever airports for GA or airports with a low volume of passenger traffic that can serve as cargo hubs. They also have access to busy metropolitan area airports at off-peak hours. Use of airports by these sectors of civil aviation is not a major driver of the airport capacity problem.

Recent efforts by FAA and local airport authorities have centered on what they perceive to be the major air transport capacity problem: accommodating the rising volume of airline passengers and air carrier operations. FAA has undertaken a multibillion dollar modernization of air traffic control facilities that will allow the system to handle more traffic, not only additional domestic and international passenger traffic but also cargo operations and expected increase in use of the system by private and business GA aircraft.

Airport authorities have concentrated on expanding gate facilities and terminal buildings to accommodate higher passenger volumes. While this has helped ease travel delays on the landside, it has had little effect on airside delays, which are caused primarily by the lack of runway capacity or by operational limits, caps or quotas, imposed for purpose of air traffic control. Proposals to increase airside capacity by adding new runways or otherwise expanding the ability to accommodate more aircraft operations have met strong community opposition in many cities, primarily on the grounds of noise but also for reasons of cost. Many observers believe that the single greatest constraint on the future growth of air travel will be the lack of adequate airport runway capacity.

In the past 20 years, only two completely new airports have been opened (Dallas-Fort Worth and Southwest Florida Regional). A new airport to replace Denver Stapleton is under construction after extended controversy and several delays: expected to open by the early 1990s. New airports are being considered in Los Angeles, Austin, and Farmington, New Mexico, but it is unlikely—if they are built at all—that they will be operational before 2000. Five other cities, Atlanta, Chicago, Minneapolis-St. Paul, San Diego, and St. Louis, are exploring the possibility of purchasing land or developing presently reserved tracts for future airport sites, but the prospects of new airports in these cities are even more remote.

If something is not done to enable airports to handle more traffic, the prospects for the early decades of the next century is bleak. If demand on the system doubles or triples, it is questionable whether sufficient capacity will be available to accommodate such an increase. Clearly, the present airport system could not safely absorb such a volume of traffic without incurring monumental delays throughout the country.

Criticism of federal policy

Certainly, the focus of federal policy since passage of the Airport and Airway Development Act of 1970, and continuing with the recently enacted AIP, has been on building and expanding airports. Some critics have argued that the bias toward capital-intensive solutions, with liberal federal aid, has distorted the evolution of the airport system. It has favored the costly—and perhaps self-defeating—approach of adding capacity wherever and whenever needed to accommodate demand. But new capacity inevitably begets new demand, which creates need for more capacity, and so on in an escalating spiral. Limitations on land available for airport expansion or building new airports, steady encroachment of urban development around airports, and community opposition to airport noise make adding capacity an increasingly expensive and difficult solution. The alternative urged by critics of present policy is to encourage demand-management techniques that would promote fuller and more efficient use of the infrastructure already in place. These critics would redirect policy away from large capital projects and toward a combination of managerial, operational, and market-oriented approaches to channel new growth to fit within the ample capacity now available in the airport system as a whole.

Another criticism of past and present policy is that it has concentrated almost exclusively on airside capacity: runways, taxiways, and other such airfield facilities. Most FAA studies of capacity have limited their concern to aircraft delay (or, even more narrowly, air carrier delay), and the calculation of benefits has been confined largely to air carrier fuel and labor savings and more efficient aircraft utilization. In part, this might be a methodological limitation. It is considerably more simple and straightforward to calculate aircraft delay costs than to quantify the intangibles of terminal and landside delay: What is the economic value of convenience or passenger time? On the other hand, FAA has traditionally interpreted aviation policy in such a way that its interest is closely circumscribed about the airfield and aircraft operations, leaving responsibility for other parts of the airport to the site manager or to other agencies of government.

Delays in terminals and on landside access roads are widespread and probably account for more of the increase in passenger travel time than delays in aircraft departures and arrivals. By concentrating on expanding the airside, the federal government has placed on airports almost the whole burden of keeping pace with terminal and landside improvements. A broader targeting of federal funds, it is argued, will be needed to deal with all forms of delay associated with air transportation. An extension of this argument is that federal policy should broaden its sphere of concern to encompass the airport as part of the overall urban or regional transportation system.

Another way in which federal policy—or at least FAA interpretation of federal policy—has been faulted is that it has led to an overly broad definition of what constitutes airports of national importance. The last edition of the NPIAS contains more than 3,000 airports that are eligible for federal aid. Most of these airports are small general aviation facilities serving only a relatively few aircraft. While there is a distinction between eligibility for federal aid and actual receipt, the existence of a trust fund and a federal policy that seeks to spread aid broadly to all classes of airports has created a very large roster of airports competing for a share of federal monies, with each believing that it can and should receive support for capital projects. At the national level, this leads to inflated estimates of "needs," which exert pressure for more and more federal outlays in a continuing program of airport building and expansion. A more restrictive definition of the federal government's interest might be necessary to clarify the distinction between those airports that serve a nationwide air transportation function and those that serve purely local and specialized needs that are national only in an aggregate sense.

A somewhat different criticism that is partially contradictory to the argument above is that federal aid has favored air carrier airports while neglecting the needs of other users of the airspace, chiefly those who frequent general aviation and reliever airports. To some extent, the provisions in AIP to increase that share allocated to general aviation are a response to this criticism; however, this argument is not simply a plea for more aid to general aviation, rather, it is directed to the larger issue of financial self-sufficiency.

Some contend that federal aid should be targeted toward those airports that do not have adequate revenues or access to debt capital in the private market. The largest airports, which collectively serve almost 90 percent of air travelers, are or could be virtually self-supporting. If so, these critics maintain, it is not an appropriate use of federal monies, even perhaps monies from a dedicated trust fund, to help those that can help themselves. This is the argument of those who would defederalize large and medium airports, and it has found favor both among small airport operators, who see it as an opportunity to obtain more federal aid, and those who seek market-oriented solutions that would reduce the federal budget.

This brief critique of past and present federal policy points to a basic issue: In promoting aviation by providing abundant capacity at low cost to airport and airspace users, has the federal government in effect subsidized airlines, general aviation, aircraft manufacturers, and local development? The evidence suggests that the answer is "yes." But the more important question is motive, not effect. In the earliest days of aviation, the aim of federal policy seems to have been to foster a fledgling industry for reasons of national defense and development of an economically valuable new mode of transportation. Without this support, aviation might have lagged or withered altogether. In the years after World War II, the rationale of civil aviation as a buttress of national defense became less important, and considerations of the national economy and regional development came to predominate. They still do. Aircraft manufacturing and the aviation industry are important contributors to the balance of trade. Available, efficient, and low-cost air travel stimulates all sectors of the economy. An airport is an important economic resource to a community, both in and of itself and because it can be used to leverage additional highly desirable development. In this sense, aviation is a general boon to the economy, and it can be argued that the federal government's policy is amply justified.

Key terms

Kelly Act of 1925
Air Commerce Act of 1926
Bureau of Air Commerce
Civil Aeronautics Act of 1938
Civil Aeronautics Board (CAB)
Civil Aeronautics Administration (CAA)
Development of Landing Areas for National Defense (DLAND)
Federal Airport Act of 1946
Airways Modernization Act of 1957
Federal Aviation Act of 1958
Federal Aviation Agency
Department of Transportation (DOT)
National Transportation Safety Board (NTSB)
Federal Aviation Administration (FAA)
Airport and Airway Development Act of 1970
Airport and Airway Revenue Act of 1970
Planning Grant Program (PGP)
Airport Development Aid Program (ADAP)
Airport and Airway Development Act Amendments of 1976
Airline Deregulation Act of 1978
Essential Air Service
Aviation Safety and Noise Abatement Act of 1979
Airport and Airway Improvement Act of 1982
Airport Improvement Program (AIP)
Airport and Airway Safety and Capacity Expansion Act of 1987
National Plan of Integrated Airport Systems (NPIAS)

Review questions

1. Who established the first airmail service in the United States? How long did it last?
   What was the primary purpose of the Kelly Act?
   The Air Commerce Act of 1926?
   How did the Bureau of Air Commerce become established?

2. When did the federal government first give financial support for the development of airports?

Describe the overriding purpose of the Civil Aeronautics Act of 1938. Distinguish between the Civil Aeronautics Board and the Civil Aeronautics Administration.

What was the function of DLAND?

3. Discuss some of the recommendations made by a select committee in November 1944 that led to the passage of the Federal Airport Act of 1946. How many dollars were appropriated by the Federal Airport Act during the first seven years? How was the money apportioned?

What were some of the provisions which had to be adhered to before federal aid was granted?

4. Describe the state of the air transportation industry during the middle 1950s that led to the passage of the Federal Aviation Act of 1958.

What was the purpose of the Curtis Committee?

Why was the Airways Modernization Board disbanded?

Identify the federal aviation administrator's major responsibilities under the 1958 act.

What was the purpose of the Department of Transportation Act of 1966?

5. Discuss some of the factors that led to the passage of the Airport and Airway Development Act of 1970. How were revenues raised under the Airport and Airway Revenue Act of 1970?

What are some advantages of the user charge/trust-fund approach? Compare and contrast the provisions of ADAP with the Federal Airport Act.

What is the PGP? How does it work?

Compare the funding for the first five years of ADAP with the 24-year history under the Federal-Aid Airport Program.

6. Discuss some of the important amendments under the Airport and Airway Development Act Amendments of 1976.

How has the Airline Deregulation Act of 1978 affected the airport system in the United States?

What is the "Essential Air Service" program?

What is the purpose of the Aviation Safety and Noise Abatement Act of 1979?

Discuss some of the major changes under the Airport and Airway Improvement Act of 1982.

What was the primary purpose of the Airport and Airway Safety and Capacity Expansion Act of 1987.

What is included in the NPIAS?

7. How has the tremendous growth in air travel during the 1980s affected the airport system?

   What is the biggest problem faced by the airport system in the 1990s and beyond?

   Discuss some of the frequently heard criticisms of the Federal Airport Policy as it has been conducted over the years.

Suggested readings

Air Commerce Act of 1926, Public Law 254, 69th Congress, May 20, 1926.

Airport and Airway Development Act of 1970 (Title I) and the Airport and Airway Revenue Act of 1970 (Title II), Public Law 258, 91st Congress, May 21, 1970.

Airport and Airway Development Act Amendments of 1976, Public Law 353, 94th Congress, July 12, 1976.

Airport and Airway Improvement Act of 1982, Public Law 248, 97th Congress, September 15, 1982.

Arey, Charles K., *The Airport*. New York: Macmillan Co., 1943.

Briddon, Arnold E., Ellmore A. Champie, and Peter A. Marraine. *FAA Historical Fact Book: A Chronology 1926−1971*. DOT/FAA Office of Information Services. Washington DC: U.S. Government Printing Office, 1974.

Civil Aeronautics Act of 1938, Public Law 706, 76th Congress, June 23, 1938.

Department of Transportation Act of 1966, Public Law 670, 89th Congress, October 15th, 1966.

Federal Airport Act of 1946, Public Law 377, 79th Congress, May 13, 1946.

Federal Aviation Act of 1958, Public Law 726, 85th Congress, August 23, 1958.

Frederick, John H., *Airport Management*. Chicago: Richard D. Irwin, Inc., 1949.

Kelly Air Mail Act of 1925, Public Law 359, 68th Congress, February 2, 1925.

Richmond, S., *Regulation and Competition in Air Transportation*. New York: Columbia University Press, 1962.

Smith, Donald I., John D. Odegard and William Shea, *Airport Planning and Management*. Belmont, California: Wadsworth Publishing Co., 1984.

The airport system

Outline

Introduction
Classification of airports
The economic role of airports
Current issues in airport system development
Airport information sources

Objectives

When you have completed this chapter, you should be able to:

△ Recognize the size and scope of the airport system in the United States.

△ Explain the FAA method of classifying airports.

△ Discuss the economic role of airports.

△ Summarize several major current issues in airport system development.

△ Identify 10 prominent airport information sources and briefly describe their primary function.

Introduction

The system of airports in the United States is the largest and most complex in the world. As of June 30, 1990, there was 17,451 civil landing areas (airports, heliports, seaplane bases, and the like) in the U.S. This includes more than 10,000 private-use airports that were built by individuals or corporations to accommodate their own aircraft and are not available to the public, and 4,046 heliports, of which only 104 are open to the public. There are 3,534 airports open for public use that also have at least one paved and lighted runway. There are 3,285 existing and 407 proposed new airports included in the NPIAS. Of the new airports, 17 will have scheduled air carrier service and 390 will be used primarily be general aviation. Figure 2-1 shows the division of the airports by ownership and availability for public use.

Airport ownership

While only about one-third of the airports on record are publicly owned, most of the busier airports are owned by governmental or quasi-governmental bodies. In the U.S., public airports are typically owned by cities and counties, or by semi-independent authorities formed by these jurisdictions. A few states, notably Alaska, Hawaii, and Rhode Island, operate broad airport systems. The federal government's ownership and operation of civil airports is limited to the airport at Pomona (Atlantic City), New Jersey, which is part of the FAA Technical Center.

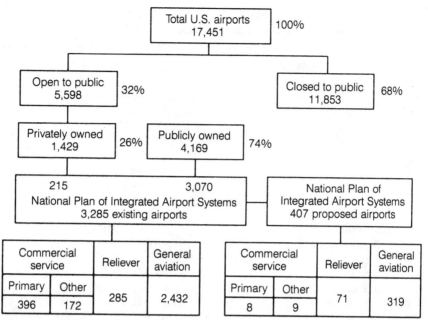

Fig. 2-1. Number of airports by ownership and public use as of June 30, 1990.

The transfers of most of these airports, both surplus and those of the World War II programs, were made with provisions that permit the federal government to recapture its interests under certain conditions and also to review and approve any transfer of former federal properties destined for non-airport use. Approximately 644 civil airports have these encumbrances. Army and Air Force Reserve and National Guard units operate out of a number of civil airports, usually under some type of lease arrangements.

Joint-use airports

Approximately 21 domestic military-owned airports permit civil use. These airports are usually located close to civilian population centers and have the type of military activity that can coexist with civil operations. Joint-use airports normally have separate civil aviation areas that might include terminal buildings, aprons, and taxiways built specifically for civil use. The runway system is normally shared. It is FAA policy to explore and coordinate the possibilities of civil use of military bases when safety and defense considerations permit. In general, the FAA and some local and state governments would prefer that greater civil use be made of some of these airfields, but the controlling factor is often the compatibility between civil operations and military missions. There are 18 joint-use airports in the National Plan of Integrated Airport Systems (NPIAS) (TABLE 2-1). Three joint-use airports are not included in the NPIAS because of low activity or restrictions on civil use at those facilities.

Table 2-1. National plan of integrated airport systems current joint-use airports, June 30, 1990. Source: FAA

State	Associated city	Airport name
AK	Delta Junction	Allen AAF
AZ	Yuma	Yuma MCAS-Yuma Int'l
AZ	Fort Huachuca/Sierra Vista	Libby AAF-Sierra Vista Muni
CA	Palmdale	Palmdale Plant 42
CA	Fairfield	Travis AFB
DE	Dover	Dover Air Force Base
FL	Valparaiso	Eglin Air Force Base
HI	Mokuleia	Dillingham Airfield
KS	Ft. Leavenworth	Sherman AAF
MA	Chicopee	Westover AFB
MI	Grayling	Grayling Army Airfield
MO	Fort Leonard Wood	Forney AAF
OH	Columbus	Rickenbacker Airport
SC	Charleston	Charleston AFB/Int'l
SC	Myrtle Beach	Myrtle Beach Air Force Base
TX	Wichita Falls	Sheppard AFB/Wichita Falls Municipal
WI	Sparta	McCoy AAF
GU	Agana	Agana NAS

Private airports

Many privately owned airports, open to the public, provide access to the air transportation system. When a privately owned airport is shown to be important to national transportation, it is included in the NPIAS. The current NPIAS includes 215 privately owned airports, including 48 reliever airports and six commercial service airports that are eligible to receive federal aid provided the owner is willing to make adequate assurance regarding the continued operation of the airport.

Airport activity

The activity, services, and investment at individual airports vary greatly. They are generally as active as the cities they serve. Indeed, the largest of our airports are almost self-contained cities. Table 2-2 lists the 10 busiest airports in three categories: total commercial passengers, aircraft operations, and based aircraft.

Total passengers is the sum of the enplaning (those who get on aircraft) and deplaning passengers (those who get off). Total passengers is a good indicator, especially of terminal building activity, because airports must provide service for passengers, both before and after they use the aircraft. Total operations is also a good indicator of airport activity, especially the use of the runway system. An aircraft operation is either a takeoff or a landing, including practice touch-and-goes.

Based aircraft is an important indicator of general aviation activity. At most airports there is a fleet of aircraft that is locally owned, "based," which accounts

Table 2-2. Activity at the 10 busiest airports. Source: FAA

Total commercial passengers CY 1988 (millions)		Total aircraft operations FY 1989 (thousands)		Based aircraft 1989	
Chicago-ORD	57	Chicago-ORD	789	Anchorage-Merrill	1,009
Atlanta	46	Dallas-Ft. Worth	694	Van Nuys	973
Dallas-Ft. Worth	44	Atlanta	670	Santa Ana	924
Los Angeles	43	Los Angeles	632	Centennial	894
New York - JFK	30	Santa Ana	534	Tamiami	830
Denver	30	Van Nuys	499	Deer Valley	820
San Francisco	30	Ft. Worth	493	Pontiac	804
Miami	24	Phoenix	480	Ft. Lauderdale	801
New York-LGA	24	Denver	468	Gillespie	799
Boston	23	Long Beach	462	Chino	788

for a large percentage of total activity. At major airports with airline service, however, there are relatively few based aircraft, most of the activity being transient.

Landing areas

The total number of landing areas increases each year, but the number that are open to the public is decreasing. More and more privately owned airports are being closed to the public, often because of insurance costs and liability considerations. Table 2-3 shows how the number of airports available to the public has decreased since 1970.

Table 2-3. U.S. landing areas 1970-1990. Source: FAA

Year	Total locations	Public-use	Private-use	Heliports (also in preceding columns)
1970	11,261	7,084	4,177	790
1975	13,251	7,005	6,246	1,524
1980	15,161	6,519	8,642	2,336
1981	15,476	6,290	9,186	2,507
1982	15,831	6,127	9,704	2,712
1983	16,029	5,987	10,042	2,918
1984	16,075	5,919	10,156	2,980
1985	16,319	5,858	10,461	3,120
1986	16,582	5,775	10,807	3,336
1987	17,015	5,723	11,292	3,653
1988	17,327	5,680	11,647	3,913
1989	17,446	5,626	11,820	4,016
1990	17,451	5,598	11,853	4,046

Classification of airports

Because of the sheer number of airports and the variety of size and function, the term airport system has little meaning when applied to all the airports and landing fields in the United States as a whole. Many airports exist only for the convenience of a few aircraft owners and operators and only play a small role in public air transportation. For this reason, FAA has identified a smaller group of airports that serve public air transportation either directly or indirectly and can be deemed of national importance and eligible for federal aid.

Since 1970, FAA has published a list of such airports, classified by size and function, in a planning document known as the National Airport System Plan (NASP). Under the Airport and Airway Improvement Act of 1982, FAA was charged with preparing a new version of this plan, called the National Plan of Integrated Airport Systems (NPIAS). First published in 1986, the second edition came out in 1991. A complete discussion of the NPIAS as part of the planning process at the national level is included in chapter 3.

In 1982, FAA revised the method of classifying airports and now lists them in four major categories: commercial service, primary, general aviation, and reliever (see TABLE 2-4).

Table 2-4. Federal-aid airports
by service level, June 30, 1990.
Source: FAA

Service level	Airports
Commercial service	568
Primary	(396)
Other	(172)
Reliever	285
General aviation	2,432
Total	3,285

Airports with scheduled services

Airports with scheduled passenger service have a number of classifications. *Commercial service airports* are defined as those airports receiving scheduled passenger service and having 2,500 or more annual enplanements, currently 568. *Primary airports* are defined as those commercial service airports having 10,000 or more enplanements, currently 396 primary airports among 568 commercial service airports. Airports with fewer than 2,500 annual enplanements are included under the general aviation category.

Hubs The term *hub* has more than one meaning in air transportation. It was first used by the Civil Aeronautics Board to describe the geographic areas that generate substantial portions of the nation's airline traffic. Later, it was adapted to categorize airports by the amount of passengers enplaned. It is also used to describe an airline route structure in which flights radiate from a major (hub) airport, much like spokes from the hub of a wheel, with the major airport serving as a transfer point for passengers changing flights. The strong competition among airlines in recent years has encouraged the use of such hubs. Urbanization and airline use of transfer hubs tends to concentrate traffic at the nation's largest airports. This point is illustrated in TABLE 2-5, in which commercial service airports are classified as large, medium, small, or nonhub airports, depending upon the percentage of the total national enplanements for which they account.

Table 2-5. Airport activity-revenue passenger enplanements 1988. Source: FAA

Hub airport category	Number of airports in category	Percentage of total national enplanements at airports	Number of annual enplanements at airports
Large (L)	29	1% and more	4,830,895 or more
Medium (M)	42	0.25 – 1.00	1,207,724 – 4,830,895
Small (S)	74	0.05 – 0.25	241,545 – 1,207,724
Non (N)	423	Less than 0.05%	Less than 241,545

The busiest airport in the nation, Chicago O'Hare International, enplaned 5.85 percent of all the passengers in the United States in 1988, and the 29 large hub airports together 67 percent of the national total.

Service in Alaska Scheduled service in Alaska is somewhat different from service in other states; the most important difference being the large number of small communities served by small aircraft. This is due to a unique lack of other adequate transportation modes. Approximately 200 communities are currently served. Many Alaskan communities are served infrequently, although on a scheduled basis. Once or twice a week is not unusual, and even less frequent service can be cited.

International About 265 foreign flag carriers, scheduled and nonscheduled, representing 94 countries, are authorized to serve the United States. Approximately 50 certificated U.S. carriers have specific authority to provide scheduled service to 87 foreign countries. About 150 other U.S. carriers may provide ser-

Metropolitan Dade County Tourism Department

Concorde SST at Miami International Airport.

vice to foreign countries, particularly to Canada, Mexico, and the Caribbean, on a nonscheduled basis.

International passengers (excluding Canadian traffic) account for only 6.5 percent of total U.S. passengers, but are important factors at New York, Miami, Los Angeles, and Honolulu. They account for only about 5 percent of the passengers at O'Hare, but 53 percent at JFK International Airport. International travel is important to airport planners because it requires special areas for customs and immigration procedures.

The general aviation system

General aviation airports account for the bulk of civil aircraft operations. It encompasses everything from crop dusting in small aircraft to passenger and cargo charters in the largest aircraft. It includes 98 percent of all registered civil aircraft and 95 percent of all airports; at other than the large and medium hub airports, most of the aircraft activity at commercial service airports is general aviation. Pipeline patrol, search and rescue operations, medical transport, business and executive flying in fixed-wing aircraft and helicopters, charters, air taxi, flight training, personal transportation, and the many other industrial, commercial, and recreational uses of airplanes and helicopters fall in the province of general aviation.

The airports serving general aviation are likewise varied. Typically, they are small, usually with a single runway and only minimal navigation aids. They serve primarily as a base for a few aircraft. There are notable exceptions. A few GA airports located in major metropolitan areas handle extremely high volumes of traffic (particularly business and executive aircraft) and are busier and more congested than all but the largest commercial airports. Such GA airports as Van Nuys, Long Beach, and Santa Ana in California fall into this category.

An important aspect of general aviation airports is that they serve many functions for a wide variety of aircraft. Some GA airports provide isolated communities with valuable links to other population centers. This is particularly true in areas of northern Alaska where communities are often unreachable except by air, but many parts of the Western United States also depend heavily on air transportation. In such areas, the GA airport is sometimes the only means of supplying communities with necessities and is vitally important in emergency situations.

The principal function of general aviation airports, however, is to provide facilities for privately owned aircraft used for business and personal activities. The role of GA airports in providing facilities for business aircraft is of growing importance. The business aircraft fleet is largely made up of twin-engine propeller or jet aircraft, typically equipped with sophisticated avionic devices comparable to those of commercial airliners. General aviation airports serving business aviation play an important role by providing facilities comparable to those at major air carrier airports, thereby permitting diversion of some GA traffic from congested hubs.

Although the general aviation fleet includes transport type equipment similar to that used by the major airlines, 78 percent of general aviation aircraft are single-engine piston aircraft. There are 184,447 aircraft currently based at NPIAS airports, of which approximately 71,540 are based at general aviation airports and 60,339 are based at reliever airports.

The FAA has established general aviation airport categories based on airport planning considerations. The *Basic Utility (BU) airport* accommodates most single-engine and many of the small twin-engine aircraft, approximately 95 percent of the general aviation fleet. *General Utility (GU) airports* accommodate virtually all general aviation aircraft. Typical runway lengths, at an assumed elevation of 500 feet above mean sea level and at a temperature of 85 °F, are 3,200 feet for BU airports and 4,300 feet for GU airports. Other general aviation airport designs are based on transport aircraft or business jets.

The reliever airport system

Reliever airports are a special category of general aviation airports. They are located in the vicinity of major air carrier airports and are specifically designated by FAA as "general aviation type airports which provide relief to congested major airports." To be classified by FAA as a reliever, an airport must have at least 50 based aircraft, or handle 25,000 itinerant operations or 35,000 local operations annually either at present or within the last two years. *Local operations* are aircraft flights that originate and terminate at the same airport. An *itinerant opera-*

tion originates at one airport and terminates at another. The reliever airport must also be located in an SMSA with a population of at least 250,000 or where passenger enplanements reach at least 250,000 annually. As the name suggests, reliever airports are intended to draw traffic away from crowded air carrier airports by providing facilities of similar quality and convenience to those available at air carrier airports.

They also provide the surrounding areas with access to air transportation. In the early 1960s, special legislation was passed to help develop these airports. By separating them from other general aviation airports, Congress gave them the equivalent of priority funding. The Airport and Airway Improvement Act of 1982 provided that a minimum of 10 percent of the Airport Improvement Program funds be reserved for reliever airports.

Relievers now account for most of the aircraft landings and takeoffs in major metropolitan areas. The 11 designated reliever airports in Atlanta had a total of 1,085,000 operations versus 802,000 at Hartsfield International. In Denver, operations at its three relievers totaled 558,000 versus 522,000 at Stapleton International. Another measure of their importance is the number of aircraft that are based at them. The 285 existing reliever airports accommodate 60,399 based aircraft, which is 29 percent of the total civil aircraft fleet.

Cessna Skywagon parked at a small general aviation airport.

The economic role of airports

Transportation is basic to the economy of any region, but little credit is given to the vital role it plays in linking suppliers, manufacturers, and consumers into a productive and efficient pattern of distribution. This is especially true from the aviation standpoint.

Everyone is aware of the contribution of highways to the transportation system because almost everyone drives a car, and almost every 18-wheeler has a sign on the back advertising that "This truck pays $5,000 in taxes every year."

Aviation is a key element in the transportation network but this fact is not publicized as well. The airlines do a fairly good job of letting the public know the importance of scheduled service at primary airports, but the public is usually unaware of the benefits derived from the general aviation industry.

A transportation link

The local airport is the principal gateway to the nation's transportation system. A community's lack of an airport can be as detrimental to its development as being bypassed by the railroads a century ago, or left off the highway map 50 years ago.

Communities that are not readily accessible to the airways might suffer economic penalties that can affect every local citizen, whether they fly in a general aviation aircraft, use the airlines, or never have occasion to travel at all.

The airlines provide excellent service to many major metropolitan areas of the country, but thousands of smaller cities, towns, and villages also need air transportation service. There are close to 20,000 incorporated communities in the 48 contiguous states and an additional 15,000 unincorporated communities. Because scheduled airlines serve fewer than 5 percent of the nation's 17,000 airports with approximately 5,000 aircraft, there are a large number of communities and their citizens without immediate access to the fine airline system.

The role of general aviation airports serving more than 200,000 aircraft, or 98 percent of the total active aircraft in the United States, in providing air access is increasing. By having air access to all the nation's airports, general aviation aircraft can bring the benefits and values of air transportation to the entire country.

Attracting industry

Cities and towns that years ago decided not to build an airport have learned that lack of an airport jeopardizes community progress. Time and again the lack of an airport has proved to be the chief reason why a community has been bypassed as a location for a new plant or a new industry.

While scheduled air service is concentrated in major metropolitan areas, business and industry are moving to less populated areas. Prior to World War II, nine out of 10 new industrial plants were built in metropolitan centers. By the early 1960s, this had shifted to approximately 50/50, and today nine out of 10 new industrial plants are being built in non-metropolitan areas. Room to expand, lower taxes, and better living and working conditions for employees are just several of the reasons causing this exodus. With branch plants, the source of production is nearer the distribution points—but management is farther away from its responsibilities. Without flexible air transportation provided by corporate aircraft and general aviation airports, management faces the dangers of absentee management—both in the widely spread branches and in the home office because of extended trips.

The airport has become vital to the growth of business and industry in a community by providing air access for companies that must meet the demands of supply, competition, and expanding marketing areas. Communities without airports place limitations on their capacity for economic growth.

Stimulate economic growth

Airports and related aviation and nonaviation businesses located on the airport represent a major source of employment for many communities around the country. The wages and salaries paid by airport-related businesses can have a significant effect on the local economy by providing the means to purchase goods and services while generating tax revenues as well. But local payrolls are not the only measure of an airport's economic benefit to the community. Indirectly, the employee expenditures generate successive waves of additional employment and purchases that are more difficult to measure but nevertheless substantial.

In addition to the local economic activity generated by the regular expenditures of resident employees, the airport also stimulates the economy through the use of local services for air cargo, food catering to the airlines, aircraft maintenance, and ground transportation on and around the airport. Regular purchases of fuel, supplies, equipment, and other services from local distributors inject additional income into the local community. The airport retail shops, hotels, and restaurants further act to recycle money within the local community as dollars pass from one person to another, supporting many people and many businesses. This so-called *multiplier effect* operates in all cities as aviation-related dollars are channeled throughout the community.

Airports provide an additional asset to the general economy by generating billions of dollars per year in state and local taxes. These tax dollars increase the revenues available for projects and services to benefit the residents of each state and community. Whether the extra tax dollars improve the state highway system, beautify state parks, or help prevent a tax increase, airport-generated tax dollars work for everyone.

Cities with good airport facilities also profit from tourist and convention business. This can represent substantial revenues for hotels, restaurants, retail stores, sports and night clubs, sightseeing, rental cars, and local transportation, among others. The amount of convention business varies with the size of the city, but even smaller communities show a sizable income from this area.

Influence on real estate value

Beyond the benefits that an airport brings to the community as a transportation facility and as a local industry, the airport has become a significant factor in the determination of real estate values in adjacent areas. Land located near airports almost always increases in value as the local economy begins to benefit from the presence of the airport. Land developers consistently seek land near airports, and it follows inexorably that a new airport will inspire extensive construction around it.

Current issues in airport system development

In recent years, a number of issues have arisen concerning airport system development where the interests of several parties have come into sharp conflict. One such group of issues relates to the strategic policy of the federal government in development of the airport system. Some have suggested that past federal policy has placed too much emphasis on capital investment in new facilities and not enough on methods to make more effective use of existing facilities.

A second set of issues involves funding. Some observers have suggested that the federal role has become too large and pervasive and that responsibility for airport development should devolve either on the airports and their local sponsors or on state governments.

Other issues arise from the legal and contractual arrangements traditionally concluded between airports and airlines. These arrangements have evolved over several decades, during a period of extensive federal regulation of the airlines. There is some concern that these airport-airline agreements might be inappropriate in a deregulated era, either because they might be too rigid to allow airports and airlines to meet new challenges or because they might have anticompetitive features that do not allow the market to operate freely.

Another issue is the problem of aircraft noise, which has been a growing environmental and political problem for many airports despite technological advances in reducing noise of jet aircraft.

Finally, there are issues surrounding the planning of future airport development, particularly the timing and location of demand growth and the role that the federal government will play in defining and meeting airport needs.

Federal policy and strategy

Historically, federal airport development policy has sought to promote the aviation industry and to accommodate growth of traffic demand. Where forecasts of future traffic demand have exceeded existing airport capacity, the solution has generally been to provide capital aid to build new facilities. The Airport Development Aid Program (ADAP), funded with user fees earmarked for the Airport and Airway Trust Fund, was established in 1970 as a response to the congestion and delay problems that plagued airports in the late 1960s. ADAP provided federal matching grants to airports to pay for certain types of capital improvements, principally construction of new runways, taxiways, and aprons to relieve airside congestion. Federal assistance for capital improvements continues through the Airport Improvement Program (AIP), created by the Airport and Airway Improvement Act of 1982.

FAA projections of future traffic demand indicate that there could be severe airside congestion at a number of major airports over the next 20 years. Although some of the delays might be eased by improved air traffic control technology, the FAA view is that the primary constraint on the growth of the system will be "a lack of concrete" and that there is a need for more runways, taxiways, and ramps.

Thus, basic strategy has been challenged on the grounds that it biases the outcome toward capital-intensive solutions. Critics argue that federal development grants have, in some cases, encouraged airport operators to overbuild. In other cases, the facilities built with federal support are substantially different in form and more expensive than needed to accomplish their intended function. But more fundamentally, the existence of a federal program providing aid for only certain types of capital improvements at airports has distorted investment decisions and led airport operators to build not necessarily what they *need*, but what the government is willing to help pay for. By accommodating demand wherever and whenever it occurs through increasingly large and complex new capital facilities, more growth is encouraged at precisely those locations where it will be most difficult and expensive to absorb.

Other critics have suggested that projections of traffic growth are too high. Recent changes in the airline industry—such as deregulation, the growth of commuter air carriers, sharp rises in fuel costs, and escalating operating costs—might have caused permanent structural changes in the airline industry such that the great traffic growth of the 1960s, '70s, and '80s will not continue. The general aviation industry has also experienced a sharp downturn in sales since the late 1970s; thus, policies aimed at accommodating high projected levels of growth might lead to overbuilding and excess capacity, and misallocation of resources within the system.

Congestion and delay in the airport system are not evenly distributed, concentrated at a few airports, while many others operate far below their design capacity; thus, an alternative strategic response might be to manage or direct growth of air activity in ways that make more productive use of existing, uncrowded airport facilities.

Some observers believe that growth can be managed through administrative or economic means requiring only limited new capital investments. Administrative responses to growth include rules adopted by airport operators or various levels of government to divert traffic from congested airports to places or times where it can be handled more easily. Economic responses rely on market competition to determine access to airport services and facilities. To some extent, both administrative and economic measures for managing demand are already in use at a number of busy airports; however, legal, contractual, and even constitutional barriers might preclude wider use of such techniques. Some of these barriers could be lowered through federal government action. A discussion of possible administrative and economic options is presented in chapter 8.

Funding issues

Before World War II, the federal government was inclined to the view that airports, like ocean and river ports, were a local responsibility, and the federal role was confined to maintaining the navigable airways and waterways connecting those ports. At the onset of World War II, the federal government began to develop airports on land leased from municipalities. Federal investment was justified on the grounds that a strong system of airports was vital to national defense. After the war, many of these improved airports were declared surplus and turned over to municipalities. Federal assistance to airports continued throughout the 1950s and 1960s at a low level and was aimed primarily at improving surplus airports and adapting them to civil use. Major federal support of airport development resumed in 1970 with the passage of the Airport and Airway Development Act, which was in large part a response to the congestion and delay then being experienced at major airports. This act established the user-supported Airport and Airway Trust Fund and ADAP.

Federal assistance to airports under ADAP was distributed as matching grants for capital improvement projects. There were several formulas for allocation—entitlement (calculated from the number of passengers enplaned at the airport), block grant (based on state area and population), and need (discrepancy funds). Over the 10-year life of ADAP, outlays from the trust fund amounted to approximately $4 billion. ADAP expired in 1980, but a similar program of airport development assistance, AIP, was established in 1982. Before AIP was enacted, there was extensive debate about the future direction of federal airport aid, spared by proposals to withdraw assistance for ("to defederalize") major air carrier airports.

Supporters of *defederalization* advanced two arguments: that the federal government is overinvolved in financing airport development and that federal assistance is not necessary for large airports because they are capable of financing their own capital development. By excluding large airports from eligibility for federal grants, the government could reduce the overall cost of the aid program and at the same time provide more aid to small air carrier and general aviation airports. The advantage to large airports, as pointed out by supporters of defederalization, would be freedom from many legal and administrative requirements involved in accepting federal assistance.

Opponents of defederalization contend that the proposal is unwise for several reasons. First, it would eliminate federal assistance for the very airports that provide the bulk of passenger service and have the greatest problems of congestion and delay. It is at these airports, the backbone of the national system, where a federal presence can most easily be justified. Further, passengers using large airports pay approximately three-quarters of the taxes supporting the Airport and Airway Trust Fund; thus, defederalization would lead to subsidy of smaller airports by larger ones. Some observers also questioned the ability of many airports to carry out necessary capital improvements without federal participation. While agreeing that federal grants form only a small percentage of total capital budgets at large airports, they argued that it was a needed revenue source for all but the very largest 5 or 10 airports.

Some proponents hold that defederalized airports should be allowed to charge a "passenger facility charge" or "head tax" to make up for the loss of federal funds. Federal law now prohibits airports from taxing passengers. Others object to the head tax while supporting the concept of defederalization, holding that airports could raise sufficient funds through retained earnings or through the private bond market to cover their capital needs. One major objection to the head tax is that passengers would have to bear a double tax when using a defederalized airport. They would have to pay a ticket tax supporting the Airport and Airway Trust Fund plus a head tax at the arrival or departure airport.

The major airlines, as represented by the Air Transport Association, are indifferent on the question of defederalization but opposed to the head tax. The airlines hold that the tax would impose unnecessary administrative burdens on them and would be unfair to passengers. Other observers note that the underlying reasons for the air carriers' objection is that head taxes would give airports an independent source of revenue and weaken the voice that airlines now have in airport investment decisions.

Airport operators are divided. Some very large airports, such as Chicago O'Hare, support defederalization on the condition that it be accompanied by the freedom to impose a head tax. The Airport Operators Council International, an organization representing airports of all sizes, expresses qualified support of the concept of "optional defederalization" where airports could choose whether or not they wished to receive federal aid, rather than having the decision made for them on the basis of size and passenger volume. Many airports oppose defederalization and the head tax.

The question of defederalization is still open. Although the Airport and Airway Improvement Act of 1982 passed without a defederalization provision, it directed the Department of Transportation to study the effects of defederalization. As of early 1990 there was no definitive answer to the problem.

Another approach to airport financing was also raised during the debate over AIP. Under the general concept of *new federalism*, it was proposed to turn increased responsibility for decisions on airport funding and programming over to state aviation agencies and departments of transportation. Supporters contended that state agencies are in a better position to determine the needs of local airports and could distribute grants with less red tape than the federal government. They pointed out that some states already have active aviation agencies that evaluate airport improvement projects and approve all applications for federal assistance. In these cases, the needs of the airports and the state might better be served by allowing state agencies more latitude in distributing airport grants.

A stronger role for state agencies could reduce the federal role to basically that of a tax collector. Because of the interstate nature of air transportation, it would probably be more efficient to continue to collect ticket taxes, fuel taxes, or other aviation taxes at the national level; however, the funds could be passed through to the states on a formula basis, and the actual decisions on how funds were spent could be made at the state level.

There are several objections to the concept of new federalism. First, the state agencies vary in strength. Many do not have the staff or the expertise to take on the responsibilities of evaluating airport development projects or administering grants. A period of transition would be necessary while these states prepared to accept new responsibilities. Others argue that setting up 50 separate agencies to do the work of FAA would add an additional layer of bureaucracy because FAA involvement could not be completely eliminated. Still others see interstate or multistate cooperation as a major stumbling block. For example, a state government, perhaps lacking perspective of the airport system as a whole, might find little incentive to aid development of an airport outside its borders or to enter into regional compacts to compensate citizens of adjacent states for airport noise impacts.

Airport management issues

Deregulation has led to changes in the relationship between airports and airlines. Airports traditionally maintained long-term use agreements (of 20 to 30 years) with the airlines that served them. These agreements covered such arrangements as landing fees and the leasing of terminal space. As a result of these agreements, airlines have had a strong influence on the creditworthiness of airports in the revenue bond market because their financial stability and continued presence was a guarantee of the long-term economic viability of the airport. In some instances, airlines have been party to airport revenue bonds, agreeing to be jointly and severally liable for payment of debt and interest. In return for such guarantees, airlines have gained approval rights for capital improvement projects to be undertaken at the airport.

Since deregulation, however, air carriers' routes and service points are not as stable, and the airlines themselves have experienced financial difficulties. Long-term contracts written in the era of regulation might now inhibit the carriers' freedom to change routes. Conversely, they may also make it difficult for airports to accommodate new carriers. In some cases, carriers with long-term agreements whose service to the airport has declined might be occupying gate and counter space that a new entrant might be able to use more effectively.

Some observers have questioned whether long-term agreements—especially majority-in-interest clauses—might not have anticompetitive effects in the deregulated environment. They point out that incumbent carriers might make use of their agreements to deny new entrants access to the aiport, or at least to place them at a competitive disadvantage with respect to terminal space and facilities. They also point out that carriers often negotiate with airport management as a group in a "negotiating committee" or "top committee" and question whether group negotiations involving competing firms are appropriate in a deregulated market.

It has also been pointed out that a capacity limit at a major airport has the effect of reducing free competition among carriers and works as a form of "reregulation" of the industry. Airport operators must be careful that actions taken to manage or control the growth of traffic at individual airports do not have anticompetitive effects. This issue was raised in connection with two events, the 1981 air traffic controllers' strike and the Braniff bankruptcy, which brought attention to the question of who owns airport operating slots. A *slot* is a block of time allocated to an airport user to perform an aircraft operation (takeoff or landing).

During the strike, FAA imposed quotas on 22 airports, limiting the number of operations that could be performed each hour. Several methods of allocation were tried: administrative assignment, exchanges among incumbent carriers, and, briefly, auction. New entrant airlines complained that all of these methods were unfair.

When Braniff stopped operating, FAA redistributed its slots among other carriers, despite Braniff's claims that the slots were the airline's property for which it should be paid. Throughout this period there was controversy over whether or not a slot should be considered property, and whether the proceeds from a slot sale should go to the airline, the airport, or the federal government.

This issue arose again in connection with slot auctions at Washington National and New York LaGuardia. Finally after continued controversy, the FAA granted the airlines the right to buy and sell the slots they held. While the buy-sell slot rule has stabilized the situation somewhat for the airlines, most airport authorities would prefer to see the funds from any sale go toward expanding the capacity of the air transportation system. Authorities also question the rationale for allowing private airlines who obtained federally authorized landing slots at no cost, to sell these slots to other airlines at large profits. New entrant air carriers also claimed that the slot-holding airlines stifle competition. Regional carriers are also concerned about the slots available.

Unquestionably slots represent one of the most significant barriers to entry in the airline business today. Their impact on the industry extends far beyond the few airports where they are imposed because markets critical to many communities either begin or end at one of these facilities.

This question might become particularly acute if problems of delay and congestion spread to more airports, and airport operators seek to employ traffic management techniques. If an airport imposes a quota, it must devise some method for allocating slots to present users and for accommodating new entrants. Until the question of slot ownership is finally resolved, any attempt to use selling or auction as an allocation method is likely to reignite this controversy.

Noise and environment issues

Noise has been a major problem at airports since the introduction of the commercial jet aircraft. Recent technological advances in airframe and jet engine design have made new aircraft much quieter, but many industry experts believe that further large-scale reductions in aircraft noise will not be possible.

The public is very sensitive to noise, which has become an emotionally charged political issue. Noise is probably the single most important constraint on the expansion of airports or the building of new ones. The problem is in large part one of land use, and land use decisions are usually beyond the control of FAA and the airport proprietor. Zoning and land use planning are the responsibility of local jurisdictions, and many jurisdictions have not applied land use controls to prevent residential communities from growing up near airports. Often, intergovernmental cooperation is needed because major airports might be surrounded by several municipalities, each with different zoning policies. The federal government has sometimes complicated the issue by financing and approving residential development projects in high-noise areas.

At present, citizens with complaints about airport noise have recourse only to the airport proprietor. While FAA and air carriers have some responsibility for abating aircraft noise, only the airport operator is legally liable. In many cases, airports have had to pay nuisance and damage claims for noise. To reduce their liability and to protect themselves, airports have instituted noise abatement programs that involve restricting aircraft flight paths or hours of operation so as to reduce noise impact on residential areas. Noise abatement procedures can have a detrimental effect on airport capacity, and many airports with serious congestion and delay have found that the need to control nose restricts their freedom of action. In some cases, airports have had to purchase surrounding land or install noise-absorbing insulation in buildings under flight paths.

Some states and localities have enacted special regulations to limit aircraft noise at airports under their jurisdiction. There are several concerns about the proliferation of local noise standards. First, the standards vary from one location to another, adding confusion and complexity to the system. Second, the standards might act as a restraint on interstate commerce. Airlines might have to accelerate their purchases of quiet aircraft in order to serve many points with stringent noise standards. If they are not financially able to make these purchases, the only alternative might be to curtail operations at some locations.

Some argue that the federal government should set and enforce a uniform national standard for airport noise; however, FAA has been reluctant to embark on such a policy, in part because the federal government might then have to assume liability for violations of the standard.

Planning issues

Many of the difficulties in planning a national airport system arise from its size and diversity. Each airport has unique problems, and each airport operator—although constrained by laws, regulations, and custom—is essentially an independent decision-maker. While airports collectively form a system, it is not a system that is comprehensively planned and centrally managed. FAA's role in planning the system has traditionally been one of gathering and reporting information on individual airport decisions and discouraging redundant development.

Since 1970, the National Airport System Plan and subsequent NPIAS has been prepared by FAA regional offices, working in conjunction with local airport authorities. NPIAS presents an inventory of the project capital needs of more than 3,200 airports "in which there is a potential federal interest and on which federal funds may be spent." because the funds available from federal and private local sources are sufficient to complete only a fraction of the eligible projects, many of the airport improvements included in NPIAS are never undertaken.

NPIAS has been criticized on three principal points.

First, it is not really a plan, in the sense that it does not present time phasing or assign priorities to projects. FAA has attempted to meet this criticism by categorizing projects and needs according to three levels of program objectives: Level I—Maintain the existing system; Level II—Bring airports up to standards; and Level III—Expand the system. Some, however, see this categorization as inadequate.

Second, the criteria for the selection of the airports and projects to be included in the plan have come under criticism. Some have argued that most of the 3,200 airports in NPIAS are not truly of national interest and that criteria should be made more stringent to reduce the number to a more manageable set. On the other hand, there are those who contend that the plan cannot be of national scope unless it contains all publicly owned airports. It is argued that because NPIAS lists only development projects eligible for federal aid and not those that would be financed solely by state, local, and private sources, the total airport development needs are understated by the plan.

A final criticism is that NPIAS deals strictly with the development needs of individual airports, without regard to regional and intermodal coordination.

Airport information sources

Many of the national aviation organizations are deeply interested in helping to develop and preserve airports because of their role in the national air transportation system and their value to the areas they serve. These groups provide facts and figures, films, speakers, and other types of assistance to airport management and other proponents in order to present a strong, positive case to community leaders and others. Many provide publications, which range from mimeographed newsletters and bulletins to first-class magazines. Most are headquartered in the Washington, D.C., area where they compete with hundreds of other lobbying groups for the attention of Congress and federal agencies. Some are frequently called to testify at congressional and federal hearings, where their influence and expertise can be significant.

Each of the organizations is particularly concerned with the interests of their constituents; however, there are numerous times when they close ranks and work together for mutual goals affecting the aviation community in general. The following is a brief listing of the most prominent associations. A complete listing can be found in the *World Aviation Directory* published by McGraw-Hill, Inc.

AEROSPACE INDUSTRIES ASSOCIATION (AIA)—1919
1250 Eye Street, NW
Washington, DC 20005
(202)371-8400

First called the Aeronautical Chamber of Commerce, its name was changed to Aircraft Industry Association in 1945 and finally its present name in 1959. Member companies represent the primary manufacturers of military and large commercial aircraft, engines, accessories, rockets, spacecraft, and related items.

AIRCRAFT OWNERS & PILOTS ASSOCIATION (AOPA)—1939
421 Aviation Way
Frederick, MD 21701
(301) 695-2000

With over 270,000 members, AOPA represents the interests of general aviation pilots. It provides insurance plans, flight planning, and other services, and sponsors large fly-in meetings. The Air Safety Foundation is affiliated with AOPA.

AIR LINE PILOTS' ASSOCIATION (ALPA)—1931
1625 Massachusetts Avenue, NW
Washington, DC 20036
(703) 689-2270

Founded in 1931, it is the oldest and largest airline pilots' union.

AIRPORT OPERATORS COUNCIL INTERNATIONAL (AOCI)—1948
Suite 200, 1220 19th Street, NW
Washington, DC 20036
(202) 293-8500

Members are governing and operating bodies of 150 U.S. and 70 foreign air carrier airports enplaning 75 percent of the free-world air passengers and 92 percent of the U.S. This organization deals with all kinds of technical and economic problems facing airports.

AIR TRANSPORT ASSOCIATION (ATA)—1938
1709 New York Avenue, NW
Washington, DC 20006
(202) 626-4000

Represents the nation's certificated air carriers in a broad spectrum of technical and economic issues.

AMERICAN ASSOCIATION OF AIRPORT EXECUTIVES (AAAE)—1928
4212 King Street
Alexandria, VA 22302
(703) 824-0500

A division of the Aeronautical Chamber of Commerce at its inception, AAAE became independent in 1939. Membership includes over 1,000 airport managers at 650 airports, plus affiliates. The AAAE Foundation was formed in 1957 to encourage education.

AVIATION DISTRIBUTORS & MANUFACTURERS ASSOCIATION (ADMA)—1943
1900 Arch Street
Philadelphia, PA 19103
(215) 564-3484

Represents the interests of a wide variety of aviation firms including FBOs and component parts manufacturers. A strong proponent of aviation education.

AVIATION/SPACE WRITERS' ASSOCIATION (AWA)—1938
Suite 1200, 17 S. High Street
Columbus, OH 43215
(614) 221-1900

Organization of news, feature writers, and public relations people.

CIVIL AIR PATROL (CAP)—1941
Maxwell AFB, Building 714
Montgomery, AL 36112
(205) 293-6019

An Air Force auxiliary with wing commands in 50 states, District of Columbia, and Puerto Rico. The CAP conducts search and rescue and other emergency flights. It provides extensive training for teenage cadets.

EXPERIMENTAL AIRCRAFT ASSOCIATION (EAA)—1953
EAA Aviation Center
Oshkosh, WI 54903
(414) 426-4800

EAA, with over 700 local chapters, promotes the interests of homebuilt and sport aircraft owners. It also hosts the world's largest annual fly-in.

FLIGHT SAFETY FOUNDATION (FSF)—1945
Suite 500, 2200 Wilson Boulevard
Arlington, VA 22201
(703) 522-8300

The primary function of FSF is promoting air transport safety. Its members include airport and airline executives and consultants.

GENERAL AVIATION MANUFACTURERS ASSOCIATION (GAMA)—1970
Suite 801, 1400 K Street, NW
Washington, DC 20005
(202) 393-1500

Originally, a part of AIA, GAMAs members include manufacturers of GA aircraft, engines, accessories, and avionics equipment.

HELICOPTER ASSOCIATION INTERNATIONAL (HAI)—1946
1619 Duke Street
Alexandria, VA 22314
(703) 683-4646

Members represent rotorcraft operators and manufacturers.

INTERNATIONAL AIR TRANSPORT ASSOCIATION (IATA)—1945
2000 Peel Street
Montreal, PQ, Canada H3A2R4
(514) 844-6311

An association of 105 international air carriers whose main functions include coordination of fares and operations.

INTERNATIONAL CIVIL AIRPORTS ASSOCIATION (ICAA)—1960
Building 226, Orly Aeroport Celex
Orly Sud 103, Paris, France 94396
01-497-54470

Represents airports in 80 countries and serves as United Nations consultant on airport organization, operations, planning, and construction.

INTERNATIONAL CIVIL AVIATION ORGANIZATION (ICAO)—1947
100 Sherbrooke Street W
Montreal, PQ, Canada H3A2R2
(514) 285-8219

ICAO's 163 member nations set standards and regulations for international air carriers operating over the worldwide airport/airway system.

NATIONAL AIR TRANSPORTATION ASSOCIATION (NATA)—1941
4226 King Street
Alexandria, VA 22302
(703) 845-9000

First called the National Aviation Training Association and later Trades Association, NATA represents the interests of Fixed-base and air-taxi operators.

NATIONAL ASSOCIATION OF STATE AVIATION OFFICIALS (NASAO)—1931
Suite 505, 8401 Colesville Road
Silver Spring, MD 20910
(301) 588-0587

Represents departments of transportation and state aviation departments and commissions from 49 states, Puerto Rico, and Guam.

NATIONAL BUSINESS AIRCRAFT ASSOCIATION (NBAA)—1947
1200 18th Street, NW, Room 200
Washington, DC 20036
(202) 783-9000

Represents companies that own or operate aircraft flown for corporate purposes. Affiliated with the International Business Aircraft Council.

PROFESSIONAL AVIATION MAINTENANCE ASSOCIATION (PAMA)—1972
Suite 809, 500 NW Plaza
St. Ann, MO 63074
(314) 739-2580

Promotes the interests of Airframe and Powerplant (A&P) mechanics.

REGIONAL AIRLINE ASSOCIATION (RAA)—1975
Suite 700, 1101 Connecticut Avenue, NW
Washington, DC 20036
(202) 857-1170

Formerly the Commuter Airline Association, RAA represents the regional air carriers.

The Federal Aviation Administration is also a major resource for airport operators. The most obvious need for coordination with the FAA is in obtaining funds. The regional offices and local airport offices are of considerable assistance in all phases of the procedure. The representatives at those offices know the state and local situations and what must be done to conform with federal policy. The airports district offices provide a ready source of technical assistance to airport administration. Most importantly, the FAA publishes numerous documents that are designated to assist management in all phases of airport planning and management.

Key terms

commercial service airports
primary airports
hub
general aviation airports
basic utility (BU) airport
general utility (GU) airport
reliever airports
multiplier effect
defederalization
new federalism
slot

Review questions

1. Identify the leading airports in the United States in terms of enplaned
      passengers, aircraft operations, and based aircraft.
   Distinguish between primary and commercial service airports.
   Describe the multifaceted role of general aviation airports.
   What are the requirements necessary to be classified as a reliever airport?

2. Why is the close proximity to an airport important in attracting businesses to
      a particular area?
   The United States has the finest scheduled air transportation system in the
      world. Why do we need all of these general aviation airports?
   How do airports stimulate economic growth?

3. Discuss several of the basic criticisms of federal policy and strategy
      regarding airport development over the years.
   Give two arguments in favor of and against defederalization.
   How do you feel about certain major airports charging a passenger "head
      tax" as an alternative to federal funding?
   What is meant by "new federalism?" Give some objections to this concept.

4. How has deregulation led to changes in the relationship between airports and airlines?

   What are some of the problems with various states and localities enacting different noise regulations?

   What are the three principal criticisms of NPIAS?

   Discuss the controversy surrounding slot allocations at congested airports.

5. List and briefly describe the primary role of five national aviation organizations. Where are most of these organizations located? What do they have in common and what is their relationship to airports?

Suggested readings

deNeufville, Richard. *Airport System Planning*. The MacMillan Press, Ltd. London, England, 1976.

Howard, George P., Ed. *Airport Economic Planning*. The MIT Press. Cambridge, Massachusetts, 1974.

National Plan of Integrated Airport Systems (NPIAS), 1990–1999. Washington, DC: FAA, June, 1991.

Ninth Annual Report of Accomplishments under the Airport Improvement Program. FY 1990. Washington, DC: FAA, April, 1991.

Wiley, John R., Airport Administration and Management. Eno Foundation for Transportation. Westport, Connecticut, 1986.

Airport
system planning

Outline

Introduction
The planning process
Need for integration among plans

Objectives

When you have completed this chapter, you should be able to:

△ Discuss the importance of airport system planning.

△ Describe the purpose and some criticisms of the NPIAS.

△ Describe the purpose and define the "levels of need" under NPIAS.

△ Distinguish between regional and state airport planning.

△ Describe the purpose and some criticisms of the SASP.

△ Explain what is meant by "Integrated Airport System Planning" as described in the NPIAS.

△ List the major objectives of an airport master plan.

△ Explain the importance of local coordination in airport system planning.

△ Discuss the need for integration among airport system plans at the national, regional, state, and local levels.

Introduction

Considering the high cost and long lead time for building or improving airports, planning is the key in determining what facilities will be needed and in creating programs for providing them in a timely manner, while making wise use of resources. Planning for airport development requires more than simply scheduling the capital improvements to be made. Airports are public entities, whose managers interact with many other public and private organizations. Airport development plans affect other aspects of community life, such as the land dedicated to aviation use or the noise or automobile traffic that the airport generates. The need for aviation development must thus be weighed against other societal needs and plans. Planning cannot be done for one airport in isolation; each airport is part of a network that is itself part of the national transportation system.

Our attention in the future must be focused on *airport system planning*, not simply airport planning. Airport plans must be developed as part of a system that includes national, regional, state, and local transportation planning.

Federal Aviation Administration

The variety of aircraft shown at this metropolitan airport demonstrates the need for airport system planning.

Determining need and programming development at individual airports has become formalized in a process called *airport master planning*. While master planning in the full sense is practiced primarily by large airports, even the smallest must make use of some elements of the process to prepare for future change. At a level above airport master planning is *regional system planning*, which is concerned with development of all airports in a metropolitan area. It often involves difficult political decisions on development priorities among competing airports. In some cases, this responsibility is assumed by a regional or metropolitan planning agency, but many state governments have also taken on the task of developing a coordinated system plan for airports serving not only major metropolitan regions but also outlying small communities and rural areas within the state. In some cases, state agencies prepare these plans themselves; in others, they provide technical assistance and review for local planning bodies. The role of the federal government in airport planning includes a broad range of activities. The most comprehensive activity is the National Plan of Integrated Airport Systems (NPIAS) of the Federal Aviation Administration, which summarizes the development needs of roughly 3,200 airports across the country. At the other extreme, FAA has responsibility to approve, on a project-by-project basis, specific development projects for which airport sponsors are seeking federal funds.

This chapter describes airport system planning at various levels, with emphasis on the planning process and the need for integrating planning at all levels.

The planning process

National level

Airport planning at the national level is the responsibility of FAA, whose interests are to provide guidance for development of the vast network of publicly owned airports and to establish a frame of reference for investment of federal funds. These interests are set forth in the *National Plan of Integrated Airport Systems (NPIAS)*, a document required under the Airport and Airway Improvement Act of 1982. The NPIAS is a 10-year plan that is revised every two years and is closely coordinated with the FAA's 10-year capital investment plan to improve the air traffic control system and airway facilities.

NPIAS is not a plan in the fullest sense. It does not establish priorities, lay out a timetable, propose a level of funding, or commit the federal government to a specific course of action. Instead, it is merely an inventory of the type and cost of airport developments that might take place during the planning period at airports eligible for federal assistance. It is a tabular, state-by-state presentation of data for individual airports, listed in a common format, indicating location, role, type of service, and level of activity (enplanements and operations) currently and for five and 10 years in the future. Projected costs of airport needs in categories—land, paving, lighting, approach aids, terminal, and other—are shown, also at intervals of five and 10 years.

Estimates of need contained in NPIAS are developed by comparing FAA national and terminal area forecasts to the present capacity of each airport. Much of the initial determination of need and the regular updating is performed by FAA regional offices, which monitor changes and developments being carried out at the airports. NPIAS is not a simple compilation of local master plans or state airport system plans, although FAA does draw on these documents as sources in forming judgments about future needs and prospective airport improvements.

NPIAS is not a complete inventory of airport needs. The plan contains only "airport development in which there is a *potential* federal interest and on which federal funds may be spent under the current Airport Improvement Program (AIP) or former Airport Development Aid Program (ADAP) and the Planning Grant Program." There are two necessary conditions in the test of potential federal interest. First, the airport must meet certain minimum criteria as an eligible recipient for federal aid, and second, the planned improvement at that airport must be of a type that is eligible for federal aid. Eligible projects include such projects as land acquisition for expansion of an airfield, paving for runways and taxiways, installation of lighting or approach aids, and expansion of public terminal areas. Improvements ineligible for federal aid are not included in NPIAS: construction of hangars, parking areas, and revenue-producing terminal areas that airports are expected to build with private, local, or state funds.

On the other hand, NPIAS probably overstates the amount that will actually be spent on airport improvements over the 10-year period. Many of the projects whose costs are included in the NPIAS will not receive federal funds and many will not be undertaken at all. Inclusion in the NPIAS does not necessarily represent federal agreement to fund a project or local commitment to carry it out. It is merely FAA's best estimate of likely future need. The goal of NPIAS is to set forth ". . . the type and estimated cost of airport development considered by the secretary to be necessary to provide a system of public airports adequate to *anticipate and meet* the needs of civil aeronautics . . . ." If and when local sponsors are ready to undertake projects, they must apply for federal funds.

NPIAS relates airport system improvements to three *levels of need*: Level I—Maintain the airport system in its current condition; Level II—Bring the system up to current design standards; and Level III—Expand the system. Maintaining the system includes such projects as repaving airfields and replacing lighting systems; bringing the system up to standards involves such projects as installing new light systems and widening runways; expanding the system includes construction of new airports or lengthening runways to accommodate larger aircraft.

The classification by three levels of need is a refinement added to subsequent editions of the NPIAS. It moves in the direction of assigning priorities to different types of projects instead of the earlier practice of presenting needs as a single sum. FAA selected this presentation because previous lump sum projections "often did not lend themselves well for use in establishing the funding levels of programs intended to implement their broad findings." The three-level system was developed as a guide to Congress, illustrating how "alternative levels of funding . . . can be blessed on relating NPIAS development needs to three levels of program objectives."

The classification system is somewhat misleading because it is not as hierarchical as it might appear, and the placement of a type of improvement at a particular program level does not necessarily reflect the priority that will be given a particular project. High-priority projects, those that FAA and a local sponsor agree must be carried out as soon as possible, might not necessarily correspond with "Level I" needs in the NPIAS. An expansion project (Level III) at an extremely congested and important airport might be more urgent than bringing a little-used airport up to standards (Level II); thus, if available funds were limited to 34 percent of total need (the amount needed to cover Levels I and II) it would not be possible, nor would FAA intend, to carry out only Level I and II projects and leave vital Level III projects unfunded. In any given year, the actual grants awarded are used for some projects in each program level.

NPIAS has been criticized for drawing the federal interest too broadly and for being more of a "wish list" than a planning document. Critics have claimed that it is merely a compilation of improvements desired by local and state authorities and that it does not represent a careful assessment of airport development projects that truly serve national airport needs as distinct from those that are primarily local or regional in character. It is true that the plan includes many very small airports of questionable importance to the national system of air transportation. The *criteria for inclusion in the NPIAS* are minimally restrictive. The principal ones are: 1) that the airport has (or is forecast to have within five years) at least 10 based aircraft (or engines); 2) that it can be at least a 30-minute drive from the nearest existing or proposed airport currently in the NPIAS; and 3) that there is an eligible sponsor willing to undertake ownership and development of the airport. Clearly there are many airports that meet these minimum criteria. As of the beginning of 1990, there were 3,285 airports qualifying for inclusion in the NPIAS, roughly a minimum of one airport per county.

Paradoxically, NPIAS has also been criticized for just the opposite reason: It is too exclusive, in that it reflects only FAA's interpretation of national importance and not those of state or regional planning agencies. Approximately 1,000 airports, not listed in the NPIAS, are integral parts of state and regional development plans; and their exclusion means that sponsors or state planning agencies cannot expect federal aid for developing these facilities.

Regional level

Regional airport planning takes as its basic unit of analysis the airport hub, roughly coincident with the boundaries of a metropolitan area. The planner is concerned with air transportation for the region as a whole and must consider traffic at all the airports in the region, both large and small. The practice of regional planning is relatively new and has been instituted to deal with questions of resource allocation and use that often arise when the airports in a region have been planned and developed individually and without coordination among affected jurisdictions. Regional planning seeks to overcome the rivalries and the jurisdictional overlaps of the various local agencies involved in airport development and operation. The goal is to produce an airport system that is optimum with respect to regionwide benefits and costs.

Thus, regional airport planning addresses one critical issue usually not dealt with in an airport master plan: the allocation of traffic among the airports in a region. This can be a sensitive subject. Questions of traffic distribution involve political as well as technical and economic issues, and they can greatly affect the future growth of the airports involved. One airport might be quite busy while another is underutilized. If traffic were to continue growing at the busy airport, new facilities would have to be constructed to accommodate that growth. On the other hand, if some of the new traffic were diverted to an underutilized airport, the need for new construction might be reduced and service to the region as a whole might be improved.

Although a planning agency might decide that such a diversion is in the interest of a metropolitan region and might prepare forecasts and plans showing how it could be accomplished, it might not necessarily have power to implement these plans. Where airports are competitors, it is probably not reasonable to expect that the stronger will voluntarily divert traffic and revenues to the other. The planning agency would likely have to influence the planning and development process at individual airports so that they will make decisions reflecting the regional agency's assessment of regional needs.

One way to influence planning decisions is through control over distribution of federal and state development grants. Before 1982, regional agencies served as clearing houses for federal funds under the review process required by *Office of Management and Budget Circular A-95*. While the award of federal airport development funds depended mainly on FAA approval of the airport sponsor's application, the A-95 process required that designated regional agencies review projects before the grants were awarded. In particular, the regional agencies were required to certify that the planned improvement was consistent with federal regulations, for example, environmental regulations.

In July 1982, President Reagan issued Executive Order 12372, outlining a new policy for intergovernmental review of direct federal grant programs. The purpose of the new policy: to "strengthen federalism by relying on state and local processes for the state and local government coordination and review of proposed financial assistance and direct federal development . . . ." The intent is to give additional weight to the concerns of state and local officials with respect to federally funded development. State and local governments are encouraged to develop their own procedures (or refine existing procedures) for reviewing development plans and grant applications. Under the new policy, agencies are to certify that federal spending is consistent with state and local objectives and priorities, instead of certifying that state and local projects comply with federal guidelines, as they did formerly. Federal agencies, such as FAA, are expected to accommodate recommendations communicated through the state review process or to justify refusal to do so.

Some states may choose to continue using the same regional planning organizations as review agencies, while others may create new procedures and new agencies. The executive order discourages "the reauthorization of any planning organization which is federally funded, which has a federally prescribed membership, which is established for a limited purpose, and which is not adequately representative of, or accountable to, state or local elected officials;" however, states may choose to retain the same regional agencies that were established under state law in the first place, but to change their function to reflect accountability to state and local rather than federal officials. It is still too early to tell how these changes in the review procedure will affect the ability of regional agencies to influence airport planning decisions.

Much of the regional agency's success might depend as much on negotiation and persuasion as on legal or budgetary authority. Often, compromises can be reached on a voluntary basis. For example, the regional airport planning commission worked with the three San Francisco area airports to help each develop a "noise budget" to comply with California's strict environmental laws. Because noise is directly related to the level of aviation activity, the noise budget plan, when completed, will affect future traffic allocation among the airports. Its implementation will most likely require some diversion of new traffic growth from busy San Francisco International to the other bay area airports.

Even where airports in a region are operated by the same authority, allocation of traffic between airports might still be difficult. For example, the Port Authority of New York and New Jersey can implement its planning decision to increase activity at Newark by instituting differential pricing, improved ground access, or other measures to increase use of that airport. Implementation of the policy, however, depends not just on control of airport development expenditures but also on the ability to influence the activities of private parties, the air carriers and passengers.

Regional airport planning authorities may also, if they have planning responsibility for other transportation modes, plan for the airport as part of the regional transportation system. When multimodal planning responsibility resides in one organization, there is greater likelihood that the planning agency will consider airport needs in relation to other forms of transportation in the region. Also, the regional agency may try to improve coordination between the various modes, so that, for example, airport developments do not impose an undue burden on surrounding highway facilities or so that advantage can be taken of opportunities for mass transit. For this to happen, however, two conditions are necessary: regionwide authority and multimodal jurisdiction.

State level

According to the National Association of State Aviation Officials (NASAO), 47 state aviation agencies carry out some form of airport planning. In 39 states, these agencies are subdivisions of the state department of transportation; in the others, they are independent agencies. Several states have an aviation commission in addition to an aviation agency. The commissions are usually appointed by the governor and serve as policymaking bodies. State involvement in airport planning and development takes several forms: preparation of state airport system plans, funding of local master planning, and technical assistance for local planning.

Airport planning at the state level involves issues that are somewhat different from those of local or regional agencies. State governments are typically concerned with developing an airport system that will provide adequate service to all parts of the state, both rural and metropolitan. Development of airports is often seen as an essential tool for economic development or overcoming isolation of rural areas. Some state aviation agencies (in Ohio and Wisconsin, for example), have set a goal to develop at least one well-equipped airport in each county. Usually the allocation of traffic between airports serving the same community is not at issue. Rather, the issue is deciding how to allocate development funds among candidate communities and to maintain a balance between various parts of the state.

Before 1970, very few states conducted extensive or systematic airport planning. An important stimulus to state agencies to initiate comprehensive planning efforts was provided by the Airport and Airway Development Act of 1970, which set aside one percent of airport aid monies from the trust fund for this purpose each year. Most states applied for these funds promptly and typically spent from one to four years in developing *state aviation system plans (SASP)* under guidelines issued by FAA, although a few took considerably longer. Most of the states sought assistance from outside consultants in some phase of the planning activity.

State plans typically encompass a planning period of 20 to 30 years; the year 2000 is a common planning horizon. Planning periods are normally divided into short, medium, and long-term segments (usually 5, 10, and 20 years, respectively). In each case, estimates of future needs have been developed by comparing existing facilities with projections of future traffic.

The major feature of the plans, and by far the bulk of each document, is a detailed listing of the actions planned by class of airport and type of improvement. The types of improvements most commonly cited are land acquisition (new sites or expansion of existing airports), pavement repair or improvement (runways, taxiways, aprons, roads, parking), installation of lighting and landing or navigation aids, and building construction (terminals, hangars, administrative facilities).

While there are surface similarities, SASPs vary greatly in scope, detail, expertise, and planning philosophy. One state system plan might basically be a wish list, prepared primarily because planning funds were available and the state DOT required it. On the other hand, some state agencies regard the SASP as a valuable working document that is kept current and serves as a guide in programming and distribution of state funds.

In many states, programming of funds is somewhat separate from the system planning process. While the SASP might have a long planning horizon of 20 years or more, the actual award of grants to complete particular projects is on a much shorter time scale. Some state agencies have developed methods for keeping current files on local airport projects planned for the near term, say, three years. When airports apply for state aid, or request state assistance in applying for federal aid, the SASP is used to assign priority for a grant award as funds become available. As a rule, only a fraction of the projects outlined in the SASP are undertaken.

Virtually all state plans estimate costs of recommended improvements and identify funding sources. Funding is the primary constraint in implementation of the SASPs. In all states, some sort of consultation, coordination, or review by persons outside the state aviation agency is part of the planning process. Often these are regional economic development or planning agencies created by state government. In many cases, airport planning is part of a general transportation planning process, but methods of interaction and feedback among the modal agencies vary considerably.

Some state agencies are involved in master planning activities for local airports, especially rural or small community airports that do not have the staff to carry out master planning on their own. State agencies might provide technical assistance or actually develop local master plans. Some states also participate in airport planning for major metropolitan areas, although most leave this responsibility with the local airport authority or a regional body. In recent years, state participation in planning at the larger airports has shown some increase, a trend that might be bolstered by current federal policy that earmarks a share of annual trust fund outlays for state aviation planning.

National plan of integrated airport systems

The Airport and Airway Improvement Act of 1982, reflects a strengthened congressional commitment to airport planning. At the regional and state levels, the law dedicates one percent of federal airport development funds for planning. As such, the new law provides an opportunity for state governments and regional agencies to institute or expand their planning efforts.

The act called for refinement of the national airport planning process by instructing the Department of Transportation to develop a *National Plan of Integrated Airport Systems (NPIAS)*. The description of this plan in the legislation makes it clear that the intent is to expand and improve planning at the national level. Specifically, the act calls for *"integrated airport system planning,"* which it defines:

> . . . the initial as well as continuing development for planning purposes of information and guidance to determine the extent, type, nature, location, and timing of airport development needed in a specific area to establish a viable, balanced, and integrated system of public-use airports.

Planning includes identification of system needs, development of estimates of systemwide development costs, and the conduct of such studies, surveys, and other planning actions, including those related to airport access, as might be necessary to determine the short, intermediate, and long-range demands that the airport must meet.

The policy declaration points out several ways in which the planning effort is to be "integrated:"

> . . . it is in the national interest to develop in metropolitan areas an integrated system of airports designed to provide expeditious access and maximum safety . . . [and it is in the national interest to] encourage and promote the development of transportation systems embracing various modes of transportation in a manner that will serve the states and local communities efficiently and effectively.

From this it is evident that the legislation requires a plan that is "integrated" in two ways: (1) geographically, in the sense that all airports in a region are to be

Port of Seattle

Aerial view of Seattle-Tacoma International Airport.

considered together; and (2) intermodally, in the sense that planning for the airport should be part of the planning for the regional transportation system as a whole. The requirements of the act will bring FAA's airport planning process into closer relation with metropolitan and regional transportation planning than ever before.

Local level

At the local level, the centerpiece of airport planning is the *airport master plan*, a document that charts the proposed evolution of the airport to meet future needs. The magnitude and sophistication of the master planning effort depends on the size of the airport. At major airports, planning might be in the hands of a large department capable of producing its own forecasts and supporting technical studies. At such airports, master planning is a formal and complex process that has evolved to coordinate large construction projects (or perhaps several such projects simultaneously) that can be carried out over a period of five years or more. At smaller airports, master planning might be the responsibility of a few staff members with other responsibilities, who depend on outside consultants for expertise and support. At very small airports, where capital improvements are minimal or are made infrequently, the master plan might be a very simple document, perhaps prepared locally but usually with the help of consultants.

An airport master plan presents the planner's conception of the ultimate development of a specific airport. It effectively presents the research and logic from which the plan was evolved and artfully displays the plan in a graphic and written report. Master plans are applied to the modernization and expansion of existing airports and to the construction of new airports, regardless of their size or functional role.

Objectives of the airport master plan   The overall *objective of the airport master plan* is to provide guidelines for future development that will satisfy aviation demand and be compatible with the environment, community development, other modes of transportation, and other airports. Specific objectives within this broad framework are as follows:

- To provide an effective graphic presentation of the ultimate development of the airport and of anticipated land uses adjacent to the airport.
- To establish a schedule of priorities and phasing for the various improvements proposed in the plan.
- To present the pertinent backup information and data that were essential to the development of the master plan.
- To describe the various concepts and alternatives that were considered in the establishment of the proposed plan.
- To provide a concise and descriptive report so that the impact and logic of its recommendations can be clearly understood by the community the airport serves and by those authorities and public agencies that are charged with the approval, promotion, and funding of the improvements proposed in the airport master plan.

Local coordination   The development and operation of an airport impacts on the entire community; therefore, recent emphasis in planning of successful airports has been on integrating the airport into a comprehensive plan. Compatibility with local community goals, residential and commercial land uses, and transportation needs are now considered essential ingredients in airport planning at the local level.

Airports begin with local initiative. The local community must decide if it needs a new airport or expansion of an existing one. Planning an airport demands careful consideration of the long-range development goals of the city or town. Effective coordination of planning at the local level requires involvement of individuals that are interested and knowledgeable about the community and the importance of airport development.

A public agency is required in order to qualify for federal airport aid. This group might be the city council, the county board of commissioners or supervisors, or other elected body, state aeronautical commission or agency, port authority, or a specially created airport authority. State legislative approval is generally required if a new authority is created. The airport public sponsor will often seek professional assistance from a consulting firm before planning and obtaining federal funds.

An airport master plan draws widespread interest from the private citizen, community organizations, airport users, areawide planning agencies, conservation groups, ground transit officials, and aviation and airport concessionaire interests. If these groups are not consulted during the development of the plan, it will likely be unsuccessful when presented to the public; therefore, it is essential that the master plan team coordinate their efforts with and seek the advice of these elements during the critical stages of the plan's development. This coordination will help pave the way for acceptance and, more important, it will permit vital input from organized interests that will lead to the evolution of a well-integrated plan.

Effective coordination between members of the planning teams is also essential to the development of a successful master plan. A balanced effort is not easy to achieve because of the many disciplines involved in the plan's preparation. For large projects, input might be required from economists, financiers, scientists, architects; civil, mechanical, electrical, and traffic engineers; pilots, air traffic controllers, airline and concessionaire advisers, and airport managers. And to put the airport in its proper perspective, the roles of the environmentalist, ecologist, and urban planner must be considered.

This is why the role of the coordinator of the master plan effort is so important. He must keep the enthusiasm of his advisers in check in order to balance the study efforts and costs of various master plan elements. If he is successful, he will develop a saleable master plan that will lead to the construction of a functional airport that blends pleasantly into the environment.

An airport doesn't exist in isolation. It is an element of the total transportation availability of an area. Its integration into a whole system is even more important in these days of intermodal shipping than it formerly was. The long-range planning of any form of transportation within an area can most effectively be done in concert with the planning for all modes.

Ground transportation reflects on an airport in at least two ways. First, the less surface transportation there is in an area, especially one of great distances, the more need there is for air facilities. (It costs considerably less to build a runway than to construct one mile of interstate highway.) Second, businesses looking to locate in a new community generally require that the airport be fewer than 30 minutes away from plant location.

A review of access roads, peak-hour traffic patterns, bus and rail transportation, and other nearby airports plays a role in the report that determines whether or not an airport proposal is approved for inclusion in the National Airport System Plan, a prerequisite to federal funding of planning and construction of an airport.

The airport master plan is most applicable to a rather narrow planning problem, the development of a single airport. Coordination efforts required for development of the master plan will be elaborated on for each stage of development of the master plan in the chapters that follow.

Need for integration among plans

Airport planning, as practiced today, is a formalized discipline that combines forecasting, engineering, and economics. Because it is performed largely by government agencies, it is also a political process, where value judgments and institutional relationships play as much a part as technical expertise. On the whole, airport planners have been reasonably successful in anticipating future needs and in devising effective solutions. Still, mistakes have been made—sometimes because of poor judgment or lack of foresight and sometimes because of certain characteristics of the planning process itself. In effect, the process and the methods employed predispose planners toward solutions that might be "correct" for a single airport but perhaps not for the community, region, or airport system as a whole. As a result, airport plans might take on a rigidity that is inappropriate in light of changing conditions or a narrowness of focus that does not make best use of resources.

Airport planning at local, regional, state, and federal levels is not well coordinated and integrated. To some extent, this arises naturally from different areas of concern and expertise. At the extremes, local planners are attempting to plan for the development of one airport, while FAA is trying to codify the needs of several thousand airports that might request aid. Local planners are most concerned with details and local conditions that will never be of interest to a national planning body.

The lack of common goals and mutually consistent approach is also evident between federal and state planning. More than 20 years ago, the federal government recognized the need to strengthen state system planning and provided funds for this purpose under ADAP, and nearly all the state airport systems plans have been prepared with federal funding; however, it does not seem that FAA has always made full use of these products in preparing the NPIAS. The state plans contain many more airports than NPIAS, and the priorities assigned to airport projects by states do not always correspond to those of NPIAS. While it is probably not desirable, or even possible, for NPIAS to incorporate all elements of the state plans, greater harmony between these two levels of planning might lead to more orderly development of the national airport system.

There is also a lack of coordination between airport planning and other types of transportation and economic planning. This is particularly evident in the case of land use, where airport plans are often in conflict with other local and regional developments. Even though the airport authority might prepare a thoroughly competent plan, lack of information about other public or private development proposed in the community (or failure of municipal authorities to impose and maintain zoning ordinances) allows conflicts to develop over use of the airport and surrounding land. This problem can be especially severe where there are several municipalities or local jurisdictions surrounding the airport property.

An additional problem is the lack of integration of airport planning with that for other modes of transportation. An airport is an intermodal transportation center, where goods and people transfer between the ground and air modes. It forms an important link in the total transportation system of a region. The ground transportation system providing access to the airport can be a significant contributor to congestion, delay, and the cost of airport operation. Yet airport operators have little authority or influence over decisions on transportation beyond the airport property line.

Key terms

airport system planning
National Plan of Integrated Airport Systems (NPIAS)
NPIAS levels of need
criteria for inclusion in the NPIAS
regional airport planning
Office of Management and Budget Circular A-95
state aviation system plans (SASP)
integrated airport system planning
airport master plan
objectives of the airport master plan

Review questions

1. "Planning cannot be done for one airport in isolation." Expand upon this statement.
   What is NPIAS? Highlight some of the criticisms it has received?
   Describe the three levels of needs under NPIAS?
   Identify the criteria for inclusion in the NPIAS.

2. What is regional airport planning?
   Discuss some problems that might arise as a result of coordinating the plans of three airports in one metropolitan area.
   How has the OMB Circular A-95 affected regional airport planning?

3. Discuss some of the concerns of state government regarding airport system planning.
   Why do individual SASPs vary so greatly? What is the major constraint in implementing SASPs?

4. How did the Airport and Airway Improvement Act of 1982 "reflect a strengthened congressional commitment to airport planning?"

5. Summarize the objectives of an airport master plan. Discuss the importance of local coordination in developing an airport master plan and give some examples.

6. Discuss some of the problems in attempting to integrate airport planning at the national, regional, state, and local levels. What can be done to overcome some of these problems?

Suggested readings

deNeufville, Richard. *Airport Systems Planning*. Cambridge, Massachusetts: The MIT Press, 1976.

DOT/FAA Advisory Circular. 150/5050-3B, Planning the State Aviation System.

DOT/FAA Advisory Circular. 150/5050-5, The Continuous Airport System Planning Process.

DOT/FAA Advisory Circular. 150/5020-1, Noise Control and Compatibility Planning for Airports.

Howard, George P. *Airport Economic Planning*. Cambridge, Massachusetts: The MIT Press, 1974.

National Plan of Integrated Airport Systems (NPIAS), 1990-1999. Washington, DC, FAA, June 1991.

Schreiver, Bernard A. and William W. Siefert. *Air Transportation 1975 and Beyond: A Systems Approach*. Cambridge, Massachusetts: The MIT Press, 1968.

Part 2
Planning and funding the airport

Airport requirements and site selection

Outline

Introduction
Inventories
Forecasting
Demand/capacity analysis
Environmental impact study
Site selection

Objectives

When you have completed this chapter, you should be able to:

△ Define airport master plan and recognize the major components of the first and second phase.

△ Describe the five major factors included in the Inventories stage.

△ Explain how public hearings can assist the airport sponsor in developing an airport master plan.

△ Identify the three basic types of forecasting methods used by airport planners.

△ List the five operational activity forecasts needed by airport planners.

△ Discuss the purpose of the demand/capacity analysis stage.

△ Highlight the major environmental concerns of airport planners.

△ List the 10 factors that must be considered by airport planners in preparing an environmental impact statement.

△ Discuss the major factors that must be given careful analysis in the evaluation of airport sites.

Introduction

While there is considerable variation in the content of the airport master plan and how it is used, its basic products are a description of the desired future configuration of the airport, a description of the steps needed to achieve it, and a financial plan to fund development. The master planning process consists of four basic phases: airport requirements, site selection, airport layout, and financial planning. This chapter will cover the major considerations included in the first two phases.

The first phase, *airport requirements*, specifies new or expanded facilities that will be needed during the planning period. This involves cataloguing existing facilities and forecasting future traffic demand. The planner compares the capacity of existing facilities with future demand, identifying where demand will exceed capacity and what new facilities will be necessary.

The process of relating future demand to existing facilities and estimating the nature and size of needed improvements is complex. It requires detailed forecasts because sizing depends not only on the number of passengers and aircraft in future years but also on the type of the traffic. For example, traffic consisting mainly of transfer passengers imposes requirements that are different from those where the majority of traffic is origin and destination passengers. Sizing of facilities is also affected by the distribution of activities throughout the day and by the size and operating characteristics of aircraft serving the airport. This process is simplified by the use of standard relationships between general measures, such as annual enplanements, and specific measures, such as peak-hour passenger demand.

The second phase, *site selection*, is most important in the construction of a new airport. When considering the expansion of an existing airport, there is usually less choice about where to locate new facilities. Requirements for safety areas and clear zones around existing runways and taxiways, for example, mean that much apparently "vacant" land at airports cannot be used for other purposes. New facilities can be located only in places where they, and the traffic they generate, will not interfere with existing facilities. The site selection phase for a new airport requires an in-depth analysis of alternative sites, looking closely at such factors as physical characteristics of the site, the nature of surrounding development, land cost and availability, ground access, and the adequacy of surrounding airspace. The final choice of one site over others is often quite subjective. For example, there is probably no objective way to compare the disadvantages of increased noise in some part of the community with the advantages of improved air service for the metropolitan area as a whole. The "right" choice depends on how decision-makers weigh various criteria, and it is often a political rather than a technical choice.

Inventories

The first step in the preparation of an airport master plan for an individual airport is the collection of all types of data pertaining to the area that the airport is to serve. This includes an inventory of existing airport facilities, area planning efforts that might affect the master plan, and historical information related to their development. This review will provide essential background information for the master plan report. It will also provide basic information for the development of forecasts and facility requirements.

Historical review of airports and facilities

The historical review traces the development of a community's airport facilities and the air traffic that they have served. A description of each airport and the date of construction or major expansion is included. Airport ownership is also mentioned. The decision to prepare an airport master plan study of a particular airport and the appropriation of funds for the study will probably have resulted from certain legislative actions and preliminary studies by the airport sponsor such as the airport authority or local governmental body charged with the responsibility of administering airports in the area. These activities are also cited in the historical review of airports and facilities. The results of recommendations by airport committees and local, state, or regional planning groups are also summarized. The dates and amounts of money included in enabling legislation by local, state, and federal authorities are also cited in the review.

The scope of the data collection is generally limited to the area that the master plan airport will serve and to national trends which will affect that area. The planner must carefully research and study data that are available from current sources such as state, regional, and national airport system plans and other local aeronautical studies.

Existing airports and their configurations are shown on a base map. Included are all air carrier, general aviation, and military airports in the area.

Airspace structure and navaids

It is necessary to identify how the airspace is used in the vicinity of each airport and throughout the area, all air navigation aids and aviation communication facilities serving the area, and natural or man-made obstructions or structures that affect the use of the airspace.

The airway and jet-route structures have a significant effect on the utility of existing and future airport locations. The dimensions and configurations of the control zones and transition areas are noted. These segments of controlled airspace are designed to accommodate only specific instrument flight (IFR) requirements such as instrument approach, departure, holding, and transition flight maneuvers; thus, the inventory will show the current use of the area's IFR airspace and the balance of the airspace available for future use. Charts that are useful in identifying the airspace structure are the federal and state aeronautical charts, instrument approach and departure charts of Jeppesen Sanderson Inc., and other aeronautical publications.

Additional maps or overlays showing the existing airspace structure are included in the inventory. Later in the planning process, proposed expansion of new airports can be related to the existing airspace structure and compatibility verified, or adjustment to proposed development made.

Airport related land use

An inventory of land uses in the vicinity of each existing airport is necessary so that later in the planning process a determination can be made on the feasibility of expansion and whether an expanded airport will be compatible with the surrounding area and vice versa. Current plans that show existing and planned land uses, highways, utilities, schools, hospitals, and so forth are obtained from areawide agencies and transportation planning agencies that have jurisdiction over the area the master plan airport is to serve. Current land use is also displayed on a map to assist in later steps of the planning process. Also, if feasible, and estimate of the land values is made.

Normally when considering airport-related land use, a survey will be conducted of all ground travel entering or leaving the airport, including the air travelers, employees, suppliers, and visitors. Information might also be collected on parking and commodity movements. Sufficient data is obtained to establish the travel patterns of airport-oriented trips and to develop relationships that will be used to determine future travel patterns.

Copies of zoning laws, building codes, and other regulations and ordinances that might be applicable to the development of an airport master plan are obtained. All of these have an effect on airport related land use.

Aeronautical activity

The principal determinant of future airport system requirements is the amount of aeronautical activity that will be generated in the metropolitan area. A record of current aviation statistics as well as a consideration of historical airport traffic data for such elements as passenger and air cargo traffic, aircraft movements, and aircraft mix is necessary to forecast aeronautical activity. The assessment of these aviation statistics, along with consideration of the socioeconomic attributes for the area, forms the basis for forecasts of aeronautical activity for the metropolitan area. The forecasts of aeronautical activity, in turn, form the basis for facilities planning for future requirements.

Aeronautical statistical data include federal, state, and regional statistics as they relate to the master plan airport and the collection of as many local statistics as can be obtained. At the local level surveys and questionnaires are used to supplement data on operations, frequency, and hours of use of aircraft and origins and destinations of travelers. The primary aviation statistics needed are taken up in this chapter's forecasting section.

Socioeconomic factors

The collection and analysis of socioeconomic data for a metropolitan area helps answer the basic questions regarding the type, volume, and concentration centers of future aviation activity in the region. Accordingly, the determinants (what causes a market to be the size it is) of a market for airports are established. What industries need air transportation? Do they have need for better air transportation facilities? How many people will be available in the future who possess the income to make use of air service? Will the people and industries having the wherewithal to utilize the airport be there? Because people are associated with a multitude of income-earning and income-spending activities at any particular location from and to which they travel, transportation facilities are needed between those points where the future travel is expected to occur.

The primary forces that measure and help determine economic change, and a general rationale for their use in determining air transportation demand, are as follows:

Demography   The size and structure of the area's population and its potential growth rate are basic factors in creating demand for air transportation services. The existing population along with its changing age and educational and occupational distributions can provide a primary index of the potential size of the aviation market and resultant airport employment over short, intermediate, and long-range forecast periods. Demographic factors influence the level of airport traffic and its growth, both in terms of incoming traffic from other states, regions, or cities, and traffic generated by the local or regional populations concerned.

Disposable personal income per capita   This economic factor refers to the purchasing power available to residents in any one period of time, which is a good indicator of average living standards and financial ability to travel. High levels of average personal disposable income provide a strong basis for higher levels of consumer spending, particularly on air travel.

Economic activity and status of industries   This factor refers to situations within the area the airport serves that generate activity in business aviation and air freight traffic. A community's population, size, and economic character affect its air traffic generating potential. Manufacturing and service industries tend to generate greater air transport activity than primary and resource industries, such as mining. Much will depend on established and potential patterns of internal and external trade. In addition, other aviation activities such as agricultural and instructional flying and aircraft sales are included in this factor.

Geographic factors   The geographic distribution and distances between populations and commerce within the area that the airport serves have a direct bearing on the type of transportation services required. The physical characteristics of the land and climatic differences are also important factors. In some cases, alternative modes of transportation might not be available or economically feasible. Furthermore, physical and climatic attractions assist in determining focal points for vacation traffic and tourism and help in establishing the demand for air services that they generate.

Competitive position   The demand for air service also depends on its present and future ability to compete with alternate modes of transportation. Also, technological advances in aircraft design and in other transportation modes, as well as industrial and marketing processes, can create transportation demands that have not previously existed.

Sociological factors The trend toward a more urbanized society, the increased mobility of the population, rising educational levels, and a shorter work week with the resultant increase in leisure time are also major factors in determining demand for air travel.

Political factors The granting of new traffic rights and routes for international air service will influence the volume of traffic at an airport. Demand for air transportation also depends on government actions such as the imposition of taxes and other fees. In addition,government might support other modes of transportation, which might result in changes in demand for air transportation services.

Aerial view of Lindbergh Field at San Diego

Community values

A very important factor in the airport master planning process is the determination of the attitude of the community toward airport development. Poor airport-community relations, unless changed, could influence the ability to implement an airport master plan. On the other hand, a recognition by the community of the need for progress in the development of air transportation can have a positive influence in minimizing complaints; thus, it is necessary to place airport development in its proper perspective relative to community values.

The Airport and Airway Development Act of 1970 established a requirement that airport sponsors must afford the opportunity for public hearings for projects involving the location of an airport, a new airport runway, or a runway extension.

Public hearings enable the airport sponsor to:

- Cite examples of nearby communities that have benefited from having an airport. Such examples can point out growth in new and existing businesses and recreational facilities.

- Identify local business and commercial reliance on air transportation.

- Identify the local airport's role in state, regional, and national airport plans.

- Explain how the airport master plan will accommodate potential local environmental problems, immediate and long-range, emphasizing plans for minimizing noise and zoning recommendations for compatible land use.

- Estimate the adverse impact on community growth and economy if the airport project is not carried forward.

- Concentrate on presenting the facts in a positive, comprehensive and forceful manner, anticipating and rebutting opposition claims.

Recognition of community values and keeping the public apprised of developments will assist in the implementation of the airport master plan.

Forecasting

Airport master plans must be developed on the basis of forecasts. From forecasts, the relationships between demand and the capacity of an airport's various facilities can be established and airport requirements can be determined. Short, intermediate, and long-range (approximately 5, 10, and 20 years) forecasts are made to enable the planner to establish a schedule of development for improvements proposed in the master plan.

The inadequacies of past forecasts raise questions as to what the forecasts should encompass to provide proper guidance for the development of a master plan for the individual airport. The planner must go beyond the aviation demand forecast discussed under this section. He must study carefully the impacts that social, environmental, economic, and technical forecasts will have on the master plan airport. The planner must incorporate these influences in the development of aviation demand forecasts; however, the necessity to take into consideration a broad scope analysis of socioeconomic forecasts does not mean that the planner has to develop a mass of far-ranging forecasts as a part of the master plan effort. The planner must first engage in a research of forecasts that exist for the area served by the airport, and then develop only those forecasts that are germane to the development of the master plan. The magnitude of development of forecasts will depend on the size of the community the airport serves and on information that might be available from earlier planning efforts such as state or regional airport system plans.

Forecasting methods

Three basic types of forecasting methods are available to assist planners in the decision-making process: causal models, time-series or trend analysis, and judgmental forecasts. *Causal models* are highly sophisticated mathematical models that are developed and tested using historical data. The model is built on a statistical relationship between the forecasted (dependent) variable and one or more explanatory (independent) variables. Some models include up to 40 or 50 independent variables. There need not be a cause-and-effect relationship between the dependent and independent variables. A statistical correlation alone is sufficient basis for prediction or forecasting. Correlation is a pattern or relationship between the two or more variables. The closer the relationship, the greater the degree of correlation.

A causal model is constructed by finding variables that explain, statistically, the changes in the variable to be forecast. The availability of data on the variables—or, more specifically, their specific values—is largely determined by the time and resources the planner has available. Prominent independent variables used in forecasting various segments of the air transportation industry include gross domestic product (GDP), disposable personal income (DI), and consumer spending on services.

Another reasonably sophisticated statistical method of forecasting is *time-series analysis* or *trend extension*, the oldest and in many cases still the most widely used method of forecasting air transportation demand. Time-series models show the dependent variable, time. This method is used quite frequently where both time and data are limited, such as in forecasting a single variable, such as cargo tonnage, where historical data is obtained for that particular variable.

Forecasting by time series or trend extension actually consists of interpreting the historical sequence and applying the interpretation to the immediate future. It assumes that the rate of growth or change that has persisted in the past will continue. Historical data are plotted on a graph, and a trend line is drawn. Frequently a straight line, following the trend line, is drawn for the future; however, if certain known factors indicate that the rate will increase in the future, the line might be curved upward. As a general rule, there might be several future projections, depending upon the length of the historical period studied.

Airport authorities keep numerous records of data of particular concern to them (enplanements, aircraft movements, number of based aircraft, and so forth), and when a forecast is needed, a trend line is established and then projected out to some future period. The accuracy of forecasting by historical sequence in time or trend analysis depends on good judgment in predicting those changing factors that might keep history from repeating.

The values for the forecasted variable are determined by four time-related factors: (1) long-term trend, such as market growth caused by increases in population; (2) cyclical variations, such as those caused by the business cycle; (3) seasonal phenomena, such as weather or holidays; and (4) irregular or unique phenomena, such as strikes, wars, and natural disasters.

Judgmental forecasts are educated guesses based on intuition and subjective evaluations. A judgmental forecast is an estimate made by an individual who is closely acquainted with the factors related to the variable being forecast. These factors are weighed and evaluated according to the experience and intuition of the forecaster. This method permits a broad range of information to be brought to bear on the forecast, such as national trends, growth in air travel, political situations, and so forth. It is especially advantageous when used in conjunction with causal models or time-series analysis, or where there are a large number of variables for which relatively little data are available, or when intangible factors are expected to play a major role. The resultant forecasts from use of this method alone are the most difficult to defend under close scrutiny and might be subject to strong bias from the individual involved in the forecasting process.

Forecasts of aviation demand

Forecasts of aviation demand form the basis for facilities planning. There is a need to know: (1) the types of civil airport users—certificated air carrier, commuters, general aviation, and the military services where applicable; (2) the types and volume of operational activity—aircraft operations, passengers and cargo, based aircraft, and so forth; and (3) the aircraft mix—jet and large-capacity prop transport aircraft, smaller commercial, corporate, business and pleasure aircraft, future vertical/short takeoff and landing (V/STOL) aircraft and so forth.

Civil airport users The airport planner must develop forecasts of aviation demand for the following four major *civil airport user categories* as applicable to the airport under construction:

1. Air Carrier. As used here, "air carrier" refers to airline aircraft operators holding certificates of public convenience and necessity issued by the former Civil Aeronautics Board based on the Department of Transportation authorizing them to perform passenger and cargo services. This general air carrier grouping includes the major, national, large, and medium regional air carriers.

2. Commuters. These noncertificated small regionals perform scheduled service to smaller cities and serve as feeders to the major hub airports.

They generally operate aircraft fewer than 12,500 pounds maximum gross takeoff weight.

3. General Aviation. As used here, "general aviation" refers to that segment of civil aviation that encompasses all facets of aviation except air carriers and commuters. General aviation includes air taxi operators, corporate-executive transportation, instruction, rental, aerial application, aerial observation, business, pleasure, and other special users.

4. Military. As used here, "military" refers to the operators of all military (Air Force, Army, Navy, U.S. Coast Guard, Air National Guard, and military reserve organizations) aircraft using civil airports.

Operational activity   Annual forecasts of airport traffic (for 5-, 10-, and 20-year periods) form the principal basis for future airport facility requirement planning. It is essential to develop *operational activity forecasts* by the type of major user categories (air carrier, commuter, general aviation, and military) as previously described.

In the development of the operational activity forecasts, an unconstrained approach can be used for most areas. The "unconstrained" forecast represents the potential aviation market in which all of the basic factors that tend to create aviation demand are used, without regard to any constraining circumstances (limited airport expansion capability, airspace, access, and so forth) that could affect aviation growth at any specific airport or location.

Forecasters review and relate national and/or local historical needs and forecast data to the areas under study as a guide for future planning. With this approach, it is possible to determine the theoretical development needs in accordance with the total demand potential. In the exceptionally high activity metropolitan areas, however, potential constraints and alternative methods for their reduction are also considered.

Six major types of operational activity forecasts are considered necessary to determine future facility requirements:

1. Enplaning Passengers. This activity includes the total number of passengers (air carrier, commuter, and general aviation) departing on aircraft at the airport. Originations, stopover, and transfer passengers are identified separately.

   Influencing factors considered for air carrier passenger traffic, in most forecasting methods, include: historical trends in the national percentage participation rates for both the metropolitan area and its major city—pair markets; local and regional population and socioeconomic trends; and the business/personal composition of the metropolitan area's traffic. These factors are used to develop future participation rates and ultimately to translate national projections into metropolitan area forecasts. Sometimes, two series will be correlated to a degree where one might be capable of measuring the other. For example, some communities' numbers of U.S. international passengers are sufficiently correlated with the domestic passengers to assume that the relationship will continue.

The number of enplaned general aviation passengers is frequently estimated for the area by first developing load factors for the future average number of passengers per plane and then by multiplying these factors by one-half the total number of forecasted general aviation itinerant operations (other than local operations).

2. Enplaning Air Cargo. Enplaning air cargo includes the total tonnage of priority, nonpriority, and foreign mail, express and freight (property other than baggage accompanying passengers) departing on aircraft at an airport, including originations, stopover, and transfer cargo. Where applicable, domestic and international are identified separately.

The air cargo industry (like most industries) depends on population growth, continuing gains in the gross domestic product (GDP), and the export-import increases produced by a free trade market.

Most forecasters make use of both judgment and statistical techniques to develop percentage growth factors derived from such investigative approaches as follow: (1) an extrapolation of past trends of all commerce, with particular attention to air commerce and the metropolitan regions' share of air commerce; (2) a review of national air cargo forecasts by airlines, aircraft manufacturers, governmental agencies, and trade associations; (3) consideration of the effect on the growth of mail by such factors as conflicting mail data, world conflict, changing post office policies and methods, and possible actions of Congress; (4) a projection of air transport cargo lift potential—the impact of new cargo aircraft; (5) the potential air cargo penetration into other transport modes—such as water transport for the overseas market and long-haul common carrier truck for the domestic market—due to marketing changes in air cargo transportation; (6) future costs of ground freight transport as compared with air transport and domestic shipper practices.

Two general methods of forecasting a metropolitan area's air cargo are: using area annual growth rates applied to the area's current cargo base; or calculating a percentage ratio of the area's cargo to the national total and projecting a future trend to apply to an acceptable national forecast of air cargo.

3. Aircraft Operations (movements). Aircraft operations include the total number of landings (arrivals) at and takeoffs (departures) from an

Metro-Dade Aviation Department

Air cargo depot located in the southwest corner of Miami International Airport.

airport. Two types of operations—local and itinerant—are separately identified: (1) *local operations*—performed by aircraft that (a) operate in the local traffic pattern or within sight of the tower, (b) are known to be departing for or arriving from flight in local practice and flight test areas located within a 20-mile radius of the airport and/or control tower, (c) execute simulated instrument approaches or low passes at the airport; and, (2) *itinerant operations*—all aircraft arrivals and departures other than local operations described above. Where applicable, domestic and international itinerant operations should be identified separately.

Except for local training flights at some airports, air carrier aircraft movements are itinerant operations. The basic premise underlying the methodology for forecasting air carrier operations by airport is that a relationship exists between the number of enplaned passengers and cargo shipments and the level of service provided. It is assumed that the number of aircraft seats for transiting and enplaning passengers and the number of flights by type of aircraft have been a function of the traffic demand and traffic characteristics of the community as well as the route structure and operating policies and practices of the individual carriers. It is also assumed that these same factors will continue to determine the level of operations in the future.

An often-used forecast method for air carrier operations can be summarized as follows:

The total generated seats at each airport are forecast to increase as a function of the forecast of enplaned passengers.

The analysis and forecast of aircraft mix is an internal part of the methodology to determine the number of air carrier operations because the total forecast seats are distributed among the type of aircraft the carriers are expected to operate at each airport in the forecast year. The seat totals, by aircraft type, are divided by average seating capacities to yield the number of aircraft operations by aircraft type required. Total air carriers' operations are determined by summing the operations by aircraft type.

General aviation aircraft movements can be either itinerant or local operations. Because general aviation activity is related to such parameters as population, employment, income, and based aircraft in the metropolitan region, most methods of estimating its future level are centered around historical growth trends and operations per based aircraft. Because trends can be misleading, supporting rationale is often developed before any conclusions are reached after using historical trends. Methods of forecasting general aviation operations at air carrier and general aviation control tower airports in a metropolitan area take into account such factors as: (1) the past trend of general aviation operations at each air carrier airport, (2) the air carrier activity forecast for the airport. This might be large enough to cause general aviation restrictions. Any surplus in general aviation activity is allocated to other airports in the area, (3) the number of towers planned or programmed for general aviation in the area, and (4) discussions with airport management and FAA.

Future general aviation activity at air carrier and general aviation control tower airports are generally developed from historical growth trends, considering the above factors and adjusting the trends based upon knowledge of the individual airport's potential and the economic expectation of its associated community. An alternate, approximate method for general aviation control tower airports is to determine and project their percent of U.S. towers' operations and apply the derived percentage factors to the FAA's national forecasts of tower operations, adjusted for the addition of new tower airports. (*See* the FAA publication *Aviation Forecasts*, which is issued annually.)

One approach to forecasting general aviation activity at general aviation nontower airports is to establish a relationship between operations and based general aviation aircraft, and to apply this relationship to an acceptable forecast of based aircraft. Base norms are determined for the airport's local and itinerant operations per based aircraft. These base norms are then adjusted for normal growth and multiplied by the number of projected based aircraft to obtain future activity.

Future forecasts of military operations can be projected based on past trends and information provided by military sources.

4. Based Aircraft. Based aircraft is the total number of active general aviation aircraft that use or might be expected to use an airport as "home base." General aviation based aircraft are separately identified as single-engine, multiengine, piston or turbine, or V/STOL.

Forecasts of general aviation aircraft within the metropolitan area are based upon growth rates reflected for national totals in the FAA annual publication *Aviation Forecasts*, which establishes an annual percentage increase in based aircraft for single-engine, multiengine, and turbine aircraft. These forecasts are modified to reflect special conditions at each metropolitan area.

5. Busy-Hour Operations. Busy-hour operations is the total number of aircraft operations expected to occur at an airport at its busiest hour, computed by averaging two adjacent busiest hours of a typically high activity day. One definition of typically high activity day would be the average day of the busiest month of the year. The operations are identified by major user category, as applicable.

The operations forecast is translated to reflect the total number of aircraft operations expected to occur at an airport during a busy hour of a typically high activity day. The percent this day of the annual operations is computed from previous records.

Also, the air carrier busy hour is selected. Assuming that this hour and the percent of daily passengers and aircraft operations, together with the percent of annual operations, would remain the same, it is possible to apply these percentages to future passenger and operations forecasts to obtain the busy-hour operations number for the forecast period. Also, a certain percentage of the future estimated annual cargo volumes are translated into all-cargo plane movements, by month, day of week, and hour of day, indicate that only a few of the all-cargo plane movements operate in peak periods; therefore, during the average busy hour of passenger plane movements, only a few all-cargo plane movements are expected.

The annual operations forecast also reflects the total number of general aviation operations at each airport in the metropolitan region during a busy hour of a typically high activity day. In general, the method of forecasting general aviation peak hour operations follows the steps in forecasting air carrier busy-hour operations. In addition, the number of general aviation operations expected to occur at each airport during the air carrier busy hour is also considered in estimating the total busy-hour operations at each airport.

Military operations are not normally considered in the busy hour because the military services avoid congested time periods at civil airports. At air carrier tower airports, one method of developing military busy hour is to consider that itinerant and local military busy day operations tend toward a constant percentage of annual operations for each category.

6. Aircraft Mix. In determining airport requirements, it is necessary to forecast the aircraft mix (types of categories of aircraft) that are to be accommodated at the airport. Airport management must keep abreast of technological advances in aircraft design in order to assure the provision of adequate airfield and terminal design at the airports from which they are to operate.

   Forecasts of aircraft mix are summarized into: (1) seating capacity groups for air carrier aircraft, and (2) operational characteristics groups for all four of the major airport user categories.

The annual FAA report *Aviation Forecasts* gives national and regional trends in air carrier and general aviation aircraft mix.

Demand/capacity analysis

After aviation demand has been determined, the next step in the airport master planning process is the assessment of facility requirements. The study of the *demand/capacity* relationship involves an estimation of the need to expand facilities and the cost of these improvements. This type of analysis is done in consultation with the airlines and the general aviation community. The analysis is applied to aircraft operations versus airfield improvements; to passenger enplanements versus terminal building improvements; to cargo tonnage versus cargo facility development; to airport access traffic versus access roads and rapid transit facilities; and to other improvements as might be appropriate. Airspace in the vicinity of the master plan airport is also analyzed.

Demand/capacity analysis is normally applied to short, intermediate, and long-range developments (approximately 5, 10, and 20 years). The analysis is only an approximation of facility requirements, their costs, and savings that will result from reduced delays to airport users as well as anticipated revenues that might be obtained from proposed improvements; thus, demand/capacity analysis will yield preliminary estimates of the number and configuration of runways, areas of apron, number of vehicle parking spaces, and capacities of airport access facilities. Preliminary estimates of economic feasibility may also be obtained. These approximations will provide a basis for developing the details of the airport master plan and for determining the feasibility of improvements considered in the plan.

Aircraft operational requirements

The forecasts of aviation activity will indicate the kinds of aircraft anticipated to use the master plan airport. The frequency of use, passenger/cargo load factors, and lengths of outbound nonstop flights will also be indicated. From this demand data, the planner can ascertain the required physical dimensions of the aircraft operational areas.

While a capacity analysis provides requirements in terms of numbers of runways/taxiways, and so forth, the analysis of aircraft operational requirements allows the determination of runway/taxiway/apron dimensions, strengths, and lateral clearances between airport areas. Of course, both of these analyses are interrelated and are accomplished simultaneously in order to determine system requirements.

Capacity analysis

An analysis of the existing air traffic capacity of the area the master plan airport is to serve will help to determine how much additional capacity will be required at the master plan airport. Four distinct elements require investigation, namely:

Airfield capacity   *Airfield capacity* is the rate of aircraft movements on the runway/taxiway system which results in a given level of delay.

Terminal area capacity   *Terminal area capacity* is the ability of the terminal area to accept the passengers, cargo, and aircraft that the airfield accommodates. Individual elements within terminal areas must be evaluated to determine overall terminal capacity. Terminal elements included in the analysis are: (1) airline gate positions, (2) airline apron areas, (3) cargo apron areas, (4) general aviation apron areas, (5) airline passenger terminals, (6) general aviation terminals, (7) cargo buildings, (8) automobile parking, and (9) aircraft maintenance facilities.

Airspace capacity   The proximity of airports to one another, the relationship of runway alignments, and the nature of operations (IFR or VFR) are the principal interairport considerations which will affect *airspace capacity* of the master plan airport. For example, it is not uncommon in a large metropolitan area to have major or secondary airports spaced so closely that they share one discrete parcel of airspace. In such cases there may be a reduction in the IFR capacity for the airports involved due to the intermixing of traffic within the common parcel of airspace. When this occurs, aircraft, regardless of destination, must be sequenced with the proper separation standards. This reduces the IFR capacity for a specific airport.

Ground access capacity   The establishment of capacity requirements for the master plan airport will determine the capacity required for airport access. The airport capacity figures are translated into numbers of movements by people and access vehicles. A preliminary examination of existing and planned highway and mass transit systems allows a judgment as to the availability of *ground access capacity*. In determining the volume of people, it is necessary for the planner to establish the percentage relationship between passengers, visitors, and airport employees. This can vary from one urban area to another and from one site to another.

Facility requirements are developed from information obtained in demand/ capacity analysis and from FAA advisory circulars and regulations which provide criteria for design of airport components. Demand/capacity analysis yields approximate number and configuration of runways, number of gates, square footage of terminal buildings, cargo facilities, number of public and employee parking spaces, types of airport access roads, and the overall land area required for the airport. From the mix of aircraft and the number of aircraft operations, general requirements for length, strength and number of runways, spacing of taxiways, layout and spacing of gates, and apron area requirements can be determined. These approximations are used by the planner in developing the details under the airport layout plan (discussed in chapter 5).

Environmental impact study

Environmental factors must be considered carefully in the development of a new airport or the expansion of an existing one. This requirement was first established in the Airport and Airway Development Act of 1970 and the Environmental Policy Act of 1969. The *National Environmental Policy Act of 1969* requires the preparation of detailed environmental statements for all major federal airport development actions significantly affecting the quality of the environment. The Airport and Airway Development Act of 1970 directed that no airport development project may be approved by the secretary of transportation unless he is satisfied that fair consideration has been given to the communities in or near which the project may be located.

Studies of the impact of construction and operation of the airport or airport expansion upon accepted standards of air and water quality, ambient noise levels, ecological processes, and natural environmental values are conducted to determine how the airport requirements can best be accomplished. An airport is an obvious stimulus to society from the standpoints of economic growth and the services it offers to the public; however, this generation of productivity and employment might be negated by noise and air pollution and ecological compromises if compatibility between an airport and its environs is not achieved; thus, the airport master plan must directly contend with these problems identified in the studies of environmental qualities so that the engineering of airport facilities will minimize or overcome those operations that contribute to environmental pollution.

Aircraft noise

Aircraft noise is probably the severest environmental problem to be overcome in the development of an airport. Where aircraft noise causes disturbance, it makes an airport unpopular no matter how well the airport serves its community. The resolution of the noise problem requires careful analysis, development of proper land use, and a coordinated approach on the part of the government, aircraft manufacturers, airport operators, and the community.

Improvements in design of engines used on the newer aircraft such as the Boeing 757 and 767 have had a significant effect on reducing noise. Noise abatement procedures and special operational restrictions have resulted in substantial noise reduction from existing airports. Airport layouts that direct the noise away from built-up areas have also been a principal consideration in the development of new airport facilities.

One of the most effective means of reducing noise impact is through the proper planning of land use for areas affected by airport noise. The difficulties that are encountered in establishment of land use plans depend on whether its application is preventive or remedial in nature. Methods of land use control include purchase for direct airport use; conversion to a use compatible with expected noise levels; acquisition of aviation easements; and the establishment of zoning and building codes.

Air pollution

While there is evidence that aircraft engine emission constitutes less than one percent of the total air pollutants in a typical metropolitan area, this facet of the environmental impact of airport operations cannot be overlooked in the development of the airport master plan. It is rather evident to the observer on the ground that exhaust smoke does exist and that contaminants are emitted into the environment.

The federal government and industry are keenly aware of the public reaction to engine exhaust emissions and are jointly working towards alleviating the problem. This is an easier problem to resolve from a technical and economic aspect than the noise alleviation problem, and it will probably be eliminated in the foreseeable future as a factor with which the airport planner must deal; however, the anticipated effects of air pollution and considerations given thereto are always reported in the airport master plan.

Natural environmental values

Normally, airport planners will not consider locations for airport development near national parks and wilderness areas or areas designated as wildlife and waterfowl refuges, public recreation areas and historical monuments. Expansion of existing airports into or adjacent to such areas is avoided where possible.

Water pollution

Although the means of controlling water pollution is probably the best understood aspect of the environmental problem, it is studied carefully in the development of an airport master plan and means for overcoming water pollution problems are incorporated in the plan. An airport can be a major contributor to water pollution if suitable treatment facilities for airport wastes are not provided. Sources of water pollution are: (1) domestic sewage from airport facilities, (2) industrial wastes such as fuel spills; and, (3) high temperature water degradation from various power plants at the airport.

Federal environmental policy

Section 4(f) of the Department of Transportation Act requires responsible federal action in assuring the protection of natural environmental values through the following provision:

> It is hereby declared to be the national policy that special effort should be made to preserve the natural beauty of the countryside and public park and recreation lands, wildlife and waterfowl refuges, and historic sites. The Secretary of Transportation shall cooperate and consult with the Secretaries of the Interior, Housing and Urban Development, and Agriculture, and with the States in developing Transportation plans and programs that include measures to maintain or enhance the natural beauty of the Federal-Aid Highway Act of 1968. The Secretary shall not approve any program or project which requires the use of any publicly owned land from a public park, recreation area, or wildlife and waterfowl refuge of national, State, or local significance as determined by the Federal, State, or local officials having jurisdiction thereof, or any land from an historic site of national, State, or local significance as so determined by such officials unless (1) there is no feasible and prudent alternative to the use of such land, and (2) such program includes all possible planning to minimize harm to such park, recreational area, wildlife and waterfowl refuge, or historic site resulting from such use.

This section represents an important step in an attempt to prevent further encroachment or environmental values. Today there is an awareness at all levels of government, and in the public in general, that our natural resources are being threatened and that this threat must be alleviated.

Another far-reaching federal law to protect our nation's environmental and natural resources was enacted on January 1, 1970. The National Environmental Policy Act of 1969, declares a broad national environmental policy that calls on the federal government to exercise leadership in improving and coordinating federal plans, functions, programs, and use of resources with the goals of preventing damage either to the environment or ecological systems and encouraging mutual productive harmony between man and his environment. The law also established, in the executive office of the president, a council on environmental quality to develop guidelines for agencies affected by the law.

Insofar as airport development is concerned, any required federal actions regarding proposals that significantly affect the quality of the environment must be accompanied by findings concerning:

- The environmental impact of the proposed action.
- Any adverse environmental effects that cannot be avoided should the proposal be implemented.
- Alternatives to the proposed action.
- The relationship between local short-term uses of man's environment and the maintenance and enhancement of long-term productivity.
- Any irreversible and irretrievable commitments of resources that would be involved in the proposed action should it be implemented.

In line with the above guidelines and policy, an airport master plan (including site selection) must be evaluated factually in terms of any proposed development that is likely to:

- Noticeably affect the ambient noise level for a significant number of people.
- Displace significant numbers of people.
- Have a significant aesthetic or visual effect.
- Divide or disrupt an established community or divide existing uses (e.g., cutting off residential areas from recreation or shopping areas).
- Have any effect on areas of unique interest or scenic beauty.
- Destroy or derogate from important recreational areas.
- Substantially alter the pattern of behavior for a species.
- Interfere with important wildlife breeding, nesting, or feeding grounds.
- Significantly increase air or water pollution.
- Adversely affect the water table of an area.

Site selection

The site selection process begins after a community has determined that it is feasible to plan for a new airport. Determining the proper site is undoubtedly the most important step in building an airport.

An airport planner will study many factors before recommending sites for the community's new airport. Site selection studies evaluate airspace, environmental factors, community growth, airport ground access, availability of utilities, land costs, and site development costs. The planner also gives preferential ratings to possible sites.

The results of the site selection study are always presented in a positive and persuasive fashion because the actual selection will most likely be decided in the

City of Houston-Department of Aviation

Construction work on the east taxiway at Houston Intercontinental Airport.

political arena. This is particularly true of airports that serve large urban areas where the citizenry is very sensitive to environmental and socioeconomic factors.

The site selection study is completely integrated with current local and regional comprehensive plans. During the course of study, close liaison is maintained with federal, state, regional, and metropolitan planning agencies having jurisdiction within the area to be served by the airport and with the airlines and other aviation interests operating in the area. The site selection team takes full advantage of data from recent studies that have been developed by these organizations.

The initial investigation of airport sites is the responsibility of the airport sponsor. Preliminary recommendations are presented to the FAA for review. After review, the FAA will confer with the sponsor regarding the preliminary recommendations and will assist the sponsor in evaluating the most desirable sites, if so requested. In some instances, this evaluation will result in a recommendation to the sponsor to study additional sites. When the sponsor has made a final recommendation, or recommendations, the FAA will state in writing its position on the proposed site selection. Grants for phases of an airport master plan that follow site selection will not be made until an airport site has been approved by the FAA.

In its review of proposed airport sites, the FAA will evaluate them from an airspace standpoint. Federal Aviation Regulation Part 157, Notice of Construction, Alteration, Activation and Deactivation of Airports, requires proponents of civil or joint use (civil/military) airport projects to notify the nearest FAA area or regional office before work on the project begins. During the course of the site selection study, the FAA will offer advice to sponsors regarding airspace for sites under consideration.

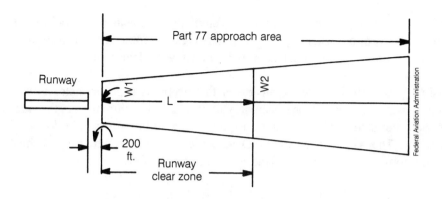

Category	W_1	W_2	L*
1. Precision instrument runway	1,000	1,750	2,500
2. Nonprecision instrument runway for larger than utility with visibility minimums as low as 3/4 mile	1,000	1,510	1,700
3. Nonprecision instrument runway for larger than utility with visibility minimum greater than 3/4 mile	500	1,000	1,700
4. Visual approach runway for larger than utility	500	700	1,000
5. Nonprecision approach for utility	500	800	1,000
6. Visual approach runway for utility	250	450	1,000

*Length of clear zone is determined by distance required to reach a height of 50 ft. for the appropriate surface.

Fig. 4-1. Runway clear zones.

Factors affecting site selection

The major factors that require careful analysis in the final evaluation of airport sites include:

Airspace analysis In major metropolitan areas, it is not uncommon for two or more airports to share common airspace. This factor might restrict the capability of any one airport to accept IFR traffic under adverse weather conditions. Airports too close to each other can degrade their respective capabilities and create a serious traffic control problem. It is important to analyze the requirements and future needs of existing airports before considering construction sites for a new airport.

Surrounding obstructions Obstructions in the vicinity of the airport sites, whether they be natural, existing, or proposed man-made structures, must meet the criteria set forth in Federal Aviation Regulation Part 77, Objects Affecting Navigable Airspace. The FAA requires that *clear zones* at the ends of runways be provided by the airport operator. Runway clear zones are areas comprising the innermost portions of the runway approach areas as defined in FAR Part 77. The dimensions of the clear zones are shown in FIG. 4-1.

The FAA requires that the airport owner have "an adequate property interest" in the clear zone area in order that the requirements of FAR Part 77 can be met and the area protected from future encroachments. Adequate property interest might be in the form of ownership or a long-term lease or other demonstration of legal ability to prevent future obstructions in the runway clear zone.

Expansion   Available land for expansion of the airport is a major factor in site selection; however, it is not always necessary to purchase the entire tract at the start because adjacent land needed for future expansion could be protected by lease or option to buy. The Airport and Airway Development Act of 1970 first established funding for communities to acquire land for future airport development.

Availability of utilities   Consideration is always given to the distance that electric power, telephone, gas, water, and sewer lines must be extended to serve the proposed site. Cost of obtaining utilities can be a major influence on the site selection.

Meteorological conditions   Sites must be carefully investigated for prevalence of ground fog, bad wind currents, industrial smoke, and smog. A study of wind direction on a year-round basis is always made because prevailing winds will influence the entire design of the airport.

Economy of construction   Soil classification and drainage can have an effect on the cost of construction. Similarly, sites lying on submerged or marshy land are much more costly to develop than those on dry land. Rolling terrain requires much more grading than flat terrain. The site that is more economical to construct will be a deciding factor in the final selection.

Convenience to population   An airport must be convenient for the people who will use its facilities. Much in the same way that shopping centers derive their success from convenient access and parking, the airport too must be accessible in terms of time, distance and cost of transportation. As a rule of thumb, the airport should be located no more than 30 minutes from the majority of potential users. Consideration in site selection is always given to the proximity of railroads, highways, and other types of transportation for movement and transfer of cargo and passengers.

Noise   Noise is the most predominant objection raised by opponents to new airports and airport expansion projects. Numerous efforts are being made by industry and government to seek new and better ways to reduce aircraft sound levels. Many of the older jet aircraft are now being retrofitted with noise kits that are designed to reduce noise. Engine manufacturers are exploring new engineering concepts and designs that will reduce this source of noise to an absolute minimum. Pilots of airliners are required to maintain certain power settings and to fly prescribed routes that reduce noise levels in the vicinity of takeoff and landing areas. Noise certification standards have been established by the FAA for new aircraft.

Cost comparisons of alternate sites A quantitative and qualitative comparison of the aforementioned factors is made from the standpoint of cost. Quantitative analysis includes an evaluation of the costs of land acquisition and easements, site developments, major utilities, foundations, access facilities, ground travel to users, and effects on surrounding areas such as noise, air and water pollution, and safety. Qualitative evaluation considers accessibility to users, compatible land users, expansion capabilities, and air traffic control compatibility.

Key terms

airport requirements
site selection
causal models
time-series analysis or trend extension
judgmental forecasts
civil airport user categories
operational activity forecasts
air carrier passenger traffic
enplaning passengers
enplaning air cargo
aircraft operations
local operations
itinerant operations
based aircraft
busy-hour operations
aircraft mix
airfield capacity
terminal area capacity
airspace capacity
ground access capacity
National Environmental Policy Act of 1969
clear zones

Review questions

1. What is an airport master plan? Describe the first two phases of the airport master plan.

   Why is it important for the planner to make a historical review of airports and facilities in the area?

   What is the chief concern of the planner from the standpoint of airspace structure and navaids when two or more airports serve the area?

2. Discuss some of the socioeconomic factors that airport planners take into con-

sideration during the early development stage. Why is it important that the airport planner involve the public in having hearings throughout the developmental process?

3. Compare and contrast the three methods of forecasting discussed in this chapter.
   List the four major civil airport user categories.
   What are operational activity forecasts? List the six major types.
   Why is the airport planner concerned with aircraft mix?

4. What is the purpose of demand/capacity analysis? Discuss the four elements to be investigated under capacity analysis.

5. What are the major environmental concerns in planning an airport?
   How has the problem of noise been addressed in recent years? Describe the guidelines established by the Council on Environmental Quality.
   List the 10 environmental areas that must be evaluated and explained in case of any proposed airport development.

6. Describe the importance of airspace analysis in the site selection phase. What is the runway clear zone?
   What is meant by economy of construction?
   Summarize some of the other factors taken into consideration by airport planners in selecting an airport site.

Suggested readings

Ashford, Norman and Paul H. Wright. *Airport Engineering*. New York: Wiley-Interscience Publications, John Wiley & Sons, 1979.

Deem, Warren H. and John S. Reed. *Airport Land Needs*. San Francisco: Arthur D. Little, Inc., 1966.

DOT/FAA Advisory Circular 150/5070-6A, Airport Master Plans.

DOT/FAA Advisory Circular 150/5060-3A, Airport Capacity Criteria Used in Long-Range Planning.

DOT/FAA Advisory Circular 150/5070-5, Planning the Metropolitan Airport System.

DOT/FAA Advisory Circular 150/5060-1A, Airport Capacity Criteria Used in Preparing the National Airport Plan.

DOT/FAA Advisory Circular 150/5050-4, Citizen Participation in Airport Planning.

FAR, Part 77, Objects Affecting Navigable Airspace.

FAR, Part 157, Notice of Construction, Alteration, Activation, and Deactivation of Airports.

FAR, Part 153, Acquisition of U.S. Land for Public Airports.

FAR, Part 151, Federal Aid to Airports.

Horonjeff, Robert. *Planning and Design of Airports*, 2nd Ed. New York: McGraw-Hill, 1975.

Additional FAA Advisory Circulars:

AC 70/7460-2A Proposed Construction or Alterations of Objects that affect the Navigable Airspace

AC 150/5060-2 Airport Site Selection

AC 150/5060-3A Airport Capacity Criteria Used in Long-Range Planning

AC 150/5070-3 Planning the Airport Industrial Park

AC 150/5060-7 Establishment of Airport Action Groups

Airport layout and land use plans

Outline

Introduction: Phase three of the master plan
Airport layout plan
Approach and clear zone layout
Land use plan

Objectives

When you have completed this chapter, you should be able to:

△ Describe the major items included in an airport layout plan drawing.

△ Identify the prominent airside facilities.

△ Describe the four basic runway configurations.

△ Highlight the importance of prevailing wind in planning runways.

△ Distinguish between the following runway classifications: visual, nonprecision instrument, and precision instrument.

△ Understand the importance of runway lighting and ILS systems.

△ Describe the basic principles involved in laying out taxiways.

△ Distinguish between holding areas and holding bays.

△ Describe the four basic aircraft parking positions.

△ Explain each of the so-called imaginary surfaces described in FAR Part 77.

△ Discuss the importance of land use planning on and off the airport.

Introduction
Phase three of the master plan

The third phase of the airport master plan includes four components: the airport layout plan, the land use plan, terminal area plans, and airport access plans. This chapter covers the former two and chapter 6 the latter two subjects.

Once the airport requirements (phase one) have been determined and the site (phase two), new or existing, has been selected, the master plan process moves on to the development of the airport layout plan. The development of the airport layout plan will establish the actual configuration of runways, taxiways, and aprons, and will set aside areas for the establishment of terminal facilities. Preliminary estimates of facility requirements were made under demand/capacity analysis in phase one of the master plan. The location of air navigation facilities and runway approach zones are also incorporated in the airport layout plan.

The land use plan within the airport boundary sets aside areas for establishment of the terminal complex, maintenance facilities, commercial buildings, industrial sites, airport access, buffer zones, recreation sites, and other possible improvements as may be appropriate to the specific airport situation. The land use plan outside the airport boundary includes those areas affected by obstruction clearance criteria and noise exposure factors.

The development of the terminal area plan and plans for facilities within the terminal area evolve from the airfield configurations and land use criteria established in the airport layout and land use plans. The airport access plan indicates the proposed routings of airport access to central business districts or to points of connection with existing or planned arterial ground transportation systems. Various modes of surface transportation are considered. The sizes of access facilities are based on airport access traffic studies. Because access facilities beyond airport boundaries are normally outside the jurisdiction of airport sponsors, careful coordination is required with other areawide planning bodies.

Airport layout plan

The *airport layout plan* is a graphic presentation to scale of existing and proposed airport facilities and land uses, their locations, and the pertinent clearance and dimensional information required to show conformance with applicable standards. It shows the airport location, clear zones, approach areas, and other environmental features that might influence airport usage and expansion capabilities.

The airport layout plan also identifies facilities that are no longer needed and describes a plan for their removal or phase-out. Some areas might be leased, sold, or otherwise used for commercial and industrial purposes. The plan is always updated with any changes in property lines; airfield configuration involving runways, taxiways, and aircraft parking apron size and location; buildings; auto parking; cargo areas; navigational aids; obstructions; and, entrance roads.

Airport layout plan drawing

The *airport layout plan drawing* includes the following items: the airport layout, location map, vicinity map, basic data table, and wind information (FIG. 5-1).

Airport layout   The *airport layout* is the main portion of the drawing. It depicts the existing and ultimate airport development and land uses drawn to scale and includes as a minimum the following information:

- Prominent airport facilities such as runways, taxiways, aprons, blast pads, extended runway safety areas, buildings, navaids, parking areas, roads, lighting, runway marking, pipelines, fences, major drainage facilities, segmented circle, wind indicators, and beacon.

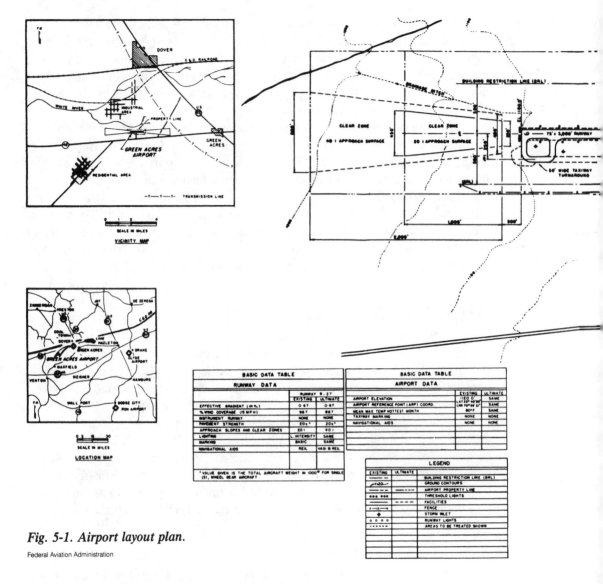

Fig. 5-1. Airport layout plan.

Federal Aviation Administration

- Prominent natural and manmade features such as trees, streams, ponds, rock outcrops, ditches, railroads, powerlines, and towers.

- Revenue-producing nonaviation-related property, surplus or otherwise, are outlined with current status and use specified.

- Areas reserved for existing and future aviation development and services such as for general aviation fixed-base operations, heliports, cargo facilities, airport maintenance, and so forth.

- Areas reserved for nonaviation development, such as industrial areas, motels, and so forth.

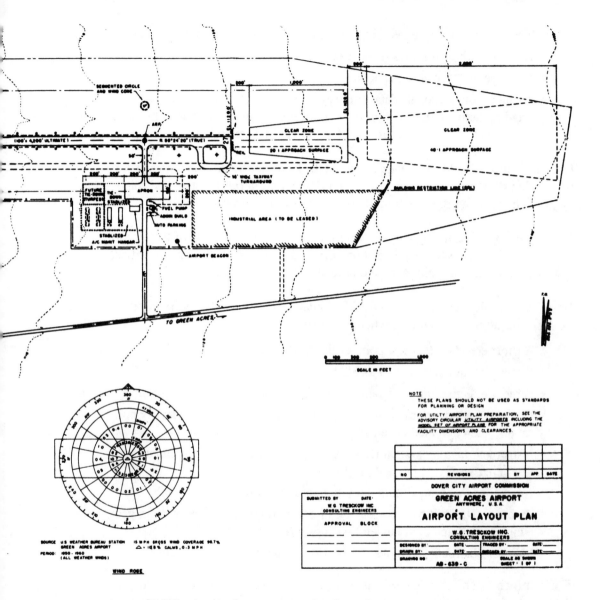

- Existing ground contours.
- Fueling facilities and tiedown areas.
- Facilities that are to be phased out.
- Airport boundaries and areas owned or controlled by the sponsor, including avigation easements.
- Approach and clear zone outlines.
- Airport reference point with latitude and longitude given based on U.S. Geological Survey grid system.

- Elevation of runway ends, high and low points, and runway intersections.
- True azimuth of runways (measured from true north).
- North point—true and magnetic.
- Pertinent dimensional data—runway and taxiway widths and runway lengths, taxiway-runway-apron clearances, apron dimensions, building clearance lines, clear zones, and parallel runway separation.

Location map The *location map* shown in the lower left-hand side of the airport layout plan drawing is drawn to scale and depicts the airport, cities, railroads, major highways, and roads within 25 to 50 miles of the airport.

Vicinity map The *vicinity map* shown in the upper left-hand side of the airport layout plan drawing shows the relationship of the airport to the city or cities, nearby airports, roads, railroads, and built-up areas.

Basic data table The *basic data table* contains the following information on existing and ultimate conditions where applicable:

- Airport elevation (highest point of the landing areas).
- Runway identification such as 6/24.
- Percent effective runway gradient for each existing and proposed runway.
- Percent of wind coverage by principal runway, secondary runway (if applicable), and combined coverage.
- Instrument landing system (ILS) runway when designated, dominant runway otherwise, existing and proposed.
- Normal or mean maximum daily temperature of the hottest month.
- Pavement strength of each runway in gross weight and type of main gear (single, dual, and dual tandem) as appropriate.
- Plan for obstruction removal, relocation of facilities, and so forth.

Wind information A *wind rose* is always included in the airport layout plan drawing with the runway orientation superimposed. Crosswind coverage and the source and period of data is also given. Wind information is given in terms of all-weather conditions, supplemented by IFR weather conditions where IFR operations are expected.

Airport components

The airport is a complex transportation hub serving aircraft, passengers, cargo, and surface vehicles. It is customary to classify the components of an airport into two major categories: airside facilities and landside facilities (FIG. 5-2).

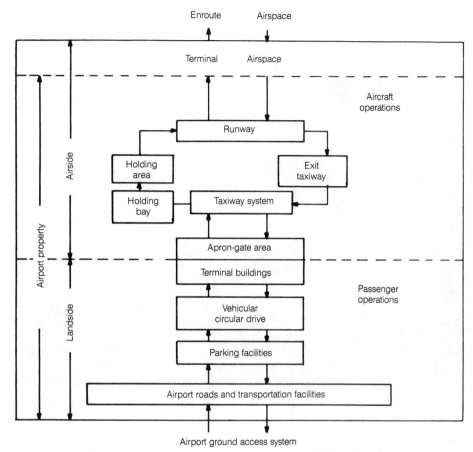

Fig. 5-2. Airport components.

Airside facilities, sometimes called the *aeronautical surfaces*, or more simply the *airfield*, are those on which aircraft operations are carried out. Principally, they are the runways where aircraft take off and land, the taxiways used for movement between the runway and the terminal, and the apron and gate areas where passengers embark and debark and where aircraft are parked. Because the airspace containing the approach and departure paths for the airfield has an important effect on runway utilization, it is also customary to include terminal area airspace as part of the airside.

The *landside facilities* are essentially those parts of the airport serving passengers, including surface transportation. It includes the terminal buildings, which include passenger loading and waiting areas, ticket counters, baggage handling facilities, restaurants, shops, car rental facilities, and the like. Loading, handling, and storage areas for air cargo and mail, often separately located, are also part of the terminal complex.

Reynolds, Smith, and Hills

An aerial view of Greensboro/High Point/Winston-Salem Airport showing airside and landside facilities.

The landside also includes the vehicular circular drive, parking facilities, and, in some cases, rail rapid transit lines and stations that are part of a larger urban mass transit system. Customarily, only roadways and transportation facilities on the airport property are considered part of the landside, even though they are actually extensions of, and integral with, the urban and regional transportation network.

The discussion that follows will focus in on the airside facilities and land use plan. Landside facilities will be taken up in the next chapter.

Airside facilities

Prominent airside facilities include runways including their classifications, marking and lighting, instrument landing system, taxiways, holding areas and bays, ground control, and parking.

Runways There are many airport runway configurations. The FAA includes 22 different layouts in their advisory circular 150/5060-3A, Airport Capacity Criteria Used in Long-Range Planning. The basic runway configurations are: (1) single

	Runway Configuration				PHOCAP(3)	
	FAA layout	Description	Aircraft Mix (1)	PANCAP (2)	IFR	VFR
Single	A	Single runway (arrivals = departures)	1	215,000	53	99
			2	195,000	52	76
			3	180,000	44	54
			4	170,000	42	45
Parallel	B Less than 3500'	Close parallels	1	385,000	64	198
			2	330,000	63	152
			3	295,000	55	108
			4	280,000	54	90
	C 3500' to 4999'	Intermediate parallels	1	425,000	79	198
			2	390,000	79	152
			3	355,000	79	108
			4	330,000	74	90
	D 5000' or more	Far parallels	1	430,000	106	198
			2	390,000	104	152
			3	360,000	88	108
			4	340,000	84	90
	H 5000' or more	Dual-line runway	1	770,000	128	396
			2	660,000	126	304
			3	590,000	110	216
			4	560,000	108	180
Open-V	K_1	Open V, dependent operations away from intersection	1	420,000	71	198
			2	335,000	70	136
			3	300,000	63	94
			4	295,000	60	84
	K_2	Open V, dependent operations toward intersection	1	235,000	57	108
			2	220,000	56	86
			3	215,000	50	66
			4	200,000	50	53
Intersecting	L_1 Direction of OPS	Two intersecting at near threshold	1	375,000	71	175
			2	310,000	70	125
			3	275,000	63	83
			4	255,000	60	69
	L_2	Two intersecting in middle	1	220,000	61	99
			2	195,000	60	76
			3	195,000	53	58
			4	190,000	47	52
	L_3 Direction of OPS	Two intersecting at far threshold	1	220,000	55	99
			2	195,000	54	76
			3	180,000	46	54
			4	175,000	42	57

Key: (1) Aircraft Mix

	Percentage			
	1	2	3	4
Type A - 4-engine jet and larger	0	0	20	60

Fig. 5-3. Airport runway configurations. *Continued on page 116.*

Key: (1) Aircraft Mix	Percentage			
	1	2	3	4
Type B - 2 and 3-engine jet, 4-engine piston, and turbo prop	0	30	40	20
Type C - executive jet and transport type twin-engine piston	10	30	20	20
Type D & E - light twin engine piston and single-engine piston	90	40	20	0

(2) PANCAP - Practical Annual Capacity
(3) PHOCAP - Practical Hourly Capacity

Fig. 5-3. Continued.

runway, (2) parallel runways, (3) open-V runways, and (4) intersecting runways (FIG. 5-3).

1. *Single runway.* The single runway is the simplest of the configurations. Under VFR conditions it can accommodate up to 99 predominantly light twin-engine and single-engine piston aircraft (type D&E) operations per hour. The capacity under IFR conditions is reduced to 42 to 53 operations per hour depending on the aircraft mix and navigational aids available at the particular field.

2. *Parallel runways.* There are basically four types of parallel runways: (1) *close* [fewer than 3,500 feet between runways], (2) *intermediate* [3,500 to 4,500 feet between runways], (3) *far* [more than 5,000 feet between runways], and (4) *dual-lane* [two-close parallel runways separated by 5,000 feet or more]. The capacities of parallel runway configurations vary considerably depending upon the number of runways and the spacing. With an aircraft mix of predominantly type D and E, operations per hour vary under IFR conditions between 64 for close parallels to 128 for a dual-lane configuration.

3. *Open-V runways.* Runways that diverge from different directions and do not intersect are classified as open-V runways. When there is little or no wind, both runways can be used simultaneously. Open-V runways revert to a single runway when winds are strong from one direction. Operations increase significantly when takeoffs and landings are made away from the V. When the operations are toward the V, the hourly capacity is reduced by almost 50 percent for Type D and E aircraft during VFR conditions.

4. *Intersecting.* Two or more runways which cross each other are referred to as intersecting runways. An intersecting runway configuration is utilized when there are relatively strong winds during the year from more than one direction. Like open-V runways, intersecting runways revert to a single runway when the winds are strong from one direction. If winds are relatively light, both runways can be used simultaneously.

The capacity of intersecting runways greatly depends upon the location of the intersection and the way the runways are operated. The highest capacity is achieved when the intersection is close to the takeoff end and landing threshold as shown in layout L_1.

From a planning standpoint, a single-direction runway configuration can achieve greater capacity and ease air traffic control. Routing aircraft in a single direction is less complex than routing in multiple directions. In general, an open-V configuration will yield higher capacities than intersecting configurations.

An analysis of the prevailing wind is essential in planning runways. The primary runway should be oriented as closely as possible to the direction of the prevailing winds. Aircraft that are landing and taking off can maneuver on a runway as long as the wind direction at right angles to the direction of travel (crosswind) is not excessive. The maximum allowable crosswind depends on the size of aircraft and the condition of the pavement surface. Large jet aircraft can maneuver in crosswinds as high as 40 knots, but it is difficult to do so and consequently lower values are used for planning purposes.

For all runways other than utility (constructed and intended for propeller-driven aircraft weighing 12,500 pounds or fewer), the FAA requires that "runways should be oriented so planes may be landed at least 95 percent of the time with crosswind components not exceeding 15 mph (13 knots)." For utility airports, the crosswind component is reduced to 11.5 mph (10 knots). The "95 percent" criteria required by the FAA is applicable to all conditions of weather.

Runway classifications and markings   The FAA classifies runways as visual, nonprecision instrument, and precision instrument. A *visual runway* is intended solely for the operation of aircraft using visual approach procedures, with no straight-in instrument procedure and no instrument designation indicated on an FAA approved layout plan. A *nonprecision instrument runway* is one having an instrument approach procedure using air navigation facilities with only horizontal guidance for which straight-in nonprecision instrument approach procedure has been approved. A *precision instrument* runway is one having an instrument approach procedure using an instrument landing system (ILS), or a precision approach radar (PAR). Figure 5-4 shows the standard markings required by the FAA for all visual and nonprecision instrument runways. Markings common to all runways include: (1) centerlines, (2) designator, and (3) holding indications. Additional markings for a nonprecision instrument runway include: (4) threshold marking and (5) fixed distance marker.

Figure 5-5 shows the detailed markings of a precision instrument runway. Additional markings for this runway include: (6) touchdown zone markers and (7) side stripes.

Figure 5-6 shows the markings for a *displaced threshold* (available for takeoff or rollout but not for touchdown) and a *relocated threshold* (area preceding

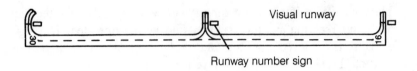

Visual runway

Runway number sign

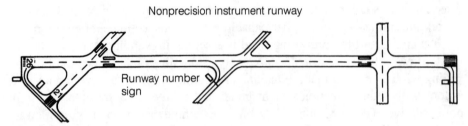

Nonprecision instrument runway

Runway number sign

Fig. 5-4. Visual and nonprecision instrument runways. Federal Aviation Administration

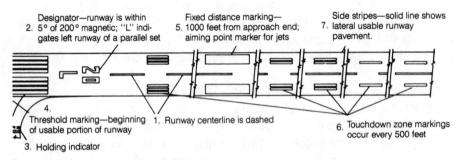

Detail of precision instrument runway

Designator—runway is within
2. 5° of 200° magnetic; "L" indi-
   gates left runway of a parallel set

Fixed distance marking—
5. 1000 feet from approach end;
   aiming point marker for jets

Side stripes—solid line shows
7. lateral usable runway
   pavement.

4.
Threshold marking—beginning   1. Runway centerline is dashed
of usable portion of runway

6. Touchdown zone markings
   occur every 500 feet

3. Holding indicator

Fig. 5-5. Detail of precision instrument runway. Federal Aviation Administration

Threshold indicators

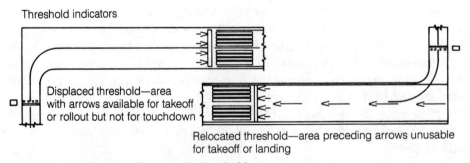

Displaced threshold—area
with arrows available for takeoff
or rollout but not for touchdown

Relocated threshold—area preceding arrows unusable
for takeoff or landing

Fig. 5-6. Displaced and relocated thresholds. Federal Aviation Administration

arrows unusable for takeoff or landing). Figure 5-7 shows the markings for inter-secting runways. Figures 5-8 and 5-9 show the markings for closed runways and heliports.

Intersecting runways

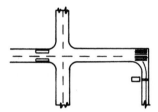

An instrument runway has priority over a visual one. Priority runway centerline markings will interrupt visual runway markings at intersection.

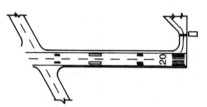

Runway 20L is a precision instrument runway whose markings have priority over both visual and non-precision instrument runways.

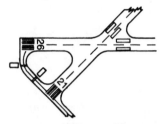

Two nonprecision instrument runways. Neither has priority at intersection.

Fig. 5-7. Intersecting runway markings. Federal Aviation Administration

Closed runways

Fig. 5-8. Closed runways.

Federal Aviation Administration

Temporarily closed runway sign is a simple cross at both ends. A permanently closed runway will have the ''x's'' at intervals along its length. Closed taxiways have the same symbols but smaller and in yellow.

Civil heliport

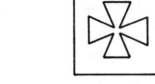

Military heliport

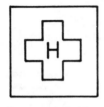

Recommended for
hospitals

Yellow "x" indicates heliport is closed.

Fig. 5-9. Heliport markings.

Federal Aviation Administration

Runway lighting   Runway lighting is extremely important for a pilot who might
have flown for long hours in darkness. Sophisticated lighting systems are also
essential for a rapid alignment check during daytime approaches if visibility is
poor. For a pilot breaking out of low clouds, high-intensity approach lights are the
only visual clue that the ground is near. In fog, even approach lights might hardly
be visible, the bright runway lights will guide the pilot after touchdown.

Fog-plagued airports might have individual lights that peak at an intensity of
30,000 candelas (twice the illumination of a set of car headlights). To prevent dis-
orientation, they can be dimmed—from 100 percent for sunlight or fog, to one
percent for a clear night.

Failure of the electricity supply could be catastrophic to a landing jet, so most
civil airports have emergency systems that switch automatically within 15 seconds
of a failure, and those with all-weather facilities have a standby system that
switches within one second. Figure 5-10 shows the lighting system for a precision
instrument runway.

Instrument runway landing system   The guidance system for approach and
landing now in use is the *instrument landing system* (ILS), which has been the
standard system in the U.S. since 1941 and is widely used by civil aviation
throughout the world. ILS provides guidance by radio beams that define a
straight-line path to the runway at a fixed slope of approximately three degrees

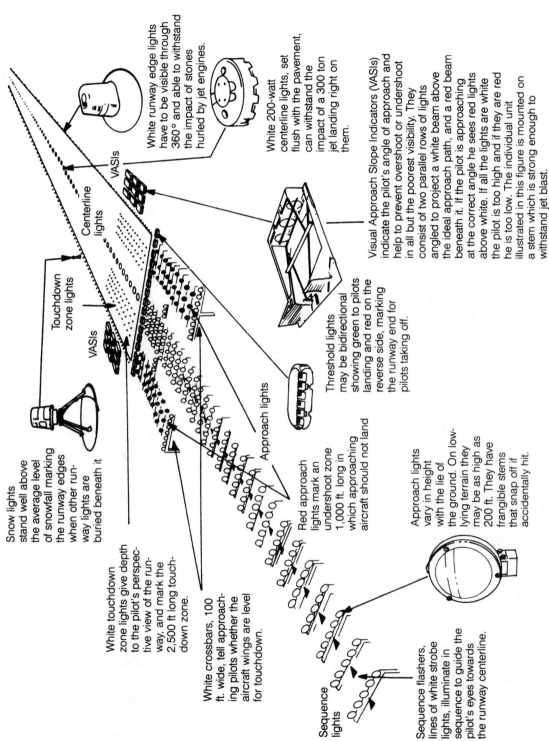

White runway edge lights have to be visible through 360° and able to withstand the impact of stones hurled by jet engines.

VASIs

Centerline lights

White 200-watt centerline lights, set flush with the pavement, can withstand the impact of a 300 ton jet landing right on them.

Touchdown zone lights

VASIs

Visual Approach Slope Indicators (VASIs) indicate the pilot's angle of approach and help to prevent overshoot or undershoot in all but the poorest visibility. They consist of two parallel rows of lights angled to project a white beam above the ideal approach path, and a red beam beneath it. If the pilot is approaching at the correct angle he sees red lights above white. If all the lights are white the pilot is too high and if they are red he is too low. The individual unit illustrated in this figure is mounted on a stem which is strong enough to withstand jet blast.

Approach lights

Threshold lights may be bidirectional showing green to pilots landing and red on the reverse side, marking the runway end for pilots taking off.

Snow lights stand well above the average level of snowfall marking the runway edges when other runway lights are buried beneath it

White touchdown zone lights give depth to the pilot's perspective view of the runway, and mark the 2,500 ft long touchdown zone.

Red approach lights mark an undershoot zone 1,000 ft. long in which approaching aircraft should not land

Approach lights vary in height with the lie of the ground. On low-lying terrain they may be as high as 200 ft. They have frangible stems that snap off if accidentally hit.

White crossbars, 100 ft. wide, tell approaching pilots whether the aircraft wings are level for touchdown.

Sequence lights

Sequence flashers, lines of white strobe lights, illuminate in sequence to guide the pilot's eyes towards the runway centerline.

Fig. 5-10. Precision instrument runway lighting. Federal Aviation Administration

and five to seven miles from the runway threshold. All aircraft approaching the airport under ILS guidance must follow this path in single file, spaced at intervals dictated by standards for safe longitudinal separation and the need to avoid wake turbulence (FIG. 5-11).

The ILS consists of a *localizer beacon* beam radiating along the straight line of approach to the runway that activates a needle on the aircraft's ILS signal receiver and guides the pilot in the direction toward the runway centerline. This signal can be considered as an electronic extension of the centerline of the runway. The *glideslope transmitter*, set approximately 450 feet to one side of the runway, sends out a different electronic signal that activates a second needle on the same ILS receiver and guides the pilot downward on a sloping path to the runway. This beam, angled at approximately three degrees to the horizontal, guides the aircraft down at a steady rate of descent.

By checking his map or chart when nearing the airport, the pilot can navigate to a point or fix close enough to receive both these signals, which will activate the two needles on the ILS receiver. The pilot then begins the descent. The needles will show how far to the right or left or how much above or below the aircraft is in relation to the precise electronic path he must follow at the center of the intersection of the localizer and glideslope signals. The pilot's job is to fly the plane so as to keep the needles on the ILS receiver as close as possible to their center positions on the instrument's face.

As the aircraft descends on the glideslope, it will pass through two electronic markers. The markers transmit vertical beams that penetrate the localizer and glideslope beams and identify precise lateral positions.

The first or *outer marker* is located from five to seven miles from the end of the runway. Its vertical beam activates a rapidly flashing blue light on the marker beacon receiver when the plane passes through. The outer marker also has an audio signal—two dashes per second at a low tone to further alert the pilot to his position on the glideslope.

About 3,500 feet from the runway, the *middle marker* vertical beam flashes an amber light on the marker beacon receiver. This marker's audio signal is a series of alternating dots and dashes at a high tone. Just seconds after passing through the middle marker, depending upon the decision height of landing category, the pilot should see the approach lights. The *decision height* is the point where the pilot has to decide whether it is safe to land, or whether he should pull up and abort the landing.

The new *microwave landing system* (MLS) is gradually being adopted at major airports. This system transmits a radio beam from left to right and right to left across the sky. By automatically timing the intervals between successive interceptions of the sweeping beam, the landing system can accurately calculate an aircraft's position relative to the runway. It is cheaper than the ILS to install at airports (although the aircraft equipment is more costly) and, because the beams spread more widely, it offers a number of alternative approach paths.

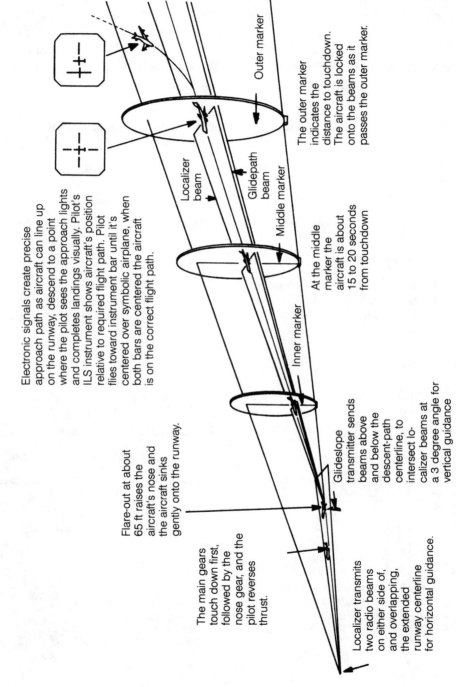

Electronic signals create precise approach path as aircraft can line up on the runway, descend to a point where the pilot sees the approach lights and completes landings visually. Pilot's ILS instrument shows aircraft's position relative to required flight path. Pilot flies toward instrument bar until it's centered over symbolic airplane, when both bars are centered the aircraft is on the correct flight path.

Flare-out at about 65 ft raises the aircraft's nose and the aircraft sinks gently onto the runway.

The main gears touch down first, followed by the nose gear, and the pilot reverses thrust.

Localizer transmits two radio beams on either side of, and overlapping, the extended runway centerline for horizontal guidance.

Glideslope transmitter sends beams above and below the descent-path centerline, to intersect lo-calizer beams at a 3 degree angle for vertical guidance.

Inner marker

At the middle marker the aircraft is about 15 to 20 seconds from touchdown

Localizer beam

Glidepath beam

Middle marker

Outer marker

The outer marker indicates the distance to touchdown. The aircraft is locked onto the beams as it passes the outer marker.

Fig. 5-11. Instrument landing systems. Federal Aviation Administration

Taxiways The major function of taxiways is to provide access to and from the runways to other areas of the airport including the terminal area in an expeditious manner. *Exit* and *entrance* taxiways are generally located at the ends of the runway and constructed at right angles to the runway. At busy airports where taxiing traffic moves simultaneously in different directions, *parallel* one-way taxiways are often provided. Taxiways are planned with the following principles in mind:

1. Aircraft that have just landed should not interfere with aircraft taxiing to take off.

2. Taxi routes should provide the shortest distance between the terminal area and the runways.

3. At busy airports, taxiways are normally located at various points along runways so that landing aircraft can leave the runways as quickly as possible. These are also referred to as *exit taxiways* or *turnoffs*.

4. A taxiway designed to permit higher turnoff speeds reduces the time a landing aircraft is on the runway.

5. When possible, taxiways are planned so as not to cross an active runway.

At busy airports, blue-edge lights mark the sides of the taxiway and sometimes green center lights mark the route to the active runway. Red stop bars might appear when another aircraft crosses its path. Standard taxiway markings are shown in FIG. 5-12.

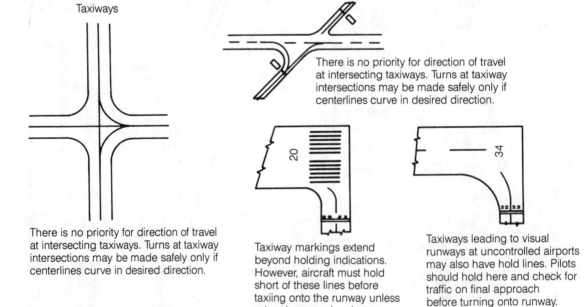

Taxiways

There is no priority for direction of travel at intersecting taxiways. Turns at taxiway intersections may be made safely only if centerlines curve in desired direction.

There is no priority for direction of travel at intersecting taxiways. Turns at taxiway intersections may be made safely only if centerlines curve in desired direction.

Taxiway markings extend beyond holding indications. However, aircraft must hold short of these lines before taxiing onto the runway unless prior clearance has been received from air traffic control.

Taxiways leading to visual runways at uncontrolled airports may also have hold lines. Pilots should hold here and check for traffic on final approach before turning onto runway.

Fig. 5-12. Taxiway markings. Federal Aviation Administration

Holding areas Holding areas (commonly referred to as *run-up areas*) are located at or very near the ends of runways for pilots to make final checks and await final clearance for takeoff. These areas are generally large enough so that if an aircraft is unable to take off, another aircraft can bypass it. The holding area normally can accommodate two or three aircraft and allow enough space for one aircraft to bypass another.

Holding bays Holding bays are apron areas located at various points off taxiways for temporary storage of aircraft. At some airports where peak demand results in full occupancy at all gate positions, ground control will often route an aircraft to a holding bay until a gate becomes available. Some holding bays, the size of a football field, are located as close as 250 feet from the active runway. During peak hours, aircraft are held in the bay until given a takeoff position at which time they move to the holding area. See FIG. 5-13 for an example of a holding area and holding bay.

Ground control and parking An aircraft landing at a major metropolitan airport might have to negotiate a mile or more of taxiways to reach the parking apron area. Pilots normally have a map of the airport layout, and taxiways are marked with lights and other signals. If a pilot loses his way despite the radioed instructions from controllers in the tower giving him the route to be taken, an airport truck with a large "Follow Me" sign might be sent to lead the pilot onto the parking apron area.

Lines painted on the concrete parking apron adjoining the taxiways lead the airline pilot to his final positioning. Linemen will greet the incoming aircraft and direct the pilot with appropriate parking signals (FIG. 5-14). The pilot will attempt to keep the aircraft's nosewheel on the appropriate line as he follows the lineman's instructions. The aircraft's stopping point must be precise if the jetways (the telescopic walkways joining aircraft to terminal) are to reach the door and be in the correct position. Various optical or electrical devices assist in this maneuver.

Aircraft can be positioned at various angles with respect to the terminal building but the nose-in parking position is the most frequently used at major airports (FIG. 5-15). Normally, an aircraft will maneuver into the nose-in parking position under its own power; however, in order to leave the gate position, it has to be towed out a sufficient distance to allow it to proceed under its own power.

The nose-in parking position requires the smallest gate area per aircraft. It also causes lower noise levels and there is no jet blast toward the terminal building. Parking close to the building also facilitates passenger loading and unloading.

Aircraft can also be parked in *angled nose-in*, *angled nose-out*, and *parallel* positions (FIG. 5-16). Generally, these positions are used at smaller airports with less traffic and fewer facilities and equipment. The big advantage of these positions is the ability of the pilot to maneuver in and out of gate positions without the need for towing.

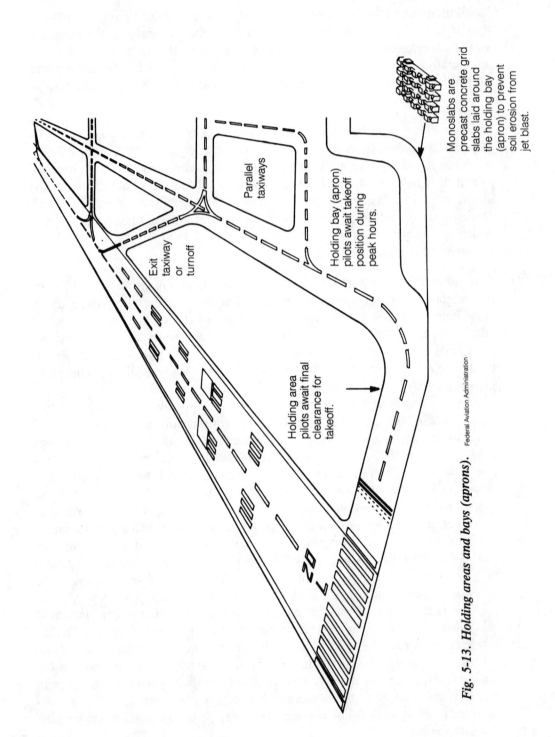

Parallel
taxiways

Exit
taxiway
or
turnoff

Holding bay (apron)
pilots await takeoff
position during
peak hours.

Holding area
pilots await final
clearance for
takeoff.

Monoslabs are
precast concrete grid
slabs laid around
the holding bay
(apron) to prevent
soil erosion from
jet blast.

Fig. 5-13. Holding areas and bays (aprons).   Federal Aviation Administration

Parking apron.

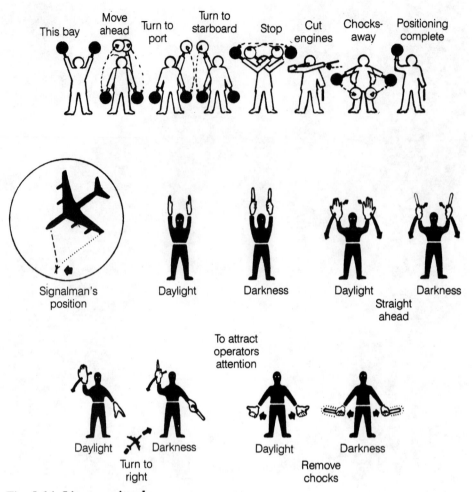

Fig. 5-14. Lineman signals. Federal Aviation Administration

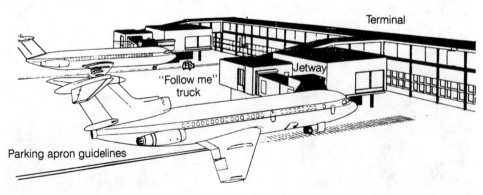

Fig. 5-15. Nose-in parking.

Northeast Orient 747 parked nose-in at Seattle-Tacoma International Airport.

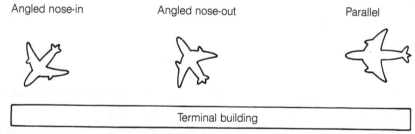

Fig. 5-16. Aircraft parking positions.

Airport layout plan report

The airport layout plan drawing is normally accompanied by a written report that documents the following items:

1. Reasoning behind the design features such as demand/capacity analysis and so forth.
2. Basis and/or computation for the runway length design.
3. Basis for runway orientation if not aligned for maximum wind coverage.
4. Low visibility wind data where available.

Approach and clear zone layout

The *approach and clear zone layout* is a graphic presentation to scale of the following items:

1. Areas under the imaginary surfaces as defined in FAR Part 77, Objects Affecting Navigable Airspace.

2. Existing and ultimate approach slopes and any height or slope protection established by local zoning ordinance.

3. A plan and profile of the clear zones and approach areas showing the controlling structures and trees therein (usually the tallest object within a cluster) and their elevations. Also, roads, railroads, and pipelines that cross clear zones and approach areas are shown.

4. Location and elevation of obstructions exceeding criteria in FAR Part 77.

5. For airports serving jet aircraft and within the boundaries defined by the imaginary surfaces given in FAR Part 77, an outline of all areas with present or potential concentrations of people is shown on the drawing. The primary type of development in these areas includes industrial developments, residential areas, ballparks, schools, and hospitals. For other airports, this information is shown for the areas under the approach surfaces and at least 1,000 feet to either side of each runway or 500 feet from the nearest aircraft operational area.

6. In the approach areas, tall smokestacks, television, and radio transmission towers, garbage dumps, or other areas attracting a large number of birds, and any other potential hazard to aircraft flight.

FAR Part 77

Obstruction clearance requirements at or near airports are contained in *FAR Part 77*, Objects Affecting Navigable Airspace. An object that protrudes above the imaginary surfaces specified in this part is considered an obstruction to air navigation. If the airport planner finds that there is an obstruction to air navigation, he must contact the airport services section of the FAA and seek advice.

In order to determine whether an object is an obstruction to navigable airspace, several imaginary surfaces are established with relation to the airport and to each runway. The size of the imaginary surfaces depends upon the type of approach planned for that runway: visual, nonprecision instrument, and precision instrument.

The principal imaginary surfaces defined in FAR Part 77 are shown in FIG. 5-17:

1. A surface longitudinally centered on a runway is called a *primary surface*. When the runway has a specially prepared hard surface, the

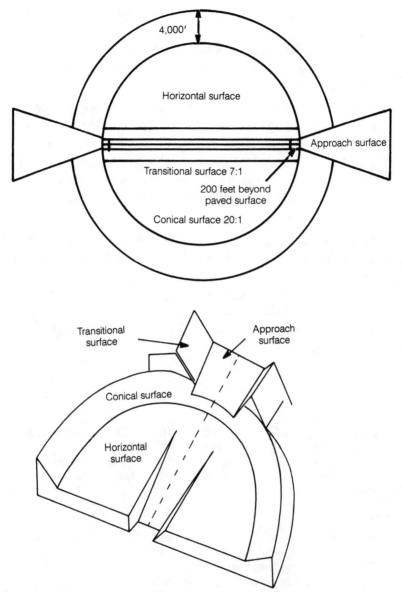

Fig. 5-17. Imaginary surfaces. <small>Federal Aviation Administration</small>

primary surface extends 200 feet beyond each end of that runway, but
when the runway has no specially prepared hard surface, or planned
hard surface, the primary surface ends at each end of that runway.

2. A *horizontal surface* is a horizontal plane 150 feet above the established
   airport elevation, the perimeter of which is constructed by swinging arcs
   of specified radii from the center of each end of the primary surface of

each runway of each airport and connecting the adjacent arcs by lines tangent to those arcs.

3. The *conical surface* extends outward and upward from the periphery of the horizontal surface at a slope of 20-to-1 for a horizontal distance of 4,000 feet.

4. A surface longitudinally centered on the extended runway centerline and extending outward and upward from each end of the primary surface is called the *approach surface*.

5. The *transitional surfaces* extend outward and upward at right angles to the runway centerline and the runway centerline extended at a slope of 7-to-1 from the sides of the primary surface and from the sides of the approach surfaces.

The dimensions of the imaginary surfaces are shown in TABLE 5-1. FAR Part 77 specifies dimensions for each category of runway coded A, B, C, and D.

Table 5-1. Imaginary surface dimensions FAR Part 77 (in feet). Source: FAA

	Visual runway		Nonprecision instrument runway			Precision instrument runway
				B		
	A	B	A	C	D	
Width of primary surface and approach width at inner end . . .	250	500	500	500	1,000	1,000
Radius of horizontal surface	5,000	5,000	5,000	10,000	10,000	10,000
Approach surface width at end	1,250	1,500	2,000	3,500	4,000	16,000
Approach surface length	5,000	5,000	5,000	10,000	10,000	*
Approach slope	30:1	20:1	20:1	34:1	34:1	*

Categories	Description
A	Utility runway—constructed for and intended to be used by propeller-driven aircraft weighing 12,500 lbs. or less.
B	Runways larger than utility.
C	Visibility minimums greater than 3/4 mile.
D	Visibility minimums as low as 3/4 mile.
*	Precision instrument approach slope is 50:1 for inner 10,000 feet and 40:1 for an additional 40,000 feet.

Land use plan

The airport *land use plan* shows an on-airport land uses as developed by the airport sponsor under the master plan effort and off-airport land uses as developed by surrounding communities. The work of airport, city, regional, and state planners must be carefully coordinated. The configuration of airfield runways, taxiways, and approach zones established in an airport layout plan provides the basis for development of the land use plan for areas on and adjacent to the airport. The land use plan for the airport and its environment in turn is an integral part of an areawide comprehensive planning program. The location, size, and configuration of the airport needs to be coordinated with patterns of residential and other major land uses in the area as well as with other transportation facilities and public services. Within the comprehensive planning framework, airport planning, policies, and programs must be coordinated with the objectives, policies, and programs for the area that the master plan airport is to serve.

Land uses on the airport

The amount of acreage within the airport's boundaries will have a major impact on the types of land uses to be found on the airport. For airports with limited acreage, most land uses will be aviation-oriented. Large airports with a great deal of land in excess of what is needed for aeronautical purposes might be used for other uses. For example, many airports lease land to industrial users, particularly those who use business aircraft or whose personnel travel extensively by air carrier or charter. In many cases, taxiway access is provided directly to the company's facility. In some instances, railroad tracks serving the company's area, company parking lots, or low-level warehousing can be located directly under runway approaches (but free of clear zones). Companies that might produce electronic disturbances that would interfere with aircraft navigation or communications equipment or cause visibility problems due to smoke are not compatible airport tenants. Some commercial activities are suitable for locating within the airport's boundaries. Recreational uses such as golf courses and picnicking areas are quite

Hangar facilities at Greater Pittsburgh International Airport.

suitable for airport land uses and might in effect serve as good buffer areas. Certain agricultural uses are appropriate for airport lands, but grain fields that attract birds are avoided.

Although lakes, reservoirs, rivers, and streams might be appropriate for inclusion within the airport's boundaries, especially from the standpoints of noise or flood control, care is normally taken to avoid those water bodies that have in the past attracted large numbers of waterfowl. Dumps and landfills that might attract birds are also avoided.

Land uses around the airport

The noise problem is the biggest objection voiced by people in areas near the airport. The responsibility for developing land uses around the airport so as to minimize the impact of noise and other environmental problems lies with the local governmental bodies. The more political entities involved, the more complicated the coordination process becomes.

In the past, the most common approach to controlling land uses around the airport was zoning. Airports and their surrounding areas become involved in two types of zoning. The first type of zoning is *height and hazard zoning*, which protects the airport and its approaches from obstructions to aviation while restricting certain elements of community growth. FAR Part 77, Objects Affecting Navigable Airspace, is the basis for height and hazard zoning.

The second type of zoning is *land use zoning*. This type of zoning has several shortcomings. First, it is not retroactive and does not affect preexisting uses that might conflict with airport operations. Secondly, jurisdictions with zoning powers (usually cities, towns, or counties) might not take effective zoning action. This is partly because the airport might affect several jurisdictions and coordination of zoning is difficult. Or the airport might be located in a rural area where the county lacks zoning powers and the sponsoring city might not be able to zone outside its political boundaries. Another problem is that the interest of the community is not always consistent with the needs and interests of the aviation industry. The locality might want more tax base, population growth, and rising land values, all of which are not often consistent with the need to preserve the land around the airport for other than residential uses.

Another approach to land use planning around the airport is *subdivision regulations*. Provisions can be written into the regulations prohibiting residential construction in intense noise exposure areas. These areas can be determined by acoustical studies prior to development. Insulation requirements can be made a part of the local building codes, without which the building permits cannot be issued.

Finally, another alternative in controlling land use around the airport is the relocation of residences and other incompatible uses. Often urban renewal funds are used for this purpose.

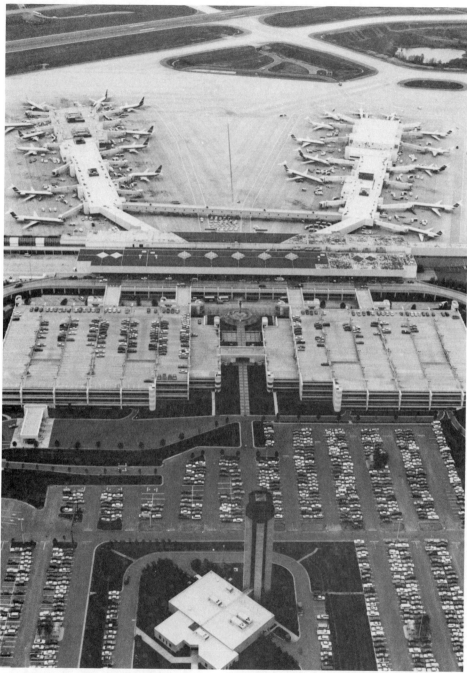

A symmetrical view of Charlotte/Douglas International Airport showing the airport's twin parking decks, terminal building and four concourses. The 150-foot FAA control tower is in the foreground and a 15-foot sculpture of Queen Charlotte, whom the city was named after, its centered between the twin parking decks.

Key terms

airport layout plan
airport layout plan drawing
airport layout
location map
vicinity map
basic data table
wind rose
airside facilities
landside facilities
single runway
parallel runways
open-V runways
intersecting runways
visual runway
nonprecision instrument runway
precision instrument runway
displaced threshold
relocated threshold
instrument landing system (ILS)
localizer beacon
glideslope transmitter
outer marker
middle marker
decision height
microwave landing system (MLS)
exit and entrance taxiways
parallel taxiways
holding areas
holding bays (aprons)
approach and clear zone layout
FAR Part 77
primary surface
horizontal surface
conical surface
approach surface
transitional surfaces
land use plan

Review questions

1. What is an airport layout plan drawing? Describe the information included in the airport layout section of the drawing. What other items are included in the drawing?

2. Define airside facilities. Describe the four basic runway configurations.
   What is the FAA's requirement with regard to runway orientation and the prevailing wind? Is it the same for utility and nonutility airports?
   Describe the following runway classifications: visual, nonprecision instrument, and precision instrument. What is meant by a displaced threshold? A relocated threshold?
   Describe the lighting system for a precision instrument runway.

3. How does the ILS system work?
   What is the microwave landing system (MLS)?
   Describe the basic principles in laying out taxiways. Distinguish between holding areas and holding bays.
   What are the four basic aircraft parking positions? Which is the most popular at major airports? Why?
   What is the airport layout plan report?

4. What is the approach and clear zone layout? Describe the "imaginary surfaces" described in FAR Part 77. What is a utility runway?

5. What nonaviation land uses would be compatible with aviation activities within the airport boundary? Which would not?
   What is the biggest problem when residential communities are built adjacent to the airport? Discuss some possible solutions to this problem.
   Which type of businesses might be appropriate airport neighbors?

Suggested readings

FAA Advisory Circulars:

150/5070-3	Planning the Airport Industrial Park
150/5300-13	Airport Design Standards
150/5060-1A	Airport Capacity Criteria Used in Preparing the National Airport Plan
150/5060-3A	Airport Capacity Criteria Used in Long-Range Planning

150/5070-6	Airport Master Plans
150/5050-2	Compatible Land Use Planning in the Vicinity of Airports
150/5100-5	Land Acquisition in the Federal-Aid Airport Program
150/5190-3	Model Airport Zoning Ordinance
150/5340-21	Airport Miscellaneous Lighting Visual Aids
150/5020-1	Noise Control and Compatibility Planning for Airports
150/5100-13	Development of State Standards for General Aviation Airports

deNeufville, Richard. *Airport Systems Planning*. Cambridge, Massachusetts: The MIT Press, 1976.

Horonjeff, Robert. *Planning and Design of Airports*, 2nd Ed. New York: McGraw-Hill, 1975

Gesell, Laurence E. *The Administration of Public Airports*, San Luis Obispo, California: Coast Aire Publications, 1981.

Federal Aviation Regulations (FAR):

Part 77	Objects Affecting Navigable Airspace
Part 153	Acquisition of U.S. Land for Public Airports
Part 157	Notice of Construction, Alteration, Activation and Deactivation of Airports

Terminal area and airport access plans

Outline

Introduction: Continuation of phase three
Terminal area plans
Airport access plans

Objectives

When you have completed this chapter, you should be able to:

△ Define "terminal area."

△ Describe the primary objective of the terminal area plans.

△ Discuss some of the factors taken into consideration by airport planners in selecting a terminal area concept.

△ Summarize the advantages and disadvantages of the centralized and decentralized passenger processing systems.

△ Distinguish between the four terminal building design concepts.

△ Explain what is meant by the passenger handling system and identify the processing links.

△ List some of the terminal building facilities occupied by airport operations and management, airline operations, and government agencies.

△ Describe the flow of domestic, international, and transfer passengers through the terminal.

△ Define "general concept evaluation" and "criteria for design and development."

△ Identify the steps involved in determining space requirements.

△ Describe the purpose of the airport access plans.

Introduction
Continuation of phase three

This chapter completes phase three of the airport master plan with a discussion of the terminal area and airport access plans. The development of the terminal area plan, plans for components within the terminal area, and airport access plans evolve from demand/capacity analysis and from the airfield configurations and land use criteria established in the airport layout and land use plans. This does not mean that the terminal area concept that is selected for a particular airport will not have a vital impact on the airport layout plan. The airfield configuration and the terminal area configuration must fit together and adjustments in both layouts must be made as the master plan evolves. Regardless of these necessary design adjustments, the details of the terminal area plan will follow the development of the airport layout plan.

The *terminal area* is the area used or intended to be used for such facilities as terminal and cargo buildings; gates, hangars, shops, and other service buildings; automobile parking, airport motels and restaurants, and garages and vehicle service—facilities used in connection with the airport; and entrance and service roads used by the public within the boundaries of the airport.

The airport terminal—the building itself and the paved areas surrounding it on the airside and the landside—is the zone of transition for passengers, providing the link between surface and air transportation. Design and operation of the terminal have an influence on both airside capacity and ground access and the overall rate at which aircraft can be handled. The basic relationship, illustrated in FIG. 6-1, dictates the design of the terminal complex.

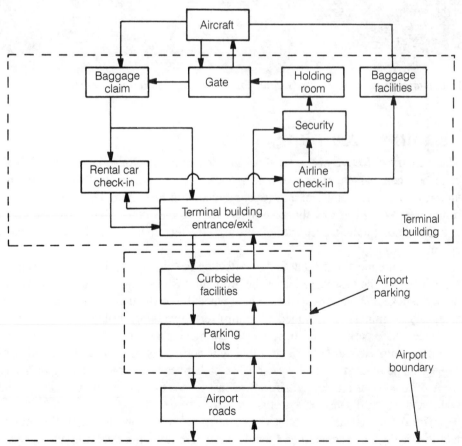

Fig. 6-1. Airport landside functional flow.

Vehicular circular drive at the Greater Pittsburgh International Airport.

Terminal area plans

The primary objective of the terminal area plans is to achieve an acceptable balance between passenger convenience, operating efficiency, facility investment, and aesthetics. The physical and psychological comfort characteristics of the terminal area should afford the passenger orderly and convenient progress from automobile or public transportation through the terminal to the aircraft and back again.

One of the most important factors affecting the air traveler is walking distance. It begins when the passenger leaves the ground transportation vehicle and continues on to the ticket counter and to the point at which he or she boards the aircraft. Consequently, terminals are planned to minimize the walking distance by developing convenient auto parking facilities, convenient movements of passengers through the terminal complex, and conveyances that will permit fast and efficient handling of baggage. The planner normally establishes objectives for average walking distances from terminal points to parked aircraft. Conveyances for passengers such as moving walks and baggage handling systems are also considered.

The functional arrangement of the terminal area complex with the airside facilities is designed so as to be flexible enough to meet the operating characteristics of the airline industry for handling passengers and for fast ground servicing of aircraft so that minimum gate occupancy time and maximum airline operating economy will be achieved.

The final objective of the terminal area plans is to develop a complex that provides all necessary services within an optimum expenditure of funds from the standpoints of capital investment and maintenance and operating costs. This takes into account flexibility and costs that will be required in future expansions of the terminal area.

Terminal area factors

In the selection of a terminal area concept, the following factors are taken into consideration by airport planners:

A. Passengers
    1. Adequate terminal area curb space for private and public transportation.
    2. Minimum walking distance—automobile parking to ticket counter.
    3. Minimum walking distance—ticket counter to passenger holding area and holding area to aircraft.
    4. Passenger transportation—where long distances must be traversed.
    5. Pedestrian walkways to aircraft—as backup to mechanical transportation systems for passengers.
    6. Efficiency of passenger interline connection.
    7. Baggage handling—enplaning and deplaning.
    8. Convenient hotel-motel accommodations.
    9. Efficient handling of visitors and sightseers at the airport.

B. Passenger vehicles
    1. Public automobile flow separation from service and commercial traffic.
    2. Public transportation to and from the airport.
    3. Public parking—long-term (three hours or more) and short-term (less than three hours).
    4. Airport employee parking.
    5. Airline employee parking.
    6. Public auto service area.
    7. Rental car parking and service areas.

C. Airport operations
    1. Separation of apron vehicles from moving and parked aircraft.
    2. Passenger flow separation in the terminal building (departing and arriving).
    3. Passenger flow separation from apron activities.
    4. Concession availability and exposure to public.
    5. Airfield security and prevention of unauthorized access to apron and airfield.

6. Air cargo and freight forwarder facilities.
7. Airport maintenance shops and facilities.
8. Airfield and apron drainage.
9. Airfield and apron utilities.
10. Utility plants, and heating and air conditioning systems.
11. Fire and rescue facilities and equipment.

D. Aircraft
1. Efficient aircraft flow on aprons and between terminal aprons and taxiways.
2. Easy and efficient maneuvering of aircraft parking at gate positions.
3. Aircraft fueling.
4. Heliport areas.
5. General aviation areas.
6. Noise, fumes, and blast control.
7. Apron space for staging and maneuvering of aircraft service equipment.

E. Safety
1. Enplaning and deplaning at aircraft.
2. Elevators, escalators, stairs, and ramps as to location, speed, and methods of access and egress.
3. People-mover systems as to location, speed, methods of access and egress.
4. Road crossings as to protection of pedestrians.
5. Provisions for disabled persons.

The planner must also take into consideration expansion capabilities to accommodate increasing passenger volumes and aircraft gate positions. In addition, the planner must provide a proper balance between capital investment, aesthetics, operation, and maintenance costs, and passengers and airport revenues.

Specific planning criteria is developed for the aforementioned factors and for major terminal area components. Information for terminal requirements are obtained from the air carriers, general aviation interests, airport concessionaires, airport management, and special technical committees. The criteria is analyzed and agreed upon by all parties involved before it is incorporated in the master plan. It is essential that coordination with airport interests and users be effected before the final selection of a terminal area concept is made.

Terminal building design concepts

Airport terminal buildings can be categorized as either centralized, decentralized, or a combination of the two (hybrid). *Centralized passenger processing* means all the facilities for ticketing, baggage check-in, security, customs, and immigration are all done in one building and used for processing all passengers using the building. Advantages and disadvantages of a centralized passenger processing terminal are as follows:

Advantages
1. Centralizes airline, airport, and international processing personnel thus reducing costs.
2. Facilitates control of passengers—transfers and security.
3. Provides for simplified vehicular and pedestrian information system.
4. Centralizes passenger services and amenities.

Disadvantages
1. Generates vehicular congestion at curbside.
2. Creates pedestrian congestion at check-in processing areas.
3. Develops long walking distances from parking areas to processing areas.
4. Limits expansion.

Decentralized passenger processing means the passenger handling facilities are provided in smaller units and repeated in one or more buildings. Advantages and disadvantages of a decentralized passenger processing terminal are as follows:

Advantages
1. Optimizes the level of service/convenience for passengers.
2. Minimizes walking distances.
3. Clarifies circulation providing direct passenger flow.
4. Disperses vehicular circulation for curbside drop-off and parking.
5. Provides potential for growth through modular construction.
6. Accommodates diverse modes of transportation for passenger access/egress.

Disadvantages
1. Necessitates decentralization of personnel for airline, airport, and governmental processing activities.
2. Increases capital costs per gate.
3. Increases operating and maintenance costs.

There are four terminal building design concepts, each of which can be used with varying degrees of centralization: (1) gate arrival, (2) pier finger, (3) satellite, and (4) transporter. These concepts are shown in FIG. 6-2.

Gate arrival The gate arrival concept is a centralized layout that is aimed at reducing the walking distance by bringing the automobile as close as possible to the aircraft. The most fundamental type of gate arrival concept is the *simple terminal*. It consists of a single common waiting and ticketing area with several exits onto a small aircraft parking apron. It is adaptable to airports with low airline activity and is also adaptable to general aviation operations whether it is located as a separate

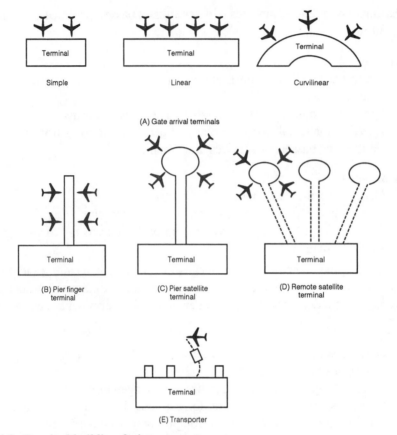

Fig. 6-2. Terminal building design concepts.

entity on a large airline-served airport or is the operational center for an airport used exclusively by general aviation. Where the simple terminal serves airline operations, it will usually have an apron that provides close-in parking for three to six commercial transport aircraft. Where the simple terminal serves general aviation only, it is within convenient walking distance of aircraft parking areas and adjacent to an aircraft service apron. The simple terminal normally consists of a single level structure where access to aircraft is afforded by a walk across the aircraft parking apron. The layout of the simple terminal takes into account the possibility of linear extension for terminal expansion.

The *linear* or *curvilinear terminal* concept is merely an extension of the simple terminal concept—that is, the simple terminal is repeated in a linear extension to provide additional apron frontage, more gates, and more room within the terminal for passenger processing. The more sophisticated linear terminals often feature a two-level structure where enplaning passengers are processed direct from curb to aircraft on one level while the other level is used by deplaning passengers for baggage claim and access to ground transportation. Passenger walking distance from curb through terminal to aircraft is short, usually 75 to 100 feet. The linear configuration also lends itself to the development of adequate, close-in public parking. Ample curb frontage for loading and unloading ground transportation vehicles is provided with each extension of the linear terminal and there is a direct relationship of enplaning or deplaning curb frontage to departing or arriving aircraft. Linear terminals can be expanded with almost no interference to passenger processing or aircraft operations. Expansion may be accomplished by linear extension of existing structure or by developing two or more linear terminal units.

The linear concept does not require long concourses, fingers, satellites, or service buildings, but it does not lend itself to common facilities such as waiting rooms, concessions, ticket counters, or hold rooms. These facilities are usually repeated with each linear extension. At large airports, the concept can also require an extensive system of directional signs because enplaning passengers must not only be directed to the correct airline area but also to the correct passenger processing module within that area. Another problem with the concept is that on a return flight to the airport, a passenger might find that his deplaning module is located a long distance from where he parked his car at his enplaning module. These factors must be taken into account in comparing the operating and construction costs of the linear terminal with other concepts. The configuration of the space occupied by the linear concept must also be compared with the space and configurations of other concepts in determining their compatibility with particular airport situations.

Pier finger The pier finger terminal concept evolved in the 1950s when gate concourses were added to simple terminal buildings. Since then, very sophisticated forms of the concept have been developed with the addition of hold rooms at gates, jetways, and aircraft loading bridges, and vertical separation of the ticketing check-in function from the baggage claim function; however, the basic concept has not changed in that the main terminal building is used to process passengers and baggage while the finger or pier provides a means of enclosed access from the central terminal to aircraft gate. Aircraft are parked at gates along the pier as opposed to the satellite concept, where they are parked in a cluster at the end of a concourse.

Walking distances through finger terminals are long, averaging 400 feet or more. Curb space must be carefully planned because it depends on the length of the central terminal and is not related to the total number of gates afforded by fingers. This is particularly true of deplaning curbs near centralized baggage claim facilities.

Although the finger concept has afforded one of the most economical means of adding gate positions to existing terminals, its use for expansion is limited because it takes valuable apron space. Planners also must be aware not to add new pier fingers without providing adequate space for passenger processing in the main terminal.

International Satellite Terminal at Miami International Airport.

Satellite terminals   The primary feature of the satellite terminal concept is the provision of a single terminal (with all ticketing, baggage handling, and ancillary services) that is connected by concourses to one or more satellite structures. The features of the satellite concept are very similar to those of the finger concept except that aircraft gates are located at the end of a long concourse rather than being spaced at even intervals along the concourse. Satellite gates are usually served by a common hold room rather than individual hold rooms. Another feature is that the concourse can be located underground (*remote satellite*), thereby providing space for aircraft taxi operations between the main terminal and the satellite.

The distance from the main terminal to a satellite is usually well above the average distance to gates found with the finger concept; therefore, people-mover systems are provided between terminal and satellite at many airports to reduce walking distances.

One of the advantages of the satellite concept is that it lends itself to a compact central terminal with common areas for processing passengers. In some instances, where terminal area space is limited, structural parking is provided above the central terminal building.

Aircraft maneuvering areas are required around satellites so that push-out tug operations do not cause aircraft to block active taxiways. Wedge-shaped aircraft parking positions around the satellite also tend to crowd the operation of aircraft servicing equipment.

Pier finger with loading bridges at Baltimore-Washington International Airport.

Terminals developed under the satellite concept are difficult to expand without reducing ramp frontage or disrupting airport operations; therefore, increases in terminal capacity are usually effected by the addition of terminal units rather than expansion of an existing unit.

Mobile lounge or transporter The mobile lounge or transporter concept is in use at a number of airports including Dulles International and Tampa International airports. It is sometimes called the *remote aircraft parking* concept. Aircraft parking aprons are remote from the terminal building. The mobile lounges transport passengers from the building to aircraft and can be used as hold rooms at terminal building gate positions. In this concept, the aircraft gate positions are placed in parallel rows at required spacings with mobile lounge and service vehicle roads running between the parallel rows of aircraft. Several sets of parallel aircraft parking rows can be provided for ultimate development of gate positions. Airline operations buildings must be provided adjacent to aircraft parking aprons.

With the mobile lounge concept, walking distances are held to a minimum because the compact terminal building contains common passenger processing facilities and curb frontage can be located directly across the terminal building from mobile lounge gates. Building and curb length, which is established in part by the number of mobile lounge gates, must be carefully planned to provide adequate frontage for enplaning and deplaning passengers.

The concept has good expansion capability in that capacity can be increased by the addition of mobile lounges and the main terminal and aprons can be expanded without the addition of extensive concourses, fingers, or satellites. With the mobile lounge concept, additions can be made with little impedance to airport operations and aircraft movements.

Aircraft maneuvering capability is excellent with this concept. Remote aircraft parking can reduce taxi time and distance to runways and avoid aircraft congestion next to terminal building facilities. This also removes the aircraft noise and jet blast problem from the building area. Mobile lounges must be capable of mating with various aircraft sill heights and terminal building floor heights.

In comparing the mobile lounge concept with other concepts, the cost of independent terminal and service buildings and the purchase, operation, and maintenance of mobile lounges must be considered. The time required to move passengers between terminal and aircraft by mobile lounge also has to be taken into consideration by the planner.

These concepts are embodied in pure form only at a few airports that have been built on entirely new sites, such as Dallas-Fort Worth (FIG. 6-3). At most

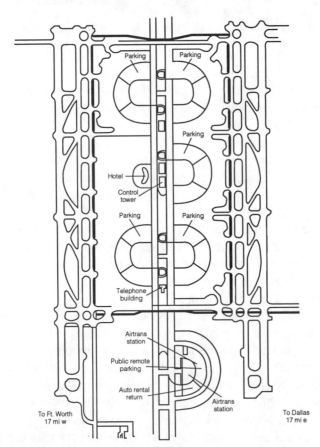

Fig. 6-3. Pure concept (curvilinear gate arrival).

airports the design of the terminal building has evolved and been modified in response to traffic growth and local conditions, giving rise to a hybrid that incorporates features of two or more of the basic concepts (FIGS. 6-4 and 6-5). At airports with land available adjacent to the existing facility, the design has tended to evolve into a pier finger arrangement, sometimes with separate unit terminals for commuter airlines or groups of new air carriers for whom there is not room in the main terminal. At airports where the terminal has grown to the limits of available land area, satellite terminals and remote parking have typically developed. Transporter and satellite terminal concepts utilizing people-moving equipment have been adopted at some airports to enhance the attractiveness of the terminal for passengers because they eliminate the extreme walking distances associated with long piers extending from central terminals.

Overestimation or underestimation of traffic volume or the type of service to be provided can sometimes render even a well-conceived design inefficient or inappropriate. Dallas-Fort Worth Airport, for example, was planned with the expectation that origin-destination traffic would predominate. Since airline deregulation, the growth of hub and spoke networks, which typically requires passen-

La Guardia Airport

Lower Level

Baggage claim area
Buses
Car rental
H/M res phones
Limousine svc
Lounges
Baggage SVC no flights
from LGA

Upper level

Approximate walking
distance from one end of
the terminal to the other is
1300 feet

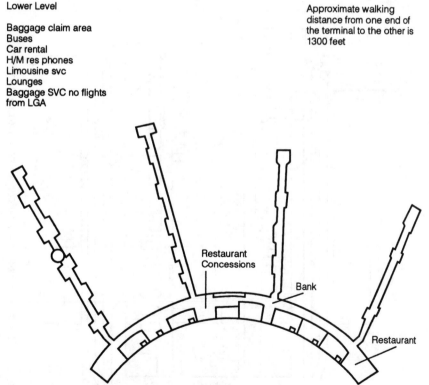

Restaurant
Concessions

Bank

Restaurant

Fig. 6-4. Hybrid concept (separate concourses with transporters).

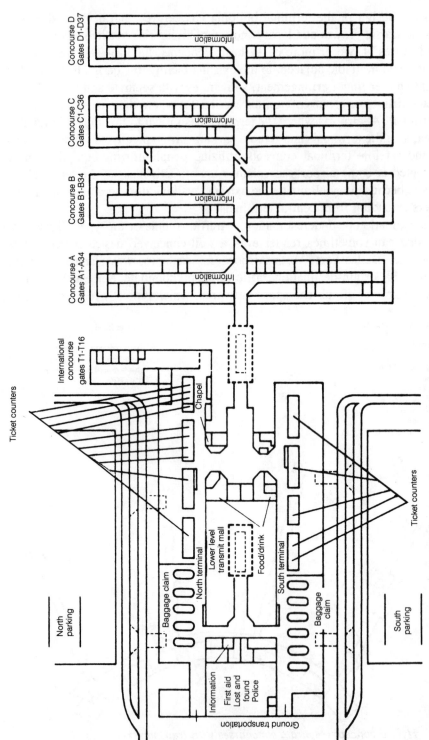

Fig. 6-5. Hybrid concept (separate concourses with transporters).

gers to change planes at the airport, has thwarted the effectiveness and convenience of the design. At Chicago O'Hare Airport, the need to adapt the concourses for passenger security screening has created long and circuitous routes for transferring passengers. Efforts to encourage greater use of Dulles Airport in Virginia for short and medium-length domestic flights have been hindered by the design of the terminal because the need to go from apron to terminal and back again by mobile lounges greatly increases the time and inconvenience of interline connection. New York Kennedy Airport, planned with separate terminals for major airlines, is well-suited for origin-destination passengers and for transfers to flights on the same airline, but very inconvenient for interlining domestic passengers and those coming in on international flights and continuing to other U.S. destinations.

Clearly, no single design is best for all circumstances. Traffic patterns, traffic volume, and flow characteristics (peaking), the policies of individual carriers using the airport, and local considerations (esthetics and civic pride) dictate different choices from airport to airport and from one time to another. The airport planner, who is required to anticipate conditions 10 to 15 years in the future, must often resort to guesswork. Even if the guess is correct initially, conditions change, and result in a mismatch between terminal architecture and the traffic to be served. To guard against this, airport planners now tend to favor flexible designs that can be expanded modularly or offer the opportunity for low-cost, simple modifications as future circumstances might demand.

The passenger-handling system

The *passenger-handing system* is a series of links and processes that a passenger goes through in transferring from one mode of transportation to another. These processes include: (1) access/egress, (2) access/processing interface, (3) processing, and (4) flight interface.

Access/egress   The access/egress link includes all of the ground transportation facilities, vehicles, and other modal transfer facilities required to move the passenger to and from the airport. Included are:

1. Highways.
2. Rail and metropolitan train service.
3. Autos, taxicabs, buses, and limousine service.
4. V/STOL facilities.
5. Transfer stations—off and on airport parking sites and rail stations.

Access/processing interface   The next link or process is the access/processing interface, in which the passenger makes the transition from the vehicular mode of transportation to pedestrian movement into the passenger processing activities.

Skyride, Miami International Airport.

Activities here include loading and unloading of passengers from vehicles at curb-side and pedestrian circulation from surface and parking facilities. Facilities include:

1. Vehicular circular drive for loading and unloading passengers.
2. Sidewalks, shuttle buses, and other automated conveyance systems to and from parking facilities.
3. Bus stops, taxi stands, and limousine stops.

Passenger processing   The passenger processing link accomplishes the major processing activities required to prepare the passenger for using air transportation. Primary activities include ticketing, baggage check-in, security, and passport check on the enplaning cycle, and baggage claim, passport check, and customs check on the deplaning cycle. Facilities include:

1. Ticketing and baggage check-in counters.
2. Counters for security, customs, health, and immigration.
3. Terminal waiting lobbies.
4. Baggage claim area.
5. Visitor departure and arrival waiting areas.
6. Space for passenger movement and circulation.

Loading bridges are part of the flight interface.

7. Visitor observation area and lounges.

8. Public service areas including restrooms, baggage lockers, firstaid facilities, lost and found, nursery, TV lounge, hotel reservation decks, post office, and place of worship.

9. Information booths and displays for flight schedules and other flight-related announcements, and for giving directions for movement within the terminal building.

10. Eating and drinking facilities including snack shops, coffee shops, bars, restaurants, private banquet rooms, kitchens, automatic food dispensers, and water fountains.

11. Concessions, including news/flowers/gifts/books/candy, beauty and barber shops, cleaning/valet, banks, car rental agencies, insurance, and duty-free shops, currency exchange services, tourist information/accommodation services (at international airports.)

Flight interface The flight interface provides the link between the passenger processing activities and the flight. Facilities include:

1. Gate lounges and counters.

2. Moving sidewalks, buses, and mobile lounges (transporters).

3. Loading facilities including jetways, nose bridges, stairs, and escalators.

4. Facilities for transferring between flights including corridors, waiting areas, and mobile conveyance facilities.

Facilities for airport operations and management

The terminal building normally houses the facilities for airport operations and management. These include:

1. Office space for airport administrative and operations personnel.
2. Storage facilities for maintenance supplies, materials, tools, and equipment.
3. Repair shops and offices.
4. Mechanical/utilities systems space such as air conditioning and heating, boilers and water supply, electrical service and equipment, elevator-escalator machinery rooms, emergency equipment (generators), and communications (telephones and radio).
5. Employee lounges, food and beverage facilities, and restrooms.
6. Fire, crash, and rescue facilities.

Facilities for airline operations

Space in the terminal building must be available for the following airline operations:

1. Operations offices adjacent to passenger handling counters.
2. Control/dispatch offices for such flight-related activities as flight planning and associated administrative duties.
3. Hospitality/VIP lounges.
4. Employee/aircrew lounges.
5. Telecommunications facilities.
6. Baggage-handling facilities, including conveyors, sorting equipment, and baggage carts.

Facilities for government agencies

While government agencies might not necessarily be housed in the terminal building, space for their functions must be provided near the passenger-handling system. These include the FAA, weather service, postal service, customs, immigration and naturalization, agriculture, health, and security services.

Passenger flow through the terminal

A terminal building is designed around the passengers' needs and wants. By locating passenger processing points conveniently and in a logical order, terminal designers aim to keep passengers moving through the system in a smooth flow with a minimum of delay; however, passenger traffic follows an irregular pattern, peaking at certain times of the day and year, so public areas must be large enough to accommodate peak crowds including friends and relatives.

Passengers can be divided into three primary groups: (1) domestic, (2) international, and (3) transfer.

Domestic passengers   The domestic long-haul or short-haul business traveler generally arrives at the terminal shortly before departure, frequently alone and with relatively little baggage. Business travelers prefer fast service. They are generally familiar with the airport and need to be processed quickly.

Leisure passengers generally arrive at the airport an hour or so before departure, bringing much more luggage than the average business traveler. They are generally unfamiliar with the airport layout, which means more time spent in the terminal. These passengers, plus their friends and relatives, frequent the concessions to a greater degree than do business travelers.

A domestic departure passenger would enter the general concourse (which is A in FIG. 6-6) and proceed to the ticket counter, where tickets are verified and baggage loads totalled. The passenger would then proceed to the security checkpoint (B) and onto the gate serving his flight. A domestic arrival would depart the aircraft, leave the gate area, go to the baggage claim area (C) to pick up luggage, and depart the airport terminal via the general concourse (A).

Hartsfield Atlanta International Airport

The underground transit mall at Hartsfield Atlanta International Airport links the terminal buildings with the four domestic concourses. It offers three modes of transportation for passengers and visitors: walk, step onto a moving sidewalk, or use the automated train system.

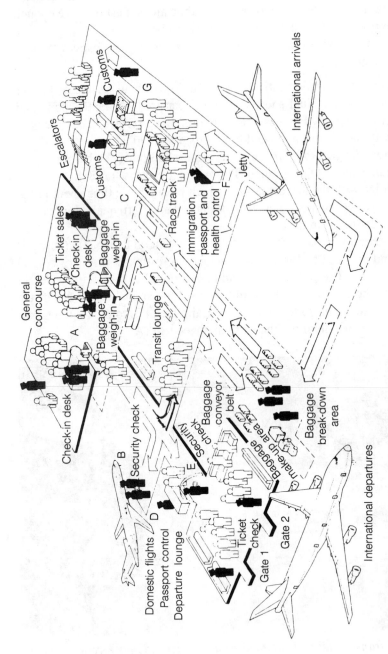

Fig. 6-6. Passenger flow through the terminal.

International passengers   International flights are similar to long-haul flights and possess many of the characteristics of leisure passengers. They tend to check in early because processing time for international flights is longer. Consequently, they tend to utilize the concessions and other facilities to a great degree.

An international departure follows a similar pattern to the domestic departure. The traveler proceeds from the general concourse (A), after ticket verification and baggage check-in to passport control (D), then through security (E) on to a specific concourse (area between the general concourse and gate area), and then gate area.

An international arrival leaves the aircraft and goes directly to immigration, passport, and health control (F). He then proceeds to the baggage claim area (C). The passenger then goes to the customs area (G) for an inspection of luggage and then on to the general concourse (A) to leave the terminal.

Transfer passengers   A transfer passenger is one who transfers from one flight to a connecting flight. The domestic transfer passenger simply proceeds from one specific concourse to the boarding gate of the next flight. The transfer passenger flow is somewhat complicated when domestic and international flights are mixed. When a domestic arrival passenger transfers to an international departure, he must go to the airline ticket counter for a passport verification before proceeding to the international gate.

An international arrival goes through immigration and baggage claim area after departing the aircraft. The traveler then proceeds through customs for an inspection check and on to the general concourse to purchase a ticket for the domestic departure. An international traveler transferring to another international flight generally goes directly to an international transit lounge. He then proceeds to the international departure gate for his flight.

Vertical distribution of passenger flow

Many of the larger airports distribute the passenger flow over several levels within the airport terminal. The primary purpose of distributing passenger processing activities over several levels is to separate the flow of arriving and departing passengers. The question of how many levels a terminal building should have depends primarily on the volume of passengers. It is also influenced by the type of passengers: domestic, international, and transfer.

Figure 6-7 shows a cross-section of the major functional areas in a multilevel passenger terminal. Departing passengers park their vehicles (1) and proceed via the bridge level (3) into the terminal or are dropped off at the vehicular circular drive (Enplane Drive-5). Ticketing lobby (6), concourse (11), and gate area (14) are all on the first level. Arriving passengers proceed from the gate area (14) through the concourse (11) to the baggage claim area (7). After claiming their baggage, they proceed to the parking facility (1) via the bridge level (3) or are

Tom Bradley International Terminal at Los Angeles International Airport.

International terminal lobby at San Francisco International Airport.

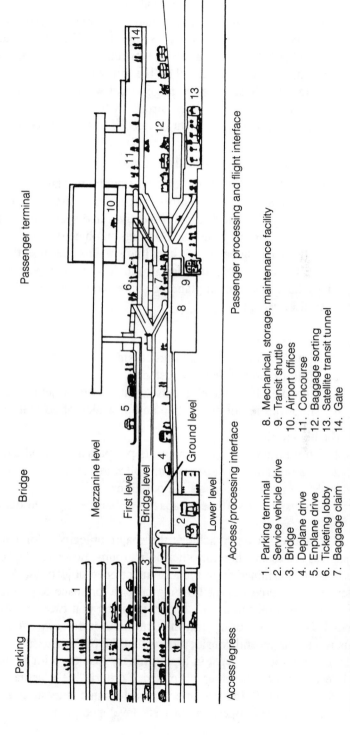

Fig. 6-7. *Vertical distribution of passenger flow through multilevel terminal.*

picked up at the ground level (Deplane Drive-4). Notice that the airport offices (10), mechanical, storage and maintenance facilities (8) and service vehicle drive (2) are located above or below the passenger flow. Transit shuttles (9) and satellite transit tunnel (13) leading to a satellite terminal (normally for long-haul domestic or international flights) is located on the lower level.

Variations in this basic design might occur when traffic volumes or type of traffic requires. For example, at large airports where intra-airport transportation systems operate, a special level might be needed to provide access to these systems.

Terminal building space requirements

The terminal building is a complex major public-use facility serving the needs of passengers, the air carriers, visitors, airport administration and operations, and concessionaires. Clearly, different objectives and space requirements are sought by each of these groups of users. Conflicts in objectives and space requirements often arise in planning passenger handling systems. Because the main users of the system are the passengers and the air carriers, it is important to recognize the objectives that are sought in planning space requirements from the viewpoints of these two user groups:

For the passengers
1. Minimization of delays in processing.
2. Minimization of walking distance.
3. Protection from the elements: weather, noise, jet blast, and so forth.
4. Simplification of orientation and provision of comfort and convenience.

For the air carriers
1. Minimization of operating costs per passenger handled.
2. Maximization of capacity per dollar invested.
3. Minimization of delays in operations.
4. Provision for sufficient capacity to handle expected demand.

The above list only includes the major objectives for two users. Planning objectives are established for other user groups; however, the space requirements are largely determined from the aforementioned objectives. A planner must consider these objectives in establishing criteria for space requirements.

It has been recognized in airport planning that two sets of space criteria are needed. One is a set of criteria that can be used for *general concept evaluation*. This is a set of general considerations that the planner uses to evaluate and select among alternative concepts in a preliminary fashion prior to any detailed design and development. The other set of space criteria is the actual *criteria for design and development*. In this set, specific performance measures are needed in order to evaluate the likely operation of well-developed plans.

Reynolds, Smith, and Hills

Adequate space to accommodate passengers is exemplified in this picture showing a portion of the terminal lobby at Jacksonville International Airport.

While general concept evaluation criteria can be developed on the basis of experience and observation of existing terminal buildings, the more specific design and development criteria require the use of a number of analytic techniques for their generation. These include network models, critical path method (CPM), queuing models, and simulation models. A complete discussion of these techniques can be found in *Planning and Design of Airports* by Robert Horonjeff.

Metro-Dade Aviation Department

A moving sidewalk at Miami International Airport.

The most important general concept evaluation criteria for space requirements are:

1. Ability of the facility to handle expected demand.
2. Compatibility with the expected aircraft fleet mix.
3. Flexibility for growth and response to advances in technology.
4. Compatibility with ground access systems.
5. Compatibility with the airport master plan.
6. Delay potential caused by the physical layout of the building.
7. Cost considerations.
8. Sociopolitical and environmental considerations.

The most important specific design and development criteria for space requirements are:

1. Processing costs per passenger.
2. Walking distances for various types of passengers.
3. Passenger delays in processing.

4. Occupancy levels for lounges and corridors.

5. Aircraft maneuvering delays and costs.

6. Construction costs.

7. Operating and maintenance expenses.

8. Estimated revenues from concessionaires.

Steps involved in determining space requirements Once the sets of criteria have been established, the next determination is the actual space requirements for the various users. The following is a general outline of the major steps involved in this process:

1. Number of passengers and types. The first step involves a forecast of the annual passenger volume. Next is a determination of the approximate hourly volume. Planners refer to this figure as the *typical peak-hour passenger volume* or *design volume*. The peak hour of an average day in the peak month is commonly used as the hourly design volume for terminal space. This figure is generally in the range of three to five percent of the annual volume.

   The type of passenger is broadly classified as domestic, international, or transfer. A further breakdown by type would include such items as: (a) arriving or departing, (b) with or without checked baggage, (c) mode of access to or egress from the airport—automobile, bus, limousine, train, or helicopter, (d) scheduled, charter, or general aviation flight, and (e) any other characteristics that might be relevant to the particular airport.

   The forecasted volume of passengers is then broken down by type including subcategories.

2. Passenger type by facility. A matrix is developed matching passenger types and volumes with the various facilities in the terminal. These would include such areas as the ticket lobby, restrooms, baggage claim area, waiting rooms, eating facilities, and so forth. Areas for servicing international passengers would include public health, immigration, customs, agriculture, and visitor waiting areas. By summing the volume of passengers in rows corresponding to the facilities, it is possible to approximate the total load on each facility.

3. Determining space requirements. The actual space requirements are determined by multiplying the estimated number of passengers using each facility with an empirical factor to arrive at the approximate area or capacity of the facility required. The empirical factor or constant is based upon experience acquired by planners and contemplates a reasonable level of service and occupancy. *See* TABLE 6-1.

Table 6-1. Terminal building space requirements (hypothetical).

Facility (example)	Space required in 1000 ft.^{2} per 100 typical peak-hour passengers (empirical factor)	Typical peak-hour passengers	Area required (sq. ft.)
Ticket lobby	1.5	400	6,000
Fast food facilities	.8	250	2,000
Customs	2.6	300	7,800
Baggage claim	1.4	275	3,850

Baggage handling.

Baggage handling services

Baggage handling services include a number of activities involving the collection, sorting, and distribution of baggage. An efficient flow of baggage through the terminal is an important element in the passenger handling system. Much of the passenger delay in the terminal can be attributed to the baggage flow (FIG. 6-8).

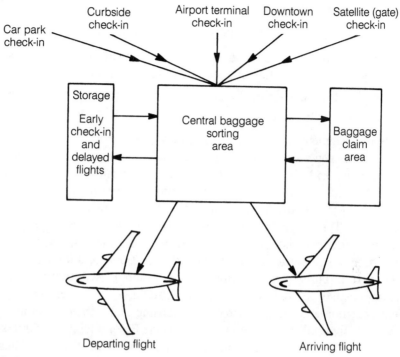

Fig. 6-8. Baggage flow.

Departing passengers normally check their baggage at one of a number of sites including curbside check-in and at the ticket counter in the terminal building. The bags are then sent to a central sorting area, where they are sorted according to flights and sent to the appropriate gate where they are loaded aboard the departing aircraft. Arriving baggage is unloaded from the aircraft and sent to the central sorting area. Sorted bags are sent to another flight (transfer passenger), to storage for later pickup, or to the baggage claim area.

Airport access plans

The *airport access plans* are an integral part of the master planning process. These plans indicate proposed routing of airport access to the central business district and to points of connection with existing or planned ground transportation arteries. All modes of access are considered including highways, rapid transit, and access by vertical and short takeoff and landing (V/STOL) aircraft. The estimated capacity requirement for the various modes considered is determined from forecasts of passengers, cargo, and aircraft operations. The airport access plans normally are general in nature because detailed plans of access outside the boundaries of the airport will be developed by highway departments, transit authorities, and comprehensive planning bodies.

Segments of airport access

Airport access is usually divided into two major segments:

1. Access from the central business district and surburban areas via highway and rapid transit systems to the airport boundary.

2. Access from the airport boundary via airport roads and rapid transit to parking areas and passenger unloading curbs at the terminal building.

The first segment is a part of the overall regional or urban transportation system and serves general and airport traffic. State and local highway departments and local transit authorities will bear the major responsibility for the administration, design, and construction of this segment. Airport sponsors are responsible for developing the requirements of airport traffic that must be served within the first segment. They are also responsible for promoting the development of facilities to serve that demand. Regional, state, and local planning bodies are relied upon to bring together the general needs of urban transportation and the specialized needs of airports by the development of comprehensive transportation plans for metropolitan or regional areas as a whole. At the federal level, the Department of Transportation and the Department of Housing and Urban Development provide national inputs through programs such as the Federal Highway Grants-in-Aid Program, and urban transportation planning funds. With this diversification of responsibility, careful coordination is required if the first segment of the airport access problem is to be effectively resolved.

The second segment of airport access, from the airport boundary to the parking area and terminal building unloading curbs, is primarily the responsibility of airport management. They plan and construct the second segment of access, although they are often assisted by the air carriers in this effort. Airport sponsors must take special care in planning on-airport access, although they are often assisted by the air carriers in this effort. Airport sponsors must take special care in planning on-airport access to ensure that it is compatible with off-airport ground transportation plans and with ultimate terminal area development.

The biggest problem concerning access stems from the fact that airport travel tends to peak in the same morning and afternoon periods as does general urban and suburban travel. The first segment of access traffic is made up of general urban travelers, and airport passengers, visitors, and employees. General urban travelers drop out after the first segment, leaving only the airport traffic in the access system. Because most visitors ride in the same vehicle with passengers during access, they do not add to the peaking problem except for congestion within the terminal building. Airport-based employees do add to the peaking problem because they ride in separate vehicles. Airport access facilities are designed on the basis of typical peak-hour traffic. At some of the busiest airports, congestion rises in the morning, remains almost constant throughout the day, and does not taper off until evening.

Rapid transit is an alternative to relieve access problems to some of the most congested airports. An example is in Cleveland, where an extension of the city subway line carries passengers from downtown to Cleveland Hopkins International Airport. In conjunction with the existing access highway system, it is a quick and practical airport access mode.

Vehicle parking

Parking facilities at or near the airport must be provided for: (1) airline passengers, (2) visitors accompanying passengers, (3) spectators, (4) people employed at the airport, (5) car rentals and limousines, and (6) people having business with the airport tenants.

A separate parking facility is normally provided for employees. At some of the major airports, an employee parking lot is often several miles from the terminal area. Employees are bused to the airport from the outlying facility. Buses run on a regular schedule around the clock.

The car-rental parking area is normally close to the terminal building in order to minimize the passenger walking distance. Normally this close-in facility will only accommodate cars that have been reserved. Other rental cars are often parked in a special area away from the terminal building and driven to the car-rental area upon request. Departing passengers normally deposit rental cars in the special area and are bused to the terminal area. This is a common arrangement at many large airports.

Public parking facilities are provided for airline passengers, visitors, and spectators. The major goal here is to locate this area as close as possible to the terminal building in order to minimize walking distance.

Most of the major airports have separate parking facilities for short-term and long-term parkers. Surveys at a number of major airports indicate that a large number (75 percent or more) park three hours or less and a much smaller group parks from 12 hours to several days or longer; however, short-term parkers typically only represent about 20 percent of the total maximum vehicle accumulation. Consequently, many airports designate the most convenient (closest area) spaces to short-term parkers, who represent the highest number of users.

At some very busy airports, long-term parking is provided off the airport property at reduced rates by private concessionaires who provide shuttle transportation to the airport for their customers.

Key terms

terminal area
centralized passenger processing
decentralized passenger processing
gate arrival

simple terminal
linear or curvilinear terminal
pier finger
satellite terminals
mobile lounge or transporter
passenger handling system
access/egress
access/processing interface
passenger processing
flight interface
general concept evaluation
criteria for design and development
typical peak-hour passenger volume (design volume)
airport access plans

Review questions

1. What is included in the "terminal area?"
   Discuss the primary objective of the terminal area plans.
   Describe the factors taken into consideration by airport planners in selecting
     the terminal area concept.

2. What are the advantages and disadvantages of the centralized and
     decentralized passenger processing system?
   Describe the four (4) basic terminal building design concepts including their
     advantages and disadvantages. How can some of the best plans be thwarted
     by the realities of present airport-airway systems?

3. Describe the four (4) components of the passenger handling system. What
     facilities are required for the following: airport operations and
     management, airline operations, and government agencies.
   Why is the terminal building primarily designed around passenger needs and
     wants? Describe the passenger flow (arriving and departing) through the
     terminal building for the following passengers: domestic, international,
     and transfer.
   What is the primary purpose of the vertical distribution of passenger flow?

4. List the primary objectives in planning space requirements for the
     passengers and the air carriers.
   Define *general concept evaluation* and *criteria for design and development*.
   Discuss the steps involved in determining space requirements.
   Describe the baggage flow through the terminal building for arriving and
     departing passengers.

5. Why must airport management and planners work very closely with other governmental bodies in developing airport access plans?
   What are the two segments of airport access? What is the biggest problem concerning access roads? Describe the parking facilities required at a major airport.

Suggested readings

Airport Access—A Planning Guide. DOT/Federal Highway Administration, Transmittal 113, Vol. 20, Appendix 55. GPO. Washington, DC, October, 1971.

Airport Ground Access. Report of the Secretary of Transportation to the United States Senate Committee on Appropriations pursuant to Senate Report No. 95-268. GPO. Washington, DC, May, 1975.

Airport Land Banking. DOT/FAA/Office of Aviation System Plans, FAA Report # ASP-77-7. GPO. Washington, DC, August, 1977.

Airport Master Plans. DOT/FAA Airports Service, Advisory Circular 150/5070-6, GPO. Washington, DC, February, 1971.

Airport Terminal Building Development with Federal Participation. DOT/FAA/Office of Airports Programs, Advisory Circular 150/5360-6. GPO. Washington, DC, October, 1976.

Planning and Design Considerations for Airport Terminal Building Development. DOT/FAA/Office of Airports Programs, Advisory Circular 150/5360-7. GPO. Washington, DC, April, 1988.

Planning the Airport Industrial Park. DOT/FAA/Office of Airports Programs, Advisory Circular 150/5070-3. GPO. Washington, DC, February, 1975.

Land Acquisition & Relocation Assistance under ADAP. DOT/FAA Advisory Circular 150/5100-11. GPO. Washington, DC, February, 1975.

Financial planning

Outline

Financial plan
Airports in the municipal bond market

Objectives

When you have completed this chapter, you should be able to:

△ Describe the purpose of the financial plan.

△ Define "break-even need" and how it relates to the economic evaluation of the fourth phase of the master plan.

△ Distinguish between nondepreciable and depreciable investment.

△ List and briefly describe five potential airport revenue sources.

△ Distinguish between general obligation bonds, self-liquidating general obligation bonds, and revenue bonds as alternate financing methods.

△ Summarize the market for airport bonds in recent years.

△ Describe the competitiveness of airport bonds from the standpoint of bond ratings, interest costs, and defaults.

Financial plan

The fourth and final phase of the airport master plan includes the financial plan. The *financial plan* is an economic evaluation of the entire plan of development. It looks at the activity forecasts of the first phase from the point of view of revenues and expenditures, analyzing the airport's balance sheet over the planning period to ensure that the airport sponsor can afford to proceed. A corollary activity in this phase is the consideration of funding sources and financing methods for the proposed development. Questions to be addressed include which portions will be funded through federal grants-in-aid, the size and timing of bond issues, the revenue from concessionaire rents, parking fees, landing fees, and so on.

Economic evaluation

Although the primary objective of the airport master plan is to develop a design concept for the entire airport, it is essential to test the economic feasibility of the plan from the standpoints of airport operation and individual facilities and services. Economic feasibility will depend on whether the users of the airport improvements programmed under the plan can produce the revenues (as might be supplemented by federal, state, or local subsidies) required to cover annual cost for administration, operation, and maintenance. This must be determined for each stage of development scheduled in the master plan. This consideration includes the cost of capital to be employed in financing the improvement, the annual operating costs of facilities, and prospective annual revenues.

The schedule of improvements proposed in the master plan, as well as the cost estimates are developed by stages (TABLE 7-1).

This preliminary cost estimate for each of the proposed improvements provides the basic capital investment information needed for evaluating the feasibility of the various facilities. Estimated construction costs are adjusted to include allowance for architect and engineering fees for preparation of detailed plans and

Table 7-1. Preliminary master plan cost estimates by stage (in thousands of dollars—hypothetical).

Description of improvement	First	Second	Third	Total
Airfield: (includes lights)				
Runway	$400	$90	$1,200	$ 1,690
Taxiways	800	400	1,000	2,200
Aprons	200	150	900	1,250
Roads:				
Terminal and service	150	100	800	1,050
Parking lot	50	-	150	200
Buildings:				
Expansion of existing				
terminal	1,130	400	-	1,530
New terminal	-	-	8,500	8,500
Fire/crash	-	-	200	200
Airport maintenance	-	-	150	150
Relocation:				
Fixed base operator	200	-	-	200
National Guard	40	100	-	140
Airport maintenance	35	-	-	35
Miscellaneous:				
Electrical	140	25	90	255
Utilities	40	-	200	240
Drainage	30	20	225	275
Landscaping	-	-	175	175
Fencing	10	-	50	60
Site preparation	300	150	800	1,250
Total estimated construction	$3,525	$1,435	$14,440	$19,400
Legal, administrative,				
engineering	800	250	2,800	3,850
Total project	$4,325	$1,685	$17,240	$23,250
Land acquisition	2,800	-	-	2,800
Total estimated cost	$7,125	$1,685	$17,240	$26,050

specifications, overhead for construction administration, allowance for contingencies, and allowance for interest expenses during construction. Estimated costs of land acquisitions as well as the costs of easements required to protect approach and departure areas are included. If the master plan provides for the expansion of an existing airport, the cost of the existing capital investment might be required to be added to the new capital costs.

The airport layout plan also indicates the stage development of the proposed facilities. The drawings are normally legended to indicate staging shown on the plan, either on single or separate sheets. Charts that show the schedule of development for various items of the master plan are developed for inclusion in the master plan report.

Break-even need The annual amount that is required to cover cost of capital investment and costs of administration, operation, and maintenance can be called the break-even need. The revenues required to produce the break-even need are derived from user charges, lease rentals, and concession revenues produced by the airport as a whole. In order to make sure that the individual components of the airport are generating a proper share of the required annual revenues, the airport can be divided into cost areas to allow allocation of costs to such areas following generally accepted cost accounting principles.

Carrying charges on invested capital include depreciable and nondepreciable items.

Nondepreciable investment Nondepreciable investment items are those that have a permanent value even if the airport site is converted to other uses. Nondepreciable investment items include the cost of land acquisition, excavation and fill operations, and road relocations that enhance the value of the airport site. The annual cost of capital invested in nondepreciable assets depends in the first instance on the source of capital used. If revenue or general obligation bonds have been issued to acquire the asset, the total of the principal and interest payments and required reserves or coverage payments called for by the bonds is used. Assets acquired with airport operating surpluses of prior years, general tax revenues, or gifts do not ordinarily impose a cash operating requirement and the treatment of these investments will require a decision by the operator based upon legal considerations and financial operating objectives of the airport. Interest or depreciation charges are not required to be recovered on amounts secured by the airport under the Airport and Airway Improvement Act of 1982 or previous acts. Treatment of funds acquired under state grants-in-aid programs are governed by the terms of the act involved.

Depreciable investment The annual cost of capital invested in plant and equipment (as distinguished from land) can be regarded as depreciable investment. The annual charge for depreciation depends on the useful life of the asset and the source of capital used in acquiring the asset. If payments of principal and interest on bonds issued to pay for the asset are required over a shorter period than the useful life of the asset, this schedule would govern and form the basis for depreciation charges unless other revenues are available to service the debt. Depreciation charges for capital assets acquired with operating surpluses of prior years, general tax revenues, or gifts do not ordinarily impose a cash operating requirement on the operator and the treatment of this investment will require a policy decision by the operator. Interest or depreciation charges are not required to be recovered on amounts secured under the Airport and Airway Improvement Act of 1982 or previous acts. Funds obtained under state grants-in-aid are governed by the terms of the act involved.

Expenses for administration, operation, and maintenance   Estimated expenses for administration, operation, and maintenance are developed for each airport cost area based on unit costs for direct expenses. For nonrevenue areas, these expenses are forecasted separately and distributed to various airport operations. For utility expenses, the net amount expected to be owed from utility purchase, after sale of utility services, is forecast.

Potential airport revenue   The sum of the estimated annual carrying charges on invested capital and the estimated average annual expenses of administration, operation, and maintenance establishes the break-even need for each revenue-producing facility and for the airport as a whole. The next step in establishing economic feasibility is to determine if sufficient revenues (that might be supplemented by federal, state, and local subsidies) can be expected at the airport to cover the break-even needs; therefore, forecasts are prepared for revenue-producing areas. These areas include:

1. Landing area. This area includes runways and related taxiways and circulation taxiways. Flight fee revenue determination is distributed between scheduled airlines, other air carrier users, and general aviation. Flight fee amounts should provide sufficient revenues to cover the landing area break-even need.

2. Aircraft aprons and parking areas. Revenues to obtain the break-even need for airline terminal aprons and cargo aprons are assigned to the scheduled airlines. Those for general aviation ramps are assigned to private aircraft. Apron and parking area fees should provide sufficient revenues to cover the break-even needs for specific aircraft aprons and parking areas.

3. Airline terminal buildings. Revenues for concessionaires and ground transportation services are usually based on a percentage of gross

income with a fixed-rate minimum for each type of service. Space for scheduled airlines and other users is paid for on a fixed-rental basis. In order to establish rental rates, forecasts of potential revenue from concessions and ground transportation must be established. Rental rates are based on the break-even need of the terminal building after giving credit for forecasted revenues from concessions and ground transportation.

4. Public parking areas. Public parking is usually operated on a concessionaire basis with revenues obtained from rentals based on a percentage of gross income with a fixed-rate minimum. The revenue amount required to meet break-even needs will depend on whether parking facilities are constructed by the airport owner or under provisions of the concessionaire contract. These revenues apply to public parking for both airline and general aviation terminals. Revenues in excess of the break-even need for public parking is allocated to the break-even need for the airport as a whole.

5. Cargo buildings. Rentals are usually charged on a rate per square foot and cover investments in employee parking, truck unloading docks, as well as building space. Rates are established to meet break-even needs.

6. Aviation fuel. Fees charged to aviation fuel handling concessionaires are established to cover the costs of fuel storage areas and associated pumping, piping, and hydrant systems.

7. Hangars. Rentals are usually based on a rate per square foot and cover investments in associated aircraft apron space and hangar-related employee parking. Hangar office space is charged on a similar basis and covers office-related employee parking.

8. Commercial facilities. Airport office buildings, industrial facilities, and hotels are usually operated on a lessee-management basis with revenues obtained from rentals on a square foot basis. The facilities are often financed by private capital. Revenues in excess of the break-even need are allocated to the break-even need of the airport as a whole.

9. Other usable areas. Various uses of ground space for activities such as gasoline stations, service facilities for rental car operators, and bus and limousine operators usually obtain revenues on a flat rate basis. Those facilities are often financed by private capital. Revenues in excess of the break-even need are allocated to the break-even need of the airport as a whole.

Final economic evaluation   After analysis of the break-even needs for individual components of the master plan has been made, economic feasibility is analyzed on an overall basis. The goal of overall analysis is to determine if revenues will equal or exceed the break-even need. This determination requires an evaluation of the scope and phasing of the plan itself in terms of the users requirements and their ability to make the financial commitment necessary to support the costs of the program. If this review indicates that revenues will be sufficient, revisions in the scheduling or scope of proposed master plan developments might have to be made, or recovery revenue rates for airport cost areas might require adjustment. These factors are adjusted until the feasibility of the master plan is established; this is to say, airport revenues, (as might be supplemented by federal, state, or local subsidies) will match capital investment throughout the master plan forecast period. When the economic feasibility of improvements proposed in the master plan has been established, capital budget and a program for financing those improvements is developed.

Financing methods

The establishment of the airport master plan's economic feasibility (the balance between annual cost of capital investment and airport revenues) is vital to the financing for the improvements proposed in the plan. The implementation of the airport master plan will depend largely on the proper financing of those capital improvements. The primary responsibility for financing the development plans rests with local operating agencies or authorities. Public financing of airport development can be accomplished many ways. Financing might be raised from taxes, general obligation bonds, revenue bonds, private financing, government assistance, or a combination thereof.

General obligation bonds   General obligation bonds are issued only by states, municipalities, and other general-purpose governments. The payments (interest and principal) to bondholders are secured by the full faith, credit, and taxing power of the issuing government agency. An advantage of general obligation bonds is that due to the community guarantee they typically can be issued at a lower interest rate than can other types of bonds; however, most states limit the amount of general obligation debt that a municipality may issue to a specified fraction of the taxable value of all property within its jurisdiction. In addition, many states require voter approval before using general obligation debt.

Fiscal pressures on local governments for all manner of activities have been especially great in recent years. The need for school construction and other essential public works has required a considerable volume of general obligation bond financing. In numerous cases, local governments have reach statutory bond limits or desire to reserve whatever margin is left for more general functions of government. It is becoming increasingly difficult to obtain taxpayer approval for general obligation bond issues for airports.

Self-liquidating general obligation bonds   Self-liquidating general obligation bonds are also secured by the full faith, credit, and taxing power of the issuing government body; however, there is adequate cash flow from the operation of the facility to cover the debt service and other costs of operation of the facility. In other words, they are self-liquidating (self-sustaining). The debt is not legally considered as part of the community's debt limitation; however, because the credit of the local government bears the ultimate risk of default, the bond issue is still considered, for purposes of financial risk analysis, as part of the debt burden of the community; therefore, this method of financing generally means a higher rate of interest on all bonds sold by the community. The amount of interest rate generally depends in part upon the degree of "exposure risk" of the bond. Exposure risk occurs when there is insufficient net operating income to cover the level of debt service plus coverage requirements, thus forcing the community to absorb the residual.

Revenue bonds   The debt service on revenue bonds is payable solely from the revenue derived from the operation of a facility that was constructed or acquired with the proceeds of the bonds. Revenue bond financing for airport improvements has become the most common financing method. Financing with revenue bonds presents an opportunity to provide those improvements without direct burden to the taxpayer.

Private financing   Specific facilities on the airport such as hangars, fuel distribution systems, and hotels are often built with private financing. Such facilities can be constructed with private capital on land leased from the airport. The obvious advantage of such an arrangement is that it relieves the community of all responsibility for raising the capital funds for the particular improvements involved. Tenant improvements within the terminal building are also typically financed by the tenant through its own funding sources.

Federal and state grants for airport construction   Federal and state assistance for development projects recommended in airport master plans is available through grants-in-aid covered by the Airport and Airway Improvement Act of 1982 and various state programs.

The development of a financial plan is the final step in the airport master plan process. Thereafter, the overall master plan must be accepted by the airport sponsor and by the public. Once the plan has been adopted and the financing has been obtained, the final design and construction of improvements proposed in the master plan can be implemented.

With a determination of the projects to be constructed and their timing, a capital budget is prepared to show on an annual basis the requirement for capital funds and the source of funds. This analysis also permits an accurate estimation of the amount of interest to be earned on capital funds held from the sale of bonds prior to the need to commit such funds for construction purposes.

Airports in the municipal bond market

After World War II, larger airports began switching from general obligation bonds to revenue bonds as a method for financing new construction and improvements to existing fields. The first airport revenue bond in the United States was a $2.5 million issue sold in 1945 by Dade County, Florida, to buy what is now Miami International Airport from Pan American World Airways.

In the 1950s, the city of Chicago and the airlines that serve it worked out what has become the basic pattern for revenue bonds underwritten by airlines in the agreement that set up the financing for O'Hare International Airport. The airlines pledged that if airport income fell short of the total needed to pay off the principal and interest on the bonds, they would make up the difference by paying a higher landing fee rate. The historic *O'Hare agreement* demonstrated that airports, backed up by the airlines that use them, could raise the money they need in the financial market without depending on general tax funds, and airport revenue bonding became the accepted way to raise money for construction and expansion.

The revenue bonds are usually issued for 25 or 30 year terms, in contrast with the customary 10 or 15 year terms for general obligation bonds. Interest rates run slightly higher on revenue bonds than on general obligation bonds.

A bond issue can be sold competitively, with the airport accepting bids and selling the issue to the bond house that offers to buy it for the lowest interest rate, or the interest rate can be negotiated between the seller and a single buyer. Often airport sponsors use the services of a bond counsel, who advises on the best way to market a particular bond issued. After a bond house buys a bond issue, it resells the bonds to commercial banks, insurance companies, pension funds, and other large investors.

The market for airport bonds

Perhaps the toughest test of an airport's financial strength is its success in competing with other municipal enterprises for private investment capital in the bond market. While the financially stronger airports are the ones most active in the bond market, even financially weaker airports can attract private capital, though often they must use the taxing power of the local government as security for bond financing.

Airports raise millions of dollars annually in the bond market. Most municipal bonds are exempt from federal income tax, a key feature that makes this financing less expensive than most other sources of private money. Predictably, the vast majority of airport debt capital is raised in the tax-exempt bond market.

The role of bond financing in overall investment varies greatly according to an airport's size and type of air traffic served. During the 1980s, investment dollars raised through the bond market for large commercial airports were three times greater than the federal grants awarded these airports. In contrast, small airport federal grants were more than double bond proceeds. Not surprisingly, debt financing plays the smallest role at GA airports, where it has accounted for approximately 10 percent of total federal state and private investment over the past seven years.

In terms of total dollar volume of bond sales, large and medium airports are by far the most prominent in the bond market. Of the total amount of municipal debt sold for airport purposes during the 1980s, 90 percent was for large and medium airports, in contrast to only nine percent for small commercial airports. GA airports accounted for a little more than one percent of total airport bond sales.

Bond ratings, interest cost, and defaults

The competitiveness of airports in the municipal bond market can be gauged by three conventional indicators of investment quality: (1) bond ratings, (2) interest costs, and (3) defaults.

Bond ratings   Bond ratings is a system used by major investor services (such as Moody's and Standard & Poor's) to grade bonds according to investment quality. The top ranked bonds are as follows:

1. Best grade. Bonds rated Aaa (by Moody's) or AAA (by Standard & Poor's) are graded best. Their exceptionally strong capacity to pay interest and repay principal offers the lowest degree of risk to investors in bonds.

2. High grade. Bonds rated Aa1 or Aa (by Moody's) or AA+ or AA (by Standard & Poor's) have very strong ability to pay interest and repay principal, but they are judged to be slightly less secure than best-grade bonds. Their margins of protection might not be quite so great, or the protective elements might be more subject to fluctuation.

3. Upper-medium grade. Bonds rated A1 or A (by Moody's) or A+, A, or A− (by Standard & Poor's) are well protected, but the factors giving security to interest and principal are deemed more susceptible to adverse changes in economic conditions or other future impairments than for bonds in the best and high-grade categories.

4. Medium grade. Bonds rated Baa1 or Baa (by Moody's) or BBB+, BBB, or BBB− (by Standard & Poor's) lack outstanding investment characteristics. Although their protection is deemed adequate at the time of rating, the presence of speculative elements might impair their capacity to pay interest and repay principal in the event of adverse economic conditions or other changes.

Although investors have considerable confidence in airport bonds, ratings vary between the top and medium grades. A medium grade means that rating firms see the investment as carrying a measure of speculative risk. General obligation bonds generally draw the best ratings. Under this form of security, ratings are determined by the economic vigor of the municipality or the entire state, and airports have little or no influence on the rating. Revenue bonds, on the other hand, draw ratings according to the fiscal vitality of the airport itself. Because more than 90 percent of all airport bonds (in terms of dollar volume) are secured with airport revenues, the criteria used by investor services to rate such bonds are central to the marketability of such bonds.

Credit analysts at the major investor services rate an airport revenue bond according to a variety of factors, including the financial performance of the airport, the strength of passenger demand, and use agreements with the airlines serving the airport. Financial strength is viewed as a direct function of passenger demand at the airport, and credit analysts review both financial indicators and underlying patterns of passenger traffic.

Airline deregulation, which has freed air carriers from virtually all obligation to serve particular airports, has caused some shift in the relative weight credit analysts give to these different factors. In response to deregulation, the investor services today place greater emphasis on local economic strength than on airport use agreements and the financial stability of the airlines serving an airport. The rationale is that if one airline withdraws service, a strong local economy would attract other airlines to pick up the travel business.

In view of the methods adopted by the investor services, it is not surprising that large airports—with their comparatively stronger financial showings—tend to draw the best revenue bond ratings. During the 1980s, credit analysts were far more likely to assign medium-grade revenue bond ratings to issues for medium and small airports than for large airports. In fact, over that period not a single large airport issuing debt was rated below the upper-medium category.

Since deregulation, bond rating organizations have emphasized that passengers are an airport's true customers and that sufficient passenger demand will provide financial incentives for some airline to offer service over the long term. In particular, for origin-destination airports (those at which most passengers either begin or end their journeys) in strong travel markets, the financial failure of one carrier might have no influence on the airport bond rating. For example, when Dallas-Fort Worth Airport sold $157 million of revenue bonds in November 1982, it retained its A rating from both Moody's and Standard & Poor's despite the collapse of Braniff Airways earlier that year. Braniff had held a significant share of the Dallas-Fort Worth market and, under a residual-cost use agreement, had agreed to pay a substantial portion of the total airline share of airport costs. Moody's municipal credit report on the issue cited the bond's security provisions, the adequacy and diversity of pledged revenues, and the airport's role as one of the major facilities serving a strong southwestern economy. The report concluded that this "combination of the sufficient revenues for all requirements and increases in scheduled commercial airline service offset the potentially adverse effects following cessation of operations this past spring of the former dominant airline serving the area."

For hub airports serving large numbers of connecting flights, the poor financial outlook for a major airline could mean a permanent loss of patronage, with important implications for bond ratings. In May 1983, for example, Moody's revised the rating of Atlanta Hartsfield on approximately $86 million "third-lien" revenue bonds downward from A to Baa1, citing as the primary reasons Eastern Airline's financial problems (reflected in a net loss of $113.8 million in fiscal year 1982), a trend of declining traffic, and reduced debt service coverage.

Interest costs   Interest costs represent the payments by airports to attract investors relative to what other municipal enterprises pay. The difference between interest costs paid by airports and by other public enterprises indicates that airports generally hold a strongly competitive position in the municipal bond market.

Like municipal bonds in general, airport bonds are sold and traded at prices that reflect both general economic conditions and the credit quality of the airport or (in the case of general obligation bonds) the creditworthiness of the issuing government. Rated revenue bonds are offered for sale in one of two ways. Under competitive bidding, the airport selects the lowest bid and thus obtains funds at the lowest cost of borrowing. Under a negotiated sale, the bond purchaser consents at the outset to purchase the bond issue at an agreed price. In either case, the entire bond issue is usually purchased by an underwriter (commonly, an investment brokerage company), or an underwriter team, who in turn markets the bond to institutional and individual investors.

In deciding the price of a particular bond issue, underwriters identify a "ballpark" interest rate on the basis of general market conditions and then refine this estimate according to the credit standing of the airport in question. General market conditions represent by far the most important determinant of interest costs on airport revenue bonds, and in this respect airports have little control over the cost of capital.

Within the range of interest costs dictated by market conditions, underwriters refine their bids on airport revenue bonds on the basis of the credit standing of the individual airport. Two factors have greatest importance here: the airport's basic fiscal condition (including its prospects for traffic growth and the strength of the local economic base), and the presence of special pressures on the airport to expand capacity, thereby necessitating extensive capital development. On average, larger airports pay lower interest costs than smaller airports, allowing for differences in types of security and average maturities of issues.

Defaults   Defaults refers to the frequency with which a given type of enterprise has defaulted on a bond issue.

This history of an enterprise, or of an entire industry, with regard to the number of defaults is an important index of investment value. By this measure, the record of airports is particularly strong. The airport industry has never suffered a single default, a fact noted by several credit analysts in citing the premium quality of airports as credit risks.

A paper presented by analyst R.H. Bates, "Airport Financing: Whither (or Wither) the Market?" at the 1982 Airport Operators' Council International Economic Specialty Conference put the bond picture in focus:

> Airport revenue bonds have a remarkable track record. In spite of recessions, inflation, oil embargoes, fare wars, deregulation, astronomical increases in the price of aviation fuel, increasingly difficult community-airport relationships, costly noise mitigation programs, slot restrictions, a controllers' strike, curfews, threats about antitrust exposure, and the like, the nation's airports have shown that they can meet the challenges, cope with change, and consistently make payments on their outstanding debt. The industry has survived without a single default. The investment community has had its "seasoning" with airport revenue bonds. As a result of the positive experience, there is a great deal of "comfort" in airports as credit risks today.

Key terms
financial plan
break-even need
nondepreciable investment items
depreciable investment
general obligation bonds
self-liquidating general obligation bonds
revenue bonds
O'Hare Agreement
bond ratings
defaults

Review questions
1. What is included in the fourth phase of the airport master plan? Why are preliminary cost estimates needed for each stage of the master plan? What is the "break-even need?"

2. Distinguish between nondepreciable investment items and depreciable investment.
   Forecasted potential revenue-producing sources are required in determining the break-even need. List and briefly describe five of these areas.

3. Compare general obligation bonds and self-liquidating general obligation bonds. Why have revenue bonds become so popular in recent years?
   What type of facilities are financed privately?
   When did the first airport revenue bonds appear?
   What is the "O'Hare Agreement?"

4. Why do larger airports rely on the bond market more than smaller airports?
   What are bond ratings? Why do general obligation bonds generally draw the best ratings? How has airline deregulation affected bond ratings?
   What is the most important determinant of interest costs? What are defaults?
   Has the airport industry ever suffered a default on its bonds?

Suggested readings

Bates, R. Airport Financing: "Whither (or Wither?) the Market?" A paper presented at the Airport Operators Council International Economic Specialty Conference, Sacramento, CA, March 31, 1982.

Bollinger, Lynn L., Alan Passen and Robert E. McElfresh. *Terminal Airport Financing and Management*. Boston: Harvard University Press, 1970.

Moody's Bond Record, September 1982.

Standard & Poor's Ratings Guide. New York: McGraw-Hill, 1979.

Weston, J.F. and E.F. Brigham. *Managerial Finance*, 5th ed. New York: Dryden Press, 1975.

Part 3
Managing growth

Airport capacity
and delay

Outline

Introduction
Capacity, demand, and delay
Factors affecting capacity and delay
Measuring delay
Approaches to reducing delay

Objectives

When you have completed this chapter, you should be able to:

△ Understand the relationship between capacity, demand, and delay.

△ Describe the factors affecting capacity and delay.

△ Discuss the methods of measuring delay.

△ Compare the "administrative management" and "demand management" approaches to reducing delay.

△ Summarize five administrative management approaches to controlling demand.

△ Describe how demand management relies on the price mechanism in determining airport access.

△ Discuss some of the factors affecting the use of demand management alternatives.

Introduction

A major concern of airport planners, users, and operators is *delay*. Flights cannot be started or completed on schedule because of the line of aircraft awaiting their turn for takeoff, landing, or use of taxiways and gates at terminal buildings. These delays translate into increased operating costs for airport users and wasted time for passengers. The cause for delay is commonly referred to as a *lack of capacity*, meaning that the airport does not have facilities such as runways, taxiways, or gates in sufficient number to accommodate all those who want to use the airport at peak periods of demand.

The solutions generally advocated by airport operators, airlines, and the FAA are to build additional facilities at crowded airports or to find ways to make more efficient use of existing facilities. The latter course is viewed as attractive because it requires less capital investment and avoids many of the problems associated with increasing the size of the airport and infringing on the surrounding communities. A third course advocated by some is not to increase capacity but to manage

Aircraft lined up awaiting takeoff clearance from Washington National Airport.

demand by channeling it to off-peak times or to alternate sites. The rationale underlying all these approaches is that capacity and demand must somehow be brought into equilibrium in order to prevent or reduce delay.

The relationship of capacity, demand, and delay is considerably more complex than the foregoing suggestions. Before addressing solutions, it is necessary to look more closely at matters of definition and to examine how and where delays occur. It is also necessary to look at specific airports where delays are now being encountered to obtain a clearer picture of the severity of the problem and the points at which it could be attacked.

Capacity, demand, and delay

Capacity generally refers to the ability of an airport to handle a given volume of traffic (demand). It is a limit that cannot be exceeded without incurring an operational penalty. As demand for the use of an airport approaches this limit, lines of users awaiting service begin to develop, and they experience delay. Generally speaking, the higher the demand in relation to capacity, the longer the lines and the greater the delay.

Figure 8-1 shows that delay is not a phenomenon occurring only at the limit of capacity. Some account of delay will be experienced long before capacity is reached, and it grows exponentially as demand increases. The term *congestion*, referring to the condition where demand approaches or exceeds capacity, is not commonly defined in the technical literature and is used in this chapter only as a descriptor of a situation where demand is high in relation to capacity.

Capacity

There are two commonly used definitions of airfield capacity: "throughput" and "practical capacity." The *throughput* definition of capacity is the rate at which aircraft can be brought into or out of the airfield, without regard to any delay they

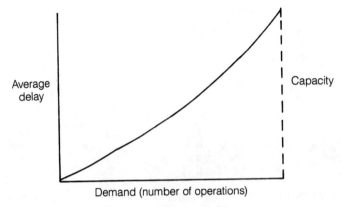

Fig. 8-1. Theoretical relationship of capacity and delay.

might experience (handled). This definition assumes that aircraft will always be present waiting to take off or land, and capacity is measured in terms of the number of such operations that can be accomplished in a given period of time. *Practical capacity* is the number of operations (takeoffs and landings) that can be accommodated with no more than a given amount of delay, usually expressed in terms of maximum acceptable average delay. Practical hourly capacity (PHOCAP) and practical annual capacity (PANCAP) are two commonly used measures based on this definition. PANCAP, for example, is defined as that level of operations that results in not more than four minutes average delay per aircraft in the normal peak two-hour operating period.

Delay

Delays occur on the airfield, whenever two or more aircraft seek to use a runway, taxiway, gate, or any other airside facility at the same time. One must wait while the other is accommodated. If all users of the airfield sought service at evenly spaced intervals, the airfield could accommodate them at a rate determined solely by the time required to move them through the facility.

Aircraft arrive and leave not at a uniform rate but somewhat randomly, which means that delay can occur even when demand is low in relation to capacity. Further, the probability of simultaneous need for service increases rapidly with traffic density, so that the average delay per aircraft increases exponentially as demand approaches throughput capacity. When demand exceeds capacity, there is an accumulation of aircraft awaiting service that is directly proportional to the excess of demand over capacity. For example, if the throughput capacity of an airfield is 60 operations per hour and the demand rate is running at 70 operations per hour, each hour will add 10 aircraft to the line awaiting service and 10 minutes to the delay for any subsequent aircraft seeking service. Even if demand later drops to 40 operations per hour, delays will persist for some time because the lines can be depleted at a rate of only 20 aircraft per hour.

Figure 8-2 indicates the relationship between practical and throughput capacity. As demand approaches the limit of throughput capacity, delays increase sharply and, theoretically, become infinite when demand equals or exceeds throughput capacity. Practical capacity, which is always less than throughput capacity, is that level of airfield utilization that can be attained with no more than some acceptable amount of delay.

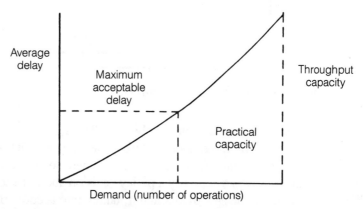

Fig. 8-2. Relationship between throughput and practical capacity.

The acceptability of delay is the key to the concept of practical capacity. Unlike throughput capacity, which can be objectively determined by analysis of airfield components and traffic patterns, practical capacity is value judgment—a consensus among airport users and operators—about how much delay they can tolerate.

Although practical capacity is usually stated in terms of an average figure, the acceptability of delay is actually determined not so much by the average but by the probability that the delay for a given aircraft will be greater than some amount. Just as demand tends to be nonuniformly distributed, so too is delay.

Figure 8-3 shows a typical distribution of delays encountered by aircraft at a particular level of demand. Note that most delays are of short duration, and that even though the average delay is low (5 minutes), there are a few aircraft encountering relatively long delays of 15 minutes or more; thus, while practical capacity is usually specified as that level of operations that —on average—will result in a given amount of delay, it is understood that the average implies that some percentage of delays will be considerably longer.

How much delay is acceptable? This is a judgment involving three factors. First, it must be recognized that some delay is unavoidable because it occurs for reasons beyond anyone's control—wind direction, weather, aircraft performance characteristics, the randomness of demand for service. Second, some delay, though avoidable, might be too expensive to eliminate, for instance, the cost of

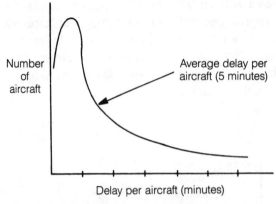

Fig. 8-3. Typical probability distribution of aircraft delay.

remedial measures might exceed the potential benefit. Third, even with the most vigorous and successful effort, the random nature of delay means that there will always be some aircraft encountering delay greater than some "acceptable" length; thus, acceptable delay is essentially a policy decision about the tolerability of delay being longer than some specified amount, taking into account the technical feasibility and economic practicality of available remedies.

Factors affecting capacity and delay

The capacity of an airfield is not constant over time; it might vary considerably during the day or the year as a result of physical and operational factors such as airfield and airspace geometry, air traffic control rules and procedures, weather, and traffic mix. When a figure is given for airfield capacity, it is usually an average based either on some assumed range of conditions or on actual operating experience.

It is the variability of capacity, rather than its average value, that is more detrimental to the overall operation of an airfield. Much of the strategy for successful management of an airfield involves devising ways to compensate for factors that, individually or in combination, act to lower capacity or to induce delay. These factors can be grouped in five categories: (1) airfield characteristics, (2) airspace characteristics, (3) air traffic control, (4) meteorological conditions, and (5) demand characteristics.

Airfield characteristics

The physical characteristics and layout of runways, taxiways, and aprons are basic determinants of the ability to accommodate various types of aircraft and the rate at which they can be handled. Also important is the type of equipment (lighting, navigation aids, radar, and the like) installed on the airfield as a whole or on particular segments. For any given configuration of runways and taxiways in use, capacity is constant; however, capacity varies as configurations change.

Airspace characteristics

The situation of the airfield in relation to other nearby airports and in relation to natural obstacles and features of the built environment determines the paths through the airspace that can be taken to and from the airport. Basically, the airspace geometry for a given airfield does not change over time; however, when there are two or more airports in proximity, operations at one airport can interfere with operations at another, causing the acceptance rate of one or both airports to suffer or requiring aircraft to fly circuitous routes to avoid conflict. In some cases, the interdependence of approach and departure paths for nearby airports can force one to hold departures until arrivals at the other have cleared the airspace or necessitate that each leave gaps in the arrival or departure streams to accommodate traffic at the other.

Air traffic control

The rules and procedures of air traffic control, intended primarily to assure safety of flight, are basic determinants of airfield capacity and delay. The rules governing aircraft separation, runway occupancy, spacing of arrivals and departures, and the use of parallel or converging runways can have an overall effect on throughput or can induce delays between successive operations. ATC rules and procedures have an especially important influence on capacity and delay at airfields where two or three runways might be in use at the same time or where there might be several arrival streams that must be merged on one final approach path.

A related factor affecting delay is the noise-abatement procedures adopted by FAA and by local airport authorities. These usually take the form of restrictions on flight paths over noise-sensitive areas or reduction (or outright prohibition) of operations during certain hours. These noise-control measures can have an adverse effect on capacity. For example, the runway configuration with the highest capacity might not be usable at certain times because it leads to unacceptably high noise levels in surrounding areas. Similarly, some noise-abatement procedures involve circuitous flight paths that may increase delays. The airport must thus make a tradeoff between usable capacity and noise control, with the usual result being some loss of capacity or increase of delay.

Meteorological conditions

Airport capacity is usually highest in clear weather, when visibility is at its best. Fog, low ceilings, precipitation, strong winds, or accumulations of snow or ice on the runway can cut capacity severely or close the airport altogether. Even a common occurrence such as a wind shift can disrupt operations while traffic is rerouted to a different pattern; if the new pattern is not optimum, capacity can be reduced for as long as the wind prevails. A large airport with multiple runways might have 30 or more possible patterns of use, some of which might have a substantially lower capacity than the others.

For most airports, it is the combined effect of weather, runway configuration, and ATC rules and procedures that results in the most severe loss of capacity or the longest delay lines. Much of the effort to reduce delays at these airports, through airfield management strategy and installation of improved technology, is aimed at minimizing the disparity between visual meteorological conditions (VMC) and instrument meteorological conditions (IMC) capacity. *Visual meteorological conditions (VMC)* and those in which atmospheric conditions permit pilots to approach, land, or take off by visual reference and to see and avoid other aircraft. *Instrument meteorological conditions (IMC)* are those in which other aircraft cannot be seen and safe separation must be assured solely by ATC rules and procedures. Under IMC, pilots must also rely on instruments for navigation and guidance to the runway.

Demand characteristics

Demand—not only the number of aircraft seeking service, but also their performance characteristics and the manner in which they use the airport—has an important effect on capacity and delay. The basic relationship among demand, capacity, and delay described earlier is that as demand approaches capacity, delays increase sharply. But for any given level of demand, the mix of aircraft with respect to speed, size, flight characteristics, and pilot proficiency will also determine the rate at which they can be handled and the delays that might result. Mismatches of speed or size between successive aircraft in the arrival stream, for example, can force air traffic controllers to increase separation, thus reducing the rate at which aircraft can be cleared over the runway threshold or off the runway.

For any given level of demand, the distribution of arrivals and departures and the extent to which they are bunched rather than uniformly spaced also determines the delay that will be encountered. In part, this tendency of traffic to peak at certain times is a function of the nature of the flights using the airport. For example, at airports with a high proportion of hub-and-spoke operations, where passengers land at the airport only to transfer to another flight, the traffic pattern is characterized by closely spaced blocks of arrivals and departures. Accommodating this pattern can cause much greater delays than if arriving and departing flights are spread and more uniformly intermixed.

Measuring delay

FAA regularly collects and analyzes data on delay, which are maintained in four data bases. The most extensive data base is that maintained by the *National Air-*

space Command Center (NASCOM). It is made up of daily reports from controllers at about 60 major airports and contains information on the number of delays, the time of beginning and end, and judgments by controllers about the primary and secondary causes. The principal value of NASCOM is that it allows FAA to monitor general trends of delay at major airports on a continuous basis. The subjective nature of controller reports limits the value of NASCOM data in analyzing the causes of delay.

The *Standard Air Carrier Delay Reporting System (SDRS)* contains reports from American and United Air Lines on their entire systems and at 32 specific airports. SDRS provides data on the flight phase where delays are incurred (taxi-out, taxi-in, at gate, and airborne), measured against a standard ground time and a computer-projected flight time. The cause of delay is not reported. Like NASCOM, SDRS is used principally to monitor trends in delay on a daily basis.

The *Performance Measurement System (PMS)* is similar in structure to NASCOM, except that it is maintained manually rather than on a computer. Delays of 15 minutes or longer are reported by controllers at about 20 airports. A fourth delay monitoring system, developed by the *FAA Office of Systems Engineering Management (OSEM)*, uses data from the Department of Transportation on operational times actually experienced by air carrier flights. Delay is measured by OSEM as the difference between an arbitrary standard flight time and the actual time reported for each flight.

All of these delay measurement and reporting systems suffer from basic faults. NASCOM and PMS are based on controller reports, and the quality and completeness of reporting vary considerably with controller workload. Further, NASCOM and PMS include only the longer delays (30 minutes or more for NASCOM, 15 minutes or more for PMS).

At the beginning of 1982, the threshold for reporting delay in the NASCOM system was lowered to 15 minutes. While this makes the NASCOM and PMS data bases more compatible, it prevents direct comparison with NASCOM data from previous years, when only delays of 30 minutes or more were reported. As a rule of thumb, FAA estimates that changing the definition of reportable delay from 30 to 15 minutes increased the number of recorded delays by a factor of between two and three.

Because delay is a highly skewed distribution, measuring only the "tail" of the distribution produces a distorted picture of the incidence and magnitude of delay. It is impossible to infer the true value of average delay from such extreme statistics, and both NASCOM and PMS probably exaggerate mean delay by a substantial margin.

All four FAA data bases measure delay against the standard of flight times published in the Official Airline Guide. This, too, probably results in an overestimation of delay because there is wide variation in the "no-delay" time from airport to airport and, at a given airport, among various runway configurations.

Many operations, when measured against a single nominal standard, are counted as delays but are within the normal expectancy for a given airport under given circumstances. There might also be a distortion in the opposite direction. Most airline schedules, especially for flights into and out of busy airports, have a built-in allowance for delay. In part, this is simply realistic planning, but there is also a tendency to inflate published flight times so as to maintain a public image of on-line operation.

Finally, all the delay measuring systems incorporate whatever delay might be experienced en route. Delays en route might not be attributable to conditions at the airport, and including them in the total for airports probably leads to over-estimation.

While it is clear from the data that delays do occur at many airports, it is probably true also that actual delay is not as great as FAA data bases indicate, either in terms of the number of aircraft delayed or the average length of delay.

NASCOM data during the late 1980s indicated that roughly 80 percent of all delays were due to weather, which either forced temporary closing of the airport or required that operations be conducted under instrument flight rules (which usually entail greater separation than under visual flight rules) in order to assure safety. The next largest category of delay was also weather-related (weather and equipment failures), typically occurring when landing aids required for instrument operations malfunction or are otherwise unavailable at a time when visibility is reduced by rain, fog, or snow. Delays caused by traffic volume in excess of throughput capacity typically accounted for six percent of all delays reported by NASCOM. Nearly all volume-related delays (more than 95 percent) were at the departure airport.

Approaches to reducing delay

Most air travel is between a few major airports and at certain times of the day. Chronic delay is limited to a very few specific times and places, and one of the principal causes is peaking of traffic flow. One approach is through technological improvements and construction of new facilities that can help airports absorb growing traffic demand and lessen delay (*See* chapters 9 and 10). Another alternative is to manage the demand to fit within existing capacity.

Two basic approaches to managing demand have the same objective: to ease congestion by diverting some traffic to times and places where it can be handled more promptly or efficiently. This might be done through *administrative management*; the airport authority or another governmental body might allocate airport access by setting quotas on passenger enplanements or on the number and type of aircraft operations that will be accommodated during a specific period. The alternative approach is economic—to structure the pricing system so that market forces allocate scarce airport facilities among competing users; thus, *demand manage-*

ment does not add capacity, it promotes more effective or economically efficient use of existing facilities.

Any scheme of demand management denies some users free or complete access to the airport of their choice. This denial is often decried as a violation of the traditional federal policy of freedom of the airways and the traditional "first-come, first-served" approach to allocating the use of airport facilities. Economists reject this argument on the grounds that it is a distortion of the concept of freedom to accord unrestricted access to any and all users without regard to the societal costs of providing airport facilities. Attempts to manage demand are also criticized for adversely affecting the growth of the aviation industry and the level of service to the traveling public. Nevertheless, as growth in traffic has outstripped the ability to expand and build airports, some forms of demand management have already come into use, and many industry observers have taken the position that some form of airport use restrictions will become increasingly important in dealing with delay and in utilizing existing airport capacity efficiently.

Administrative management

Several administrative management approaches are being adopted to manage demand at individual airports or for a metropolitan region. Among these are: (1) required diversion of some traffic to reliever airports, (2) more balanced use of metropolitan air carrier airports, (3) restriction of airport access by aircraft type or use, (4) establishment of quotas (either on the number of operations or on passenger enplanements), and (5) "rehubbing" or redistributing transfer traffic from busy airports to under-used airports.

Diversion of traffic   In some metropolitan areas, the shortage of airport capacity may not be general, but confined to one overcrowded airport. Perhaps other airports in the region could absorb some of the demand. The FAA lists 27 airports in the Chicago area, 51 in Los Angeles area, and 53 in the Dallas-Fort Worth region. The vast majority of these airports are small and suited only for general aviation (GA) aircraft, but in some cases there is also an underutilized commercial service airport.

The best regionwide solution to the problem of delay at a major airport might be to divert some traffic away from the busy airport to either a general aviation reliever airport or a lightly used commercial airport. To some extent, this can occur as a result of natural market forces. When delays become intolerable at the busy airport, users begin to divert of their own accord. While those who choose to move to a less crowded facility do so for their own benefit, they also reduce somewhat delays incurred by users that continue to operate at the crowded airport. Public policy might encourage this diversion through administrative action or economic incentives before traffic growth makes conditions intolerable or necessitates capital investment to accommodate peaks of demand at the busy airport.

Diversion of general aviation from busy air carrier airports is often an attractive solution. GA traffic, because it consists mostly of small, slow-moving aircraft, does not mix well with faster, heavier air carrier traffic. GA operators—especially those flying for recreational or training purposes—want to avoid the delays and inconveniences (and sometimes the hazards) of operating at a major airport. These fliers are often willing to make use of GA airports located elsewhere in the region if suitable facilities are available.

Diversion of GA traffic from commercial air carrier airports has been taking place for many years. As air carrier traffic grows at a particular location, it almost always tends to displace GA traffic. FAA has encouraged this trend by designating approximately 285 airports as "relievers" or "satellites" to air carrier airports, and earmarking funds especially for developing and upgrading these airports. Many other airports, although not specifically designated as relievers, serve the same function; they provide an alternative operating site for GA aircraft well removed from the main commercial airport of the region.

To be attractive to a broad spectrum of GA users, a reliever airport should be equipped with instrument approaches and provide runways capable of handling the larger, more sophisticated GA aircraft. In addition, users need facilities for aircraft servicing, repair, and maintenance, as well as suitable ground access to the metropolitan area.

Not all GA aircraft can make use of reliever airports. Some might be delivering passengers or freight to connect with commercial flights at the air carrier airport. Others might be large business jets that require the longer runways of a major airport.

In general, airport authorities do not have the power to exclude GA as a class, although this has been attempted on occasion. For example, in the late 1970s, the airport management and city government of St. Louis attempted to exclude all private aircraft from Lambert Airport. This ordinance was overturned by the courts as discriminatory.

Where they have had any policy on the matter, local airport authorities have attempted to make GA airports attractive to users by offering good facilities or by differential pricing schemes. This approach is most effective where the commercial airport and the principal reliever are operated by the same entity. The state of Maryland, owner of Baltimore-Washington International Airport, operates a separate GA airport, Glenn L. Martin Field, and has a specific policy of encouraging GA traffic to use it rather than the main airport. The master plan for Cleveland Hopkins International Airport depends on the availability of the city-owned Lakefront Airport as a reliever. If that airport should for some reason cease operation as a GA reliever, Hopkins would experience a great increase in traffic, which might necessitate additional construction that is not now planned.

Corporate aircraft and commercial jet prepare for takeoff.

Most local airport authorities, however, do not operate their own GA relievers. Some large airport authorities plan and coordinate activities with nearby reliever airports operated by other municipalities or private individuals, but this has not been the general case. The system of relievers in each region has tended to grow up without any specific planning or coordination on the regional level.

Development of GA relievers is not without problems. These airports are also subject to complaints about noise, and they experience the same difficulties as commercial airports in expanding their facilities or in developing a new airport site. Further, because many GA airports are small and function just on the ragged edge of profitability, problems of noise or competing land use can actually threaten the airport's existence. The number of airports available for public use in the United States has been declining. Between 1980 and 1990, for example, the number of public-use airports declined from 6,519 to 5,598. Although most of the airports that closed were small, privately owned facilities, some industry observers worry that the nation is irrevocably losing many potential reliever airports just as it has become clear that they are vital.

Balanced use of large airports   At the largest commercial service airports, GA activity consists primarily of flights by large business and executive aircraft. This type of GA traffic accounts for approximately 10 to 20 percent of the use of major airports, a figure that many consider the "irreducible minimum." The delays that persist at these airports are primarily the result of air carrier demand that can be satisfied only by another commercial service airport. In several metropolitan areas, it is clear that the commercial airports are not used in a balanced manner. For example, San Francisco International is experiencing delay problems while nearby Oakland airport is underutilized. Washington National is overcrowded while Dulles International and Baltimore-Washington International are looking for business.

Newark is underutilized compared with busy La Guardia and Kennedy. Similar pairs exist in Chicago (O'Hare and Midway), Dallas (Dallas-Fort Worth and Love Field), and Houston (Houston Intercontinental and Hobby). A policy designed to divert traffic from busy to underutilized airports would have a generally positive effect on the ability of metropolitan areas to accommodate air traffic. Further, It might obviate the need for expansion or expensive technological improvements designed to reduce delays at the busy airport.

Diverting air carrier traffic to alternate airports is not a simple solution; there are a number of problems. One is simply the habits of the traveling public. People are accustomed to using the busier airport. They probably prefer the better ground access, the larger choice of flight times and destinations, the greater variety of carriers, and other advantages that the busy airport offers.

Air carriers, sensitive to public preferences, tend to concentrate their service at the busier airport, where they perceive a larger market. It is in the carrier's economic interest to serve the airport where passengers want to go. The busier airport is a known and viable enterprise, while the underutilized alternate airport is a risk. Air carriers are justifiably reluctant to isolate themselves from the major market by moving all their service to the less popular airport. On the other hand, serving both airports imposes an economic burden that carriers seldom choose to bear, as they would incur the additional expense of setting up and operating duplicate ground services. In addition, splitting their passengers between two airports might make scheduling of flights more complicated and lead to inefficient utilization of aircraft.

These obstacles have sometimes been overcome in locations where airport operators have the authority to encourage a diversion of traffic from one airport to another. For example, in the New York area, the Port Authority of New York and New Jersey operates all three air carrier airports. In theory, this gives the port authority the ability to establish regulatory policies or economic incentives to encourage the diversion of some traffic to Newark. In practice, however, measures adopted to promote traffic redistribution have not been fully effective. The recent growth of traffic at Newark has been due primarily to new carriers entering the New York market and not diversion of established carriers.

In contrast, San Francisco and Oakland airports are operated by separate sponsors. San Francisco, despite severe problems of delay, would rightly be reluctant to encourage passengers and air carriers to move to Oakland. Even though more balanced regional airport use might be achieved and the long-range need for expansion at San Francisco reduced, the short-range effect would be that San Francisco would lose revenues to a competitor. There is no regional authority with the power to promote this reallocation of traffic.

Restriction of access by aircraft type   One means of diverting certain traffic from a busy airport to one with unused capacity is to restrict access to the busy airport on the basis of aircraft type or use. Restriction of aircraft access to airports by size or performance characteristics might affect airport capacity and delay in several ways. First, the mix of aircraft using a runway system helps to determine capacity. When aircraft are of similar size, speed, and operating characteristics, runway acceptance rate is greater than when performance characteristics vary widely. Similar aircraft can be more uniformly and accurately spaced on approach and departure, thereby smoothing out irregularities in the traffic stream, which is a major factor causing delay; thus, at airports where the bottleneck is in the runway system, restrictions that narrow the range of aircraft using that system might have a beneficial effect. Diversion of small GA or commuter aircraft to other airports or construction of a separate short runway dedicated to their use could improve the ability of the airport to handle larger transports or the overall traffic mix.

A second implication of limiting access to specific aircraft types is that it might reduce the need for capital improvements required to accommodate a larger variety of aircraft. For example, Washington National Airport does not accept jumbo jet aircraft. Allowing larger aircraft into National would probably necessitate changes in runways, taxiways, aprons, and gates. In addition, the larger number of passengers per aircraft would put additional strain on National's already congested terminal and landside facilities, making a number of collateral improvements necessary.

Access restrictions at Washington National are combined with a cap on passenger enplanements. Although the cap is still under debate, it is currently set at 16 million passengers annually. (National currently handles 13 million.) FAA considers the cap necessary because limiting aircraft size without also setting a ceiling on the number of passengers might lead to more aircraft operations than the airport can handle safely or efficiently and worsen the congestion that already exists at National.

The purpose of the access restrictions, the cap on passengers, and the quota system (discussed below) is to divert traffic from National Airport to Dulles. Most local airport managers would not be able to adopt such measures unless there were a nearby underutilized airport, also under their control, to handle the diverted traffic. To forbid some portion of the traffic to use an airport without an available alternative would most likely be construed as a restriction of interstate commerce or discriminatory practice.

Quotas One technique of administrative management now in use at a few airports is the quota system—an administratively established limit on the number of operations per hour. Because delay increases exponentially as demand approaches capacity, a small reduction in the number of hourly operations can have a significant effect on delay. This makes the quota an attractive measure for dealing promptly (and inexpensively) with airport congestion.

Examples of airports with quotas are O'Hare, La Guardia, JFK, and Washington National, airports covered by the *FAA high-density rule*. The quotas at these airports were established by FAA in 1973 based on estimated limits of the air traffic control (ATC) system and airport runways at that time. FAA is currently considering lifting the rule at some of these locations because of improvements made to airport facilities and slower than expected growth in air traffic. An example of a locally imposed quota is John Wayne Airport in Orange County, California, which limits scheduled air carrier operations to an annual average of 41 operations per day. This quota is based on noise considerations as well as limitations on the size of the terminal and gate areas.

During busy hours, demand for operational slots typically exceeds the quota. At the airports covered by the high-density rule, the slots are allocated among different user classes. For example, at National, where there are 60 slots available per hour, 27 are allotted to air carriers, 11 to commuter carriers, and 12 to general aviation. During visual meteorological conditions, more than 60 operations can be handled, and aircraft without assigned slots may be accommodated at the discretion of air traffic controllers and the airport manager.

At airports where the quota system is in force, slots may be allocated in various ways: a reservation system, negotiation, or administrative determination. The GA slots are generally distributed through a reservation system—the first user to call for a reservation gets the slot.

However, for commuters and air carriers, the slots at the high-density rule airports are still subject to a great deal of controversy. In 1986, FAA declared the slots the property of the airlines holding them by allowing carriers to sell or lease slots to other airlines. A few available slots were also distributed by lottery.

Under airline regulation, when the number of carriers and routes was fairly stable, airline scheduling committees would meet under antitrust immunity to negotiate the flights to be allotted to each user, which meant the incumbent carriers. From 1979 to 1986, the committees had to accommodate new entrants and the changing market strategies of incumbent carriers. On several occasions during this period, negotiations between carriers concerning available slots nearly broke down, which would have necessitated the FAA to use administrative means to distribute the slots.

Rehubbing   A systemwide response to alleviate delays at busy airports is redistribution of operations to other, less busy airports in other regions. Some air carriers, especially those with a high proportion of interconnecting flights, might voluntarily move their operations to underutilized airports located at some distance from the congested hub. Transfer passengers account for a large percentage of traffic at some large airports. About three-fourths of passengers at Atlanta, and nearly half of passengers at Chicago, Denver, and Dallas-Fort Worth arrive at those airports merely to change planes for some other destination. There is an advantage for carriers in choosing a busy airport as a transfer hub—they can offer passengers a wide variety of possible connections; however, when the airport becomes too crowded, the costs of delay might begin to outweigh the advantages of the large airport, and carriers might find it attractive to establish new hubs at smaller, less busy airports.

This rehubbing of the airport system is already a trend. Redistribution of operations has certainly been facilitated by the deregulation of the airline industry, which allowed carriers greater freedom in restructuring their routes. Medium-size airports appear to be receiving increased air carrier activity since deregulation, and some carriers are shifting their transfer operations to these less-congested facilities. For example, USAir has developed Charlotte (North Carolina), Dayton (Ohio), and Baltimore-Washington (Maryland) as regional hubs.

In addition to relief from congestion, carriers who have moved to less busy airports find another, perhaps more compelling, advantage. Because there is often little service by competing carriers at those locations, the hubbing carrier has greater control of passengers, who can transfer only to departing flights of the airline that brought them, not to a competitor's.

While it is doubtful that rehubbing has actually reduced delay problems at major airports, it does seem clear that development of transfer hubs at medium airports has allowed for growth that might not have been possible had the carriers sought to concentrate their activities at the major hubs. Further, rehubbing has taken advantage of a certain "overcapacity" in the national airport system by making greater use of the facilities available at medium airports.

Demand management

Administrative management of airport use—whether by restricted access for certain types of aircraft, by demand balancing among metropolitan area airports, or by selection imposition of quotas—offers the promise of immediate and relatively low-cost relief of airport congestion. As long-term measures, these solutions might not be as attractive. Administrative limits tend to bias the outcome toward maintenance of the status quo when applied over a long period of time. Because the economic value of airport access is not fully considered in setting administrative limits, incumbents cannot be displaced by others who would place a higher value on use of the airport. Further, incumbents and potential new entrants alike have no way to indicate the true economic value they would place on increased capacity. Economists contend that a vital market signal is missing and that airport operators and the federal government cannot obtain a true picture of future capacity needs. Administratively limiting demand, they say, creates an artificial market equilibrium that—over the long term—distorts appreciation of the nature, quality, and costs of air transportation service that the public requires. Economists, therefore, favor a scheme of allocating airport access by demand management which relies on the price mechanism.

At present, price plays a rather weak role in determining airport access or in modulating demand. Access to public use airports, except for the few large airports where quotas are imposed, is generally unrestricted so long as one is willing to pay landing fees and endure the costs of congestion and delay. Landing fees, most often based solely on aircraft weight and invariant by time of day, make up a very small fraction of operational cost—typically two to three percent for air carriers and even less for GA. Further, landing fees are not uniform from airport to airport. In many cases, landing fees are set so that, in the aggregate, they make up the difference between the cost of operating the airport and the revenues received from other sources such as concessions, leases, and automobile parking fees.

This leads economists to the conclusion that landing fees are somewhat arbitrary and do not reflect the costs imposed on the airport by an aircraft operation. Economists suggest that by including airport costs and demand as determinants of user fees, delay could be significantly reduced. The two most commonly advocated methods of achieving this are differential pricing and auctioning of landing rights.

Differential pricing   Many economists argue that weight-based landing fees are counterproductive because they do not vary with demand, and consequently provide no incentive to utilize airport facilities during off-peak hours. Further, they do not reflect the high capital costs of facilities used only during peak hours. Thus, economists contend, a more effective pricing method would be to charge higher user fees during peak hours and lower fees during off-peak hours. Theoretically, the net effect of such a pricing policy would be a more uniform level of demand.

Much of the traffic moved away from peak hours by higher landing fees would probably be GA. Correspondingly, the benefits of peak-hour fees would be greater at airports with a high proportion of GA activity. But peak-hour fees could also be structured so as to affect the pattern of air carrier activity. These charges would have to be fairly high because landing fees represent only a small fraction of air carrier operating costs and because increases can be passed on to passengers.

Despite increases in landing fees, carriers would want to continue to use the airport at peak times, either to have access to a large number of passengers or because long-haul scheduling problems require them to serve a particular airport during certain hours; thus, they would absorb some increase in landing fees—just as they absorb the cost of delays—as part of the cost of doing business; however, some flights might be moved to off-peak hours if the charges were high enough. It is possible that properly structured peak-hour prices, if they were reflected in fares, could have an effect not only on the airline's scheduling patterns but on passengers' travel habits as well. If significant savings were possible, some passengers would choose to travel during off-peak hours.

It is difficult to project accurately the changes in patterns of airport use that might be brought about by peak-hour surcharges. FAA has estimated that peak-hour surcharges, along with improvement of the ATC system, would reduce anticipated air carrier delay costs by approximately 80 percent at the nation's 25 busiest airports over the next 25 years. A recent Congressional Budget Office (CBO) report suggests that although expansion might be inevitable at many airports, peak-hour surcharges could significantly delay the need for expansion and reduce financial pressure at a number of airports. Another important aspect of peak-hour surcharges noted by CBO is that even if they do not reduce traffic levels at peak hours to the desired levels, they could provide airports with increased revenues to expand facilities and, consequently, to reduce delays.

Some observers reject this line of reasoning. They contend that to be effective in shifting demand to slack periods, peak-hour charges would have to be set so high that they would be politically unacceptable. Further, there is no assurance that airlines would not average the higher costs of peak-hour access at certain airports with the lower cost at other times and places and pass this along to all passengers as a general fare increase. Airlines would thus create an internal cross-subsidy in their fare structure to cover the higher costs of access to some airports. Because the average fare increase would likely be small, the economic signal to the public would be diminished and have scant effect on travel behavior.

A major problem with the concept of peak-hour surcharges is how to determine the level of surcharge. One widely advocated method is to charge the airport user the full marginal costs of airport facilities. In other words, each airport user pays a share of the additional capital and operating costs to the airport authority of providing service at the time demanded. For example, if a user lands at an airport during a period of peak demand where two or more runways are necessary to handle the traffic, the charge should include a contribution to the cost of building, operating, and maintaining those additional runways. On the other hand, if the user lands during an off-peak hour, when the one runway in use is not sought by others, there would be no additional charge. While both on-peak and off-peak users would pay fees to cover maintenance, wear and tear, or other costs, only peak-hour users would pay the additional costs associated with the time of use. The resulting user fees would be directly related to the levels of airport activity, producing the desired effect of higher fees during peak hours and a strong price signal to use the airport at off-peak hours.

Some contend that a system of marginal cost pricing should be based on the delay costs that each peak-hour user imposes on other users. For example, during peak hours, airport users would be charged a fee based on the delay costs associated with their operations. This creates a system of user fees where the fees become progressively larger as delays increase. Proponents contend that using marginal delay costs as the basis for pricing airport access provides a stronger incentive for off-peak airport use than a scheme based on marginal facility costs alone.

Implementing a policy of differential pricing—whether based on marginal facility cost, marginal delay cost, or some purely arbitrary scheme—is difficult. It is likely that a significant increase in airport user fees will raise questions of equity. Higher fees might be more burdensome for small airlines and new entrants than for established carriers. There are a number of examples where airport operators have attempted to increase user fees and have been challenged by air carriers and general aviation. In some cases, air carrier landing fees are established in long-term contracts that cannot be easily changed.

GA users often contend that differential pricing is discriminatory because it favors those with the ability to pay, and illegal because it denies the right to use a publicly funded facility. Economists rebut this argument by pointing out that time-of-use price is neither discriminatory nor illegal so long as price differences reflect cost differences and that it is fair and just to set prices based on the costs that each user imposes on others and on society generally.

Despite the difficulties inherent in increasing airport user fees, there are two well-documented examples of differential pricing policies that have been in effect for several years. In the early 1970s, the British Airport Authority implemented peak-hour surcharges at London's Heathrow Airport. In the late 1960s, the Port Authority of New York and New Jersey began imposing peak-hour surcharges on general aviation. Both differential pricing policies sought to move traffic to off-peak hours, even though the pricing methods employed were considerably different.

Because of the large volume of international traffic, activity at Heathrow increases significantly during the summer months, compounding delay problems. As a result, the surcharges imposed at Heathrow in 1972 were set on an hourly and seasonal basis. The hours of greatest delay were from 8 a.m. to 1 p.m. During the summer, surcharges were applied for the entire five-hour period each day. During the remaining months, surcharges were levied only for the period between 9 and 11 a.m., Monday through Friday. The effects of peak-hour surcharges at Heathrow were not clear-cut. During 1972 and 1973, there was an apparently steady movement of traffic away from peak periods. This trend, however, was reversed in the following year and fluctuated thereafter, leaving some doubt as to the effectiveness of the surcharges.

The surcharges imposed by the Port Authority of New York and New Jersey were aimed specifically at general aviation using the three major commercial airports in the New York metropolitan area. During 1968, 17 percent of all aircraft operations at the three commercial airports were delayed by more than 30 minutes. During the same month, GA traffic constituted 25 percent of the airport traffic, 30 percent during peak hours. In an effort to shift this GA traffic away from peak hours, the Port Authority increased the landing fee for aircraft with fewer than 25 seats to $25 during peak hours, a fivefold increase. The fee remained at the $5 level during off-peak hours.

Peak-hour surcharges produced significant results at all three New York airports. Following the imposition of the surcharges, GA activity during August and September decreased 19 percent overall and 30 percent during peak periods. More important, delays—in terms of the percentage of aircraft operations experiencing delays of over 30 minutes—declined markedly.

To be sure, there are factors other than surcharges that affect airport use, and, undoubtedly, some could have influenced the outcomes in both New York and London. For example, the fuel crisis of 1973 unquestionably influenced the traffic at Heathrow and masked somewhat the effects of the surcharge. A controller slowdown at New York's airports during the summer of 1968 intensified delay problems and could have accounted for some of the traffic diversion attributed to the surcharges.

In general, peak-hour surcharges represent an attempt to manage demand by charging cost-based landing fees. Access to airports is not limited except by the user's willingness to bear the additional cost imposed during peak hours. Another method of reducing peak-hour airport activity involves limiting airport access through a process by which landing rights (slots) are auctioned to the highest bidder. The auction is a hybrid process—partly administrative, partly economic—in which access is regulated, but the *right* of access is distributed through a market-oriented mechanism.

Slot auctions   Slot auctions have been advocated as the best method of allocating scarce airport landing rights on the grounds that if airport access must be limited, it should be treated as a scarce resource and priced accordingly. The method to accomplish this is a system whereby the price of airport access is determined by demand. Slot auctions allow peak-hour access only to those users willing to pay a market-determined price.

It was mentioned earlier that in 1986 the FAA granted the right to the airlines to buy and sell the slots that they held. While the buy-sell slot rule has stabilized the situation somewhat for the airlines, airports strongly argue that the funds should go toward the air transportation system, not the few air carriers who obtained the slots for free.

Critics also contend that the current slot sale process gives an advantage to the airlines already operating at the airport and denies access to competitors, providing the existing users with virtual monopolies and a financial windfall. Slot holders know that without a slot, no competitor can enter a market, and consequently, slots represent one of the most significant barriers to entry in the airline business today. Their impact on the industry extends far beyond the few airports where they are imposed because markets critical to many communities either begin or end at one of these facilities.

The carriers that control the slots contend that the system is fair because they took the risk necessary to develop the market and, as a result, they should be rewarded by retaining the slots. Contrary to FAA's expectations, the slot sale plan has not fostered an active market; available slots are scarce and expensive, with 30-minute slots at Washington National and La Guardia recently selling for more than $1 million each.

Congress has been looking very closely at the current buy-sell rule with the idea of initiating legislation to recapture the slots and require federal auctions for time-limited periods.

Factors affecting the use of demand management alternatives   The demand-management techniques enumerated above could—in theory—reduce delay. Some have actually been tried, with mixed results; however, there are factors that might affect the ability of airport operators or the federal government to implement them on a wide scale.

Some argue that regulations restricting airport access are unconstitutional because they interfere with interstate commerce and abridge the right of access for some users. Many industry observers shudder to think that the kinds of access restrictions in effect at National Airport might become common at major airports. Determination of whether they would be an undue burden is a delicate matter that must be decided on a case-by-case basis, depending on the parties involved, the location of the airport, and its importance to the national system. FAA itself does not appear to encourage the spread of quotas and other restrictions imposed by airports.

Deregulation has made the allocation of slots through negotiation or sale a more difficult process, as the scheduling committees must constantly accommodate new entrants or changes in incumbent carrier's levels of service.

Policies to encourage development of reliever airports or more balanced utilization of airports in metropolitan regions are unlikely to be implemented in locales where airports are competitors and not operated by the same sponsor. Congress has attempted to address the regional implications of airport development in its mandate for FAA to develop a National Plan of Integrated Airport Systems. It remains to be seen whether this planning document—or any other action at the federal level—can improve regional coordination of airport facilities.

The basic theory of demand-related airport access fees and the general principle that fees should be proportional to marginal delay costs are well understood. It is also commonly acknowledged that the present scheme of pricing services, especially at congested airports, is far from economically efficient; however, market-related approaches such as peak-hour pricing and congestion surcharges might be difficult to implement, and they are likely to encounter stiff opposition from some classes of users, especially GA.

Despite the theoretical attractiveness of marginal-cost pricing, it might be difficult in practice to determine the true marginal cost of a landing or a takeoff. There are analytic problems and policy issues to be resolved, as well as the underlying question of whether economic efficiency should be a primary goal of airport management. Several years of experimentation might be needed to establish the most effective fee structure for controlling delay and covering airport costs.

There are some dangers inherent in these experiments. It is possible that in a deregulated environment where carriers are frequently changing routes and levels of service, airports would be unable to determine the effects of their experiments or to guard against unpredictable (and undesirable) side effects on the airline industry or on other airports. The process of diverting air carrier operations to off-peak might be self-defeating for some airports. Rather than schedule operations in slack hours at airports that they perceive as marginal, carriers might prefer to move out of the airport altogether. While this might be a desirable effect from the system perspective, it would be the opposite for the airport operator, who would lose revenue.

Further, in order to be effective in shifting air carrier traffic to off-peak hours, landing fees during peak hours might have to be raised substantially. In many cases, use agreements between air carriers and airports would prevent such radical changes in fees. If it were determined to be in the national interest for airport operators to make such changes in their fee structures, the federal government might have to take action to abrogate or modify existing use agreements. On the other hand, some believe it is unwise for the federal government to become so directly involved in the pricing decisions of individual airports.

Economic policies or administrative actions to reduce GA traffic at congested major airports could have two effects. The intended effect would be diversion of some GA traffic to other nearby landing places; however, for some types of aircraft and for some GA users, there will be no other facility as suitable as the main air carrier airport, and they would have to pay the cost if they wish to continue using it. Alternatively, some users might find the monetary cost or inconvenience too high and choose to use commercial flights rather than continuing to operate their own aircraft.

The sale or auction of slots is controversial with regard to ownership and the right of sale. The confusion over slots following the Braniff bankruptcy, the first victim of deregulation, is a case in point. At that time, FAA's post-strike cap on operations was in effect at 22 airports, and Braniff argued that their assigned slots were assets that had monetary value that should accrue to the airline. FAA's position was that the slots were under FAA control. (FAA did reassign those slots to other carriers on an emergency basis after Braniff stopped flying.) From the airport operator's point of view, however, slots represent the essential attributes of the airport, namely runway time and space. If they are determined to be property at all, the airport operator would argue that they belong to neither FAA nor the carriers, but to the airport.

A 1981 FAA report illustrates the general benefits of demand management. The report examined projected demand and traffic mix at the 39 busiest air carrier airports to determine those with future capacity problems and to identify remedial measures that could be applied to alleviate delay. About half (19 of the 39 airports studied) were expected to face serious delay problems by 1991. Analysis of the traffic mix at these airports identified seven with a high proportion of GA traffic, and FAA concluded that demand-management techniques aimed at diverting GA to off-peak hours or to reliever airports could obviate the need for new construction to expand capacity.

Key terms

capacity
throughput
practical capacity
visual meteorological conditions (VMC)
instrument meteorological conditions (IMC)
National Airspace Command Center (NASCOM)
Standard Air Carrier Delay Reporting System (SDRS)
Performance Measurement System (PMS)
FAA Office of Systems Engineering Management (OSEM)
administrative management
demand management
FAA high density rule

Review questions

1. Compare throughput capacity and practical capacity. Define PHOCAP and PANCAP.
   How much delay is acceptable?

2. Discuss how the following factors affect capacity and delay: (1) airfield characteristics, (2) airspace characteristics, (3) air traffic control, (4) meteorological conditions, and (5) demand characteristics.

3. What are the four data bases used in measuring delay? What are some of the difficulties encountered in using them?
   According to NASCOM data, most delays are the result of which factor?

4. Distinguish between the administrative management and demand management approaches to reducing delay.
   Describe the various administrative management techniques to reduce delay.
   At airports where the quota system is in force, slots can be allocated in various ways. Describe three of them.

5. What are the two methods of demand management used to reduce delay? Discuss some of the difficulties in using these methods. Give several examples of airports using demand management methods.

    What are some of the factors that may affect the implementation of demand management methods on a wider scale?

Suggested readings

deNeufville, Richard, *Airport Systems Planning*. Cambridge, Mass. The MIT Press, 1976.

Airfield and Airspace Capacity/Delay Policy Analysis, FAA-APO-81-14, Washington, DC: FAA, Office of Aviation Policy and Plans, December, 1981.

Airside Capacity Criteria Used in Preparing the National Airport Plan, AC 150/5060-1A, Washington, DC: FAA, July, 1968.

Report and Recommendations of the Airport Access Task Force. Washington, DC: Civil Aeronautics Board, March, 1983.

Policy Analysis of the Upgraded Third Generation Air Traffic Control System. Washington, DC: Federal Aviation Administration, January, 1977.

Airport System Capacity-Strategic Choices. Washington, DC: Transportation Research Board, 1990.

Public Works Infrastructure: Policy Considerations for the 1980s. Washington, DC: Congressional Budget Office, April, 1983.

Airport Landside Capacity, Special Report 159. Transportation Research Board, National Academy of Sciences, TRB Washington, DC, 1975.

Airside technological
improvements

Outline

Introduction
Airport and airspace technology
Guidance, surveillance, and control
Airspace use procedures
Weather and atmospheric effects
Noise control and abatement
Airport surface utilization

Objectives

When you have completed this chapter, you should be able to:

△ Discuss several technological advances which are designed to improve air traffic guidance and surveillance.

△ Describe the following ATC systems: traffic management system (TMS) and advanced en route automation (AERA) program.

△ Distinguish between the following airspace use procedures as a means of improving traffic flow: reduced lateral separation, reduced longitudinal separation on final approach, and separate short runways for small aircraft.

△ Define "wake vortex" and "wind shear."

△ Give several examples of weather-related technologies designed to improve traffic flow.

△ Discuss the various approaches used by the FAA and airport management to reduce noise.

△ Give several examples of ground surveillance and control technologies designed to improve airport surface utilization.

Introduction

The airport system in place in the United States today is extensive and highly developed; in general, it serves the nation well. Still, there are problems of congestion and delay at the busiest airports, where facilities are not adequate to accommodate demand at all times and in all conditions of weather and visibility. The FAA forecasts that growth of commercial and private aviation could be constrained by lack of airport capacity, which it considers to be the most serious problem facing civil aviation through the remainder of this century.

Recent policy statements by FAA acknowledge that, with a few exceptions, the direct solution of building new airports and expanding existing ones might not be practical due to lack of suitable new airport sites, physical limitations of present facilities, and concerns about environmental impacts of aviation on surrounding communities. Similar views have been expressed in other studies of airport capacity, and there is a widely held opinion that while the airport system is expandable in the broad sense, there is little hope of creating major new facilities in those key metropolitan areas where air travel demand and aviation activity continue to outstrip available airport capacity unless airport planners can persuade surrounding communities that airports can be good neighbors.

For this reason, the aviation community and FAA have sought technological solutions that will ease congestion by allowing fuller and more efficient use of the airports we already have. This technology includes new equipment for surveillance, navigation, and communication, and revised procedures for using the airspace and airport facilities. In this way, it is hoped that additional demand can be absorbed within the infrastructure now in place without adversely affecting surrounding communities.

Chapters 9 and 10 examine *technological improvements*—either currently available or under development—that could be employed to relieve congestion and delay. These chapters provide a survey of possible improvements in airport technology, with emphasis on the circumstances in which this technology would be applicable, the extent to which it could increase the amount of traffic handled, and the prospects for development and deployment over the coming years.

In aviation, the term *technology* typically brings to mind sophisticated electronic and mechanical devices used for navigation, surveillance, communication,

United jet taking off from Seattle-Tacoma International Airport.

and flight control. Such devices are clearly of interest, but for the purposes of these chapters, technology is interpreted in a broader sense. As used here, technology refers not only to new devices and equipment but also to new operational concepts and procedures that they make possible. Also, many in the aviation community draw a distinction between technology (meaning equipment and sometimes procedures) and civil engineering (referring to the design and construction of physical components of the airport—the concrete, so to speak). While recognizing that different engineering disciplines and techniques are involved, these chapters do not make such a distinction but consider the design and construction of improved physical components such as runways, taxiways, and terminal buildings as simply one more form of technology that will add to airport capacity or permit more effective and economical use of the airport as a whole.

Airport and airspace technology

Technological approaches to expanding airport capacity or reducing delay fall into three broad categories. First, there are improved devices and procedures that will expedite the flow of air traffic into and out of the airport, essentially, techniques that will augment airside capacity or mitigate aircraft delay by increasing the runway operation rate.

The second category includes techniques to facilitate movement of aircraft on the airport surface. The purpose of these technologies is to move aircraft from the runway to the passenger loading gates and back again as expeditiously as possible, thereby shortening the taxi-in and taxi-out components of delay and easing congestion on taxiways, aprons, and loading ramps.

The third category embraces techniques that can be used to aid the transit of passengers through the terminal building and the flow of vehicles on airport circulation and access roads. In contrast with the first two categories, where the aim is to alleviate aircraft delay, the third category is intended to facilitate the movement of people and to reduce that part of delay incurred in getting to and from aircraft. The third category is examined in chapter 10.

The discussion that follows addresses the broad question of airport capacity, not just airside capacity or aircraft delay. The intent is to examine ways to improve the overall adequacy and efficiency of the airport as a transportation hub. The underlying proposition is that delay—*any* form of delay—ultimately affects the passenger through the loss of time and increased cost of air transportation service. In this sense, it is parochial to speak only of aircraft delay because the basic purpose of the air transportation system is to move people from origin to destination, in safety, with minimum expenditure of time and money. All measures taken at airports to shorten travel time, to lower travel cost, or to lessen inconvenience are of equal importance, regardless of whether they apply to the airside or landside.

The scheme or organization for this discussion is outlined in TABLE 9-1, which lists various forms of airside, technological improvements and the purpose

Table 9-1. Airside technology to increase capacity and reduce delay.

Technology	Area of application	Purpose	Benefit
Aircraft guidance, surveillance, and control			
Microwave landing system	Airspace	Improve precision of navigation; make more flexible use of airspace	Increased capacity; reduced delay; less noise impact
Surveillance radar	Airspace	Improve surveillance; reduce separation	Improved safety; increased capacity
Traffic management techniques	Airspace	Improve traffic flow	Reduced delay
Airspace use procedures			
Reduced lateral separation for parallel and converging runways	Airspace	Increase utilization of multiple runways in IMC	Increased capacity
Reduced longitudinal separation	Airspace	Reduce in-trail separation	Increased capacity
Separate short runways for small aircraft	Airspace	Segregate air traffic by size and speed	Increased capacity; reduced delay
Weather and atmospheric effects			
Wake vortex detection	Airspace	Reduce in-trail separation	Increased capacity
Wind shear detection	Airspace	Alert pilots to wind shear	Improved safety; reduced delay
Noise control and abatement			
Control of aircraft noise	Airspace	Reduce aircraft noise	Increased capacity; reduced delay
Aircraft operating procedures	Airspace	Lessen or distribute noise impacts	Increased capacity; reduced delay
Airport surface utilization			
Surveillance and control	Taxiways	Improve surveillance, control, and guidance of aircraft on ground	Increased capacity; reduced delay; improved safety
High-speed turnoffs and improved taxiways	Runway	Reduce runway occupancy time	Increased capacity
Taxiway marking and lighting	Taxiways	Increase efficiency of taxiway use	Reduced delay
Apron and gate facilities	Ramps and aprons	Improve docking at gate; improve aircraft maintenance and servicing	Increased capacity; reduced delay

they could achieve. Discussion of specific technologies listed in TABLE 9-1 is presented in the sections that follow, which make up the bulk of this chapter.

Guidance, surveillance, and control

The position and spacing of aircraft in the airborne traffic stream is a key factor in determining airfield capacity. For the pilot, it is vital to know where the aircraft is in relation to the runway and the airspace corridors around the airport. This is accomplished by ground-based navigation equipment and airborne receivers. The air traffic controller uses surveillance radar to monitor the position of the aircraft on approach and departure paths and in relation to other aircraft using the airport. The success of these activities—navigation by the pilot and surveillance by the controller—is affected by the inherent accuracy of the equipment used. (Is the aircraft in fact where the pilot and controller *think* it is?) The data update rate is also important. (How recent is this information and what might have happened since the last position reading?)

To appreciate the magnitude of this uncertainty, consider that at typical jet approach speeds, an aircraft can travel almost 1,000 feet horizontally and descend 50 to 60 feet in the four seconds between successive scans of the radar presently used for air traffic control at airports.

In conditions of good visibility, when visual cues can be used by the pilot to confirm the position of the aircraft and to supplement guidance systems, the spacing between aircraft can be reduced to the minimum permitted by safe operating procedures. When visibility is lessened by darkness, rain, or fog, the pilot must rely on instruments and the controller on radar. In such circumstances, a margin of safety must be added to the interval between aircraft, in effect increasing the time that must be allowed for each to use an assigned portion of the airspace or to occupy the runway, and correspondingly lowering the throughput rate. If the accuracy of navigation and surveillance devices could be improved, the capacity of the airfield under instrument meteorological conditions (IMC) could be closer to that attainable under visual meteorological conditions (VMC).

Three technologies that could improve aircraft guidance, surveillance, and control are planned for deployment in the future. They are the microwave landing system, improved surveillance radar, and automated traffic-management systems for the air traffic controller.

Microwave landing system

The current guidance system for approach and landing is the instrument landing system (ILS), which has been the standard system in this country since 1941 and is widely used by civil aviation throughout the world. ILS provides guidance by radio beams that define a straightline path to the runway at a fixed slope of approximately three degrees and extending five to seven miles from the runway threshold. All aircraft approaching the airport under ILS guidance must follow this path in single file, spaced at intervals dictated by standards for safe longitudinal separation and the need to avoid wake vortex. This long, straight-in approach is a bottleneck that reduces the runway utilization rate, especially when fast and slow aircraft are mixed in the approach stream or when arrivals from different directions must be merged on the common final approach path. As a result, the capacity of the airfield under IMC, when the long ILS common approach path must be used, is usually less than under VMC.

The runway utilization rate under IMC could come closer to that attainable under VMC if aircraft could follow multiple approach paths, descend at different approach angles, or aim at different touchdown points on the runway—none of which is practical with ILS. If this flexibility were possible, as it is under VMC, airfield capacity would be less affected by weather conditions, and throughput would be governed almost exclusively by runway geometry and aircraft performance characteristics.

The microwave landing system (MLS), which has been under development by FAA for more than a decade, would overcome some of the disadvantages inherent in the ILS. Because MLS uses a beam that scans a wide volume of airspace, rather than the pencil beam of ILS, it permits aircraft to fly any of several approach angles (including two-step glideslopes) and, in the horizontal plane, to approach along curving paths that intersect the extension of the runway centerline at any chosen point. In effect, MLS offers a degree of freedom in using the airspace that is closer to that enjoyed under conditions of good visibility (FIG. 9-1).

The chief motive for FAA in seeking to develop and deploy the MLS is not the potential capacity benefits, but its operational advantages—more precise guidance, ease of installation, improved reliability, less susceptibility to electromagnetic interference, and greater number of transmission channels. The capacity benefits are secondary but still of great importance at some airports where the present ILS acts to constrain capacity in adverse weather conditions. In terms of its effect on capacity, the chief advantage of MLS is that, in IMC, it allows pilots and controllers greater flexibility in selecting an approach path so as to shorten the approach time, to avoid air turbulence generated in the wake of preceding aircraft, or to avoid noise-sensitive areas.

Another advantage is that MLS can provide guidance for the aircraft during missed approach, allowing a safe exit from the terminal airspace and smooth reentry into the approach pattern. The availability of missed approach guidance could have a significant capacity benefit at those airports with parallel or converging runways that cannot now be used in IMC. A third advantage is that MLS can be installed on runways where ILS is not possible due to siting problems and on short auxiliary runways reserved for commuter and small general aviation (GA) aircraft. On some runways, MLS can increase capacity during IMC by providing lower landing minimums than ILS and thereby allowing the airport to remain

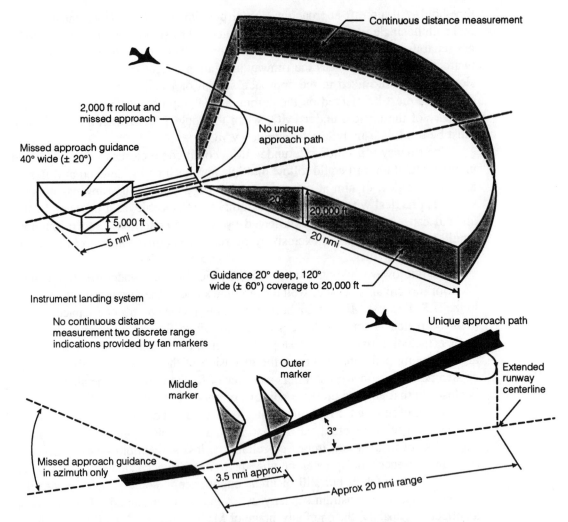

Fig. 9-1. Comparison of microwave landing system and instrument landing system. Federal Aviation Administration

open in marginal weather conditions. A fourth advantage of MLS is its capability to provide nonconflicting routes into closely situated airports, where approach or departure paths may mutually interfere and limit capacity utilization.

The capacity benefits of MLS are highly site-specific, depending on the runway configuration, the prevalence of adverse weather, the mix of aircraft using the airport, and the extent to which these aircraft are equipped with MLS receivers. Estimates by FAA indicate that the benefits could range up to 10 or 15 percent greater capacity at some airports under IMC. The overall effects on capacity at these airports would be somewhat smaller because they depend on how often instrument meteorological conditions occur.

FAA is now proceeding with MLS implementation. A contract for production and installation of 172 units was let in late 1983, with the first implementation expected by 1997. Priority will be given to large and medium hub airports and to those airports now lacking ILS because of siting restrictions or lack of available transmission channels.

Replacement of the existing ILS poses two problems that might complicate the transition of MLS and delay realization of the full benefits. There are at present about 650 ILS units in commission at some 460 airports and another 150 or so units in various stages of procurement—some as replacements for existing units, others as new installations. The MLS transition plan calls for these ILS units to remain in service for many years to come, until at least 60 percent of the aircraft routinely using the ILS/MLS runway are equipped with MLS. While ILS and MLS can be collocated and operated simultaneously without signal interference, there might be procedural difficulties in blending aircraft equipped with ILS (and therefore capable of only straight-in approaches) into a traffic stream with MLS-equipped aircraft flying curved or segmented approaches; thus, the full capacity of MLS might not be attainable at a given airport until all or nearly all aircraft are MLS-equipped and the ILS can be decommissioned.

A second factor that might delay taking full advantage of MLS at specific sites is the agreement with the International Civil Aviation Organization whereby the United States is committed to retaining ILS service at international gateway airports until 1995: 75 airports, generally the busiest U.S. airports and those most prone to capacity and delay problems. Retaining ILS service at these airports might influence some users to defer purchasing MLS equipment.

While the capacity gains attributable to MLS might be rather small for the airport system as a whole, MLS does appear to offer promise at those airports where it could be used to create a more flexible traffic pattern or to provide commuter and small GA aircraft access to an alternate runway in IMC, thereby relieving pressure on the main runway used by large air carrier aircraft. Beyond these direct benefits, moreover, MLS might permit procedural changes that could also increase capacity or reduce delay. These potential benefits of MLS are subsequently discussed in the section on airspace use procedures.

Surveillance radar

Surveillance is accomplished by radar and associated electronic and computer systems that locate, identify, and display the position of aircraft in the airspace. In terminal areas, two types of radar are presently used for this purpose: *search radar* (technically termed *primary radar*) and the *radar beacon system* (sometimes called *secondary radar*). Search radar emits signals and displays the returns reflected from the body of the aircraft, objects on the ground, and precipitation or weather fronts, thereby providing a basic two-dimensional map of the airspace. The beacon system, known as the *air traffic control radar beacon system* or

ATCRBS, displays only replies from aircraft equipped with electronic devices, called *transponders*, that send out a coded signal when interrogated by the radar beacon. This signal indicates not only the position of the aircraft but also its identity (flight number) and altitude (if the aircraft is equipped with an altitude-encoding transponder). The beacon system is presently the main source of surveillance information for air traffic control (ATC).

The radar-derived information is correlated and presented to the air traffic controller on one of four different types of display systems: TPX-42, ARTS II, ARTS III, or ARTS IIIA. The TPX-42 is the least sophisticated equipment. It is a nonprogrammable device that correlates and displays search radar data and beacon returns on each successive sweep of the antenna. The TPX-42 is used at airports with little traffic.

The *automated radar terminal system* (ARTS II) is a programmable data processor that displays primary and secondary radar data on the controller's scope but does not track aircraft or predict their position. It is used at airports with low to medium levels of activity.

ARTS III detects, tracks, and predicts the position of aircraft. This information is presented on the controller's display as computer-generated symbols (denoting altitude, ground speed, and identity) positioned alongside the secondary radar return. ARTS III also incorporates features that alert the controller when aircraft descend below minimum safe altitude or when two aircraft are approaching too closely and require action to assure safe separation—a feature known as *conflict alert*. ARTS IIIA is a refinement of ARTS III that is capable of tracking aircraft detected by search radar alone, aircraft not equipped with an ATCRBS transponder. ARTS III and ARTS IIIA equipment is installed at the 62 busiest air traffic hubs.

FAA is now in the process of replacing much of the primary radar and display equipment. The existing primary surveillance radars used at airports (ASR-4, ASR-5, and ASR-6) are based on vacuum tube technology that suffers from reliability problems and maintenance difficulties. Newer solid-state equipment (ASR-7 and ASR-8) has been installed at some locations, but these radars, like earlier versions of ASR, are adversely affected by ground clutter, false targets generated by flocks of birds, propagation anomalies, and masking of aircraft returns by weather. Of these shortcomings, weather masking is perhaps the most severe operational problem. The strong return from storms conceals the weaker return from aircraft detected on primary radar alone. To compensate, controllers alter the polarization of the radar to reduce weather echoes and make the aircraft return stand out more clearly, but this lessens the apparent severity of weather fronts and precipitation.

Between 1989 and 1992, FAA planned to install a new primary radar system (ASR-9) that will have a separate weather channel allowing the controller to assess the severity of storms while retaining the ability to detect small aircraft without transponders. The ASR-9 will also incorporate an improvement called *moving target detection* to overcome the problems of ground clutter and spurious targets. These improvements in primary radar information, when coupled with the present radar beacon display, will provide the controller with a clearer and more accurate picture of the airspace, thereby lessening workload and creating a better basis for decision-making about aircraft movement around the airport.

The immediate capacity benefit of the ASR-9 radars will be surveillance information of improved reliability and accuracy, which will provide the controller with a better picture of the airspace situation. Of even greater importance, the improved ASR-9 radar, the upgraded ARTS II and III, and the eventual installation of new sector suites for controllers will support changes in traffic management techniques that will help the controller make more efficient use of the airspace. These prospects are discussed next.

Traffic management techniques

A major task of the air traffic controller is management of traffic so as to maintain a smooth flow of aircraft to and from the airport with minimum delay. This is done by the techniques of metering, sequencing, and spacing. *Metering* is regulating the arrival time of aircraft in the terminal area so as not to exceed a given acceptance rate. *Sequencing* entails specifying the exact order in which aircraft will take off or land. *Spacing* involves establishing and maintaining the appropriate interval between successive aircraft, as dictated by considerations of safety, uniformity of traffic flow, and efficiency of runway use.

With current technology, these are largely matters of controller art that depend heavily on the individual's skill and experience. On a typical day, the controller must make literally hundreds of related decisions about the order and timing of aircraft movements in the traffic pattern under the prevailing conditions of wind and weather. The chief problems that the controller must deal with in performing these activities are randomness in the arrival and departure streams and differences in the speed and flight characteristics of successive aircraft using the airspace. The extent to which the controller is successful in applying the techniques of traffic management has a significant influence on delay and efficient use of airport capacity.

It has long been recognized by ATC experts that the key to more effective traffic management, especially in circumstances of heavy demand, it to involve computers in the decision-making process. In some instances, this means providing the controller with computerized aids to decision-making—devices to collect, integrate, and display information that will give a better picture of the traffic situation and help in executing a control strategy. In other instances—particularly where decision-making is routine, repetitive, and reducible to unambiguous rules—the approach is to substitute the computer for the human operator, relieving him of workload and guarding against human error and inconsistency.

As part of the planned modernization of the ATC system, FAA is developing new software packages that will assist in traffic management at and around airports. Known under the collective designation of *traffic management system (TMS)*, this new software will perform several important functions to increase the efficiency of airport and airspace utilization: airspace configuration management, dynamic planning and computation of acceptance rate, tactical execution of control strategy, runway configuration management, and departure flow metering.

For incoming flights, TMS will establish an acceptance rate and order of landing based on estimated arrival time and predetermined flight paths. As aircraft progress toward the runway, TMS will adjust landing time and spacing between aircraft as necessary to eliminate gaps or surges in the traffic stream and to make efficient use of airspace and runways. In the earlier stages of implementation, the computer will generate recommended instructions and command messages for the controller to relay to pilots by voice radio. In later stages, the computer will transmit commands directly to individual aircraft by the *Mode S data link*.

Mode S (for selective) is a proposed addition to the ATCRBS transponder that will permit direct, automatic exchange of digitally encoded information between the ground controller and individual aircraft.

Other components of TMS will contribute to more efficient traffic management in other ways. *Runway configuration management*, a software program that has been under development at Chicago O'Hare since the middle 1980s, will assist controllers in establishing the most efficient combination of arrival and departure runways for given conditions of weather and demand. Departure flow metering will help assure an appropriate blend of takeoffs and landings and will feed aircraft out of the terminal area and into en route airspace.

FAA plans do not call for implementation of TMS all at once. The components are being developed separately and will be tested and put in place when ready and where needed. The overall timetable is contingent on the development and installation of new computers and sector suites in terminal area control centers and on the development of companion software packages for the en route ATC system, the *advanced en route automation (AERA)* program. Full implementation of TMS, AERA, and related technological changes will not occur until 1998 or later.

TMS and AERA are tied together because FAA's long-term response to air traffic growth involves a general application of the flow management concept so as to provide strategic and tactical planning, continuous performance monitoring, and flexible and adaptive exercise of control for the airspace as a whole. For example, en route metering, which is a feature of AERA, will contribute to efficient runway use by treating all arrivals along all routes as a single traffic pattern and adjusting in-trail separation so as to achieve a steady rate of delivery into the terminal area. The present method of flow management, which uses uniform, preestablished in-trail separation, can result in inefficient runway utilization (surges and gaps in the traffic flow) because it cannot adapt readily when flow along arrival routes does not exactly match the nominal rate used as the basis for selecting in-trail spacing.

The capacity benefits of TMS are difficult to estimate on a systemwide basis. The anticipated benefits are highly specific to conditions at the airport site and particular patterns of demand. Further, it is not always possible to distinguish between the benefits of TMS and those that would result from other planned improvements in the ATC system.

Airspace use procedures

Procedures governing the use of terminal airspace and airport runways, which are designed primarily to assure safety, sometimes slow or disrupt the flow of traffic. In general, these procedures consist of rules and standards pertaining to the permissible distances between aircraft in various weather conditions and approach patterns. Actually, there are two sets of procedures: one for use in visual meteorological conditions (VMC) and another, more stringent, set for use in instrument meteorological conditions (IMC). Instrument flight rules often cause delays at busy airports because of the increased separation standards and special safeguards that must be applied in restricted visibility.

A widely held (but not unanimous) view among airspace users is that revisions of the existing instrument flight procedures are practical and that they would be warranted in the interest of reducing delay. While these revisions are sometimes spoken of as capacity improvements, they would not in most cases actually increase the capacity of airports. Instead, they would allow existing capacity to be used more fully or with greater efficiency and would bring the throughput attainable under IMS closer to what prevails under VMC.

In response to urging from airspace users, FAA instituted a comprehensive examination of airspace use procedures in October 1981. This effort, known as the *National Airspace Review (NAR)*, was a 42-month joint undertaking by FAA and the aviation industry "to identify and implement changes which will promote greater efficiency for all airspace users and simplify [the ATC] system. Additionally, the NAR will match airspace allocations and air traffic procedures to technological improvements and fuel efficiency programs." The portion of NAR concerned specifically with terminal area ATC procedures was completed in July 1984.

Many of the procedural changes sought by airspace users and under study by FAA in NAR were also examined by a special aviation industry task force convened at the request of FAA under the auspices of the Airport Operators Council International. The task force report strongly urged FAA to revise present airspace use procedures, especially those pertaining to the use of multiple runways under instrument meteorological conditions.

Reduced lateral separation

Several of the proposed revisions would permit changes in the standards for lateral separation of aircraft under instrument flight conditions. The present standards often severely restrict throughput because they preclude use of all the available runways when visibility is reduced. If the airport could continue to operate these runways, the disparity between IMC and VMC acceptance rates could be substantially narrowed. The following are the major capacity-related changes under consideration.

Converging runways   Converging runway extended centerlines meet at a point beyond the runways. Simultaneous approaches to converging runways are presently authorized only during VMC. The proposed procedures would extend this authorization to IMC in certain circumstances. The major problem to be overcome in using converging runways under instrument conditions is development of procedures to assure separation in the event of a blunder by one of the aircraft during the approach or in case both aircraft must execute a missed approach at the same time. These procedures, in turn, depend on the availability of improved surveillance radar, MLS to provide missed approach guidance, and perhaps automated aids for the controller to coordinate simultaneous approaches to two runways.

In time, it might be possible to extend these procedures to the case of intersecting runways: surfaces actually cross at some point. In addition to the problems of blunder protection and separation assurance during missed approaches, this configuration poses the risk of collision between two aircraft on the ground, and there must be adequate safeguards that aircraft on both runways can stop or turn off before reaching the intersection. Because of the inherent safety problems, most observers are skeptical about the feasibility of using this type of runway layout for instrument operations.

Dependent parallel runways   At present, instrument approaches may be conducted on parallel runways that are as close as 3,000 feet apart so long as a diagonal separation of 2 nautical miles (nmi) is maintained between adjacent aircraft. For parallel runways separated by 2,500 feet, the diagonal spacing requirement is 2.5 nmi. In addition, aircraft must be separated by 1,000 feet vertically and 3 nmi horizontally as they turn onto their parallel approach paths. These runways are termed dependent because the approaches to each must be coordinated to maintain the prescribed diagonal spacing; hence, the operational rate attainable on either is constrained by the movement of aircraft on the other.

FAA studies suggest that the diagonal spacing requirements for IFR operation on dependent parallel runways could be reduced. For runways separated by 2,500 feet, the standard could be reduced from the present 2.5 nmi to 2 nmi with current technology and no other changes in existing procedures. Reducing the spacing requirements for approaches to parallel runways less than 2,500 feet apart requires: 1) that the pilot be able to confirm that he is on approach to the proper runway because radar surveillance would no longer be sufficient; and 2) that wake vortices from aircraft approaching one runway do not interfere with operations on the other. Because of wake vortex, current procedures require that aircraft approaches to closely spaced parallel runways (less than 2,500 feet apart) be treated as approaches to a single runway and separated accordingly.

An operational solution to the wake vortex problem on closely spaced parallel runways entails that the following additional conditions be met:

1. There must be a steady crosswind to diminish the effects of wake vortex, but the wind velocity must be less than maximum crosswind limitation.

2. Small aircraft that are vulnerable to wake vortices must use the upwind runway of the closely spaced pair.

3. The threshold of the upwind runways must be displaced from that of the downwind runway.

4. The upwind runway must have a high-angle glideslope to allow for a steeper descent by vulnerable aircraft so that they can remain above, and hence avoid, wake vortices.

5. Wind monitors must be set up along the approach path to ascertain that conditions are favorable for the dissipation of wake vortices.

Satisfying these five requirements might be difficult at airports that do not have runways with suitably staggered thresholds and a sufficiently large number of aircraft that can approach at a steeper-than-normal glideslope to avoid wake turbulence. In addition, there are operational difficulties that might limit the applicability or the capacity benefits of this procedure. First, the wake vortex generated by a heavy aircraft carrying out a missed approach could interfere with operations on the other runway. One possible solution would be to require that both the leading and trailing aircraft execute missed approaches along diverging paths whenever the leading heavy aircraft misses the approach. Second, interference from departures could limit capacity gains because it might be necessary to retain present longitudinal separation standards between heavy aircraft departing on one runway and small aircraft landing on the other in order to avoid wake turbulence. Finally, as the distance between parallel approaches is reduced, there will be a need for more accurate surveillance to verify that aircraft are on approach to the proper runway. The radar now in use, which has a 5-milliradian accuracy and a 4-second update rate, is probably not adequate for this purpose and might have to be replaced with new radar capable of 1-milliradian accuracy and 1-second update. Such radar performance has been achieved in the precision approach radar system formerly installed at some airports but now decommissioned. Military radar also has this capability, but would have to be adapted and tested before use in civil aviation.

Independent parallel runways   Independent instrument approaches to parallel runways separated by at least 4,300 feet are presently authorized under the following conditions: (1) when aircraft are turned onto the approach path, they must be separated vertically by at least 1,000 feet or laterally by 3 nmi from aircraft turning on approach to the other runway; and (2) a "No Transgression Zone," at least 2,000 feet wide, must be maintained between the approaches, with a separate controller assigned to monitor this zone. A study by FAA indicates that, as with dependent parallel runways, reducing lateral spacing for independent parallel runways from 4,300 to 3,000 feet would require installation of radar with improved accuracy but no other changes in current procedures.

Triple parallel runways   Demand at some of the busier airports, such as O'Hare, Atlanta, Dallas-Forth Worth, Pittsburgh, and Detroit, sometimes exceeds the capacity of the runway system in IMC, and addition of a third approach stream would be desirable. Current ATC procedures allow approaches to triple parallel runways only during VMC. Revision of separation standards to permit their use during IMC would significantly expand the time that maximum airfield capacity is available at these few very busy airports.

   While the requirements for three parallel approaches are similar to those for two parallel approaches, the addition of a third runway complicates the approach procedures and limits possible gains in capacity utilization. To be most effective, at least the outside pair of approaches should be independent from each other, although both might be dependent on the middle runway. If all three parallel runways were dependent, there would be only a minor increase in throughput compared to that attainable with two dependent runways. Also, because a blunder on one of the outside approaches could affect more than one other aircraft, establishment of triple independent parallel approaches necessitates two "No Transgression Zones," with a separate controller assigned to monitor each. Because the 1,000 foot vertical separation rule for aircraft turning onto parallel approach paths sill applies, final approach courses, particularly for the center runway, would be longer—thereby diminishing somewhat the throughput gain attainable with the triple parallel configuration.

   A few airports have runway layouts that allow a converging approach to be added to two existing parallel approaches. This third approach is used during VMC, but in IMC the converging runway must be closed because separation between aircraft executing missed approaches cannot be assured visually.

   The requirements for three approaches, one of which is converging, are similar to those for two converging approaches; however, establishing the third converging approach for use with a parallel pair involves additional safeguards because a blunder by an aircraft on one of the outside approaches affects more than one other aircraft. The missed approach path for the converging runway must be coordinated with those of the other two runways—a procedure that is quite complex and cannot be implemented without further research and evaluation. In particular, FAA is studying whether MLS will be required to provide nonconflicting missed approach paths.

Reduced longitudinal separation on final approach

Current procedures require longitudinal (in-trail) separation of 3 nmi between aircraft conducting instrument approaches to the same runway. When there is a hazard of wake turbulence, these longitudinal separation standards are increased to 4 to 6 nmi depending on the size of the leading and following aircraft. In VMC, in-trail separations of 2.5 nmi and even 2 nmi are not uncommon depending on the runway geometry, the observed runway occupancy time, and the mix of aircraft. Proposals have been advanced to reduce the IMC standard to 2.5 nmi immediately, and perhaps to 2 nmi eventually for certain airports and runway configurations.

One determinant of the longitudinal separation standard is the length of time needed for aircraft to leave the runway after landing (runway occupancy time). As a safety measure, current ATC procedures do not permit two aircraft to occupy a runway at the same time. FAA studies have shown that runway occupancy time at many major airports averages between 41 and 63 seconds. For those airports where runway occupancy time averages fewer than 50 seconds, FAA studies indicate that minimum in-trail separation of 2.5 nmi could be allowed in circumstances where wake vortex and ATC workload permit. Flight tests conducted by the U.S. Air Force have demonstrated the feasibility of 2.5-mile separation for military use. However, safety standards for commercial operations are different than those for military operations, and analysis of radar accuracy and update rates, controller and pilot response times, and aircraft performance characteristics will be needed to determine whether 2.5-mile separation during IMC is safe for civil aviation. Because there is a direct relationship between in-trail separation and throughput, this procedural change would be a very effective method to reduce delay under instrument flight conditions.

Present ATC procedures specify that the nominal longitudinal separation standards for VMC or IMC be adjusted to compensate for the possible effects of wake turbulence. These separation standards are based on a three-way classification of aircraft according to gross takeoff weight and an attempt to account for the wake-turbulence characteristics of aircraft and their vulnerability to wake vortex encounters:

1. Heavy aircraft: maximum gross takeoff weight (GTW) in excess of 300,000 pounds.
2. Large aircraft: maximum GTW between 12,500 and 300,000 pounds.
3. Small aircraft: maximum GTW fewer than 12,500 pounds.

Definition of aircraft categories based on GTW alone is not necessarily an accurate index of wake vortex generation for all aircraft, notably those aircraft whose GTW is slightly over 300,000 pounds such as the DC-8 and B-767. As the number of B-767 aircraft in the fleet grows and as the reengining program for DC-8s proceeds, aircraft whose GTW is roughly 300,000 pounds will become an increasingly large proportion of the commercial aircraft fleet. If these aircraft continue to be classified as "heavy," greater arrival separations will be required, with adverse effects on capacity and delay.

If aircraft were classified on the basis of more precise analytical or empirical data concerning their specific aerodynamic and wake vortex characteristics, it might be possible to reduce the in-trail separation rules for some types. As a minimum, the use of approach weight rather than maximum GTW as the basis for separation criteria could be considered.

Separate short runways for small aircraft

The current practice in air traffic control is to organize aircraft on approach according to time of arrival, not type of aircraft. So long as the traffic mix is reasonably uniform, this practice has a minor effect on throughput. At many airports, however, small aircraft represent a significant portion of traffic. To avoid wake turbulence generated by the heavy and large classes of transports, these small aircraft are required to follow in-trail at distances of 4 to 6 nmi from the larger aircraft. Because many of these small aircraft operate at slow speeds, safety requires that larger and faster aircraft be spaced more than 3 nmi behind so that the leading small aircraft are not overtaken on approach. One way to overcome these operational penalties would be to segregate small general aviation and some commuter aircraft into a separate traffic stream using a different (short) runway. At some airports such a runway is already available but not usable for instrument approaches because of inadequate instrumentation; at others, new runways would have to be built and equipped with MLS.

There is some disadvantage to separate short runways in that they do not provide as much operational flexibility as a full-length additional air carrier runway; however, the separate short runway can be built at a fraction of the cost of an air carrier runway, and runway siting problems as well as local environmental issues might be easier to resolve.

Ideally, the separate short runways for small aircraft should be parallel to and operate independently from the main runway used by large air carrier traffic. A short runway that is not parallel to the main runway would not be available for use in IMC unless revised procedures for converging instrument approaches are also implemented; but even so, dependency on the main runway would limit the throughput gain because of the need to coordinate the two traffic streams. If the procedures described above to reduce spacing requirements for independent and dependent parallel approaches prove feasible, the siting of these short secondary runways could become easier.

Another development that would facilitate siting of short runways and broaden the applicability of the concept would be installation of MLS to allow curved approaches and steeper glideslopes by small aircraft, not only to alleviate wake turbulence problems but also to achieve a greater rate of runway use.

Weather and atmospheric effects

Perhaps the single greatest technological need in improving capacity and reducing delay at airports, aside from improved radar to monitor aircraft more closely spaced in terminal airspace, is development of techniques to improve the detection and prediction of weather and atmospheric effects. Weather-related technologies are typically viewed as safety improvements rather than capacity improvements, but there are significant exceptions, notably methods to protect from wake vortices. Current aircraft arrival and departure separations are predicated in large part on avoidance of wake vortices, and the key to many of the revised approach procedures described above is a better method to detect or to predict the occurrence of wake turbulence.

Beyond this, improvement in the ability to predict weather and atmospheric phenomena could lead to general reductions in delay. Present technology does not always permit sufficiently accurate prediction of the time and magnitude of adverse weather conditions, making it necessary to increase safety margins and thereby reduce throughput. The ability to foresee disruptions due to weather would permit planning to compensate for the impacts on traffic flow.

Wake vortex

Wake vortex or *wake turbulence* is an aerodynamic disturbance that originates at the wingtips and trails in corkscrew fashion behind the aircraft. Because the strength of the turbulence increases with lift, the strongest vortices occur behind heavy aircraft. These vortices spread downward and outward in the wake of the aircraft and might persist along the flight path for as long as two or three minutes in still air. When the aircraft is within 300 feet of the ground, the vortices can bounce off terrain and rise back toward the flight path, creating even more disturbance. Wake turbulence can be of such strength and duration that it poses a hazard to following aircraft (especially smaller aircraft), and present procedures require separation of 3 to 6 nmi depending on the size of the leading and following aircraft and the movement of the airmass.

Alternatives to the present procedural method of avoiding wake turbulence are being sought both in the interest of safety and for the capacity benefits that could be realized through closer spacing of aircraft in the approach zone. Two avenues are being taken. FAA has concentrated on development of techniques to detect wake vortex and to predict its movement and persistence. NASA has focused on aerodynamic research to provide better understanding of the mechanics and causes of wake vortex and to develop designs to alleviate it at the source. NASA research indicates that certain combinations of flaps, spoilers, and protrusions on wing surfaces can reduce turbulence or cause it to dissipate more quickly. Unfortunately, many of these techniques also tend to increase noise and reduce energy efficiency. Work is continuing on ways to minimize wake vortex at an acceptable price in terms of noise and fuel consumption, but no ready solution is in sight. This is an important area of research and development because the alternative, wake vortex detection and avoidance, has not been perfected to the point that pilots have confidence in its reliability.

FAA has sought to develop equipment and a concept of operation that provide real-time vortex sensing capability and to devise a predictive algorithm that will warn pilots and controllers. An experimental device, known as *vortex advisory system (VAS)*, was installed and tested at O'Hare in 1978. VAS is made up of wind sensors mounted on towers along the approach path, a central computer to process wind data and predict the strength and movement of wake turbulence, and a display to alert the controller when a hazardous condition exists. VAS has not yet proven operationally acceptable, and FAA plans further development and testing.

The disadvantage of VAS is that it does not detect wake vortices; it only measures wind direction and velocity, from which an inference can be made about the presence and strength of wake turbulence. This deficiency is particularly evident farther out on the approach path (beyond the middle marker) and in crosswind conditions where turbulence on one approach path might migrate to a parallel approach. To overcome these limitations, FAA is also investigating other technological approaches such as short-wave radar, lasers, and infrared devices that could provide better long-range sensing and wider coverage.

No practical solution is now in view, and it seems likely that procedural methods to avoid wake turbulence will continue to be employed. So long as wake vortices cannot be reliably detected and predicted, the present separation standards (perhaps with some modification to account for the aerodynamic characteristics of specific types of aircraft) will remain in force and preclude any throughput gains that might be achieved through reduced in-trail spacing.

Wind shear

Wind shear is any sudden change in wind velocity or direction. It may be associated with warm and cold fronts, low-level jet streams, or mountainous terrain. One of the most dangerous types of wind shear is a downward surge of air striking the ground and spreading out in all directions. This kind of wind shear is often associated with thunderstorms, but it might occur in other weather conditions. These downdrafts, called *microbursts*, are difficult to predict because they are small and localized, extending only two or three miles and often lasting fewer than five minutes.

For the pilot of an aircraft, wind shear is experienced as an abrupt increase or decrease of lift (or often one rapidly followed by the other) caused by a sudden shift in the wind. In this condition, the aircraft might gain or lose altitude unexpectedly and become difficult to control in angle of attack and flight path. If this occurs near the ground on takeoff or landing, there can be extreme hazard. While the primary concern is safety of flight, wind shear also disrupts airport activities and can cause suspension of operations until the condition abates.

In 1982, the federal government undertook a project known as Joint Airport Weather Studies (JAWS) to provide a better understanding of wind shear, thunderstorms, and related weather hazards and to identify weather conditions that could be warning signs to pilots: A multiagency effort involving the National Science Foundation, the National Aeronautics and Space Administration, the National Oceanic and Atmospheric Administration, and the Federal Aviation Administration. JAWS collected data on downbursts at Denver Stapleton Airport during a three-month period in the summer of 1982. The knowledge of wind shear gained through JAWS will contribute to the *low level wind shear alert system* (LLWSAS) that provides the air traffic control tower with information on wind conditions near the runway. LLWSAS consists of an array of anemometers that read wind velocity and direction around the airport and signal the sudden changes that indicate wind shear.

Over the longer term, FAA is developing other systems intended to provide better and more timely weather information at airports, both to improve safety and to help in traffic management. The *automated weather observing system* (AWOS) will gather weather data from unmanned sensors, automatically formulate weather reports, and distribute them to airport control towers. AWOS will also broadcast this information to pilots as voice synthesized messages over VHF radio. Implementation of the system, scheduled for the period 1985–94, began with a one-year demonstration program in 1985 when 21 units were put into operation at towered and nontowered airports in various locations. Full deployment at 745 airports is scheduled to begin in 1994. A similar system, *joint automated weather observation system* (JAWOS), is planned for installation at some medium and large hub airports. JAWOS will automatically gather local weather data and distribute it to other air traffic control facilities and to the National Weather Service.

In cooperation with the Department of Defense and the National Oceanic and Atmospheric Administration, FAA is also developing a next generation nationwide weather network based on pulsed Doppler radar (NEXRAD). This network will provide precipitation, reflectivity, wind velocity, and turbulence information with better accuracy. NEXRAD will probably not provide the minute-to-minute observations needed to detect small localized downbursts that produce wind shear, or detect wind shear in the absence of precipitation. Still, NEXRAD will greatly improve the quality and comprehensiveness of the weather information available to air traffic controllers and will be a significant aid in managing traffic to compensate for adverse weather conditions. A total procurement of 160 units is planned.

Noise control and abatement

Aircraft noise, especially the noise of jet aircraft, is one of the greatest barriers to airport utilization and expansion, and it is the most common subject of complaint by airport neighbors. The areas of severest noise impact are just beyond the ends of runways, but noise levels can be unacceptably high elsewhere along approach and departure paths where aircraft are close to the ground. In legal actions brought by airport neighbors, the courts have generally found that the airport operator is responsible for injury due to reduced property value or nuisance and have awarded damages to property owners and others affected by noise.

Noise is reduced two ways. One is to quiet the aircraft themselves, notably the engines, and FAA has imposed progressively stricter noise standards for aircraft in FAR 36 and FAR 91. FAR Part 36 defines noise requirements for certification of new aircraft and engines. FAR Part 91 sets the timetable for compliance and calls for retirement or retrofit of aircraft (both foreign and domestic) that did not comply with FAR Part 36 by 1985. To protect air service to small communities, FAR Part 91 allowed three additional years (until 1988) for twin-engine aircraft with 100 or fewer seats to achieve compliance.

As a result, new aircraft entering service are much quieter than earlier models, and some older aircraft have been equipped with new, quieter engines. While research is continuing on aircraft noise, airframe and engine manufacturers tend to the view that large-scale and cost-effective advances in the technology of noise suppression will be increasingly difficult to find.

The other approach has been to impose operational restrictions on airports— principally in the form of limits on the hours of use, frequency of flights, and the approach and departure routes that may be taken. Airport operators and airlines have resisted these measures because they reduce the capacity of the airport overall or at peak times and because noise abatement flight procedures often result in lengthier, less fuel-efficient paths to and from the airport. Recent studies by the FAA and others have suggested the need to loosen some of these restrictions in the interest of increasing airport capacity and promoting efficient utilization of aircraft.

The discussion that follows addresses prospective improvements in aircraft technology that might lessen noise and examines procedural solutions to alleviate the noise problem.

Aircraft noise

Aircraft noise has two components: engine noise produced by moving engine parts and by air flow through the engine, and airframe noise caused by the passage of air over aircraft surfaces. In early jet aircraft, the engine was the predominant noise source. Advances in engine technology over the past 20 years have reduced engine noise to the point where the engine and the airframe are now about equal contributors to aircraft noise on landing. The engine is still the major noise source on takeoff.

Engine noise   The principal sources of noise in a jet engine are: (1) the fan, (2) the compressor and turbine, and (3) the exhaust. The relative importance of these sources varies somewhat with the design of the engine and the operating regime, but exhaust noise is generally the greatest of the three.

Efforts to reduce fan noise have centered on altering the design of the fan blades and incorporating sound absorbing material in the fan case and the inlet and discharge ducts. Typically, this sound absorption is accomplished by a liner of porous material backed by cavities to trap sound. The newer aircraft engines now in service incorporate these design concepts, but further, small noise reductions might still be achieved.

Compressor and turbine noises are generated inside the engine by the compression, heating, and expansion of the air passing through. Methods for reducing compressor and turbine noise have included redesign of compressor parts and turbine blades to modify their sound characteristics, and use of sound-absorbing material. Because the ability to alter the design or configuration of the compressor or turbine is limited by mechanical and aerodynamic considerations and engine load requirements, it is expected that the principal method to attain further reductions in compressor and turbine noise will be acoustic treatment in the intake ducts. Research is now aimed at development of improved acoustic material capable of withstanding the hot and cold environment of the compressor and turbine, and at reducing the cost of these noise suppression treatments.

Exhaust noise results from the turbulent mixing of hot, high-speed exhaust gases with the ambient air. The way to reduce this noise is through techniques that lower the temperature and velocity differential between the exhaust and the outside air, but without loss of engine efficiency and thrust. In the early, pure turbojet engines, all of the intake air was passed through the hot section of the engine, from which it exited at high velocity. These engines were very noisy. A later development diverted some of the air from the compressor around the combustion chamber and turbine and merged it with the exhaust stream—thus shielding the high-velocity exhaust with a cooler, slower moving sheath of air from the compressor. These low-bypass ratio engines were more efficient and proved, on average, to be about 8 decibels (dB) quieter than pure turbojets. The bypass ratio is the amount of air diverted around the combustor relative to that which passes through it. Engines introduced in the 1970s made use of an even higher bypass ratio to achieve both greater fuel efficiency and a further 8-to-10 dB reduction of noise. For reference, a change of 3 dB is just perceptible to the human ear. A reduction of about 10 dB is perceived as halving the annoyance of a sound source.

Engine manufacturers are continuing to explore techniques such as high-pressure turbines, exhaust diffusers, and improved internal cooling methods—principally to increase engine efficiency but also for their potential to reduce noise. They are also evaluating internal flow mixers to combine low-velocity bypass air with higher velocity engine flow to produce an exhaust stream with less turbulence and a more uniform exit velocity. These efforts are yielding diminishing returns because further noise reduction involves very tightly coupled tradeoffs with fuel efficiency, production techniques, and maintenance costs. Attainment of noise levels significantly lower than those of FAR Part 36 appears to be very difficult without a sacrifice of fuel efficiency or a large cost penalty.

Airframe noise   Airframe noise stems primarily from turbulent air flow past the undercarriage, leading and trailing edges of high-lift devices, aircraft cavities, and projections from the aircraft surface. For an aircraft in flight, these noises intermingle and are not usually distinguishable as to source. The principal methods available to reduce aerodynamic noise are wing design, high-lift systems, and aircraft streamlining.

Recent development in aircraft wing design has included supercritical airfoil sections and winglets. Fundamentally, the supercritical airfoil and winglets reduce drag and provide additional lift, but they also serve to reduce aerodynamic noise somewhat. Drag is exhibited as turbulence in the wake of aircraft, and turbulence produces noise. Further, insofar as reduced drag and increased lift permit the aircraft to be operated at lower power settings on takeoff and landing, these aerodynamic improvements might provide a secondary benefit of reduced engine noise.

Advanced high-lift systems make use of two-segment trailing edge flaps and a variable camber on the leading edge of the wing. High-lift devices of this sort are currently used on short takeoff and landing (STOL) aircraft such as the deHavilland DHC 7. They have also been incorporated in some large transport aircraft. The 747 and later model 727 aircraft have triple-slotted flaps, and the 767 has both variable camber leading-edge flaps and double-slotted trailing edge flaps. These systems do not necessarily produce quieter aircraft, they might be noisier; however, high-lift devices permit steeper approach and takeoff paths, thereby reducing the size and severity of the aircraft noise footprint on the ground and leading, in effect, to less aircraft noise overall.

Techniques to streamline aircraft include placement of fairings around extended landing gear and other projections from the aircraft surface and enclosure of wing and body cavities. Such features are intended primarily to improve the aerodynamic performance of the aircraft, but they could also lessen aerodynamic noise. Another streamlining technique involves strategic placement of the engines at locations where the airframe can act as a shield for engine noise. There are critical tradeoffs between engine placement and aircraft performance and safety that need to be treated carefully. There is also a need for additional research to improve the understanding of how the engines and airframe interact in the production and suppression of noise.

Many of the techniques described above might lessen aerodynamic noise, but the overall reduction would probably be rather small. There is a widely held view among aircraft designers that the newest aircraft are close to the practical lower limit of aerodynamic noise and that further reductions will be technically difficult, prohibitively costly, and perhaps disadvantageous for other aspects of aircraft performance. While some of these techniques will be pursued and might be incorporated in future aircraft, the general opinion is that there are no aerodynamic solutions that will lead to large-scale reductions in aircraft noise.

Aircraft operating procedures

In addition to technological measures to reduce noise at the source, there is the procedural solution of operating aircraft in a way that alleviates the effect on noise-sensitive areas. Many such measures have already been adopted—some locally, some more generally—and work is continuing to improve these procedures, to devise new ones, or to extend their application more widely.

Procedures in use today are limited, in some cases, by safety and capacity considerations and by the capabilities of the ATC system. The ability to apply these procedures is also affected by conditions of wind, weather, and visibility. Perhaps the greatest deficiency is that restrictions are applied airport by airport, often as a result of local ordinance, in a fashion that is fragmentary, confusing, and inefficient. Aircraft operators complain that both airport capacity and aircraft utility are wasted and that market opportunities are lost. The Airport Access Task Force of the former Civil Aeronautics Board (CAB) devoted major attention to the question of noise abatement procedures and urged the federal government to reduce the number of locally imposed aircraft operating restrictions and to develop nationally applicable procedures that would appropriately balance public concerns about noise with the interests of air commerce.

Prospective advances in technology might make some of the procedures in use today more effective or less onerous to aircraft operators. One such procedure is departure thrust management, which necessitates adjustments in power settings during climbout and exit from the terminal area. As newer aircraft with better performance characteristics and quieter engines come to dominate the fleet, these departure practices might be easier to implement, or—in some instances—they may not be required as often. The CAB Airport Access Task Force estimated that phasing out aircraft with low-bypass engines (from 94 percent of the fleet in 1980–81 to 10 percent by 2000) would produce an average noise reduction of almost 6 dB systemwide, even if operations were to increase by 50 percent.

Preferential runway use is another method for reducing the extent or severity of noise impact on the surrounding community. This involves using, whenever possible, those runways that minimize the number of people or the area exposed to aircraft noise. The effectiveness of preferential runway use is site-specific because it depends on the runway layout in relation to land use patterns, the prevailing wind and weather, and the installation of navigation and landing aids. Implementation of the traffic management system and deployment of MLS might make it possible to extend this practice to other airports or allow it to be used in a wider spectrum of weather conditions.

On the other hand, preferential runway use has the effect of exposing the unfortunate few who live or work in affected areas to more unremitting noise than might be considered their ''fair share.'' For this reason, it might be more equitable to temper preferential runway use with some variation of runway use patterns. Distributing noise more uniformly among areas surrounding the airport would lessen the impact on some, but at the risk of antagonizing perhaps far more who are not presently exposed to aircraft noise.

Preferential flight paths are prescribed routines for arriving and departing aircraft to avoid overflight of noise-sensitive areas. This procedure is frequently combined with preferential runway use, but may be used even where the airport has only a simple runway layout. At some airports, the use of preferential flight paths is limited by the availability or capability of the installed landing and navigation aids. It is expected that MLS will enhance the ability to use noise-avoidance flight paths because it provides more precise and flexible approach guidance with a wider range of coverage than the existing ILS. MLS would permit multiple final approach paths, including curved approaches. The ability to fly curved approach paths will enable aircraft to avoid noise-sensitive areas in IMC much as they do now in VMC and will aid in the reduction of noise levels for airports with noise-sensitive land uses located under the straight-in approach path. MLS would also allow some aircraft to fly steeper approach paths, which—by keeping aircraft higher as they pass over development around the airport—will reduce the area of high noise impact. In FAA studies of the application of MLS to specific sites, it was found that the use of curved and segmented IMC approaches made possible by installation of MLS at airports such as LaGuardia, Minneapolis, San Francisco, Seattle, and Washington National could lead to significant noise reductions.

Airport surface utilization

An airport is an interconnected set of physical facilities and components. For it to function efficiently, the capacities of each of these elements must be matched. Relief of a bottleneck in one part of the airport will not have the desired effect on overall throughput unless other parts are capable of absorbing a greater influx of traffic. Indeed, a common experience is that enlargement of one part of the airport complex simply shifts the delay elsewhere, to the next most constraining element.

Nowhere is this more evident than on the airport surface. Measures to augment runway capacity or to increase the flow of traffic through the airspace might be of little practical benefit unless aircraft are able to move expeditiously on and off runways and to and from the terminal building. It is on airport taxiways and aprons that aircraft are closest together and that their speed is lowest. If the movement of aircraft on the airport surface is constrained by runway and taxiway design and layout, by operational procedures, or by poor visibility, the effect ripples throughout the airport and airspace, and delays accumulate.

This section examines three types of technology deployed on the airport surface: surveillance and control systems, taxiway design and lighting, and equipment used at parking aprons and gates. In general, new airport surface utilization technologies will not lead to major increases of airside capacity, which is largely determined by available runways and airspace use procedures. The primary capacity benefits are indirect—increased safety, especially during inclement weather, and relief of operational impediments to making efficient use of the airside.

Surveillance and control

Surveillance and control of aircraft movement on the airport surface is accomplished largely by visual means. In darkness or fog—and even in good visibility at large, complex airports—*airport surface detection equipment (ASDE)* is used by air traffic controllers and augment and confirm information obtained from visual surveillance of the airport surface. Used primarily at high activity airports, ASDE allows controllers to locate and monitor the movement of aircraft and ground equipment on runways, taxiways, and apron areas.

Federal Aviation Administration

Federal Aviation Administration controllers at the air traffic control tower at North Philadelphia Airport.

The existing equipment, designated ASDE-2, utilizes tube technology, which presents reliability and maintenance problems. In addition, utility of ASDE-2 is limited by display resolution, brightness, airport map definition, and poor weather penetration capability. The last is particularly significant under conditions of precipitation or fog, when the system is needed the most. Under these conditions, visual surveillance is virtually impossible, and ASDE is the controller's primary means to obtain the necessary information.

A new system utilizing solid state technology is programmed for deployment by 1991–94. This system, ASDE-3, is expected to increase reliability and reduce system maintenance, in addition to improving display resolution and weather penetration. More accurate information on the specific location and movement of aircraft and ground equipment on the airport surface provided by ASDE-3 might allow reductions in safety-dictated separation of aircraft and promote more efficient utilization of runways and taxiways. Ultimately, small gains in airfield capacity could result.

Research and development on more advanced systems will be needed, since even ASDE-3 cannot identify aircraft and surface vehicles under all weather conditions or be used by the controller to guide them to their destinations. At present, the capability of navigation systems to help aircraft land in very low visibility (category IIIC operations) exceeds that of surveillance and control systems to guide them after they are on the airport surface.

The *tower automated ground surveillance system (TAGS)* is a display enhancement intended for use in conjunction with ASDE at major airports. The ASDE-3 search radar provides a map of the airport and the location of aircraft on the airport surface, which are shown graphically on the ASDE display. TAGS will provide, for transponder-equipped aircraft, a flight identification label alongside the position indicator on the ASDE display. Because TAGS operates by receiving a signal transmitted directly by aircraft equipment, the system would be virtually immune to weather. Presentation of flight identity by TAGS would also improve ground control capability in good visibility. TAGS is presently in the exploratory phase of development and probably will not be ready for deployment until the middle 1990s.

Taxiways

The design and layout of taxiways—particularly those that provide egress from runways—have an important effect on *runway occupancy time (ROT)*. Runway occupancy time is measured from the time an approaching aircraft crosses the threshold until it turns off the runway or from the time a departing aircraft takes the active runway until it clears the departure end. Current ATC rules prohibit two aircraft from occupying the runway at the same time.

The placement of exit taxiways, where landing aircraft turn off the runways, and the angle at which these taxiways intersect the runways can be crucial. Poorly placed exit taxiways prolong runway occupancy by forcing incoming aircraft to taxi at low speed for some distance before clearing the runway. Taxiways that leave the runway at right angles force the aircraft to come almost to a complete stop before turning. Because the runway occupancy rule (with a few exceptions in VMC) does not allow an approaching aircraft to cross the runway threshold while the preceding aircraft remains on the runway, longer runway occupancy either forces the air traffic controller to increase arrival spacing or causes some approaching aircraft to execute a go-around, both of which are disruptive of throughput.

At some airports, relocating taxiways so that aircraft with shorter stopping distances can leave the runway sooner would lower ROT by as much as 20 to 30 percent. At others, providing a drift-off area alongside the runway or redesigning taxiways so that they diverge from the runway gradually and allow aircraft to turn off at higher speeds (sooner after landing) would have much the same effect; however, translating reduced ROT into a corresponding throughput gain is not straightforward because it depends on whether the runway layout, the airspace geometry, and the ATC procedures will permit closer arrival spacing to take advantage of the shorter runway occupancy.

Marking and lighting of taxiways can be as important as their design and physical layout in expediting ground movement of aircraft. For runway exits to be used to their full potential, pilots must be able to detect their location and identify the one they are to use with ample lead time. This is especially critical at night and during periods of poor visibility. A taxiway marking and lighting system that conveys the necessary information to pilots in a clearly understandable fashion promotes more efficient utilization of airfield pavements.

Research and development are in progress on several aspects of marking and lighting. For exit taxiways, the major efforts are to improve the lighting pattern and the configuration, spacing, and orientation of components in a way that promotes ready identification of the exit and provides visual guidance for safe and prompt transition from the runway to the taxiway. Among the areas under study are improved lighting and signing for taxiway intersections, traffic control signals and lighting systems for ground guidance, and methods for controlling lighting patterns and intensity from the tower. Development is also proceeding on new lighting techniques such as lights that use low voltage electricity, light-emitting diodes, and electroluminescent components to relieve some of the deficiencies of present lighting, which pilots characterize as "the blueberry pie maze."

To optimize the use of airport pavements and to make proper decisions related to safety, pilots and controllers must have accurate and up-to-date information on surface conditions that affect aircraft ground movement and stopping characteristics. Perhaps the most noticeable changes in these characteristics are aircraft braking and stopping distance on wet or icy pavement, which are important not only from a safety standpoint but also because of the effect on capacity.

One major effort is to devise pavement designs and surface treatments that will improve traction. Research is also being conducted on means to provide information that will allow pilots and controllers to predict aircraft stopping capability and skid risk more accurately under various runway surface conditions. Items such as pavement sensors that continuously monitor pavement condition and coefficients of friction are being examined. Attention is also directed at development of better methods to convey this information to the pilot and, ideally, to provide braking guidance or warning of specific hazardous conditions and locations. The primary concern is safety, but better information about pavement condition and aircraft performance when traction is reduced would also yield a capacity benefit in that a more accurate delineation of safety limits might make it possible to relax some of the present conservative rules governing aircraft movement on the surface in slippery conditions.

Apron and gate facilities

Opportunities to relieve airport surface congestion extend up to the parking spaces at the gates. Aircraft docking is typically accomplished by a ramp agent with flashlights and hand signals guiding the flight crew for proper parking of the aircraft and assuring that the wingtips have safe clearance from buildings, ground equipment, and other aircraft. New optical, electrical, electronic, and mechanical devices are being developed to provide flight crews with positive visual guidance that will permit more rapid and accurate docking. This technology will allow apron space to be used more efficiently and help prevent the delays that arise when aircraft must be repositioned in order to mate with fixed ground support systems and passenger loading bridges.

Jet aircraft parked on the ramp area preparing for departure.

While needs and procedures vary by airline and by airport, the aircraft servicing functions commonly performed at an airport include fueling, engine start, galley and cabin service, electrical ground power, towing, passenger stair or loading bridge operation, and handling of baggage, mail, and cargo. In addition, various routine or special aircraft maintenance functions are conducted.

Several technological advances offer reductions in servicing time and cost. At some airports, ground power is now being provided by fixed systems mounted on the passenger loading bridge or in undergound pits. Similarly, fixed pneumatic systems are being developed to provide ground power and aircraft engine start. These installations ease the congestion caused by mobile units clustered around aircraft on the ramp and provide for a more efficient servicing operation. Auxiliary power units now provided on most newer aircraft alleviate congestion by replacing ground equipment needed for electric service, air start, and air conditioning. These self-contained units also assist in quick turnaround, thereby reducing gate occupancy time. Special pallets and handling equipment provide for efficient transfer and loading of bags and cargo. While use of this technology saves time at the gate, the loading and unloading of the pallets themselves can sometimes be time-consuming due to mechanical problems and alignment difficulties.

These improvements in technology help ease surface congestion in two ways. Those that speed turnaround lessen gate delays and enhance throughput. Those that reduce the apron space needed for service vehicles and equipment allow more aircraft to be parked in a given area, thereby directly increasing apron capacity and helping to ease airport surface congestion in general.

Key terms

technological improvements
search radar (primary radar)
radar beacon system (secondary radar)
automated radar terminal system (ARTS)
moving target detection
metering
sequencing
spacing
traffic management system (TMS)
Mode S data link
runway configuration management
National Airspace Review (NAR)
converging runways
wake vortex
vortex advisory system (VAS)
wind shear

low level wind shear alert system (LLWSAS)
automated weather observing system (AWOS)
joint automated weather observation system (JAWOS)
airport surface detection equipment (ASDE)
tower automated ground surveillance system (TAGS)
runway occupancy time (ROT)

Review questions

1. Why has there been more attention directed to better utilization of existing
    facilities in recent years? Why not simply build more airports?
    What is meant by "technological measures" as used in this chapter?
      Technological approaches to expanding airport capacity or reducing delay
      fall into three broad categories. Explain.

2. Describe how the following three technologies could improve aircraft
    guidance, surveillance, and control: microwave landing system, improved
    surveillance radar, and automated traffic-management systems.
    Define: metering, sequencing, and spacing.
    How will TMS and AERA improve air traffic flow management?

3. What was the purpose of the National Airspace Review (NAR)?
    Discuss several proposed procedural changes designed to improve terminal
      airspace and runway utilization.
    What are the advantages and disadvantages in having a separate short runway
      for small aircraft?

4. Define *wake vortex* and *wind shear*.
    What is the vortex advisory system (VAS)? Low level wind shear alert
      system (LLWSAS)?
    What is the function of the automated weather observing system (AWOS) and
      the joint automated weather observation system (JAWOS)?

5. Discuss the two primary ways of reducing noise.
    What are the sources of noise in a jet engine? What is being done to correct
      problems emanating from these sources?
    Discuss several of the proposed aircraft operating procedural changes to
      alleviate the noise problem.

6. The primary capacity benefits from airport surface technologies are really
    indirect. Do you agree with this statement? Why?
    Discuss the three types of technology deployed on the airport surface. What
      is the purpose of airport surface detection equipment (ASDE)?

How can runway occupancy time be shortened?

What new technologies are being employed in the apron and gate area to permit more rapid and accurate docking? To ease congestion caused by mobile units clustered around an aircraft? To load cargo and baggage more efficiently?

Suggested readings

National Airspace System Plan, revised edition. Washington, DC: FAA, April, 1983.

Capital Investment Plan. Washington, DC: FAA, December, 1990.

Airport System Capacity: Strategic Choices. Washington, DC Transportation Research Board, 1990.

Report of the Industry Task Force on Airport Capacity Improvement and Delay Reduction. Washington, DC: Airport Operators Council International, September, 1982.

Report and Recommendations of the Airport Access Task Force. Washington, DC: CAB, March, 1983.

Horonjeff, Robert and F.X. McKelvey. *Planning and Design of Airports*, 3rd. ed. New York: McGraw-Hill, 1983.

Airport and Air Traffic Control System. Washington, DC: U.S. Congress, Office of Technology Assessment. OTA-STI-175, January, 1982.

Improving the Air Traffic Control System: An Assessment of the National Airspace System Plan. Washington, DC: Congressional Budget Office, August, 1983.

An Analysis of the Requirements for, and the Benefits and Costs of the National Microwave Landing System (MLS), FAA-EM-80-77. Washington, DC Federal Aviation Administration, June, 1980.

Preliminary Analysis of the Benefits and Costs to Implement the National Airspace System Plan. DOT/FAA/EM-82-22. Washington, DC: Federal Aviation Administration, June, 1982.

Response to the Industry Task Force on Airport Capacity Improvement and Delay Reduction. Washington, DC: Federal Aviation Administration, FAA Management Steering Group, May, 1983.

Analysis of Runway Occupancy Times at Major Airports, FAA-EM-78-9. Washington, DC: Federal Aviation Administration, May, 1978.

Parameters of Future ATC Systems Relating to Airport Capacity/Delay. Washington, DC: Federal Aviation Administration, June, 1978.

Landside technological improvements

Outline

Introduction
Terminal facilities and services
Landside access
Applications of technology to airport problems

Objectives

When you have completed this chapter, you should be able to:

△ Describe several technologies designed to improve passenger movement through the terminal.

△ Define "computerized ticket systems" and "computerized aircraft manifest."

△ List three ways to expedite the baggage handling process.

△ Explain how the Federal Inspection Service (FIS) is improving the process of clearing passengers and cargo through customs, immigration, and agriculture.

△ Discuss several management techniques designed to improve landside access.

△ Describe the pros and cons of rail transit as a solution to the airport access problem.

Introduction

The terminal and associated landside facilities such as the parking areas and access roads provide the zone of transition for passengers, providing the link between surface and air transportation. Basically, the landside facilities are long-term installations with relatively stable use. They are largely independent of the specialized aircraft and activities that occur on the airside. In contrast, the airside is characterized by short-term, impermanent use that is closely tied to changing aircraft technology with a useful life of about 10 to 15 years. The principal effect of the terminal on the airside is through the design of aprons and gates, which determines the number of aircraft that can be accommodated at one time and the turnaround time for passenger boarding and aircraft servicing. As seen in the previous chapter, gate and apron operations can also have a wider—though not major—effect on airside throughput capacity.

Overall, the influence of the terminal on the functional requirements and performance of airside facilities is relatively small compared with the inverse effect that the airside exerts on the terminal. The primary purpose of the terminal is to transfer passengers and their baggage between surface and air transportation with minimum time, confusion, and inconvenience. The functional requirements and choice of design for a terminal complex must take into account the passenger and baggage flows resulting from aircraft size, traffic mix, schedules of operation, and type of service provided (origin-destination or connecting flights). As a design task, this involves the integration of three major parts of the terminal: airside gates, passenger collection and service areas, and landside access and egress. Because these parts are highly interactive, it is important that the separation between them be kept to a minimum and that traffic flow smoothly among the parts.

This would be a fairly straightforward task were it not for the need to design the airside interface so that it can be adapted to accommodate continually changing aircraft technology, airline service patterns, and traffic volumes. At some large hubs, the steadily increasing size of aircraft and their fixed-point servicing requirements, when coupled with growing passenger and automobile traffic, have led to terminal complexes of a size that imposes inconvenience and delay on passengers. In response, airport designers have been forced to add an intermediate transportation mode within the terminal itself (moving sidewalks, transport buses, fixed rail systems, and other such people movers) to aid passengers in transferring between the airside and the landside.

This chapter discusses the various landside technological improvements that are aimed at facilitating passenger movement or to reduce passenger inconvenience and delay. It should be recognized that these aspects of design and operation will have little, if any, effect on airside capacity and throughput even though they might lead to substantial reductions in the overall trip time for air travel. It should also be recognized that such matters have been of little interest to FAA or to policymakers in the federal government. They are, of course, keenly important to airport operators and to a lesser extent airlines because they constitute investment needs that must be balanced against airside capacity expansion in the overall program of capital improvements for airports.

The discussion that follows is outlined in TABLE 10-1, which lists various forms of landside technological improvements and the purpose they could achieve.

Terminal facilities and services

Many airports will continue to suffer from inappropriate or outdated designs that lead to congestion and delay in passenger areas and diminish the overall utility of the airport as a transportation hub. For such airports, an alternative to a new or expanded terminal as an avenue of relief from congestion is to correct specific features that cause bottlenecks by applying improved technology that will compensate for design inadequacies. Some of these partial technological remedies are discussed next.

Table 10-1. *Landside technology to increase capacity and reduce delay.* Source: FAA

Technology	Area of application	Purpose	Benefit
Terminal facilities and services			
Passenger movers	Terminal	Improve circulation in terminal; reduce walking distance	Reduce delay; greater passenger convenience
Ticketing	Terminal	Expedite ticket purchase and passenger check-in	Reduced delay
Baggage handling	Terminal	Expedite baggage check-in, transfer, and pickup	Reduced delay
Passenger security screening	Terminal	Make screening faster and more reliable	Reduced delay; improved security
Federal Inspection Service	Terminal	Expedite customs and immigration clearance	Reduced delay
Airport access			
Terminal curbfront	Terminal; landside	Facilitate airport entrance and exit	Reduced delay
Airport circulation roads	Landside	Facilitate automobile traffic flow	Reduced delay
Airport ground access	Landside	Reduce access time; lessen road congestion	Reduced delay

Hartsfield Atlanta International Airport

A busy concourse at Hartsfield Atlanta International Airport.

Passenger movers

To speed passenger movement through the terminal and to lessen the inconvenience of walking long distances to board flights or to reach landside exits, some airports have turned to *passenger movers*. Several technologies are available, covering a broad spectrum of cost: buses, mobile lounges, moving sidewalks, and automated guideway systems. The choice of any of these involves a tradeoff between their service characteristics and cost (capital and operating) against those of adding new gates or terminal wings. This tradeoff is very sensitive to the rate of use, the specific vehicle chosen, and the cost of gate construction. Passenger movers tend to be more cost-effective than gates if the rate of use is high. Variation in traffic load is also important, and analysis indicates that passenger movers are best suited to serving those locations and intraterminal trips where there is a great fluctuation in demand.

Buses and mobile lounges add to airside surface traffic; they are also labor-intensive and therefore costly to operate. For these reasons, airports with finger piers or satellite terminals have sometimes opted for automated vehicles such as moving sidewalks or guideway transit systems. Moving sidewalks are not an entirely satisfactory option. They are costly to operate and maintain, and their speed must be slow to allow passengers time to step on and off safely; thus, they provide only a marginal decrease in passenger movement time, although they greatly reduce the effort of long passages through the terminal complex. Some experimentation with accelerating devices and transition techniques would permit greater line speeds and still afford comfortable and safe boarding and descent. If these experiments are successful, the utility of moving sidewalks will be greatly increased.

Reynolds, Smith, and Hills

Passenger movers such as the automated guideway system shown here at Tampa International Airport can shorten walking distances and speed passenger processing.

For longer distances or where the volume of traffic is large, automated guideway systems are sometimes practical. Several different types are available, varying principally in terms of propulsion, vehicle size, and complexity of the guideway network and control system. Reliability and train control system design were problems in the first systems installed at airports (Dallas-Fort Worth, for example), but the technology has improved rapidly and now appears to give good service at airports such as Atlanta and Orlando. Capital costs of vehicles and guideway construction remain high, and they are still difficult and expensive to maintain. The view of airport designers is that these systems are cost-effective only at a few very large airports, and there is reluctance to utilize this technology except as a last resort.

Ticketing

The ticket counter serves three major functions: ticket transactions, baggage check-in, and flight information. Of these, the most time-consuming are ticket transactions (which often include baggage check-in for the individual passenger). Technologies to speed ticket counter operations or to eliminate them altogether are being explored, both to reduce delays in the terminal and to cut airline personnel costs. *Computerized ticket systems* available today offer passengers advance reservations and sales, preassignment of seats, and automatic tagging of baggage. They will probably be used more widely by the major air carriers, some of whom might also offer them to small carriers under a service contract. A companion development is the *computerized aircraft manifest* that has been implemented by

Delta Air Lines, Inc.

Delta Air Lines ticket counter at Hartsfield Atlanta International Airport.

some airlines. These systems typically produce aircraft load sheets, passenger manifests, and automatic telex reservations. They greatly reduce the administrative work at the counter and expedite airline dispatch from the gate.

Ticket dispensing machines similar to those used for banking are now in limited use by some airlines at a few locations and for selected routes. Improvement of these machines so that they can handle a larger number of routes and fare structures could promote wider use, with corresponding reduction in the amount of activity that must be conducted at the ticket counter. This technology could also be extended to sale of tickets off the airport property. With the deregulation of travel agencies, the range of services provided by these firms has expanded, offering passengers an alternative to purchasing tickets at the airport. Travel agents now account for more than 70 percent of airline ticket sales in the United States. The entry of mass-marketing firms such as Sears and Ticketron into the air travel field could further decrease the need for ticketing at airport terminals, reducing airline personnel and equipment requirements, and alleviating congestion at terminal ticket counters.

Baggage handling

The handling of baggage, especially baggage claim at the end of a flight, is a common and—for passengers—particularly onerous form of delay in terminals. At most airports, baggage handling is the responsibility of the individual air carriers, but some airports operate a consolidated baggage service—either with airport personnel or on a contract basis—in the interest of speeding the process and reducing the cost. Reduction of the delays and passenger inconvenience associated with baggage handling has been approached in three ways: more efficient procedures for check-in and claim, automated handling and sorting, and elimination of some baggage handling by encouraging carry-on luggage.

One of the simplest and most widely applied methods to expedite baggage handling is *curbside check-in*. This separates baggage handling from other ticket counter and gate activities, thereby disencumbering those locations and allowing baggage to be consolidated and moved to aircraft more directly. Another method is replacement of the baggage claim carrousel with loop conveyor belts that allow passengers greater access to their luggage without increasing the size of the claim area.

Sorting baggage, moving it to and from the apron, and aircraft loading and unloading are time-critical and labor-intensive operations. Technologies to improve this process include high-speed conveyors to transport baggage between the terminal and the flight line, often used in conjunction with pallets or containers that can be put on and taken off aircraft with labor-saving equipment. *Computerized baggage sorting equipment*, capable of distributing bags with machine-readable tags, has been installed at some airports. These devices are not yet fully satisfactory because the encoding and reading of tags are time-consuming and somewhat unreliable.

To handle peak loads, automated systems must have a larger capacity because they are less flexible than manual systems. Redundancy is a must with an automated system, which increases the capital cost. As those automated systems improve and come into wider use, a further step is to install self-service systems that allow passengers to check and claim luggage either in the terminal, at the curbside, or at remote locations on or off the airport property. While such a development would be primarily a labor-saving measure by airlines and airport operators, it might also speed transit through the airport for many passengers.

The functional equivalent of automated, self-service baggage handling systems—and one that might be cheaper and more reliable—is expanded capacity within the aircraft for carry-on luggage. With the advent of stronger and lighter materials, aircraft designers have been able to reconfigure cabins to provide larger and more secure storage space on board. New aircraft universally contain such overhead storage bins, and many airlines have converted older aircraft to incorporate similar enclosed overhead storage. A further development might be provision

Port Authority of New York and New Jersey

Curbside baggage check-in at LaGuardia Airport.

of a common baggage space either within the cabin or in a special module that could be transferred to the cargo bay. Passengers entering and leaving the aircraft would pass through this space and handle their own baggage.

Passenger security screening

To deter aircraft hijacking, the federal government has established regulations to ensure safe passage for the traveling public. These regulations, implemented in January 1973, require security screening of passengers and carry-on articles. Screening has become an accepted fact of life for air travelers and a problem for airport designers and operators because the security checkpoints tend to disrupt passenger flow and in some instances force remodeling of the terminal.

The equipment used today consists of X-ray machines with moving belts and magnetometers for metal detection. This system, which replaced manual search, significantly increased the capacity and capability of the screening process. The chief drawback of the existing equipment is that, while effective in detecting metal, it has limited capacity to detect explosives and volatile substances.

New technology for screening cargo and baggage is being investigated. The aim is both to speed the screening process and to increase the thoroughness and reliability of detection. The new systems under development make use of improved bomb and explosive sensing techniques such as vapor detection, bulk detection, and computerized tomography.

Federal Inspection Service

The United States has 24 airports of foreign entry where Federal Inspection Service (FIS) for clearing passengers and cargo is provided by customs, immigration, and agriculture officials. Clearance procedures are rigid and time-consuming, and FIS processing has been a major cause of delay at high-volume ports of entry.

The U.S. Department of State is issuing machine-readable passports that might help expedite FIS clearance. Additional procedures and technologies are being investigated to achieve greater capacity, reduced clearance time, and higher agent productivity. Alternative procedures and physical arrangement of facilities are the principal areas of concentration.

The system employed at most airports of entry is the *customs accelerated passenger inspection service* (CAPIS), which provides separate immigration and customs checkpoints. CAPIS is highly time-consuming for passengers and labor-intensive to operate. Another system, referred to as *one stop*, combines immigration and customs functions at a single station. Although promising, this system has not yet achieved its expected capacity in tests and demonstrations. Chicago O'Hare and Houston Intercontinental Airport are experimenting with another approach that uses a modified version of the standard European system known as *red-green*, where travelers who do not have goods to declare are separated from those who do, with only the latter passing through a secondary inspection station. Also under study are hybrid systems that combine features of CAPIS, one stop, and the red-green concepts.

Landside access

It is a truism that nearly every airplane trip begins and ends with an automobile ride, and there is no clearer manifestation of our dependence on the automobile than at the terminal curbside and on the access roads to the airport. While the figures vary among airports, it is generally estimated that more than 90 percent of all airline passenger trips to and from airports are by private automobile or taxi. At medium and small airports, the figure is probably close to 100 percent because these communities tend not to have well-developed public transit providing a practical alternative to the automobile.

A further indication of the symbiosis between the airplane and the automobile is the emergence and growth of the car rental industry. This business has its origin in the need for air travelers to have transportation to and from airports in cities away from home. While many car rental firms have since branched out into other markets, the bulk of their business is still rentals to airline passengers, and revenues from this activity are a major source of income for airport operators.

Not all trips to the airport are made by airline passengers or those who come to meet travelers or drop them off. For airport workers (accounting for perhaps one-third of access trips) and calls by delivery vans, service representatives, and others with business on the airport property (also about one-third of all access trips), the automobile likewise predominates. Some (especially airport workers) come at times when public transit is not available or when service is infrequent, and they have almost no alternative but to drive to the airport and park.

At many airports, automobile traffic is a principal source of landside congestion and delay. A recent review of airport problems by FAA found that 23 of 41 major metropolitan area airports are suffering from capacity constraints imposed by landside congestion or lack of adequate access.

Perhaps the best known example of the effect that landside access can have on airport operations is at Los Angeles International Airport (LAX). Because of limited capacity of airport circulation roads and the inability of the freeways and city streets near the airport to absorb a greater volume of automobile traffic, regional transportation authorities imposed a cap on aircraft operations and annual passenger volume permitted at the airport. Much of the impetus for the expansion at LAX was to relieve this landside constraint, and a large share of the $700 million modernization program was expended to double-deck roads leading to and from the terminal and to remodel the terminal complex so as to segregate arriving and departing automobile traffic.

LAX is not an isolated example. Chicago O'Hare (ORD) is undergoing a $1 billion program of airport modernization, a large share of which has been to "bring aging and congested terminal and roadway facilities into balance with under-utilized airside capacity." The Port Authority of New York and New Jersey has launched a $1.5 billion modernization plan for the three New York airports.

Important parts of this plan are new roadways and local transportation to improve airport access and additional parking space around the terminals.

Only a few landside improvements and airport access projects are eligible for federal aid from the Airport and Airway Trust Fund. The Federal Highway Administration (FHWA) and the Urban Mass Transportation Administration (UMTA) also provide funds for landside development, and the airport operator or local airport authority contributes an important share through retained earnings and revenue bonds. Funding of landside investments is a complex multijurisdictional arrangement with wide variation from airport to airport. The capital improvements sponsored by FAA are limited to on-airport roadways, guideways, and walkways. Off the airport property, projects to improve landside access may receive FHWA and UMTA grants (FIG. 10-1) or be supported by state and local funds.

In general, the solution to landside access problems does not appear to be new technology, but application of management techniques to make better use of the facilities available and construction of new facilities (based on existing technology) to add to landside capacity. In a larger sense, there is also a need to look at the question or airport access from the perspective of the regional transportation system and to find ways to integrate the airport more effectively into the urban

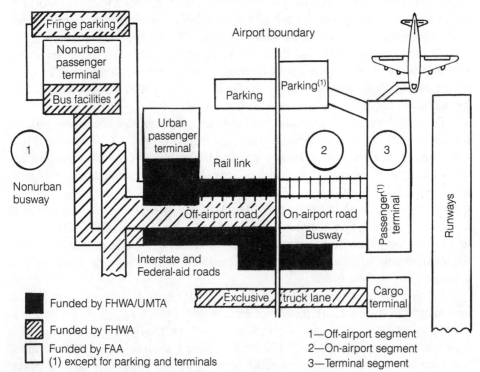

Fig. 10-1. Federal capital funding of airports and related facilities.

area it serves. Subsequent book sections focus on approaches that can be taken or applied more widely to alleviate the problem of traffic flow on the airport property and to reduce the cost and inconvenience of access from the surrounding metropolitan area.

Terminal curbfront design

The terminal curbfront provides temporary vehicle storage during passengers' transition between the terminal and the landside, and it is at the curbside that all passengers, except those using nearby parking or transit facilities, either enter or leave some form of ground transportation. Curbfront congestion is a particularly difficult problem to solve because the facilities there are intimately tied to the design of the terminal building and airport characteristics such as activity level (peak passenger volume), user characteristics (mode of transportation, mix of passengers and well-wishers, and number of bags), and vehicle characteristics (type, number of passengers, and dwell time at the curb). The most practical approaches are physical expansion or modification of facilities and procedural changes to improve passenger and vehicle flow.

The most common forms of physical improvement are additional curb frontage, bypass lanes, multiple entry and exit points in the terminal building, remote park and ride facilities, and pedestrian overpasses or underpasses. These

Upper roadway in front of the international terminal at San Francisco International Airport.

improvements are intended to increase the utilization of curb frontage by vehicular traffic or, in the case of park and ride, to reduce demand on the curbfront by diverting passengers from private cars to high-volume vehicles. Walkways to segregate foot and vehicular traffic promote pedestrian safety and facilitate roadway traffic by eliminating conflicts between pedestrians and vehicles.

In some cases, procedural changes—either alone or in conjunction with low-cost physical modifications such as signing or lane dividers—are an effective alternative to expensive construction or remodeling of the curbfront. For example, parking restrictions combined with strict enforcement will reduce curbside congestion and dwell time in discharging and boarding passengers. Short-term parking islands or reserved sections along the curbfront, defined by roadway marking or simple dividers, could segregate vehicles picking up or discharging passengers from those that must handle baggage or enter the terminal for brief errands. Similarly, separation of private cards from taxis, buses, and limousines can diminish conflicts among these kinds of traffic and improve the flow to and from the curbfront. An effective approach at some airports has been provision of bus service from remote parking to the terminal and regulations to discourage bringing private automobiles to the terminal building. None of these measures is a substitute for adequate curbside capacity, but they can lead to more efficient use of the facilities available and perhaps compensate for deficiencies in terminal and curbfront design.

Airport ground access

Aside from expansion or improvement of the road network leading to the airport, most effort to facilitate airport ground access has focused on substitutes for the automobile. Bus or airline limousine service has proved workable in some cities, but patronage is generally low because of the infrequency of service or the inconvenience of getting between origin or destination and a centrally located bus terminal. Helicopter shuttle between the airport and city center has been tried, but it is expensive, unreliable because of weather, and objectionable to the community because of noise.

A solution that has been advocated by many planners is a rail rapid transit system, either operated exclusively to and from the airport or as part of a regional network. Cleveland, for example, built a rapid transit extension to Hopkins International Airport in 1968; and the Washington, D.C., Metro system includes a station near—but not at—the main terminal at National Airport. Proposals to provide such service—either by construction of a new line to the airport or by linking an existing line to the airport by a feeder bus—have been advanced for several other cities.

In part, this interest has been stimulated by examples in foreign countries, which either have or are planning rail service to airports. Charles de Gaulle Airport in France has a rail station a little over a mile from the terminal with connec-

Access road leading to Tampa International Airport.

tion provided by shuttle bus. Amsterdam (Schiphol), Birmingham, Dusseldorf, Frankfort, Gatwick, Heathrow, Orly, Vienna, and Zurich already have rail stations in or immediately adjacent to the airport terminal. Haneda Airport in Japan has a monorail line from the center of Tokyo to the terminal, which brings passengers to within 300 feet of check-in counters. Toronto and Montreal (Dorval) in Canada have rail lines that are close by but not integral with the terminal (a connecting bus or taxi trip is needed to complete the link), and Montreal International (Mirabel) will soon have direct service from the airport to the downtown area with 13 intermediate stops.

Unfortunately, rail transit is not a universal solution to the airport access problem. In most major U.S. cities, there is not a regional rail network to be tied into the airport, and without it there is little prospect that an exclusive line between downtown and the airport would be viable. Few passengers want to travel between the airport and the central business district, and even fewer want to go during rush hour. Rail transit, with its fixed routes and corridor structure, does not serve well in the U.S. setting, where there is wide dispersion of origins and destinations for airport passengers. The capital costs of such systems are likely to be high, and it is doubtful that operating expenses could be covered from the fare box, necessitating subsidy from the municipality or the airport.

There might be public resistance to building a system to serve airport users exclusively when other parts of the metropolitan area could profit perhaps more from rail rapid transit service. Finally, the service characteristics of rail transit do not lend themselves particularly well to airport trips. Passengers encumbered by baggage find rail transit inconvenient because there is no storage space on trains and narrow aisles might be difficult to negotiate with luggage in hand. If there are intermediate stops—as there almost certainly would be if the rail line attempts to serve more than a few who want to travel from city center to the airport—the trip is prolonged, and trains might be crowded with passengers riding for other purposes.

These arguments do not necessarily deny the validity of foreign experience, but they raise doubts about the viability of rail transit access to airports in this country—where we do not have the population densities, the existing urban rail network, and the tradition of public transit that are characteristic of Europe and Japan.

An alternative rail transit, which accomplishes the same purpose but with greater flexibility and somewhat lower cost (FIG. 10-2), is the remote airline terminal.

This is a facility for processing arriving and departing passengers at a site off the airport property and transferring them to the terminal by group transportation. The off-airport terminal might include facilities for ticketing, baggage handling, and parking. Connection with the airport might be provided by public transit, special airport bus, or helicopter shuttle. The technology to implement this concept exists, and it has been tried in several cities.

The popularity of the remote terminal concept has waned in recent years, largely because indirect costs tend to offset the benefits. Trip origins and destinations are becoming more and more scattered throughout the urban area, to the extent that trips to and from the city center now account for less than a quarter of airport patronage. On the other hand, the increasingly tighter restrictions on airport terminal and landside expansion might make this concept worth reexamining, particularly if a way can be found to build and operate a network of small dispersed facilities adapted to the urban-suburban pattern of business and residence in major metropolitan areas.

Applications of technology to airport problems

In the search for solutions to capacity and delay problems, the value of new technology is typically measured by its ability to achieve one or more of the following:

1. Increased capacity.
2. Higher efficiency.
3. Greater safety.

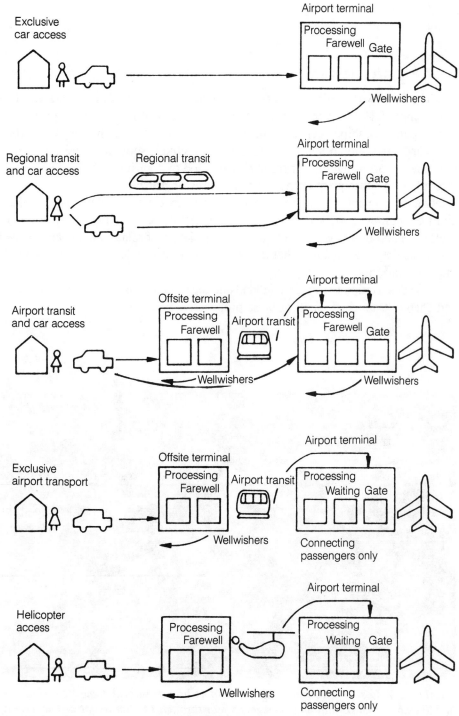

Fig. 10-2. Off-site passenger terminal concepts.

4. Improved reliability.

5. Greater accuracy.

6. Lower cost.

7. Greater convenience.

The first two are direct benefits; they constitute relief of the problem of how to accommodate a higher level of demand. Safety is of prime importance, but it has little relationship to capacity and delay unless—as is often the case with procedures and rules—the requirement for safety precludes some measure for increasing capacity or throughput. If some new method of assuring safety is found and it also allows a subsequent change in procedures or utilization of airport facilities, safety improvements might give rise to a secondary capacity-related benefit. Reliability, accuracy, cost, and convenience are operational benefits. They are worth seeking in and of themselves, but they have little direct relation to capacity except insofar as they are attributes that lead to adoption of new technology or hasten its implementation.

The description of airside and landside technologies presented in this chapter and chapter 9 touched on all of these prospective benefits.

Terminal 1 at Los Angeles International Airport houses several domestic airlines and handles more than six million passengers a year through 14 aircraft gates. The terminal became operational in 1984 as part of the airport's $700 million improvement program.

The emphasis has been on their potential to relieve capacity and delay problems, but other attributes have been cited where they appear relevant either to the future use of the technology or to the choice of one form of technology over another.

Key terms

passenger movers
computerized ticket systems
computerized aircraft manifest
curbside check-in
computerized baggage sorting equipment
customs accelerated passenger inspection service (CAPIS)
one stop clearance
red-green clearance

Review questions

1. Describe some of the passenger movement systems in the terminal designed to lessen the inconvenience of walking long distances.
   What are some problems associated with automated guideway systems?

2. What are the major functions of the ticket counter? Describe several technologies designed to speed ticket counter operations. What is the major problem associated with ticket dispensing machines?

3. What is curbside check-in? What is the purpose of computerized baggage sorting equipment?
   What is being done to promote carry-on luggage?
   Define *one stop* and *red-green* clearance of passengers.

4. How are airports such as LAX and ORD addressing the problem of landside access?
   If only a few landside improvements and airport access projects are eligible for federal aid from the Airport and Airway Trust Fund, how can this problem be addressed?

5. The solution to landside access problems does not appear to be in new technology, but application of management techniques. Do you agree? Why?
   What are some of the common forms of physical improvement to the terminal curbfront?

6. What is the major problem with helicopter shuttle service between the airport and city center?

Discuss some of the pros and cons of rail transit between the airport and city center.

Suggested readings

Kozicharow, "New York Port Authority Boosting Airport Capacity," *Aviation Week & Space Technology*, May 9, 1983.

Ott, J., "$1 Billion Upgrade Planned at O'Hare," *Aviation Week & Space Technology*, August 8, 1983.

Sweetman, B. "The New LAX Prepares for 1984," *Interavia*, July, 1983.

deNeufville, Richard. *Airport Systems Planning*. Cambridge, Massachusetts. The MIT Press, 1976.

Report of the Industry Task Force on Airport Capacity Improvement and Delay Reduction. Washington, DC: Airport Operators Council International, September, 1982.

Airfield and Airspace Capacity/Delay Policy Analysis: FAA-APO-81-14. Washington, DC: Federal Aviation Administration, Office of Aviation Policy and Plans, December, 1981.

Airport and Terminal-Area Operations of the Future. Washington, DC: Transportation Research Board, 1987.

Airport Landside Capacity. Washington, DC: Transportation Board, 1975.

Measuring Airport Landside Capacity. Washington, DC: Transportation Board, 1987.

Part 4
The management process

Financial management

Outline

Airport accounting
Planning and budgeting
Approaches to financial management at commercial airports
Pricing of airport facilities and services
Trends in airport financial management since deregulation

Objectives

When you have completed this chapter, you should be able to:

△ Discuss the importance of accounting to airport financial management.

△ Summarize the five major revenue sources under a typical airport's operating statement.

△ Explain why it is so difficult to compare operating expenses between different airports.

△ Discuss the importance of planning and budgeting in the financial management process.

△ Distinguish between the residual-cost and compensatory approaches on airport-airline relationships.

△ Define "majority-in-interest" and describe its implication for residual-cost airports.

△ Describe the major sources of revenue for the airfield area, terminal area concessions, airline leased areas, and other leased areas.

△ Discuss some of the effects of deregulation on airport financial management.

Airport accounting

Financial management of a major airport is comparable to that of a complex and highly diversified business enterprise. The airport provides a wide range of facilities and services for a diverse group of businesses and individuals. As a result, the impact of the airport's financial management not only affects the airport users, but also represents an important element in the growth and economic well-being of the community in which it is located.

Airport accounting involves the accumulation, communication, and interpretation of economic data relating to the financial position of an airport and the results of its operations for decision-making purposes. It differs from accounting procedures found in business firms because airports vary considerably in terms of goals, size, and operational characteristics. As such, it is very difficult to derive a unified accounting system that can be used by all airports. A system tailored to the needs of a large commercial airport might be impractical for a small GA airport or vice versa. Many airports have different definitions of what elements constitute operating and nonoperating revenues and expenses and sources of funds for airport development. Anyone attempting to compare the financial data of one airport to another, or against a group of similar airports, finds it extremely difficult to draw valid conclusions. Nevertheless, a good accounting system is needed for a number of reasons:

1. Financial statements are needed to inform governmental authorities and the local community regarding details of the airport's operations.
2. A good accounting system can assist airport management in allocating resources, reducing costs, and improving control.
3. Negotiating charges for use of airport facilities can be facilitated.
4. Financial statements can influence the decisions of voters and legislators.

One of the most important financial statements is the *operating statement*, which records the airports' revenues and expenses over a particular time period (quarterly and annually). Table 11-1 includes a sample of an operating statement for a fiscal period. The following discussion includes the major items appearing on an operating statement.

Table 11-1. Sample airport operating statement for the fiscal period.

Operating revenues		$740,000
Airfield area	$250,000	
Terminal area concessions	300,000	
Airline leased areas	110,000	
Other leased areas	70,000	
Other operating revenue	10,000	
Nonoperating revenues		20,000
Total operating revenues		$760,000
Operating expenses		$605,000
Airfield area	120,000	
Terminal area	260,000	
Hangars, cargo facilities, other buildings and grounds	75,000	
General and administrative expenses	150,000	
Nonoperating expenses		40,000
Total operating expenses		$645,000
Total operating income		$125,000
Depreciation		100,000
Net income		$ 25,000

Operating revenues

Airport operating revenues can be divided into five major groupings: (1) airfield area, (2) terminal area concessions, (3) airline leased areas, (4) other leased areas, and (5) other operating revenue.

Airfield area The airfield area or airside of the airport produces revenues from sources that are directly related to the operation of aircraft:

1. Landing fees—scheduled and unscheduled airlines, itinerant aircraft, military or governmental aircraft.
2. Aircraft parking charges—paved and unpaved areas.
3. Fuel flowage fees—FBOs and other fuel suppliers.

Terminal area concessions The terminal area concessions include all of the nonairline users of the terminal area:

1. Food and beverage concessions (includes restaurants, snack bars, and lounges).
2. Travel services and facilities (includes checkrooms and lockers, flight insurance, restrooms, car rentals, and telephones).
3. Specialty stores and shops (includes boutiques, newsstands, banks, gift shops, clothing stores, duty-free shops, banks, and so forth).
4. Personal services (includes beauty and barber shops, valet shops, and shoeshine stands).
5. Amusements (includes video arcades, movie and TV rooms, and observation decks).
6. Display advertising.
7. Outside terminal concessions (includes auto parking, ground transportation, hotels and motels).

Airline leased areas Airline leased areas include revenue derived from the air carriers for ground equipment rentals, cargo terminals, office rentals, ticket counters, hangars, operations, and maintenance facilities.

Other leased areas All of the remaining leased areas on the airport that produce revenue are brought together under other leased areas. Freight forwarders, fixed-base operators, governmental units, and businesses in the airport industrial area would be included under this category. All revenue derived from nonairline cargo terminals and ground equipment rentals to nonairline users would also be included.

Other operating revenue   Other operating revenue includes revenues from the operation of distribution systems for public utilities such as electricity and steam, and jobbing and contract work performed for tenants. Other miscellaneous service fees are also included under this category.

Nonoperating revenues

Nonoperating revenues include interest earned on investments in governmental securities, local taxes, subsidies or grants-in-aid, and selling or leasing of properties owned by the airport but not related to airport operations. The magnitude of nonoperating income can vary considerably between airports.

Operating expenses

Operating expenses, unlike revenues, can vary considerably between similar airports. The nature of airport expenses depends upon a number of factors including the airport's geographical location, organizational setup, and financial structure. Airports in the sunbelt do not experience the sizable snow removal and other cold-weather-related expenses that airports in colder climates must face. Some municipalities, counties, or local authorities absorb the costs of certain staff functions such as accounting, legal, planning, and public relations. Certain operating functions such as emergency service, policing, and traffic control might also be provided by local fire departments and local law enforcement agencies at some airports.

Operating expenses can be divided into four major groupings: (1) airfield area, (2) terminal area, (3) hangars, cargo, other buildings and grounds, and (4) general and administrative expenses.

Airfield area   All maintenance and operating expenses associated with the airfield are included under this category:

1. Runways, taxiways, apron areas, aircraft parking areas, and airfield lighting systems maintenance.
2. Service on airport equipment such as cars and trucks.
3. Other expenses in this area might include maintenance on fire equipment and airport service roads.
4. Utilities (electricity) for the airfield.

Terminal area   All maintenance and operating expenses associated with the terminal area:

1. Buildings and grounds—maintenance and custodial services.
2. Improvements to the land and landscaping.

3. Loading bridges and gates—maintenance and custodial services.

4. Concession improvements.

5. Observation facilities—maintenance and custodial services.

6. Passenger, employee, and tenant parking facilities.

7. Utilities (electricity, air conditioning and heating, and water).

8. Waste disposal (plumbing)—maintenance.

9. Equipment (air conditioning, heating, baggage handling)—maintenance.

Hangars, cargo facilities, and other buildings and grounds   All maintenance and operating expenses associated with hangars, cargo facilities, other buildings, and grounds:

1. Buildings and grounds—maintenance and custodial services.

2. Improvements to the land and landscaping.

3. Employee parking—maintenance.

4. Access roadways—maintenance.

5. Utilities (electricity, air conditioning and heating, and water).

6. Waste disposal (plumbing)—maintenance.

General and administrative expenses   All payroll expenses for the maintenance, operations, and administrative staff are included under this account. Other operating expenses for materials and supplies are included under general and administrative expenses.

Nonoperating expenses

Nonoperating expenses include the payment of interest on outstanding debt (bonds, notes, loans, and so forth), contributions to governmental bodies, and other miscellaneous expenses.

Depreciation

Some airports compute depreciation on the full value of facilities including federal and other aid, while other airports limit depreciation to only their share of the construction costs.

Planning and budgeting

Planning and budgeting are integral parts of any financial management process. Every airport must make short-term decisions about the allocation and scheduling of its limited resources over many competing uses; it must make long-term decisions about rates of expansion of capital improvements and funding sources. Both short-term and long-term decisions require planning. Planning is important:

1. It encourages coordinated thinking. No one department can act independently. A policy decision in a particular department affects the airport as a whole.

2. Planning helps develop standards for future performance. Without plans, the airport's measure of financial performance can only be based on historical standards. While past operating statements help to set these standards for the future, they should not necessarily serve as standards themselves.

3. Planning assists management in controlling the actions of subordinates. By planning, employees are provided a goal or standard to achieve.

4. Planning ahead might reveal potential problems for which remedial measures can be taken earlier.

5. Operations run smoothly with good planning. For example, new equipment can be ordered in advance of its anticipated usage. With smooth, uninterrupted operations, the overall efficiency of the airport can be increased.

Once the airport has decided upon a plan of action for the future, these plans are incorporated into a written financial budget. *Budgets* are simply the planned dollar amounts needed to operate and maintain the airport during a definite period of time such as a year. Budgets are established for major capital expenditures such as runway resurfacing, taxiway construction, and new snow removal equipment as well as for operating expenses during the planning period.

In an airport maintenance department, there are labor expenses and a variety of other expenses for supplies, minor equipment purchasing and repair, and mechanical systems maintenance. The real expenses incurred during the year are a measure of the actual performance. The differences between actual expenses and the budgeted amount is called a *variance*. The variance measures the efficiency of the department.

Airports generally operate under one of three different forms of budget appropriation:

1. Lump-sum appropriation. A lump-sum appropriation is the simplest form of budget and generally only utilized by small GA airports. There are no specific restrictions as to how the money should be spent. Only the total expenditure for the period is stipulated. Obviously, this is the most flexible form of budget.

2. Appropriation by activity. Under this form of budget, appropriated expenses are planned according to major work area or activity with no

further detailed breakdown. Appropriation by activity enables management to establish capital and operating expense budgets for particular areas such as airside facilities, terminal building area, and so forth. It also permits flexibility in responding to changing conditions.

3. Line-item budget. The line-item budget is the most detailed form of budgeting and is used quite extensively at the large commercial airports. Numerical codes are established for each capital expense item. Budgets are established for each item and often adjusted to take into consideration changes in volume of activity. For example, as the number of passenger enplanements changes, budgets for the terminal building maintenance can be adjusted accordingly.

A very popular approach to budgeting today at many airports is the zero-base budget. The *zero-base budget* derives from the idea that each program or departmental budget should be prepared from the ground up or base zero. This is in contrast to the normal budgeting practice, which builds on the base of a previous period. By calculating the budget from a zero-base, all costs are newly developed and reviewed entirely to determine their necessity. Various programs are reviewed and costed thoroughly and then ranked in degree of importance to the airport. Managers are presumably forced to look at a program in its entirety rather than as an expense add-on to an existing budget.

In drawing up a budget, the first step normally involves an estimate of revenues from all sources for the coming year. The next step is to establish budgets for the various areas of responsibility. When budgets are being investigated, predetermined, and integrated, the department managers who must live within the budgets are consulted about the amount of money available and help draw up budgets for their departments for the coming period. A manager who has some say about the budget and expenses is more inclined to make an added effort to keep down the actual expenses of the department.

Actual expenses are then checked against budgeted expenses frequently during the period that the budgets are in effect. Managers are supplied with figures of actual expenses so that they can compare them with budgeted expenses and investigate variances.

Approaches to financial management at commercial airports

At most commercial airports, the financial and operational relationship between the airport operator and the airlines is defined in legally binding agreements that specify how the risks and responsibilities of running the airport are to be shared. These contracts, commonly termed airport use agreements, establish the terms and conditions governing the airlines' use of the airport. *Airport use agreement* is used generically here to include both legal contracts for the airlines' use of airfield facilities and leases for use of terminal facilities. At many airports, both are combined in a single document. A few commercial airports do not negotiate airport use agreements with the airlines, but instead charge rates and fees set by local ordinance. The airport use agreements also specify the methods for calculating rates airlines must pay for use of airport facilities and services; and they identify the airlines' rights and privileges, sometimes including the right to approve or disapprove any major proposed airport capital development projects.

Although financial management practices differ greatly among commercial airports, the airport-airline relationship at major airports typically takes one of two very different forms, with important implications for airport pricing and investment:

1. The residual-cost approach, under which the airlines collectively assume significant financial risk by agreeing to pay any costs of running the airport that are not allocated to other users or covered by nonairline sources of revenue.

2. The compensatory approach, under which the airport operator assumes the major financial risk of running the airport and charges the airlines fees and rental rates set so as to recover the actual costs of the facilities and services that they use.

The residual-cost approach

A majority of the nation's large commercial airports have some form of residual-cost approach to financial management. Under this approach, the airlines collectively assume significant financial risk. They agree to keep the airport financially self-sustaining by making up any deficit—the residual cost—remaining after the costs identified for all airport users have been offset by nonairline sources of revenue (automobile parking and terminal concessions such as restaurants, newsstands, snack bars, and the like).

Although applications of the residual-cost approach vary widely, a simplified example can illustrate the basic approach (TABLE 11-2).

Most airports have a number of different cost centers. These include the airfield area, terminal area, and so forth as indicated earlier in this chapter. At a residual-cost airport, the total annual expenses, including administration, maintenance, operations, and debt service (including coverage) is calculated for each cost center, and offset by all nonairline revenues anticipated for that center. *Debt service coverage* is the requirement that the airport's revenue, net of operating and maintenance expenses, be equal to a specified percentage in excess of the annual debt service (principal and interest payments) for revenue bond issues. The coverage required is generally from 1.25 to 1.40 times debt service, thereby providing a substantial cushion that enhances the security of the bonds.

Table 11-2. Comparison of residual-cost and compensatory methods of calculating airport fees. Source: FAA

Requirement	Residual Cost		Compensatory	
	Terminal	Airfield	Terminal	Airfield
Maintenance, operations, and administration	$ 40,000	$ 40,000	$ 40,000	$ 40,000
Debt service	40,000	20,000	40,000	20,000
Debt service coverage	10,000	5,000	10,000	5,000
Deposits to special funds	5,000	20,000	5,000	20,000
Other	5,000	15,000	5,000	15,000
Total requirement	$ 100,000	$ 100,000	$ 100,000	$100,000
Cost center revenue from nonairline sources	−$50,000	−$50,000	NA	NA
Airline share (percent)	NA	NA	65	75
Residual cost	50,000	50,000	NA	NA
Activity level	6,500 ft^2	100,000 lb gross landing weight	6,500 ft^2	100,000 lb gross landing weight
Rental rate (per square foot)	$ 7.69	NA	$ 10.00	NA
Landing fee rate (per 1,000 pound gross landing weight)	NA	$ 0.50	NA	$ 0.75

This is not a comparison of actual rate calculations but a simplified illustration. Rates are not necessarily higher under either approach but differ according to the volume of traffic, amount of debt, and other factors.

NA = Not applicable

The residual between costs and revenues provides the basis for calculating the rates charged the airlines for their use of facilities within the cost center. Any surplus revenues would be credited to the airlines and any deficit charged to them in calculating airline landing fees or other rates for the following year.

The compensatory approach

Under a compensatory approach, the airport operator assumes the financial risk of airport operation, and airlines pay rates and charges equal to the costs of the facilities they use as determined by cost accounting. In contrast to the situation at residual-cost airports, the airlines at a compensatory airport provide no guarantee that fees and rents will suffice to allow the airport to meet its annual operating and debt service requirements.

Although individual airports have adopted many versions of the compensatory approach, the simplified example set out in TABLE 11-2 illustrates the basics. First, for each cost center, a calculation would be made of the total annual expense of running the center, including administration, maintenance, operations, and debt service (with coverage). The airlines' shares of these costs would then be based on the extent of their actual use of facilities within each cost center. The airlines would not be charged for the costs of public space, such as terminal lobbies. Nor would they receive any credit for nonairline revenues, which offset expenses in the residual-cost approach but are disregarded under a compensatory approach in calculating rates and charges to the airlines.

Comparison of residual-cost and compensatory approaches

These two major approaches to financial management of major commercial airports have significantly different implications for pricing and investment practices. In particular, they help determine:

1. An airport's potential for accumulating net income for capital development.
2. The nature and extent of the airlines' role in making airport capital investment decisions, which can be formally defined in majority-in-interest clauses included in airport use agreements with the airlines.
3. The length of term of the use agreement between the airlines and the airport operator.

These differences, discussed below, can have an important bearing on an airport's performance in the municipal bond market.

Net income   Although large and medium commercial airports generally must rely on the issuance of debt to finance major capital development projects, the availability of substantial revenues generated in excess of expenses can strengthen the performance of an airport in the municipal bond market. It can also provide an alternative to issuing debt for the financing of some portion of capital development. Residual-cost financing guarantees that an airport will always break even—thereby assuring service without resort to supplemental local tax support—but it precludes the airport from generating earnings substantially in excess of costs.

By contrast, an airport using a compensatory approach lacks the built-in security afforded by the airlines' guarantee that the airport will break even every year. The public operator undertakes the risk that revenues generated by airport fees and charges might not be adequate to allow the airport to meet its annual operating costs and debt service obligations. On the other hand, because total revenues are not constrained to the amount needed to break even, and because surplus revenues are not used to reduce airline rates and charges, compensatory airports may earn and retain a substantial surplus, which can later be used for capital development. Since the pricing of airport concessions and consumer services need not be limited to the recovery of actual costs, the extent of such retained earnings generally depends on the magnitude of the airport's nonairline revenues. Market pricing of concessions and other nonairline sources of revenue is a feature of both residual-cost and compensatory airports.

Because the residual-cost approach is not designed to yield substantial revenues in excess of costs, residual-cost airports, as a group, tend to retain considerably smaller percentages of their gross revenues than do compensatory airports. A few residual-cost airports, however, have modified the approach to permit accumulation of sizable retained earnings for use in capital projects. For example, at Miami International, certain airport-generated revenues are excluded from the revenue base used in calculating the residual-cost payable by the airlines; the revenues flow instead into a discretionary fund that can finance capital development projects.

Majority-in-interest   In exchange for the guarantee of solvency, airlines that are signatory to a residual-cost use agreement often exercise a significant measure of control over airport investment decisions and related pricing policy. These powers are embodied in so-called majority-in-interest clauses, which are a much more common feature of airport use agreements at residual-cost airports than at airports using a compensatory approach.

Majority-in-interest clauses give the airlines that represent a majority of traffic at an airport the opportunity to review and approve or veto capital projects that would entail significant increases in the rates and fees they pay for the use of airport facilities. The combination of airlines that can exercise majority-in-interest powers varies. A typical formulation would give majority-in-interest powers to any combination of "more than 50 percent of the scheduled airlines that landed more than 50 percent of the aggregate revenue aircraft weight during the preceding fiscal year" (standard document wording).

This arrangement provides protection for the airlines that have assumed financial risk under a residual-cost agreement by guaranteeing payment of all airport costs not covered by nonairline sources of revenue. For instance, without some form of majority-in-interest clause, the airlines at a residual-cost airport could be obligating themselves to pay the costs of as-yet-undefined facilities that might be proposed in the 15th or 20th year of a 30-year use agreement. Under a compensatory approach, where the airport operator assumes the major financial risk of running the facility, the operator is generally freer to undertake capital development projects without consent of the airlines that account for a majority of the traffic. Even so, airport operators rarely embark on major projects without consulting the airlines that serve the airport. Potential investors in airport revenue bonds would be wary of a bond issue for a project lacking the airlines' approval.

Specific provisions of majority-in-interest clauses vary considerably. At some airports, the airlines that account for a majority of traffic can approve or disapprove all major capital development projects—any project costing more than $100,000. At other airports, projects can only be deferred for a certain period of time (generally six months to two years). Although most airports have at least a small discretionary fund for capital improvements that is not subject to majority-in-interest approval, the general effect of majority-in-interest provisions is to limit the ability of the public airport owner to proceed with any major project opposed by the airlines. Sometimes, a group of just two or three major carriers can exercise such control.

Term of use agreement   Residual-cost airports typically have longer term use agreements than compensatory airports. This is because residual-cost agreements historically have been drawn up to provide security for long-term airport revenue bond issues; and the term of the use agreement, with its airline guarantee of debt service, has generally coincided with the term of the revenue bonds. The vast majority of residual-cost airports have use agreements with terms of 20 or more years and 30 years or longer is not uncommon.

By contrast, probably only 50 percent of the compensatory airports have use agreements running for 20 years or more. Many of the compensatory airports have no contractual agreements whatever with the airlines. At these airports, rates and charges are established by local ordinance or resolution. This arrangement gives airport operators maximum flexibility to adjust their pricing and investment practices unilaterally, without the constraints imposed by a formal agreement negotiated with the airlines, but it lacks the security provided by contractual agreements.

Pricing of airport facilities and services

Major commercial airports are diversified enterprises that provide a wide range of facilities and services for which fees, rents, or other user charges are assessed. It was pointed out earlier in the chapter that most commercial airports, regardless of size, type, or locale, offer four major types of facilities and services: (1) airfield area, (2) terminal area concessions, (3) airline leased areas, and (4) other leased areas.

The facilities and services provided to users generate the revenues necessary to operate the airport and to support the financing of capital development. Smaller commercial airports and GA airports typically offer a much narrower range of facilities and services, for which only minimal fees and charges often are assessed. Revenue bases shrink as airports decrease in size, and many of the smallest do not generate sufficient revenue to cover their operating costs, much less capital investment. Among GA airports, those that lease land or facilities for industrial use generally have a better chance of covering their costs of operation than do those providing only aviation-related services and facilities.

The combination of public management and private enterprise uniquely characteristic of the financial operation of commercial airports is reflected in the divergent pricing of airport facilities and services. The private enterprise aspects of airport operation—the services and facilities furnished for nonaeronautical use—generally are priced on a market pricing basis. On the other hand, the pricing of facilities and services for airlines and other aeronautical users is on a cost-recovery basis, either recovery of the actual costs of the facilities and services provided (the compensatory approach) or recovery of the residual costs of airport operation not covered by nonairline sources of revenue. This mix of market pricing and cost-recovery pricing has important implications for airport financing, especially with regard to the structure and control of airport charges and the distribution of operating revenues.

The structure and control of fees, rents, and other charges for facilities and services are governed largely by a variety of long-term and short-term contracts, including airport use agreements with the airlines, leases, and concession and management contracts. For each of the four major groups of facilities and services outlined earlier in the chapter, the basic kinds of charges assessed at residual-cost and compensatory airports can be compared in terms of: (1) method of calculation, (2) term of agreement, and (3) frequency of adjustment.

Airfield area   The major fees assessed for use of airfield facilities are landing or flight fees for commercial airlines and GA aircraft. Some airports also levy other airfield fees, such as charges for the use of aircraft parking ramps or aprons. In lieu of landing fees, many smaller airports—especially GA airports—collect *fuel flowage fees*, which are levied per gallon of aviation gasoline and jet fuel sold at the airport.

At residual-cost airports, the landing fee for airlines is typically the item that balances the budget, making up the projected difference between all other anticipated revenues and the total annual costs of administration, operations and maintenance, and debt service (including coverage). Landing fees differ widely among residual-cost airports, depending on the extent of the revenues derived from airline terminal rentals and concessions such as restaurants, car rental companies, and automobile parking lots. If the nonairline revenues are high in a given year, the landing fee for the airlines might be quite low. In recent years, several airports—including Los Angeles and Honolulu International—have approached a "negative" landing fee. At some residual-cost airports, the landing fee is the budget-balancing item for the airfield cost center only. At such airports, the surplus or deficit in the terminal cost center has no influence on airline landing fees, and terminal rental rates for the airlines are set on a residual-cost or a compensatory basis.

The method of calculating landing fees at residual-cost airports is established in the airport use agreement and continues for the full term of the agreement. To reflect changes in operating costs or revenues, landing fees are typically adjusted at specified intervals ranging from six months to three years. At some airports, fees might be adjusted more often if revenues are significantly lower or higher than anticipated. Often, the nonsignatory airlines (those not party to the basic use agreement) pay higher landing fees than the signatory carriers. General aviation landing fees vary greatly from airport to airport, ranging from charges equal to those paid by the commercial airlines to none at all. Most landing fees are assessed on the basis of certificated gross landing weight. This practice of basing landing fees on aircraft weight tends to promote use of commercial airports by general aviation. Because most GA aircraft are relatively light (under 10,000 pounds), they pay very low landing fees at most commercial airports. The smallest GA aircraft often pay no fee. Residual-cost and compensatory airports alike have landing fees for GA aircraft that are generally so small as to be negligible, either as a source of revenue to the airport or as a deterrent to use of congested facilities.

At compensatory airports, airline landing fees are based on calculation of the average actual costs of airfield facilities used by the airlines (TABLE 11-3). As in the case of residual-cost airports, each airline's share of these costs is based on its share of total projected airline gross landing weights (or, in a few cases, gross takeoff weight). In addition to fees determined by this weight-based measure, three compensatory airports—Boston Logan International and John F. Kennedy and LaGuardia airports in New York—assess a surcharge on GA aircraft during hours of peak demand. Presently, no major airports impose such peak-hour surcharges on commercial airlines to help ease congestion problems. Some airport managers and federal authorities feel that peak-hour surcharges could reduce congestion by giving airlines and other providers of air transportation services the opportunity to save money (and lower fares) by flying during uncongested periods. If peak-period demand continued to cause congestion, the increased revenue generated by the surcharges could help finance the expansion necessary to accommodate peak-hour traffic.

Landing fees at compensatory airports are established either in airport use agreements with the airlines or by local ordinance or resolution. The frequency of adjustment of the fees is comparable to that at residual-cost airports.

Terminal area concessions The structure of terminal concession and service contract fees is similar under both pricing approaches. Concession contracts typically provide the airport operator with a guaranteed annual minimum payment or

Table 11-3. *Profile of landing fees at four major airports, 1991.* Source: FAA

Basis of fee	Method of calculation	Airline landing fee Fee[a]	General aviation landing fee
Boston Logan International Compensatory; based on recovery of all costs of providing and operating "public aircraft facilities"[b]	Fee = public aircraft facilities costs divided by total projected scheduled airline landing weights; adjusted annually	$1.59	$1.59 per 1,000 lb. of maximum gross landing weight, subject to $50 minimum during peak periods and $25 in offpeak periods.
Denver Stapleton International Compensatory; based on recovery of maintenance, operations, and debt service costs for airfield area	Fee = airfield cost center expenses divided by total projected airline landing weights; adjusted annually	$1.61	$1.61 per 1,000 lb. of maximum gross landing weight, subject to $16 minimum during peak periods and $10 offpeak periods.
Los Angeles International Residual cost; based on recovery of all costs (maintenance, operations, and debt service), net of all revenues other than landing fees	Fee = residual cost divided by estimated total landing weights of all airlines; adjusted semi-annually	$0.50[c]	$0.50 per 1,000 lb. of maximum gross landing weight, subject to $10 minimum for aircraft under 12,500 lb. and $15 minimum for aircraft from 12,500 to 25,000 lb.
New Orleans International Residual cost; based on recovery of all costs (maintenance, operations, and debt service), net all revenues other than landing fees	Fee = residual cost divided by estimated total landing weights of all airlines; adjusted every 3 years	$2.76	$3.06 per 1,000 lb. of maximum gross landing weight

[a]Fee per 1,000 lb. of maximum gross weight. A typical commercial jet airliner (727-200) weighs about 200,000 lb; a typical general aviation jet (Lear 25D) weighs 15,000 lb.

[b]Defined as including the capital costs of public aircraft facilities; cost of equipment; replenishment of maintenance reserve fund; administration, operations, and maintenance costs, and allocated portions of payments in lieu of taxes.

[c]$0.55 for nonsignatory carriers.

a specified percentage of the concessionaire's gross revenues, whichever is greater. Restaurants, snack bars, gift shops, newsstands, duty-free shops, hotels, and rental car operations usually have contracts of this type. Terminal concession contracts are often bid competitively, and they range in term from month-to-month agreements to contracts of 10 to 15 years duration. (Hotel agreements generally have much longer terms, often running for 40 years or more.) Airport parking facilities might be operated as concessions; they might be run by the airport directly, or they might be managed by a contractor for either a flat fee or a percentage of revenues.

Airline leased areas   At both residual-cost and compensatory airports, airlines pay rent to the airport operator for the right to occupy various facilities (terminal space, hangars, cargo terminals, and land). Rental rates are established in the airport use agreements, in separate leases, or by local ordinance or resolution. Terminal space might be assigned on an exclusive-use basis (to a single airline), a preferential-use basis (if a certain level of activity is not maintained, the airline must share the space), or on a joint-use basis (space used in common by several airlines). Most major commercial airports use a combination of these methods. In addition, airports can charge the airlines a fee for use of any airport-controlled gate space and for the provision of federal inspection facilities required at airports serving international traffic. Some airports have long-term ground leases with individual airlines that allow the airlines to finance and construct their own passenger terminal facilities on land leased from the airport.

Among residual-cost airports, the method of calculating airline terminal rental rates varies considerably. If airline fees and charges are calculated on a residual-cost basis within each cost center, the method of calculating rental rates resembles that of the simplified example shown in TABLE 11-2. To arrive at the airline fee, total nonairline revenues generated within the terminal cost center are subtracted from the total costs of the center (administration, operations and maintenance, and debt service). Each airline's share is based on the square footage it occupies, with proration of jointly used space.

On the other hand, at residual-cost airports where receipts from airline landing fees alone are used to balance the airport budget, the terminal rental rates for the airlines can be set in various ways—on a compensatory basis (recovering the average actual costs of the facilities used), by an outside appraisal of the property value, or by negotiation with the airlines. In all cases, each airline's share of costs is based on its proportionate use of the facilities. Rental rates might be uniform for all types of space leased to the airlines, or they might differ according to the type of space provided—for example, they might be significantly higher for leases of ticket counters or office space than for rental of gate or baggage claim areas.

At residual-cost airports, the rental term for airline leased areas generally coincides with the term of the airport use agreement with the airlines. The frequency of adjustment of terminal rental rates ranges considerably—annually at many airports, but up to three to five years at others.

At compensatory airports, the method of calculating terminal rental rates for the airlines is based on recovery of the average actual costs of the space occupied. Each airline's share of the total costs is based on the square footage leased. Typically, rates differ according to the type of space and whether it is leased on an exclusive, preferential, or joint-use basis. The rental term for airline leased areas often coincides with that of the airport use agreement. (It is set by ordinance at airports that operate without agreements.) Rates are typically adjusted annually at compensatory airports.

Other leased areas   A wide variety of arrangements are employed for other leased areas at an airport, which might include agricultural land, fixed-base operations, cargo terminals, and industrial parks. The methods of calculating rental rates and the frequency of adjustment differ according to the type of facility and the nature of use. What these disparate rentals have in common is that, like terminal concessions and services, they are generally priced on a market basis, and the airport managers have considerable flexibility in setting rates and charges in the context of market constraints and their own policy objectives.

Variation in the source of operating revenues

In general, revenue diversification enhances the financial stability of an airport. In addition, the specific mix of revenues might influence year-to-year financial performance. Some of the major sources of airport revenue (notably landing fees and terminal concessions) are affected by changes in the volume of air passenger traffic, while others (airline terminal rentals and ground leases) are essentially immune to fluctuations in air traffic.

The distribution of operating revenues differs widely according to factors such as passenger enplanements, the nature of the market served, and the specific objectives and features of the airport's approach to pricing and financial management. Airport size generally has a strong influence on the distribution of revenues. The larger commercial airports typically have a more diversified revenue base than smaller airports. For example, they tend to have a wider array of income-producing facilities and services in the passenger terminal complex. In general, terminal concessions can be expected to generate a greater percentage of total operating revenues as passenger enplanements increase. On average, concessions account for at least one-third of total operating revenues at large, medium, and small commercial airports, compared to about one-fifth at very small (non-hub) commercial airports and a smaller fraction still at GA airports.

Factors other than airport size also affect distribution of operating revenues. At commercial airports, for example, parking facilities generally provide the largest single source of nonairline revenues in the terminal area. Airports that have a high proportion of connecting traffic might, however, derive a smaller percentage of their operating income from parking revenues than do so-called "origin and destination" airports. Other factors that can affect parking revenues include availability of space for parking, the volume of air passenger traffic, the airport pricing policy, availability and cost of alternatives to driving to the airport (mass transit and taxicab service), and the presence of private competitors providing parking facilities at nearby locations off the airport property.

The approach to financial management, because it governs the pricing of facilities and services provided to airlines, significantly affects the distribution of operating revenues. Because so many other factors play an important role in determining revenue distribution, however, the mix of operating revenues at an airport cannot be predicted on the basis of whether the airport employs a residual-cost or compensatory approach. The mix of revenues varies widely among residual-cost airports. With airline landing fees characteristically picking up the difference between airport costs and other revenues at residual-cost airports, airfield area income differs markedly according to the extent of the airport's financial obligations, the magnitude of terminal concession income and other nonairline revenues, and the volume of air traffic. In 1989, for example, airfield area revenues provided anywhere from 10 percent (Tampa International) to more than 50 percent (Chicago O'Hare International) of total operating revenues at residual-cost airports. By contrast, compensatory airports show a considerably smaller range of variation in the distribution of revenues.

Trends in airport financial management since deregulation

Federal deregulation of the airline industry has radically changed the market in which airlines—and airports—operate. Once subject to strict regulation of routes and fares, commercial air carriers are free to revise routes, adjust fares, and introduce or terminate service to particular airports as market conditions seem to warrant. This new freedom from federal intervention has had pronounced effects on the airline industry. It has spurred intense competition and even price wars among the airlines, led to reconfiguration of the route system, and encouraged the startup of new carriers. For some of the established airlines, serious financial difficulties have ensued. Although deregulation has not caused radical changes in the financial management of airports, recent trends do reflect the uncertainties of a new, open market. Deregulation also appears to have accelerated certain shifts in management policy and practice that were underway before deregulation.

Since the early days of commercial air travel, would-be investors in airport revenue bonds have held long-term use agreements in high regard, considering them evidence of the airlines' commitment to serve an airport for long periods—spans usually coincident with the terms of bond issues. As the industry has matured, however, investors and analysts have increasingly recognized that an airport's financial stability—hence its capacity to generate a stream of revenue adequate to secure revenue bond issues—depends more on the underlying strength of the local air travel market than on long-term use agreements.

Deregulation has reinforced this shift, as the strength of the airlines' financial commitment to an airport is significantly diluted by their new flexibility to withdraw from a market virtually at will. Confidence has also been shaken by the financial problems now plaguing many airlines. Although changes in airport financial management occur very slowly (many standing use agreements run through the 1990s or later), three important trends in financial management are now emerging at major commercial airports:

1. Shorter term contracts. Shorter terms for airport use agreements, nonairline leases, and concessionaires' contracts, and more frequent adjustment of rates and charges.

2. Modification of residual-cost approach. Modification of residual-cost rate making and majority-in-interest provisions, with movement in the direction of more compensatory forms of financial management.

3. Maximization of revenues. Concerted effort by airport managers to maximize revenues by means of a variety of strategies intended to strengthen and diversify the revenue base of the airport.

Shorter term contracts

Deregulation appears to have hastened a trend toward shorter term airport use agreements that was already under way prior to 1978. Shorter term contracts give airport operators greater flexibility to adjust pricing, investment policies, and space allocation to meet shifting needs in a deregulated environment. For example, several airports with long-term use agreements in force have given much shorter term agreements to air carriers that have begun serving the airport since 1978. Contracts for such recent entrants often run for five years or less, and they might take the form of yearly or even month-to-month operating agreements (similar to those used for air taxi and commuter operators). As existing long-term use agreements expire, many airport operators are negotiating shorter term use agreements with all carriers serving the airport. In part, this reflects the fact that many post-deregulation agreements have not involved major capital development programs requiring long-term bond financing.

Many airports are also shortening the terms of nonairline leases and contracts with concessionaires. Some are also moving to more frequent adjustment of rates and charges under existing agreements to meet the escalating costs of airport operation.

Modifications of residual-cost approach

In recent years, some airports have introduced changes to the residual-cost approach, such as more compensatory methods of calculating airline fees and charges, weakening or elimination of majority-in-interest clauses, and provisions allowing for greater retention of earnings usable for capital development. In general, the compensatory approach becomes attractive as airports develop strong markets and thus increase their revenue-generating potential. Such airports are better able to assume the financial risks of airport operation without relying on "break-even" guarantees by the airlines, and they can maximize revenues by adopting a compensatory approach.

Maximization of revenues

No matter how they approach financial management, many commercial airports are now seeking to increase and diversify their revenues by a variety of strategies. These include raising existing fees and rental rates, seeking more frequent adjustment of charges, using competitive bidding for concessionaires' contracts, increasing the airport's percentage of gross profits, and exploiting new or untapped sources of revenue: videogame rooms, industrial park development, and leasing of unused airport property. Some airports are looking to future possibilities, as well. For example, two large airports that recently renegotiated airport use agreements—Chicago O'Hare and Greater Pittsburgh International—included clauses in the new contracts protecting the airport's right to levy a passenger facility charge (or head tax). In general, this effort to diversify and expand revenue sources reflects the paramount importance of a guaranteed stream of income to assure an airport's financial success.

Key terms

airport accounting
operating statement
budgets
variance
lump-sum appropriation
appropriation by activity
line-item budget
zero-base budget
airport use agreement
residual-cost approach
compensatory approach
debt service coverage

majority-in-interest clauses
fuel flowage fees

Review questions

1. Define airport accounting. What is the purpose of a good accounting system?
   Describe the five major areas under a typical airport's operating revenues. Why is it difficult to compare operating costs between airports?
   Describe the major maintenance and operating expenses under the airfield area and terminal area.

2. List the primary reasons for planning and budgeting. What is a "variance?"
   Describe the following forms of budget appropriation: (1) Lump-sum appropriation, (2) Appropriation by activity, and (3) Line-item budget. What is a "zero-base" budget?

3. Define *airport use agreement.* Compare the residual-cost approach with the compensatory approach to airport-airline relationships. What is *debt-service coverage?* What effect does the two major approaches to financial management have on net income, majority-in-interest, and term of use agreements?

4. What are the major sources of revenue for the following areas? (1) airfield, (2) terminal concessions, (3) airline leased areas, and (4) other leased areas.
   Discuss some of the factors that determine the variations in revenues between different airports.

5. Discuss some of the effects that deregulation has had on airport-airline relationships.

Suggested readings

Gesell, Laurence E. *The Administration of Public Airports,* 2nd ed. Chandler, Arizona: Coast-Aire Publications, 1986.

Campbell, George E. *Airport Management and Operations.* Baton Rouge, Louisiana: Claitor's Publishing Division, 1972.

Eckrose, Roy A. and William H. Green. *How to Assure the Future of Your Airport.* Madison, Wisconsin: Eckrose/Green Associates, 1988.

Organization and administration

Outline

Airport ownership and operation
The airport organization chart
Airport management as a career
The airport manager and public relations

Objectives

When you have completed this chapter, you should be able to:

△ Describe the five types of public airport ownership and operation in the United States.

△ Explain the purpose of an organization chart.

△ Summarize the major responsibility and discuss the principal duties of the following positions: airport director, assistant director—finance and administration, assistant director—operations, and assistant director—maintenance.

△ Identify at least 10 other positions found at a commercial airport.

△ Discuss the educational and training requirements for an individual considering a career in airport management.

△ Explain the importance of airport public relations.

△ List the primary objectives of an airport public relations campaign.

Airport ownership and operation

Public airports in the United States are owned and operated under a variety of organizational and jurisdictional arrangements. Usually, ownership and operation coincide: commercial airports might be owned and operated by a city, county, or state, by the federal government, or by more than one jurisdiction (a city and a county). In some cases, a commercial airport is owned by one or more of these governmental entities but operated by a separate public body, such as an airport authority specifically created for the purpose of managing the airport. Regardless of ownership, legal responsibility for day-to-day operation and administration can be vested in any of five kinds of governmental or public entities: (1) a municipal or county government, (2) a multipurpose port authority, (3) an airport authority, (4) a state government, or (5) the federal government.

A typical *municipally operated airport* is city owned and run as a department of the city, with policy direction by the city council and, in some cases, by a separate airport commission or advisory board. County-run airports are similarly organized. Under this type of public operation, airport policy decisions are generally made in the broader context of city or countywide public investment needs, budgetary constraints, and development goals.

Some commercial airports in the United States are run by multipurpose port authorities. *Port authorities* are legally chartered institutions with the status of public corporations that operate a variety of publicly owned facilities, such as harbors, airports, toll roads, and bridges. In managing the properties under their jurisdiction, port authorities have extensive independence from the state and local governments. Their financial independence rests largely on the power to issue their own debt, in the form of revenue bonds, and on the breadth of their revenue bases, which might include fees and charges from marine terminals and airports as well as proceeds (bridge or tunnel tolls) from other port authority properties. In addition, some port authorities have the power to tax within the port district, although it is rarely exercised.

Another type of arrangement is the single-purpose *airport authority*. Similar in structure and in legal charter to port authorities, these single-purpose authorities also have considerable independence from the state or local governments, which often retain ownership of the airport or airports operated by the authority. Similar to multipurpose port authorities, airport authorities have the power to issue their own debt for financing capital development, and in a few cases, the power to tax. Compared to port authorities, however, they must rely on a much narrower base of revenues to run a financially self-sustaining enterprise.

Since the early 1950s, there has been a gradual transition from city and county controlled airports to the independent single or multipurpose authorities. The predominant form is still municipally owned and operated, particularly the smaller commercial and GA airports, however, there are reasons for this transition:

1. Many airport market or service areas have outgrown the political jurisdiction whose responsibility the airport entails. In some cases there is considerable, actual or potential, tax liability to a rather limited area. In these cases the creation of an authority to "spread the potential or actual tax support" for the airport might be recommended. By spreading the tax base of support for the airport, more equitable treatment of the individual taxpayer can result and the taxpayers supporting the airport in most cases more nearly match the actual users of the facility.

2. Another advantage of authority control of an airport is that such an organization allows the board to concentrate and specialize on airport matters.

3. Aviation authorities can also provide efficiency of operation and economies of scale when several political jurisdictions, each with separate airport responsibilities, choose to combine these under one board. This has been done quite successfully in many areas of the

country. Normally, the staff required by an airport authority will be quite small compared to the personnel requirements of a city or county government. This factor generally results in better coordination with the airport management team.

4. Authorities can also provide on-scene decision makers, rates, and charges unclouded by off-airport costs, and less political impact on the business of running the airport.

State-operated airports are typically managed by the state's department of transportation. Either general obligation or revenue bonding might be used to raise investment capital, and state taxes on aviation fuel might be applied to capital improvement projects.

Although several states run their own commercial airports, only a handful of large- and medium-size commercial airports are operated in this way, primarily in Alaska, Connecticut, Hawaii, Maryland, and Rhode Island. The federal government owns and operates the airport at Pomona (Atlantic City), New Jersey, which is part of the FAA Technical Center. The FAA manages this facility with capital development financed through congressional appropriations. The federal government also levies user taxes and disburses funds for the capital development of other airports through FAA's Airport Improvement Program discussed in chapter 1.

The airport organization chart

An *organization chart* shows the formal authority relationships between superiors and subordinates at various levels, as well as the formal channels of communication within the organization. It provides a framework within which the management functions can be carried out. The chart aids employees to perceive more clearly their position in the organization in relation to others and how and where managers and workers fit into the overall organizational structure.

The organization chart is a static model of the airport because it shows how the airport is organized at a given point in time. This is a major limitation of the chart, because airports operate in a dynamic environment and thus must continually adapt to changing conditions. Some old positions might no longer be required, or new positions might have to be created in order that new objectives can be reached; therefore, it is necessary that the chart be revised and updated periodically to reflect these changing conditions.

Airport management has changed so significantly over the past 25 years that it is difficult to say that any organization chart is typical or that the chart of one airport at any particular time is the one still in effect even a few months later; however, all airports do have certain common functional areas into which airport activities are divided. Understandably, the larger the airport, the greater the specialization of tasks and the greater departmentalization. Figure 12-1 shows the major functional areas and typical managerial job titles for a commercial airport.

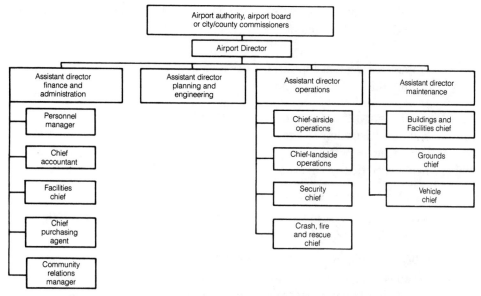

Fig. 12-1. Organizational chart for a commercial airport.

Job descriptions

The following is a brief job description for each position shown in FIG. 12-1.

Airport director   The airport director is responsible for the overall day-to-day operation of the airport. He reports directly to the airport authority, the airport board or governmental commission charged with the development and administration of the airport. This individual directs, coordinates, and reviews through subordinate supervisors, all aircraft operations, building and field maintenance, construction plans, community relations, financial, and personnel matters at the airport. Other functions include:

1. Supervision and coordination with airline, general aviation and military tenants regarding use of airport facilities.
2. Reviews airport tenant activities for compliance with terms of leases and other agreements.
3. Supervises enforcement of aircraft air and ground traffic and other applicable regulations.
4. Confers with airlines, tenants, the FAA, and others regarding airport regulations, facilities, and related matters.
5. Participates in planning for increased aircraft and passenger volume and facilities expansion.
6. Determines and recommends airport staffing requirements.
7. Compiles and submits for review an annual airport budget.

8. Coordinates airport activities with construction, maintenance, and other work done by departmental staff, tenants, public utilities, and contractors.

9. Promotes acceptance of airport-oriented activities in surrounding communities.

Assistant director—finance and administration The assistant director—finance and administration is charged with the reponsibility for overall matters concerning finance, personnel, purchasing, facilities management and office management. Specifically, this individual's duties include:

1. Fiscal planning and budget administration.

2. Assuring accomplishment of basic finance functions such as accounts receivable and payable, auditing, and payroll.

3. Administering the purchasing function.

4. Responsible for administration and use of real property including negotiation of tenant leases and inventory control.

5. Personnel functions including compensation, employee relations, and training.

6. Assuring adequate telephone and mail service.

7. Community relations.

Personnel manager The personnel manager is responsible for administering the airport personnel program. In such capacity, this individual's duties include:

1. Personnel problems involving position classification, compensation, recruitment, placement, transfers, layoffs, promotions, leaves of absence, supervisor-subordinate relationships, and working conditions.

2. Serves as equal rights and equal opportunity officer for the airport.

3. Handles Workmen's Compensation cases.

4. Evaluates organization patterns; reviews and recommends on proposed departmental organization changes; and prepares position descriptions.

5. Confers with employees and their supervisors on personnel problems.

6. Prepares personnel documents and maintains personnel records.

7. Interviews or supervises the interviewing of applicants for airport positions.

Chief accountant The chief accountant is responsible for financial planning, budgeting, accounting, payroll, and auditing. His principal duties include:

1. Coordinating, consolidating, and presentation of financial plans.

2. Administration of basic accounts such as general accounts, cost accounting, and accounts receivable and payable.

3. Administers budget; reviews and analyzes actual performance at budget review sessions.

4. Responsible for all receipts and disbursements.

5. Responsible for the payroll administration.

6. Conducts periodic internal audit of all airport functions.

Facilities chief   The facilities chief establishes criteria and procedures for the administration of all airport property. In this capacity, he is responsible for inventory control of all equipment and facilities. Principal duties and responsibilities of this individual include:

1. Identification and control of all property and equipment including periodic audits.

2. Evaluates and makes recommendations concerning the most efficient use of airport real property utilization.

3. Solicits tenants and concessionaires.

4. Develops policy and rate structure applicable to use of property by tenants and concessionaires.

5. Coordinates with purchasing and legal staff concerning tenant and concessionaire leases.

Chief purchasing agent   The chief purchasing agent directs the procurement of materials and services to support the airport; he prepares, negotiates, interprets, and administers contracts with vendors. This individual's principal duties include:

1. Coordinates requirements for materials and services to be purchased.

2. Purchases all materials and services.

3. Establishes bidding policies and procedures.

4. Works closely with facilities' chief and legal staff regarding contracts associated with purchasing equipment.

Manager of community relations   The manager of community relations is the chief liaison officer between the airport and the surrounding community. In this capacity, he is responsible for all public relations activities including the development of advertising and publicity concerning the airport. This individual is also responsible for handling all noise and other environmental matters. Principal duties include:

1. Consults with and advises airport management regarding public relations policies and practices.

2. Coordinates all publicity releases to the various media.

3. Responsible for all airport guides and information booths.

4. Coordinates VIP visits to the airport.

5. Receives and analyzes all public complaints regarding such things as noise and other environmental concerns.

6. Prepares answers to complaints and advises management as appropriate.

7. Sponsors activities and special events to generate goodwill and public acceptance.

Assistant director—planning and engineering   The assistant director—planning and engineering provides technical assistance to all airport organizations, and ensures the engineering integrity of construction, alteration, and installation programs. This individual also establishes industrial safety standards. Principal duties and responsibilities include:

1. Developing standards and specifications for construction, alteration, and installation programs; monitors such programs to ensure compliance therewith.

2. Reviews all construction plans to determine technical integrity and conformance to aesthetic design standards.

3. Develops and publishes standards and procedures for industrial safety.

4. Participates in the negotiation of construction contracts.

Assistant director—operations   The assistant director—operations is responsible for all airside and landside operations including security and crash, fire, and rescue operations. Principal duties include:

1. Directing the operations and security programs for the airport.

2. Coordinates and supervises security activities with field maintenance personnel, police, and fire departments, federal agencies, and airport tenants.

3. Recommends and assists in promulgating operational rules and procedures.

4. Supervises investigations of violations of airport regulations.

5. Prepares annual operations budget.

6. Directs monitoring of noise levels and coordinates noise level studies.

7. Participates in special programs relating to or affecting airport operations, such as studies of height limits around airport property and studies of noise control.

Federal Aviation Administration

Airside operations at Washington National Airport.

Chief—airside operations   The chief—airside operations is responsible for all airfield operations. In this capacity, his principal duties include:

1. Enforcing operating and security rules, regulations, and procedures concerning landing, taxiing, parking, servicing loading and unloading of aircraft, operation of vehicular traffic on the airfield, airline activities, and emergency situations.

2. Inspects conditions of airfield lighting, runways, taxiways, and ramp areas.

3. Corrects hazardous conditions.

4. Coordinates airfield activities with maintenance and security personnel.

5. Assists in all airfield emergency calls and disasters by notifying control tower to close runways, directing maintenance personnel, directing security officers in crowd control, and overseeing other safety considerations and activities necessary to resume normal airport operations.

6. Investigates and reports on complaints and disrupted airport operations, including unscheduled plane arrivals, aircraft accidents, rule and procedure violations, airline activities, and other operations of the airport.

7. Assigns gate and parking spaces to all aircraft.

8. Coordinates special arrangements for arrivals and departures of important persons.

9. Completes all report forms pertaining to operations activities on assigned shifts.

10. Assists in directing noise level studies with other departmental personnel.

Chief—landside operations   The chief—landside operations is responsible for all landside operations. In this capacity, his principal duties include:

1. Enforcing operating and security rules, regulations, and procedures concerning buildings, access roads, and parking facilities.

2. Exercises authority to halt hazardous or unauthorized activities by tenants, employees or the public in violation of safety regulations and procedures.

3. Answers inquiries and explains terminal use procedures and safety regulations to tenants.

4. Coordinates terminal building and other facility activities with maintenance and security personnel.

5. Coordinates all parking facility activities with tenants and transit companies.

6. Prepares personal injury and property damage reports and general incident reports.

7. Completes all report forms pertaining to operations activities on assigned shifts.

Security chief   The security chief enforces interior security, traffic, and safety rules and regulations and participates in law enforcement activities at the airport. This individual also provides the public with information regarding locations and operations. His principal duties include:

1. Enforcing ordinances and regulations pertaining to parking, traffic control, safety, and property protection.

2. Patrols facilities to prevent trespass and unauthorized or hazardous use.

3. Prevents public entry into dangerous or restricted areas.

4. Issues citations and warnings for violations of specific provisions of airport rules and regulations.

5. Secures gates and locks and watches buildings and facilities for indications of fire, dangerous conditions, unauthorized entry, and vandalism.

6. Responds to emergencies and takes immediate action to control crowds, direct traffic, assist the injured, and turn in alarms.

7. Responds to calls for police service; participates in arrests; apprehends, or assists members of the police department, in apprehending law violators.

8. Provides information to the public regarding locations and operations of the airport.

9. Assigns uniformed and armed personnel to patrol and stand watch, on a 24-hour basis, to protect and safeguard all persons and property on the airport.

Crash, fire, and rescue chief   The crash, fire, and rescue chief develops procedures and implements crash, fire, and disaster plans. His principal duties include:

1. Conducts a training (continuing) program for all crash, fire, and rescue personnel.

2. Develops and implements all crash, fire, and rescue programs.

3. Staffs and operates all crash, fire, and rescue equipment on the airport.

4. Inspects and tests all types of fixed fire prevention and extinguishing equipment on the airport.

5. Inspects all facilities for fire and/or safety hazards.

Assistant director—maintenance   The assistant director—maintenance is responsible for planning, coordinating, directing, and reviewing the maintenance of buildings, facilities, vehicles, and utilities. Principal duties include:

1. Develops, directs, and coordinates policies, programs, procedures, standards, and schedules for buildings, utilities, vehicle maintenance, and field facilities.

2. Coordinates work done by tenants and contractors.

3. Inspects maintenance work for compliance with plans, specifications, and applicable laws.

4. Makes recommendations as to adequacy, sufficiency, and condition of buildings, facilities, and vehicles.

5. Oversees maintenance contracts.

Buildings and facilities chief   The buildings and facilities chief is responsible for assuring that buildings are adequately maintained with a minimum of cost. Types of maintenance required are primarily electrical, mechanical, plumbing, painting, carpentry, masonry and cement work. His principal duties include:

1. Developing an approved maintenance schedule for all building maintenance requirements.

International terminal building at San Francisco International Airport.

2. Assigns qualified personnel to perform maintenance.

3. Inspects work for adequacy and compliance with requirements.

4. Develops special maintenance methods where necessary.

Grounds chief   The grounds chief is responsible for assuring that the grounds are maintained in good repair and that the landscape is adequately maintained. His principal duties include:

1. Develops approved schedules for maintaining all airport surface areas including paving, landscaping, and drainage systems.

2. Assigns qualified personnel to accomplish ground maintenance.

3. Inspects work for adequacy and compliance with maintenance standards.

Vehicle chief The vehicle chief is responsible for the maintenance of all vehicles utilized by the airport. Vehicle maintenance includes tune-up, minor maintenance, washing and polishing, tires and batteries, lubrication, and fueling. His principal duties include:

1. Developing an approved vehicle maintenance schedule.
2. Coordinates schedule with users of airport vehicles.
3. Assigns qualified personnel to perform maintenance.
4. Inspects all work to determine compliance with establishing maintenance standards.
5. Coordinates with purchasing to obtain vendor services as required.
6. Maintains vehicle usage and maintenance records.
7. Coordinates with purchasing in developing a vehicle disposal and replacement program.

While the aforementioned positions represent a typical managerial structure at a commercial airport, there are numerous employees with a wide variety of job skills reporting to them. Some of the typical job titles found at major airports include the following:

- Accountant
- Administrative assistant
- Airport guide
- Airport noise abatement officer
- Data processing analyst
- Programmer
- Secretary
- Key punch operator
- Public relations representative
- Buyer
- Auditor
- Student intern
- Contract analyst
- Personnel representative
- Facility planner
- Architect
- Draftsman
- Custodian
- Electrician
- Elevator mechanic
- Equipment mechanic
- Equipment operator

- Heavy-duty equipment operator
- Painter
- Carpenter
- Plumber
- Air conditioning mechanic
- Cement finisher
- Auto mechanic
- Groundskeeper
- Sheet metal mechanic
- Welder
- Plasterer
- Tilesetter
- Construction inspector
- Civil engineer
- Security officer
- Fireman
- Supervisor of operations
- Bus driver
- Maintenance foreman
- Tree surgeon
- Traffic painter and sign poster
- Truck operator
- Toolroom keeper
- Window cleaner
- Maintenance and construction laborer

Airport management as a career

There are many career paths within the field of airport management as evidenced by the wide variety of job descriptions under the previous section. Even the job of airport manager varies greatly. At one extreme is the manager of a large metropolitan airport, an appointee or civil service employee of the city government or airport authority, who heads a large staff of assistants and specialists through which he manages a highly complex organization. At the other extreme is the owner-manager of a small private field near a rural community. The latter might combine his activities as airport manager with work in some other business.

Between these two extremes is the manager of a municipally-owned or privately-owned airport where there are a limited number of scheduled airline flights each day. Based at the airport are several FBOs and a number of aircraft owned by individuals and corporations. The typical manager of a medium-size airport deals with all segments of the aviation community including the airlines, general aviation, and federal and state agencies.

In the early days of aviation, an individual could become an airport manager if he was a pilot and had several years experience in some segment of the industry. Although he had to be able to manage the operation for the owner, his experience was likely to be in some area of flying rather than in business management.

Today an airport manager must be primarily a skilled and experienced executive with a broad background in all facets of aviation. It is no longer necessary that he be a pilot. Almost every airport manager's job situation is unique in some major respects because of the wide variety of size of airport and type of ownership and operation. There are also wide variations in government procedures in different communities. This sometimes causes the responsibilities, salaries, and authority of airport managers to be completely different from one city to the next. Even the job title varies. *Director of aviation, airport superintendent, executive director, airport director, general manager,* and other titles are often used instead of *airport manager.*

Duties of an airport manager

An airport manager is often part landlord and part business executive. As a landlord, the safe condition and operation of the airport is his greatest responsibility. The maintenance of the airport buildings and land are also important. As a business executive he is in charge of public relations; financial planning; profitable and efficient day-to-day operation; and coordination of airline, concession, and airport facilities to best serve the tenants and flying public.

The airport manager's primary duty is the safe and efficient operation of the airport and all its facilities regardless of its size. However, at least in the larger commercial airports, he does not have direct control over most flying activities. He must deal with all groups and individuals who use the airport facilities. These include (1) representatives of the airlines that schedule flights, maintain, and service their aircraft, and process passengers; (2) all segments of the general aviation community, including FBOs and individual and corporate owners and operators of aircraft; and (3) the government-employed staffs of the air traffic control facilities, customs, and so forth.

All of these groups can be regarded as tenants of the airport, carrying on their independent activities. Besides dealing with the companies and individuals directly concerned with flying, the manager is in contact with concessionaires who operate restaurants, shops, parking facilities, and with the traveling public.

The size of the airport and the services it offers its tenants and the public play an important part in determining the airport manager's specific duties. Some of these duties were enumerated earlier in this chapter under job descriptions. A manager must formulate fiscal policy, secure new business, recommend and enforce field rules and regulations, make provisions for handling spectators and passengers, oversee construction projects, and see that the airport is adequately policed and airplane and automobile traffic is regulated.

The manager interprets the functions and activities of the airport to the city or other local government and to the public; he is a public relations expert as well as a business manager. This public relations function is extremely important and will be taken up at the end of this chapter in a separate section.

Not all of these duties are required of managers of airports. Many are too small to have FAA-staffed control towers; other have no scheduled airline flights. In these airports the job is simpler, but the manager must usually do all of the work himself. In large airports, he has many assistants and supervises the work.

The job of airport manager is obviously not completed between 9 and 5. The hours are often irregular and most managers have some weekend and holiday work. They will often have to work at night. In emergency situations they will usually work additional hours. Difficult weather conditions, labor problems, personnel irregularities, and flight schedule changes are only some of the things that will affect job hours. Even when not actually working, most airport managers are on call.

Education and training

The major requirement for the job of airport manager is business and administrative ability; this means the ability to make decisions, to coordinate details, to direct the work of others, and to work smoothly with many kinds of people. Probably the best college program to follow is one that leads to a degree in aviation management. College courses in engineering, management, accounting, finance and economics, business and aviation law, airline, general aviation, and airport management are good preparation for a career in airport management. Many schools who are members of the University Aviation Association (UAA) offer programs and courses that can be applied to the problems of managing an airport.

A number of the primary airports in the United States have one- or two-year internship programs which train college graduates for various aspects of airport management. Other individuals have started at a small GA airport where they become involved in all aspects of airport management—from maintenance and repair to attending city commission meetings. Some college graduates have taken jobs with aviation or airport consulting firms and after several years have moved into airport management. Many others have acquired experience in some other area of aviation before entering the field.

Because the position of airport manager is the top job in most airports, advancement generally comes by changing jobs—usually by working for a larger airport. In a large metropolitan airport, an individual usually works his way up from managing various departments to become an assistant manager or director and finally manager or director.

The important public service an airport provides along with its economic advantages to a community has caused city governments to recognize the need for professional management of airports. To meet the need, the American Association of Airport Executives (AAAE) initiated a program of accreditation for airport managers. A minimum of three years' work experience in airport management, an original paper on an airport problem, and the completion of a comprehensive examination are the major requirements of the accreditation program. The applicant must also be at least 21 years of age and of good moral character. Once an airport manager has completed these requirements the person may use the initials A.A.E. (Accredited Airport Executive) after his or her name and is eligible to vote at the business meetings of the American Association of Airport Executives. The airport managed by him or her may be designated as an AAAE field.

Many career opportunities in airport management should become available in the years ahead due to expansion of facilities and attrition. As the number of new airports increases and the facilities of many existing airports expand, new managerial positions will be created. Many of these will not be top jobs, but the airport of the future will require assistant managers specializing in one part of the huge operation. Also, qualified people will be needed to replace those who retire. Many of the present airport managers are World War II and Korean War veterans who will face retirement in the next few years.

Because the job of managing a medium-to-large commercial airport is a fascinating one that requires high qualifications, there will be tough competition for jobs; however, the motivated individual with a solid educational background and varied experience in the fields of aviation and management will find openings in a field of work that is and will remain comparatively small—but one that provides an interesting and challenging profession.

The airport manager and public relations

Unquestionably, one of the most important and challenging aspects of an airport manager's job is that of public relations. *Public relations* is the management function that attempts to create goodwill for an organization and its products, services, or ideals, with groups of people who can affect its present and future welfare. The most advanced type of public relations not only attempts to create goodwill for the organization as it exists, but also helps formulate policies, if needed, that of themselves result in a favorable reaction.

Aviation and airports have such great impact on our lives, and upon the life of our nation, that it is difficult to find a person who has no knowledge or opinion of airports. Despite the tremendous growth in all segments of aviation over the past 25 years, and the resulting challenges, problems, and opportunities, aviation has not been exempted from the controversies that inevitably are part of any endeavor affecting or touching the lives of a large number of people. This controversy is the reason why every opinion, whether positive or negative, will be a strong one. The net result is that every airport has an image—either good or bad.

The landmark theme building at the center of Los Angeles International Airport has 135-foot parabolic arches that accent an observation deck with a 360-degree view of the airport and surrounding area, a restaurant, offices, and employee cafeteria.

The great problems of airports are always related to the original and elemental images resulting from the collective opinions of the public. These images are really the balancing or compensating factors that correspond with the problems the public encounters with airports. These images are deposits representing the accumulated experience of jet noise, hours of struggle to reach the airport on clogged highways under construction, the frustration of trying to find a close-in parking place, the lines to obtain tickets, the time in waiting for luggage, and other inconveniences.

In this respect, some of the public will have an image of the airport as a very exciting place that makes major contributions to our society through commercial channels, and even more valuable contributions of a personal nature, by offering a means to efficient travel, and thus greater personal development and greater enjoyment of life.

Despite the hundreds of positive impacts of aviation, negative images do arise. Perhaps such negative images result from the fact that the industry has been so intent on the technological aspects of resolving problems that it has overlooked the less tangible components. The industry has the technology and resources to resolve many of the problems of the airport-airway system; however, the important link or catalyst in bringing together technology and community opinion is the airport public relations effort.

Both the airport and the community have a responsibility to work together to solve their mutual problems, attain desired goals, and ultimately achieve a better community. It takes continuing contributions—and sometimes sacrifices as well—

to the general welfare on the part of individual citizens and the aviation industry to earn the opportunities and rewards of a good community for the public. This two-way relationship has its problems too. Many are spawned by misunderstanding that can arise and grow to disproportionate size, and in our context, result in a negative image for the airport and a loss of public confidence in the aviation industry. Ensuring that problems are met head-on, with full and explicit information made continuously available to the public to prevent misunderstanding, is the point at which airport public relations enters the picture.

Regardless of the size of an airport, there are several basic principles underlying the public relations process. They might be summarized as follows:

1. Every airport and every company and interest on the airport has public relations, whether or not it does anything about them.

2. Public goodwill is the greatest asset that can be enjoyed by any airport, and public opinion is the most powerful force. Public opinion that is informed and supplied with facts and fair interpretation might be sympathetic. Public opinion that is misinformed or uninformed will probably be hostile and damaging to an airport.

3. The basic ingredient of good relations for any airport is *integrity*. Without it, there can be no successful public relations.

4. Airport policies and programs that are not in the public interest have no chance of final success.

5. Airport public relations can never be some kind of program that is only used to respond to a negative situation. Good public relations has to be earned through continuing effort.

6. Airport public relations goes far beyond press relations and publicity. It must interpret the airport interests to the public, and it should be a two-way flow with input and interpretation of public opinion to airport management and community leadership. It must use many means of reaching the various segments of the public interested in airport operations, and it must try to instill the public relations spirit into all facets of the airport's operation.

The airport and its public

Basically, every airport has four "publics" with which it deals, and despite the wide variance in size and scope of activities of airports, these publics are basically the same for all airports:

1. The external business public. These are the past, present, and future airport customers for all the services offered on an airport. It includes all segments of the business, government, educational, and general flying public.

Corporate aviation represents a significant amount of flight operations at commercial airports.

2. The external general public. These are the local citizens and taxpayers, many of whom have never been to the airport but who vote on airport issues or who represent citizen groups with particular concerns.

3. The internal business public. These are the businesses and enterprises whose interests are tied directly to the airport—the airlines, FBOs, other members of the general aviation community, government officials, and other aviation and travel-oriented local businesses and trade organizations, and the employees of all of these enterprises.

4. The internal employee public. This group includes everyone who works for the airport and its parent organization.

These are the most important airport publics. These are the sources of vital information that management must have to know what and how it is doing, and they are the ones who must be informed and persuaded if any airport objective is to be achieved.

Public relations objectives

The primary objectives of an airport's public relations activities are as follows:

1. Establishing the airport in the minds of the external public as a facility that is dedicated to serving the public interest. Many airports work closely with the local chamber of commerce in developing a brochure or pamphlet citing various accomplishments and activities at the airport that would be of interest to the local business community and the community in general.

2. Communicating with the external public with the goal of establishing and building goodwill. The airport manager and other members of his staff often serve as guest speakers at various civic and social

organizations. They also become active members of local or civic organizations in order to informally promote the airport and determine the pulse of the community. Public announcements of new developments at the airport are made through all media. This is a continuing part of the communications process.

3. Answering general and environmental complaints on an individual basis. It is important that the airport develop a good rapport with its neighbors and concerned citizen groups. Working closely with the airlines and other internal business publics, airport management attempts to work out such problems as noise by changing traffic patterns and adjusting hours of flight operation. Tours of the airport are given to various community groups in order for them to get a better understanding of operations. Civic-oriented activities are also conducted at the airport to improve relations with airport neighbors and address their concerns. Citizen participation in airport planning and public hearings is another means by which airport management is continually apprised of community feelings about airport related activities.

4. Establishing good working relationships with internal business publics whose interests are similar to those of airport management.

5. Promoting programs designed to enhance and improve employee morale.

Like any other facility that serves the total community, an airport requires total community understanding. A well-executed public relations program can make the community aware of the airport and its benefits and create an atmosphere of acceptance. Attitudes are not changed overnight, so the public relations effort must be a continuous campaign to build understanding and develop attitudes of acceptance.

Key terms

municipally operated airport
port authorities
airport authority
state-operated airports
federal government-operated airports
organization chart
airport director
assistant director—finance and administration
personnel manager
chief accountant
facilities chief

chief purchasing agent
manager of community relations
assistant director—planning and engineering
assistant director—operations
chief—airside operations
chief—landside operations
security chief
crash, fire, and rescue chief
assistant director—maintenance
building and facilities chief
grounds chief
vehicle chief
public relations

Review questions

1. Distinguish between a port authority and airport authority form of airport ownership and operation.

   Why have a number of formerly municipally owned airports transitioned into airport authorities over the past 30 years?

2. What is the purpose of an organization chart?

   Describe the principal responsibility of the four assistant directors.

   Describe some of the duties of the following positions: facility chief, community relations manager, chief—landside operations, and buildings and facilities chief.

   List 10 other positions found at a commmercial airport.

3. Describe the principal duties of a typical airport manager at a medium-sized commercial airport.

   What educational and training requirements would best prepare an individual for such a position? What is the AAAE program of accreditation for airport managers?

4. Why is public relations such an important function of airport management?

   Describe some of the basic principles underlying the public relations process at an airport.

   What are the airport's "publics?"

   List and briefly describe the primary objectives of an airport's public relations activities.

Suggested readings

Odegard, John D., Donald I. Smith and William Shea. *Airport Planning and Management*. Wadsworth Publishing Co., Belmont, California, 1984.

Eckrose, Roy A. and William H. Green. How to Assure the Future of Your Airport. Eckrose/Green Associates. Madison, Wisconsin, 1988.

Gesell, Laurence E. *The Administration of Public Airports*. Coast Aire Publications. San Luis Obispo, California, 1981.

Wiley, John R. Airport Administration and Management. Eno Foundation for Transportation. Westport, Connecticut, 1986.

Airport operations

Outline

Pavement maintenance
Snow removal
Safety inspection program
Bird hazards
Crash, fire, and rescue
Security
Ground support equipment

Objectives

When you have completed this chapter you should be able to:

△ Describe some of the maintenance problems with asphalt and concrete runways.

△ Define vibratory testing.

△ Describe how runway grooving helps reduce hydroplaning.

△ Identify the three basic methods of removing rubber deposits and other contaminants from runways.

△ Describe the major items included in a snow removal program.

△ Describe how the three basic mechanical methods of snow removal are used.

△ Identify four or five areas of concern under the following headings in an airport safety self-inspection program: ramp/apron, runways, taxiways, fueling facilities, and buildings.

△ Discuss several approaches to eliminating bird hazards.

△ Describe the minimum CFR requirements under FAR Part 139.

△ List the basic requirements under FAR Part 107.

△ Describe some of the major ground servicing equipment found at major airports.

Pavement maintenance

The airport surface is the beginning and end of every successful flight. The inspection, maintenance, and repair of the runways, taxiways, and apron areas ranks along with navigational aids and lighting in importance to airport management.

The first concrete runway was constructed in 1928 at the Ford Terminal in Dearborn, Michigan. During the next five years Cheyenne, Wyoming; Glendale, California; Louisville, Kentucky; and Cincinnati, Ohio, were concrete-paved. By the middle of the 1930s, paving the airport surface became popular at civilian as well as military airports.

The technical advances during World War II brought a whole new concept to the aircraft industry, and required like attention to the takeoff and landing facility as well. No longer was the paved surface considered a luxury; there was load-bearing equipment to consider—large aircraft, heavily loaded, twisting, and grinding at the airport surface.

The criteria for airport paving was borrowed from the highway builders, who themselves had only 30 years in the business and were making new discoveries each day. It was soon apparent that a building experience in Miami carried little relevance for construction in Chicago—as the geology changes, so must the paving method.

Although early efforts at paving simply related the intended load, and some evaluation of the strength of subgrade material, to determine the thickness of pavement, by 1945 it was recognized that many other factors influenced pavement performance such as material quality, repetitions of load, climatic effects, distributions of load, mixed traffic, roughness, and maintenance. All of these factors were considered in pavement life.

Today, the average airport operator has inherited an airport surface constructed more than 30 years ago, and with it, arrivals and departures of aircraft that have grown in size, weight, and landing speed operating in all-weather conditions.

Runway pavement

A wide range of materials and construction procedures is available for the construction of airport runways and taxiways. These are usually surfaced with Portland cement concrete or with some form of asphalt, which is more commonly used. In some cases, an asphalt course is laid over a concrete runway to renew the surface or to provide needed additional strength.

Because of its nonrigid character, asphalt paving requires no visible joints or seams. Asphalt might be less expensive to install than concrete, but generally requires much more maintenance in the long run. Much depends on the preparation and grading, as well as vigilance and prompt attention to maintenance needs. Moisture is the primary enemy. If water does not drain off the surface and away from the pavement edging quickly, it will filter through to the subbase and weaken it to the point where the overlying courses sag and break open. Potholes appear as heavy rains wash away loose material.

After years of use, asphalt runways begin to lose their elasticity. Oxidation brings about physical changes in the asphalt material, which begins to lose its elastic qualities. Skin cracks will develop, allowing moisture to penetrate, unless the surface is resealed periodically. Patching of weakened areas as soon as weather conditions permit and renewal of the surface course can prolong the life of the runways considerably.

Concrete runways or taxiways are usually found at large airports with heavy air carrier traffic. Concrete has high load-bearing capacity in relation to thickness and high resistance to the destructive effects of weather. It also resists deterioration from oil or fuel spillage better than asphalt, and for this reason is generally used for parking ramps and around hangars at all types of airports. Jet fuel, incidentally, causes more harm than gasoline, because it evaporates more slowly.

Concrete, being a rigid material that expands and contracts with temperature change, is laid down in slabs separated by contraction and expansion joints. The joints are filled with flexible binder, which either compresses and extrudes or shrinks as the concrete contracts or expands. Over the winter, as the concrete contracts, the joints might separate enough to admit material that is essentially incompressible, such as sand or water when frozen.

When incompressible materials infiltrate the joints in concrete, tremendous pressures are generated during later expansion of the slabs, and the concrete might fracture in the joint area. This is known as *spalling*. The fractured edges permit rainfall to enter the subsurface with progressively destructive effect. Washing away of subbase can lead to empty spaces under the slabs, which in turn causes the slabs to rock and sometimes to break.

Incompressible material in the expansion joints can also cause the slabs to pop out—that is, to rise and slide over adjacent blocks. It can also cause slabs to buckle upward, cracking the surface and providing hundreds of avenues for water to enter the subbase. Considerable yardage of concrete surface can be destroyed in a relatively short time because an insignificant-appearing expansion joint has become filled with sand.

Even if the concrete slabs are misaligned only to a small degree they present a hazard. Landing gear, particularly nosewheels, can be damaged or sufficiently bent to prevent their retraction. Irregular surfaces can blow tires and wrench an airplane out of control.

Periodic on-the-ground inspections can easily spot joint openings, surface cracks, and other problems before the runway becomes a hazard to aviation (FIG. 13-1). Most airport operations personnel are especially attentive to this precaution in the spring. The following are a few of the obvious indications of potential runway problems:

1. Ponding of water on or near runways and taxiways.

2. Buildup of soil or heavy turf at pavement edges, preventing water runoff.

3. Clogged or overgrown ditches.

4. Erosion of soil at runway edges.

5. Open or silted-in joints.

6. Surface cracking or crumbling.

7. Undulating or bumpy surfaces.

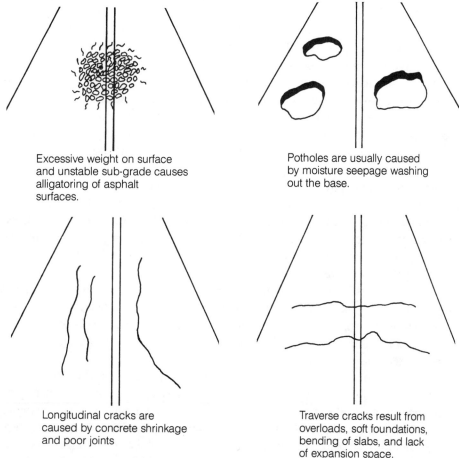

Excessive weight on surface and unstable sub-grade causes alligatoring of asphalt surfaces.

Potholes are usually caused by moisture seepage washing out the base.

Longitudinal cracks are caused by concrete shrinkage and poor joints

Traverse cracks result from overloads, soft foundations, bending of slabs, and lack of expansion space.

Fig. 13-1. Runway pavement problems.

Testing pavements

An accurate and complete evaluation of the existing pavement system is one of the key factors contributing to the success of a maintenance project. Major strides are being made in this area with the development and application of nondestructive testing (NDT).

One of the most effective and valuable of the nondestructive techniques is *vibratory* (or *dynamic*) *testing*. This technique measures the strength of the composite pavement system by subjecting it to a vibratory load and measuring the amount the pavement responds or deflects under this known load. Of the many devices available to perform these tests, one of the most popular is the Road Rater. This device can perform a test in approximately 12 seconds and is very maneuverable.

Pavement evaluations in the past normally included large numbers of expensive and time-consuming destructive tests such as cores, borings, test pits, and so forth. Selected on a visual or random basis, the locations at which these tests were performed yielded results of varying degrees of success. Unfortunately, taking enough tests to provide reasonable assurance that the results were meaningful also meant high costs and expensive runway shutdown time.

Taking advantage of the economy and speed of vibratory testing, it is possible to saturate the pavement system with tests to determine a very minimum number of locations at which destructive tests can be performed for a complete and accurate evaluation of a pavement and its components. Additionally, the results frequently point out other factors contributing to pavement weakness such as drainage deficiencies.

Rigid (concrete) pavements may also be examined with this technique to evaluate the likelihood of voids, extent of pumping, load transfer qualities, and the degree to which cracked sections reseat themselves under traffic loadings. These considerations determine the amount and type of remedial or preventive maintenance appropriate to prepare the concrete pavement system so that it will perform adequately after it is overlayed.

As for the service roads, flexible pavement methodology is used to translate the vibratory test results directly into the thickness of asphalt overlay required to strengthen the pavement to serve present and projected traffic loads with a minimum of maintenance. Particularly weak areas requiring additional investigation for possible digout are also examined.

The testing of the airport surface will reveal maintenance needed to upgrade the pavement system to the specifications as outlined in the airport manager's long-range plan. Products and methods for pavement maintenance are changing rapidly. Environmental conditions require different applications of similar materials and methods of construction. Solutions to the problem of pavement maintenance take on specific characteristics as they apply to individual airport problems.

Maintenance in general substantially reduces the need for extensive repairs or replacement of deteriorating airport surfaces. The ultimate solution to pavement difficulties is to discover and repair them before they get expensive. Airport operations personnel normally make daily inspections of pavement surfaces, note emerging problems, and call for technical assistance. Periodically, an inspection with a civil engineer is made to check on the more subtle forms of pavement distress.

Runway surface friction

Runway pavement surface friction is threatened by normal wear, water, contaminants, and pavement abnormalities. Repeated traffic movements wear down the

Phillips Fibers Corporation

Resurfacing an apron area.

runway surface. Wet weather can create dynamic or viscous hydroplaning. *Dynamic hydroplaning* is a condition where landing gear tires ride up on a cushioning film of water on the runway surfaces. *Viscous hydroplaning* occurs when a thin film of oil, dirt, or rubber particles mixes with water and prevents tires from making sure contact with pavement. Contaminants, rubber deposits, and dust particles accumulate over a period of time and smooth the textured surface. The pavement itself might have depressed surface areas that are subject to ponding during periods of rainfall.

An aircraft makes contact with the runway. The tires spin up to the speed of the aircraft and slippage occurs—heat is generated, a thin layer of rubber vulcanizes and bonds with the asphalt or concrete runway. With each successive landing, the layer of rubber builds and the antiskid character of the runway decreases. If it rains, it is possible that 100 percent of the braking ability will be lost.

The most effective and economical method of reducing hydroplaning is *runway grooving*. One-quarter inch grooves spaced approximately one and one quarter inch apart are made in the runway surface generally using diamond blades. These safety grooves help provide better drainage on the runway surface, furnish escape routes for water under the tire footprint to prevent dynamic hydroplaning, and offer a means of escape for superheated steam in reverted rubber skids. Grooving also assists in draining surface areas that tend to pond, reducing the risks of spray ingestion, fluid drag on takeoff, and impacting spray damage.

Unfortunately, the grooves become filled with foreign matter and must be cleaned periodically. The FAA suggested schedule for friction surveys is shown in TABLE 13-1.

Table 13-1. FAA suggested schedule for friction surveys.

Annual aircraft operations	Friction survey
Less than 12,000	When required
12,000 - 30,000	Once every two months
30,000 - 50,000	Once every month
50,000 - 100,000	Once every two weeks
100,000 - 200,000	Once every week
200,000 and above	Twice a week or more as required

Source: FAA

The removal of rubber deposits and other contaminants includes: (1) high-pressure water, (2) chemical solvents, and (3) high-velocity impact techniques.

1. The *high-pressure water* method has been used very successfully. The principle is based on high-pressure water jets aimed at the pavement surface to blast contaminants off the pavement surface. The technique is clean and removes deposits in a minimum of runway downtime. High-pressure water equipment operates between 5,000 and 8,000 psi and is capable of pressures exceeding 10,000 psi, and may be used when the temperature is 40 °F and rising.

2. *Chemical solvents* have also been used successfully to remove contaminants from both portland cement and asphalt runways. Chemicals must meet Environmental Protection Agency (EPA) requirements. Acid-based chemicals are used on concrete runways and alkaline chemicals on asphalt.

3. The *high-velocity impact* method consists of throwing abrasive particles at high velocity at the runway surface. This technique blasts contaminants from the surface and can be adjusted to produce the desired surface texture. The abrasive material is propelled mechanically from the peripheral tips of radial blades in a high-speed, fan-like wheel. This reconditioning operation may be carried out during all temperature conditions and seasons except during rain, in standing water, slush, snow or ice.

Snow removal

In the northern states, snow removal represents a significant portion of an airport's maintenance budget. How effective this expenditure will be depends on the ability of management to plan and execute an efficient snow removal program. Such a plan normally includes the following items:

1. A brief statement of the purpose of the plan.

2. A listing of the personnel and organizations (airport and other) responsible for the snow removal program. Many airports hire additional personnel during the winter months or utilize personnel from the streets and sanitation department on an emergency basis.

3. Standards and procedures to be followed. There are a number of excellent sources that airport management uses in preparation of this aspect of their snow removal program. They include the *Air Transportation Snow Removal Handbook* published by the ATA and FAA Advisory Circular 150/5200-23 *Airport Snow and Ice Control*. The AAAE also sponsors an annual International Aviation Snow Symposium at which workshops are held covering all aspects of snow removal.

4. Training. Because the airport snow removal program requires special skills, a training program is normally an integral part of the plan. This includes classroom training in such areas as airport orientation, snow removal standards and procedures, use of various types of equipment, aircraft characteristics (capabilities and limitations), description of hazards and problem areas on the airport, communications, and safety procedures. On-site training includes a review of operational areas and hazards, test runs with equipment to accustom operators with area dimensions and maneuvering techniques, and communications practice while on the job.

5. Air traffic control, safety considerations, inspection standards, and NOTAM responsibility.

Timing

Knowing when to implement the snow removal program in order to maintain safe operations and avoid unnecessary repetition of certain activities is critical and generally learned through experience. Weather forecasts including the following information can be helpful in this regard:

1. Forecasted beginning of the snowfall.
2. Estimated duration, intensity, and accumulation.
3. The types of precipitation expected.
4. The wind direction during the snowfall and anticipated wind direction changes and associated velocities.
5. Temperature ranges during and after the snowfall.
6. Cloud coverage following the snowfall.

Snow removal is generally geared to the operational limitations of the most critical aircraft using the airport. Large jet aircraft have a takeoff limitation of one-half inch of heavy wet snow or slush, and one inch of snow of medium moisture content. This means that removal operations must get underway before such conditions occur, and must continue without interruption until the storm is over and snow removal has progressed to the point where aircraft operations may be carried on with safety.

Snow removal operations normally are started on the active "into the wind" runway, and progress to other inactive runways and taxiways. At the same time this work is proceeding, snow clearing from ramps, aircraft loading positions, service areas, and public facilities also takes place, as all of these areas are closely related in the overall operation of an airport facility.

Equipment and procedures

There are two basic methods of removing snow and ice: (1) mechanical and (2) chemical. Most removal is accomplished by mechanical means since the chemical methods available for use in aviation are costly and not as effective as those available for highway use. Underground hot water and electrical heating systems are used in the ramp area at some large airports, but these are very expensive to construct and maintain.

The three mechanical methods of snow removal include plows, blowers or throwers, and brushes. These are illustrated in FIG. 13-2. Snowplows available for airport use do not differ significantly from those used on the highway. Blades are available in steel, steel with special carbide steel cutting edges, rubber, and polyurethane. The traditional steel edge works most effectively on dry-packed snow, but is not as effective in slush removal and will not last as long as the rubber or polyurethane edges. The carbide steel edge gives longer life than the traditional steel edge, cuts packed snow more effectively, and can be more effective in the removal of ice that is not bound to the pavement surface.

The rubber blades have a longer life than the steel blades, make less noise and vibration (which contributes to the operator's comfort), and work well on slush, although not as well as steel on a dry or packed snow. The rubber blades cost considerably more than the steel blades, but generally last five to ten times longer, depending on how carefully they are maintained.

The snow blower or thrower is the primary mechanical device for removal of hazardous snow accumulations such as windrows and snow banks. Blowers are frequently used to clear taxiways, ramps, and parking areas prior to windrow removal on the runway.

Snow brushes are primarily used to clean up the residue left on the surface by the plow or the blower. They are also used to clear surfaces of a light snow and to remove sand spread on the runway to improve friction. The brush is the only unit of the three basic types of equipment that has year-round use on the airport. Runways and taxiways can be kept clean and free of debris with the brush, which prevents foreign object damage (FOD) to propellers or turbine engines. The brush will ordinarily have the slowest operating speed of the three types, and due to its

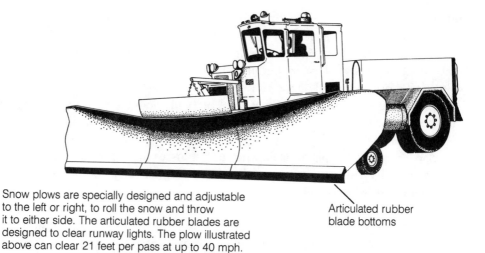

Snow plows are specially designed and adjustable
to the left or right, to roll the snow and throw
it to either side. The articulated rubber blades are
designed to clear runway lights. The plow illustrated
above can clear 21 feet per pass at up to 40 mph.

Articulated rubber
blade bottoms

A snow blower or thrower such as the one illustrated
above can clear windows at speeds of 35 mph
and handle as much as 3,000 tons per hour.

A snow brush shown above can clear a heavy snowfall
in one operation. Angled up to 45 degrees, the 14 foot long brush scatters snow
up to 50 yards to either side. Variable speed control can be set to slow
speeds for sweeping surface dirt up to 550 rpm to clear heavy slush. By means
of an air deflector snow is thrown high to be carried away by the wind, or low to
avoid blowback.

Fig. 13-2. *Snow removal equipment.*

relative ineffectiveness in removing any appreciable snow accumulation, will not be useful as the initial attack machine on most snowfalls. Its use, however, can eliminate the problems caused by freezing residue on the surfaces and the concern that aircraft operators have regarding turbine ingestion and propeller erosion caused by loose, dry sand on the runway.

Brushes are available with either steel or synthetic bristles. The steel bristle cuts better, but the nylon or polypropylene bristle is more effective on very wet snow or slush.

Snow removal equipment is expensive, but losses in revenue sustained by an airport closed by snow for several days would almost pay for the equipment needed to clear it.

Snow removal procedures Snow removal normally begins as soon as there are traces of precipitation on the runways and continues until the job is done. Snow is usually allowed to accumulate to one inch on ramp areas before airport personnel or contractors are called in to remove it. This accumulation is normally trucked to a snow dump in an outlying area of the airport.

Snow clearance operations on the runways are normally carried out by a chain of four or five vehicles working in an echelon formation. First the plows move down the runways at speeds up to 35 mph and move the snow to the pavement edges. This is normally followed by the snow blowers or throwers, which disperse the windrowed snow into the open areas beyond. The snow brushes are used for cleaning snow from semiflush type fixtures such as in-runway lighting installations, and for the removal of slush and very light snow accumulation.

At O'Hare International, the world's busiest airport, clearing the longest runway (11,600 feet) of two to three inches of snow takes about two hours. Under the worst conditions it can take six hours or longer.

Ice accumulation Although snow is an important and serious problem in airport maintenance operations, ice is the most difficult problem to cope with and presents the greatest hazards to aircraft operations. Many airports attempt to control such conditions through the use of sand. Unfortunately, dry sand spread on runways and taxiways is quickly removed by aircraft engine blast, so a means of securing the sand to the ice is necessary. The most successful method uses conventional weed-burning equipment. The procedure is to apply sand to the icy surface by hydraulically powered and operated truck spreaders. These lay down a uniform layer of sand. This is immediately followed by the flame-thrower type burner units, which heat the sand particles and melt the ice sufficiently to produce a coarse, sandpaper-like surface upon refreezing. Very satisfactory results are obtained, which normally last until thawing temperatures cause the sand particles to sink into the ice and the process must be repeated. This method of ice control normally is used when the ice thickness is one-quarter inch or more. It has the

Snowplows move the snow to the pavement edges where snow blowers disperse the windrowed snow.

additional advantage of dissipating some of the ice through evaporation and weakening the ice structure by a honey-combing effect that takes place when the open flame embeds the sand particles into the ice.

Safety inspection program

Clearly one of the most important concerns of airport management is safety. The Federal Aviation Act of 1958 and FAR Part 139 Certification and Operations of Air Carrier Airports were primarily established in the interest of promoting safety. To ensure that these regulations are continuously met—and, in fact, exceeded—airport management carries out an extensive airport safety inspection program. The frequency of inspection of each item will vary, but certain facilities and equipment must be inspected daily. Some of these items include runways, taxiways, and navigational aids. Other elements are normally ranked in order of importance to safety and the frequency of inspection is established.

The FAA *Airport Certification Program Handbook* suggests the following general categories in which emphasis on elimination, improvement or education should be placed:

1. Hazards created due to weather conditions, such as snow, ice, and slush on or adjacent to runways, taxiways, and aprons.

2. Obstacles in primary and transition surfaces and in approach, takeoff, taxi, and apron areas.

3. Protection of the public.

4. Hazards created by erosion, broken or damaged facilities in the approach, takeoff, taxi, and apron areas.

5. Hazards occurring on airports during construction activity, such as holes, ditches, obstacles, and so forth.

6. Bird hazards on or adjacent to the airport.

7. Inadequate maintenance personnel or equipment.

Additionally, FAA Advisory Circular 150/5200-18 *Airport Safety Self-Inspection* establishes a checklist primarily designed for operators of GA airports. This list includes some of the more important items that are often overlooked and result in damage to aircraft and injury to people. The following example taken from this source is not all-inclusive, but it does give an idea of the areas of major concern to an airport manager at a typical GA airport.

A. *Ramp/apron—aircraft parking areas*
1. Unsealed pavement cracks, weak or failing pavement, buildup of shoulders causing entrapment of water, poor drainage, and growth of vegetation.
2. Adequate parking and tiedown areas are provided and they are well clear of taxiways and are prominently marked.
3. Free of obstructions such as blocks, chocks, loose gravel, baggage carts, and so forth.
4. Deadlines are provided for spectator areas, passenger loading and unloading, cargo handling, and so forth.
5. Fuel trucks and other airport vehicles are parked in specified area away from aircraft.
6. No unauthorized vehicles permitted on ramp or apron.
7. "NO SMOKING" signs are prominently displayed in all areas where aircraft are being fueled.
8. Fire bottles are provided at apron and/or ramp and are in good working condition.
9. Directional signs are provided to direct aircraft.
10. Yellow center lines are provided.
11. Flood lights, power outlets, and grounding rods in good condition.

B. *Taxiways*
1. Unsealed pavement cracks, weak or failing pavement, buildup or erosion of shoulders, poor drainage, and so forth.
2. Free of weeds or other obstructions.
3. Shoulders are firm, marked as necessary for easy reference, no washouts, and so forth.

4. Center (yellow) line is provided and is in good condition.
5. Hold line is provided and is clearly visible. No unauthorized vehicles and no livestock permitted on taxiways.
6. Necessary directional signs are provided and are so located as to be well clear of taxi areas.
7. Delineators and/or lights are provided and are in good order.
8. Is there a reminder sign at runup area? "USE YOUR CHECKLIST"

C. Runways

1. Runway lights and markers are clearly visible, are operated at correct brilliance, properly leveled and oriented, equipped with usable lamps of correct wattage, clear, clean lenses in runway lights, clean green lenses in threshold lights, unobstructed by vegetation.
2. Threshold properly marked and lighted.
3. Runway numbers in good condition (hard surface).
*4. End of runways flush with surrounding area (no lip).
*5. Overrun areas in good condition.
*6. Shoulders firm, no washouts, no holes or ditches and are clearly marked.
7. Clear line (white) in good condition.
8. Approach areas clear of obstructions. It should be noted whether views of ends of other runways are unobstructed by vegetation, trees, terrain or other obstructions, and whether unauthorized vehicles or livestock have access to the runways or airfield.
9. Procedures for removal of disabled aircraft from runways available at office.

(*Items 4, 5, and 6: Make a note of any unsealed pavement cracks, weak or failing pavement, poor drainage, birdbaths, buildup or erosion of shoulders, obstructing shoulders, and the like.)

D. Fueling facilities

1. Area is clearly defined and is located away from aircraft parking area.
2. Pumps are placarded as to octane and/or fuel grade.
3. Grounding means is provided for all refueling operations.
4. Fire bottles are provided and are in good condition.
5. Fuel hose and nozzle units are stored in clean area for protection from weather and contamination.
6. Filters are checked regularly and recorded.
7. Tanks are checked for water/contamination and recorded.
8. Locks are provided and used on fuel tank filler caps to avoid possibility of sabotage.
9. Fuel tank vents are checked.
10. Fueling area is kept clean, free of debris, and so forth.

11. Rags are stored in closed containers.
12. Oil is kept in storage bin or closet.
13. Oil cans are kept in drum or container.
14. "NO SMOKING" signs posted in area.
15. Stepladder is provided, properly stored, clean, and in good repair.

E. *Buildings, hangars, shops*

1. Clean and free of debris, junk, oil cans, used aircraft parts of no value, old batteries, tires, and so forth.
2. Fire protection with an adequate number of fire bottles in good operational condition and with dates of service record available. Fire and rescue equipment and first aid and emergency services. Smoke detectors and emergency lighting.
3. All tools, equipment, and so forth properly stored.
4. Paints, oils, dopes, and so forth kept in separate area, preferably fire proof.
5. "NO SMOKING" signs properly posted.
6. Restricted area signs posted.
7. Exit signs posted.
8. Buildings numbered—legible.
9. All rags and so forth in metal containers with lids.
10. Building provided with locks for security.
11. Area around buildings clean, free of weeds, junk, and so forth.
12. Signs properly posted to identify occupants of building.

Bird hazards

A flock of birds sucked into a jet engine at takeoff can cause a dangerous stall, while a single large bird hitting an engine with the force of a bullet might smash a fan blade that can cost thousands of dollars to replace.

Airport managers, as well as all other members of the aviation community, are aware of the hazards to flight that can be caused by birds. FAR Part 139 requires that airport operators must show that they have established instructions and procedures for the prevention or removal of factors on the airport that attract—or might attract—birds.

Many airport managers call upon the expertise of an ornithologist to help analyze bird problems at their particular location. The ornithologist can provide useful data such as identification of species, estimates of the number of birds involved, habitat and diet, migrating characteristics, tendency to fly in flocks, and flight patterns.

Most allowable control techniques are intended to cause birds roosting or feeding on the airport to go elsewhere and overflights to use different routes away from the airport. There are a variety of control techniques available that can be used singly or in combination including:

1. Elimination of food sources.
2. Elimination of habitat such as trees, ponds, building ledges, and other roosting areas.
3. Physical annoyance such as noisemakers, high-pressure water from fire hoses, and even papier-mâché owls to frighten birds.
4. Chemical treatment to cause dispersal and movement of flocks or death.
5. Use of firearms or other mechanical means of killing.

Some of these techniques are not feasible. If large numbers are involved, the use of shotguns is generally ineffective. Chemical poisoning of nuisance birds is generally not allowed by the Environmental Protection Agency due to possible harmful side effects from the toxic agents and large concentrations of dead birds, both of which can pose significant public health hazards. Chemicals are available that, when mixed with food (usually grains), cause birds to exhibit erratic behavior and distress cries. These alarming reactions result in dispersal of flocks and the movement of individual birds to different locations. These chemicals are not for sale to the general public and may be applied only by personnel licensed by the EPA. If this control procedure is used, the airport manager has to obtain the services of a pest control firm or use other men and equipment available to him, after proper training and licensing of personnel.

Evaluation of the various control techniques is the next step. Evaluation is relatively simple because it involves observations to determine if the presence of birds has been acceptably reduced. The airport manager cannot ignore possible bird hazards, even if a recent control program has been successful. Continuous monitoring is accomplished through the self-inspection program required by FAR Part 139.

Crash, fire, and rescue

Seventy-five percent of all aircraft accidents occur within half a mile from the airport. Aircraft fires are rare, but an airport is not permitted to operate without an efficient fire service. Crash, fire, and rescue (CFR) services will turn out on full emergency standby on the slightest indication that something is wrong with a landing aircraft—a deflated tire, a circuit breaker out in any important system, a warning light in the flight deck. CFR units turn out on average once a day at a major airport, and are always on standby in bad weather or fog. During an emergency, CFR personnel provide general emergency help, carrying stretchers and aiding disabled people.

*Crash, fire, and rescue (CFR) vehicles such as the ones shown here at Detroit Metro-
politan Airport are ready to leave at a moment's notice.*

Aircraft fires are unusual because of the speed with which they develop and
the intense heat they generate. Thousands of gallons of fuel could be spilled, presenting a complicated rescue effort that could involve an area of more than 18,000
square feet. It is imperative for the first vehicle or vehicles reaching the crash
scene to be capable of controlling 90 percent of the fire within the practical critical area surrounding the fuselage within a minute or less. Such action would prevent the fuselage skin from parting and would keep the temperature inside the
fuselage from reaching an intolerable degree.

Vehicles required and response time

Table 13-2 shows the minimum CFR vehicles and extinguishing agents required
under FAR Part 139 for various categories of certificated air carrier airport.

Table 13-2. Minimum CFR requirements under FAR part 139. Source: FAA

Airport category	Type aircraft	Vehicle	Extinguishing agent
Index A	More than 90'	One lightweight	500 lbs. of dry chemical or 450 lbs. of dry chemical and 50 gals. of water for foam production.[†]
Index B	More than 90' but less than 126'	One lightweight and one self-propelled fire extinguishing vehicle	Same dry chemical requirements as Index A and 1,500 gals. of water for foam production
Index C	More than 126' but less than 160'	One lightweight and two additional self-propelled fire extinguishing vehicles	Same dry chemical requirements as Index A and 3,000 gals. of water for foam production.
Index D	More than 160' but less than 200'	Same as Index C	Same dry chemical requirements as Index A and 4,000 gals. of water for foam production
Index E	More than 200'	Same as Index C	Same dry chemical requirements as Index A and 6,000 gals. of water for foam production.

[†]If the airport expects to serve Index B turbine aircraft 500 gallons of water for foam production is required.

The index system shown in TABLE 13-2 is based on an area that must be secured to effect evacuation or protection of aircraft occupants should an accident involving fire occur. The protected area is equal to the length of the aircraft times a 100-foot width, the latter consisting of 40 feet on each side of the fuselage plus a 20-foot allowance for fuselage width. The indexing system was based on this critical area concept, expressed in aircraft length, to provide more equitable protection to all aircraft using the airport.

FAR Part 139 indicates that a lightweight vehicle—which it theorizes would be the first one on the scene of the crash—must be able to reach the midpoint of the farthest runway from its assigned post within three minutes from the time the alarm is sounded. The second vehicle must be able to fulfill the same requirements in four minutes, and any subsequent vehicle in four and a half minutes.

Until the 1960s, airport firefighting equipment consisted of little more than modified versions of the gear used by municipal fire services. Now, every major airport is equipped with rapid intervention vehicles (RIVs) able to reach the runways within two minutes of an alarm. Heavy-duty vehicles are designed to cross rough ground to reach a distant runway (by a circuitous route; they cannot drive across active runways) or the overshoot or undershoot areas where most fatalities occur.

RIVs are fast trucks that carry foam, water, medical and rescue equipment, and lights for use in fog and darkness. Their crews begin holding operations to contain the fire and clear escape routes. Heavy-duty foam tenders follow. They are large, but fast and maneuverable, and carry about 10 times more foam than the RIVs. Turret-mounted foam guns swivel to project the foam up to 300 feet. Figure 13-3 shows several typical vehicles used by CFR units.

Extinguishing agents

Most airport CFR facilities are based on the quick delivery of foam extinguishing agents to the scene of a crash. Foam is the general selection because of the two basic ingredients—foam concentrate and water—can be brought to the scene and applied to the fire, if any, in a matter of minutes.

Foam smothers the flames and cools the surrounding area to prevent further outbreak of fire. Water is only really effective as a coolant. Dry powder (either sodium or potassium bicarbonate base) is most effective on localized fires in wheels or tires, or in electrical apparatus.

Foam does have some limitations as an extinguishing agent. It must be applied in large quantities in what the National Fire Protection Association describes as "a gentle manner so as to form an impervious fire-resistance blanket" when dealing with large flammable (usually fuel and/or hydraulic fluids) liquid spills.

Heavy-duty foam tender.

Oshkosh Truck Corporation

The light rescue unit illustrated on the left can carry 300 lb of dry powder sodium bicarbonate in two units pressurized by carbon dioxide. Each discharge nozzle can eject powder at the rate of 3 lb per second over a range of 39 feet.

The heavy-duty fire tender illustrated on the right can discharge over 10,000 gallons of water or foam a minute through its monitor and over 1,000 gallons through each of its two hand-lines, while moving forward or backward.

The tank holds 200 gallons of foam concentrate and is designed so that the base slopes down to a sump.

The four-man four door cab is made of double-skinned insulated aluminum.

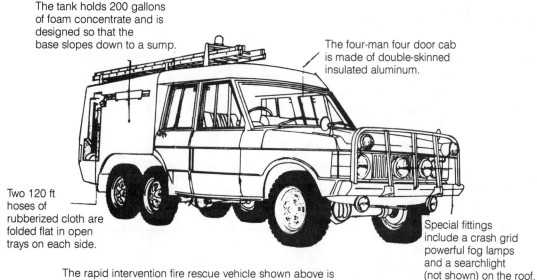

Two 120 ft hoses of rubberized cloth are folded flat in open trays on each side.

Special fittings include a crash grid powerful fog lamps and a searchlight (not shown) on the roof.

The rapid intervention fire rescue vehicle shown above is designed to accelerate to 70 mph as fast as a sports car, despite the weight of foam and equipment carried. It carries 240 gallons of a concentrated ready-mixed water and foam solution, first aid and rescue equipment which is used to contain the fire and keep aircraft escape routes open until the main fire fighting force arrives. This versatile chassis can be fitted with stretchers and other special equipment, for use as an ambulance.

Fig. 13-3. Typical CFR vehicles.

The foam blanket, once applied, can be broken by wind, or clear water streams, or turbulence, or even the "heat baking" generated by residual heat in metals or burned-over surfaces. Applying a good blanket of foam and keeping it intact is a primary objective of any CFR training program.

Foam is produced by mixing water, air, and a concentrate with suitable agitation, and then spraying it either as a stream or as a fog, depending on the type of fire faced. Properly applied, it will flow over a burning liquid and form a long-lasting blanket that seals off combustion-supporting air and quickly smothers the flames of even volatile vapors. Properly mixed and applied, it will be tough in the sense that it resists rupture from wind or heat or outside flames. A good foam will even reseal itself in the event that the "blanket is torn."

Training

Training is a key ingredient in the overall effectiveness of the CFR team. There are two basic challenges to airport management in this regard. The first challenge can best be described as a requirement to initially train CFR personnel and then to maintain a high state of readiness for extended periods of time during which they are seldom called upon to fully utilize the training they have received. Many airport CFR personnel never become involved in a full-scale aircraft crash that would demand utilization of all training skills.

The second challenge is maintaining a suitable degree of interest and alertness within all members of the team. This aspect is primarily accomplished through an intensive in-service training program.

Crash, fire, and rescue personnel must develop a complete understanding and proficiency in the following areas:

1. All special hazards on the airport and surrounding area.
2. Airport water systems including the location of all fire hydrants.
3. Radio procedures.
4. Use of apparatus and equipment.
5. Aircraft types using the airport.
6. Hot drill fires.
7. Self-contained breathing equipment.
8. Emergency medical care.
9. Salvage and overhaul.
10. Building construction.

Security

FAR Part 107—Airport Security prescribes security rules for airport operators serving certificated air carriers. It became effective on March 18, 1972, and was largely in response to a wave of bomb threats and hijacking attempts in the early 1970s. Under this regulation, airport operators are required to prepare and submit to the FAA in writing a security program containing the following elements:

1. A listing of each "air operations area" (those used or intended to be used for landing, takeoff, or surface maneuvering of aircraft).
2. Identification of those areas with little or no protection against unauthorized access due to a lack of adequate fencing, gates, doors with locking means or vehicular/pedestrian controls.
3. A plan for upgrading the security for air operations areas with a time schedule for each improvement project.

Further, under this part, the airport operator must implement a master security plan in the time frame approved by the FAA and also require persons and vehicles allowed in the air operations areas to be suitably identified.

In effect, the guidelines for Part 107 are "if you find a door open, lock it; an unprotected area, fence it; an area in darkness, light it; and someone you don't know, find out who he is." Adherence to these rules keeps honest people out of restricted areas and makes it easier to spot those people with dishonest intentions.

FAA's interest in aviation security under Part 107 is limited to security "as it affects or could affect safety in flight." It does not extend to security in automobile parking lots or terminal areas distant from the landing area. However, compliance with these regulations unquestionably has beneficial fallout in other areas of the airport. Most airport operators include such areas in their master security program.

Airport security starts at the perimeter fence, which normally has a 10-foot clear area on either side. Some airports use microwave fences in remote areas, which flash a warning of intruders to airport security personnel. Other remote facilities such as cargo terminals are often targets for thieves and pilferers. Security in this area has been strengthened considerably in recent years. Most cargo areas are well-lit and only allow trucking firms in certain designated areas. Armed security guards, closed circuit TV with zoom lens cameras, videotape recording, and a twin-lock system for high value articles (one key held by security personnel and the other by designated airline personnel) are all part of the cargo area security program. At most major airports, bonded stores for duty-free goods and surveillance cages for valuable cargo reduce all but organized pilferage and theft during delivery or loading.

Terrorism is the worst threat, and airports and airlines at risk may have air cargo X-rayed or containerized cargo is routinely decompressed for 12 hours in remotely-sited chambers to reduce the possibility of bombs exploding in aircraft cargo holds.

When smuggling was the major airport crime, the passenger was rarely subjected to the indignity of personal search. The scourge of hijackings by politically motivated terrorists has changed that. Mechanical aids are increasingly being used in the search process at most commercial airports (FIG. 13-4).

TV monitor has a zoom control to allow close-up inspection of any suspicious object. Full tilt control enables the operator to examine a suitcase from various angles. Metal shows up densely, other materials as shadows.

Combined check-in desk, electronic weighing unit and X-ray security screening.

Conveyor belt leading to airport's main baggage conveyor system

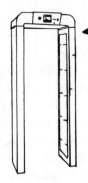

This metal-detection gateway has an electromagnetic field between doorframe-sized metal columns. Ferrous or non-ferrous metal carried through by a passenger disturbs the magnetic field, the disturbance registers on a control panel and an alarm sounds. Sensitivity can be reduced so as not to pick up the metal fastenings on clothes. The machine can be controlled by one person stationed away from the gateway and will not affect heart pacemakers, magnetic recording tape or magnetically-coded credit cards.

A portable explosives detector gives an audible alarm within four seconds of detecting explosive vapor. The probe, inserted into a handbag or suitcase, or passed over hands, clothing or containers, takes a sample of air. This is fed into the briefcase, which contains an electronic sensor unit, a rechargeable nickel-cadmium battery and a bottle containing argon gas, to detect and register the contents. The detector can respond to explosive vapor concentrations of one part per several million parts of air, and can detect traces of explosives on any material hours after contact, but it will ignore vapors from lighter fluid and cleaning fluid.

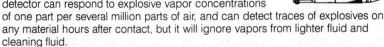

Probe

Fig. 13-4. Passenger security devices.

A combined check-in desk, electronic weighing unit with digital readout, and X-ray security is replacing the airline check-in desk at some major airports. One monitor can cover several desk points. A specially trained operator monitors the TV screen. If a suspicious object is detected, the doors leading to the main baggage conveyor system can be closed while the object is examined from all angles and from close up. If the contents are passed, the operator opens the doors to release the baggage.

Passenger carry-on luggage is handled in much the same manner in the area leading to gate positions. Luggage is placed on a small conveyor belt that moves it past cameras that take an automatic X-ray television picture of the contents. This picture is transmitted onto the screen, where an operator can immediately pick out any objects that look as if they might have an aggressive purpose.

The owner of any luggage that arouses suspicion is then asked to open it. In the vast majority of cases, what showed up on the television screen as possibly a weapon turns out to be an innocent household item such as an aerosol spray or a cigarette lighter.

More often than might be expected, lifelike toy pistols or knives being taken home as souvenirs are found by the process. Usually they are taken from the owner, given to the airline cabin staff for the journey, and returned to the owner at the end of the flight. Very infrequently a real weapon that just might have been intended for a hijacking attempt is found. A police investigation always follows such discoveries.

Meanwhile, the passengers themselves are passing through a magnetic gate which sounds an alarm when it detects metallic objects upon the person. As in the case of the baggage, most of the items picked up by the gateway prove to be innocuous—keys, lighters, cameras, and so forth—but an alert is immediately followed by a body search.

The security staff is also trained to recognize the "profile" of the typical hijacker—his facial appearance, the manner in which he is likely to comport himself during the security procedures, his dress, and the baggage he is likely to be carrying.

Ground support equipment

A considerable amount of specialized ground handling equipment is used to service aircraft at a major airport. This equipment represents a major and ever-increasing investment for the airlines, airline contracting services, or airport operators. Its adequacy and reliability are also a primary factor in airline operating efficiency and on-time performance. A quick turnaround is essential to airline profitability but just as important to airport management in assigning gate positions to new arrivals in an expeditious manner.

Between landing and takeoff an aircraft must be unloaded, cleaned, refueled, loaded up with passengers, baggage, food, water, cargo, and duty-free goods in the case of international flights, all in the shortest possible time. Figure 13-5 shows a typical positioning of servicing and loading equipment for a B-747 with cargo side door on the main deck. The B-747 is designed so that 250 to 300 passengers and their baggage can be unloaded, and the plane refueled, serviced, and reloaded, within a normal turnaround time of 30 minutes. To do this, 16 or more vehicles might be assembled around the plane at once. Routine maintenance checks of the airframe, engines, tire pressure, lights, brakes, and other essentials take about 25 minutes. Minor problems reported by the crew are also corrected. Refueling at a rate of 20 gallons a second takes about 20 minutes. All other servicing goes on simultaneously. Figures 13-6 through 13-9 illustrate some of the major ground support equipment servicing aircraft on the apron area.

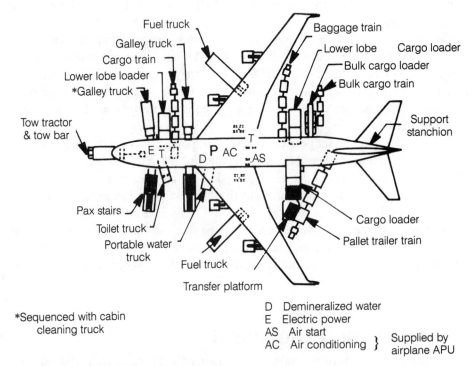

D	Demineralized water
E	Electric power
AS	Air start
AC	Air conditioning } Supplied by airplane APU

*Sequenced with cabin cleaning truck

Fig. 13-5. Boeing 747 turnaround service.

Push-out tugs are used to maneuver aircraft backwards into oddly-positioned parking positions by attaching to the nosewheel and pushing it.

Heavy tugs weighing an eighth of the B-747s they pull, can have a single cab or one at each end. These can be raised and lowered to fit beneath different aircraft fuselages.

Drinking-water supply trucks holding approximately 800 gallons can refill an aircraft tank at 20 gallons a minute.

This hydraulic platform, used to service and clean inaccessible parts of an aircraft such as the windshield. The cage first moves out, and then up to its maximum working height of 33 feet. The controls cannot be accidentally operated.

Fig. 13-6. Ground support equipment for aircraft movement and servicing.

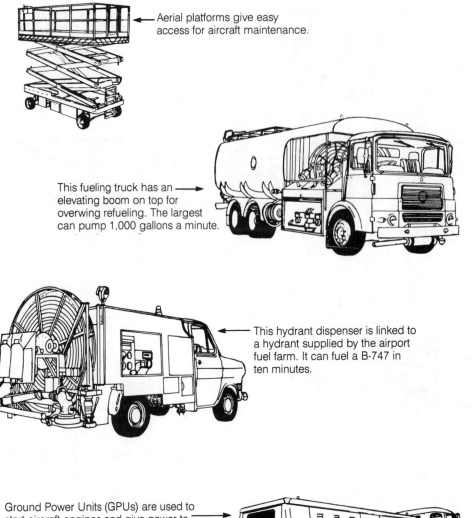

Aerial platforms give easy
access for aircraft maintenance.

This fueling truck has an
elevating boom on top for
overwing refueling. The largest
can pump 1,000 gallons a minute.

This hydrant dispenser is linked to
a hydrant supplied by the airport
fuel farm. It can fuel a B-747 in
ten minutes.

Ground Power Units (GPUs) are used to
start aircraft engines and give power to
their electrical systems on the ground
when the engines are not running. Though
useful on busy aprons, they are not
needed at airports that supply power from
a central power source, or by aircraft
with airborne power units (APUs). These
are auxiliary engines that provide an
alternative power supply independent of the
main engines.

Fig. 13-7. Ground support equipment for aircraft movement and servicing.

Fork lift trucks with rapid left and lower speeds may load small cargo units.

A double deck loader used to load air cargo pallets, has two scissor-lift platforms. The lower rises to nine feet and the upper deck, mounted on a nine foot chassis, can extend up to the 18 foot deck height of a Boeing 747. This arrangement facilitates faster air cargo handling. While the top pallet is being unloaded, the next one is readied for collection on the deck below.

Transporters are very specialized pieces of equipment designed and used to carry containers and pallets 20 inches level over the ground and transfer them to or from other rollerized equipment such as dollies, fixed racks or loaders.

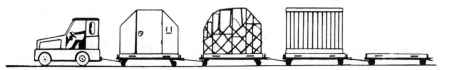

Pallet dollies are one of the most numerous pieces of equipment found on the apron area. The tractors come in various designs and can be used to tow baggage or cargo dollies.

Fig. 13-8. Ground support equipment for cargo loading.

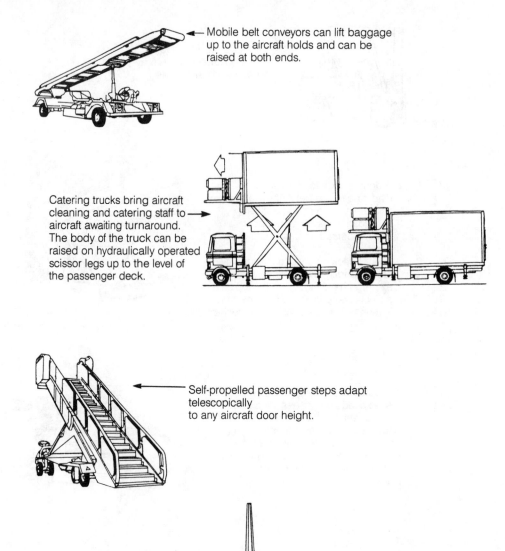

Mobile belt conveyors can lift baggage up to the aircraft holds and can be raised at both ends.

Catering trucks bring aircraft cleaning and catering staff to aircraft awaiting turnaround. The body of the truck can be raised on hydraulically operated scissor legs up to the level of the passenger deck.

Self-propelled passenger steps adapt telescopically to any aircraft door height.

Mobile lounges reduce congestion by coneying passengers to aircraft parked away from the terminals. Their extendible and lateral moving gangways scissor-lift to enclose any aircraft door-or terminal gate. They protect passengers from noise and weather. A mobile lounge can carry up to 150 passengers up to 20 mph.

Fig. 13-9. Ground support equipment for passenger and commissary servicing.

Key terms

spalling
vibratory (dynamic) testing
dynamic hydroplaning
viscous hydroplaning
runway grooving
airport safety self-inspection
FAR Part 107 Airport Security

Review questions

1. Asphalt runways might be less expensive to install than concrete, but
    generally require much more maintenance in the long run. Explain why.
   What is the major problem with concrete runways?
   List some of the obvious indications of potential runway problems.
   What is meant by vibratory (or dynamic) testing?

2. Distinguish between dynamic and viscous hydroplaning. How does runway
    grooving help reduce hydroplaning?
   Describe the three common methods of removing rubber deposits and other
    contaminants from runways.

3. Identify and briefly describe the major considerations in a snow removal
    program. Give two sources of additional information regarding snow
    removal.
   Why is timing so important in an effective snow removal program?
   Describe how the three mechanical methods of snow removal are used
    together in clearing a runway.
   Describe one successful method of removing ice from the runway.

4. List and briefly describe four or five major concerns in a safety
    self-inspection for the following areas: ramp/apron area, taxiways,
    runways, fueling facilities, and building areas.
   Why would an airport manager want to consult with an ornithologist? List
    four or five bird control techniques.

5. What are the minimum requirements under PAR Part 139 for CFR vehicles
    and extinguishing agents?
   What are RIVs?
   Why is foam the most prevalent extinguishing agent?
   What are some of the key elements in a CFR training program?

6. What are the basic requirements under FAR Part 107?
   Describe some of the major security devices used at a typical commercial airport.
   Why is aircraft turnaround time so important to airport management?
   Describe some of the major ground support equipment used in moving and servicing aircraft; in loading cargo, baggage, and passengers.

Suggested readings

FAR Part 139 Certification and Operations of Air Carrier Airports

FAR Part 107 Airport Security

Advisory Circulars:

150/5200-4	Foaming of Runways
150/5200-6A	Security of Aircraft at Airports
150/5200-8	Use of Chemical Controls to Repel Flocks of Birds at Airports
150/5200-13	Removal of Disabled Aircraft
150/5200-18	airport Safety Self-Inspection
150/5200-23	Airport Snow and Ice Control
150/5210-2	Airport Emergency Medical Facilities and Services
150/5210-5	Painting, Marking, and Lighting of Vehicles Used on an Airport
150/5210-6B	Aircraft Fire and Rescue Facilities and Extinguishing Agents
150/5210-7A	Aircraft Fire and Rescue Communications
150/5210-9	Airport Fire Department Operating Procedures During Periods of Low Visibility
150/5210-10	Airport Fire and Rescue Equipment Building Guide
150/5210-12	Fire and Rescue Service for Certificated Airports
150/5210-13	Water Rescue Plans, Facilities, and Equipment
150/5220-4	Water Supply Systems for Aircraft Fire and Rescue Protection
150/5220-10	Guide Specification for Water/Foam Type Aircraft Fire and Rescue Trucks
150/5220-11	Airport Snowblower Specification Guide
150/5220-14	Airport Fire and Rescue Vehicle Specification Guide
150/5230-3	Fire Prevention during Aircraft Fueling Operations
150/5230-4	Airport Fuel Storage, Handling, and Dispensing on Airports
150/5280-1	Airport Operations Manual
150/5370-11	Non-Destructive Testing Devices in the Evaluation of Airport Pavements

Airport relations with tenants and the public

Outline

The airport as landlord
Liability insurance
Aircraft noise

Objectives

When you have completed this chapter you should be able to:

△ Describe how airport-airline relations concerning use agreements have changed since deregulation.

△ Describe a typical airport-concessionaire agreement.

△ Discuss some of the liability exposures that an airport experiences.

△ Summarize the coverages afforded under an airport premises liability policy.

△ Highlight the FAA's role in noise abatement.

△ Discuss some of the problems of noise as it relates to land use around the airport.

△ Identify the noise abatement programs eligible for federal aid.

△ Describe some of the restrictions imposed upon aircraft operators to control noise.

The airport as landlord

A major commercial airport is a huge public enterprise. Some are literally cities in their own right, with a great variety of facilities and services. While the administration of these facilities is generally the responsibility of a public entity, such as a department of city government or aviation authority, airports also have a private character. They must be operated in conjunction with airlines that provide air transportation service and with concessionaires, FBOs, and other firms doing business on airport property. This combination of public management and private enterprise creates a unique landlord-tenant relationship.

Airport-airline relations

From the airlines' perspective, each airport is a point in a route system for the loading and transfer of passengers and freight. In order to operate efficiently, air carriers need certain facilities at each airport. These requirements, however, are not static; they change with traffic demand, economic conditions, and the competitive climate. Before airline deregulation in 1978, response to changes of this sort was slow and mediated by the regulatory process. Carriers had to apply to the Civil Aeronautics Board (CAB) for permission to add or to drop routes or to change fares. CAB deliberations involved published notices, comments from opposing parties, and sometimes hearings. Deliberations could take months, even years, and all members of the airline-airport community were aware of a carrier's intention to make a change long before the CAB gave permission. Since the Airline Deregulation Act of 1978, air carriers can change their routes without permission and on very short notice. With these route changes, airline requirements at airports can change with equal rapidity.

In contrast to airlines, which operate over a route system connecting many cities, airport operators must focus on accommodating the interests of a number of users at a single location. Changes in the way individual airlines operate might put pressures on the airport's resources, requiring major capital expenditures on making obsolete a facility already constructed. Because airports accommodate many users and tenants other than the airlines, airport operators must be con-

Delta Air Lines gate area at Hartsfield Atlanta International Airport.

cerned with efficient use of landside facilities that are of little concern to the carriers, even though carriers' activities can severely affect (or be affected by) them.

Despite their different perspectives, air carriers and the airport management have a common interest in making the airport a stable and successful economic enterprise. Traditionally, airports and carriers have formalized their relationship through airport use agreements (discussed in chapter 11) that establish the conditions and methods for setting fees and charges associated with use of the airport by air carriers. Most agreements also include formulas for adjusting those fees from year to year. The terms of a use agreement can vary widely, from short-term monthly or yearly arrangements to long-term leases of 25 years or more. Within the context of these use agreements, carriers negotiate with the airport to get the specific airport resources they need for day-to-day operations. For example, under the basic use agreement, the carrier may conduct subsidiary negotiations for the lease of terminal space for offices, passenger lounges, ticket counters, and other necessities.

Long-term agreements between airports and major airlines have traditionally been the rule. One reason is the long-lived nature of the investments involved. A runway might have an economic life of a decade or more, a terminal even longer. When an airport undertakes such an improvement for the benefit of the airlines, the airport might want long-term leases to help ensure that carriers will continue to use the facility and help pay for it. At some airports the use agreements and leases might hold all signatory carriers jointly and severally responsible for payments; at others, airlines might be individually responsible for improvements made for their benefit.

In the past, the major airlines operated as virtual regulated monopolies with clearly defined markets and better credit risks than individual airports. In recent years, the perception of airlines as stable and the airports as risky has begun to change. Since deregulation, airlines are no longer under an obligation to serve a particular city, nor are they protected from competition by other carriers. They are free to compete, to change their routes, and to go out of business. On the other hand, certain airports have demonstrated that they are creditworthy and have strong travel markets. Regardless of what happens to an individual airline, these strong airports will continue to be served. In these locations, long-term agreements with individual carriers have become less important for airports seeking financing than the underlying economic strength of the community.

Due to the frequent route changes since deregulation, short-term use agreements and leases are becoming more common. Although the cost to the carrier of a short-term lease might be higher, it has the advantage of allowing greater flexibility for both the carrier and the airport. A carrier testing a new market might not be able or willing to enter a long-term agreement or to assume responsibility for capital improvements until it is sure that the market will be profitable. At the same time, an airport might not want to enter into a long-term agreement with a new carrier that has not yet established a reputation for reliability. At some airports, several different kinds of use agreements may be in effect simultaneously.

As with major airport planning decisions, negotiations related to the day-to-day needs of the carriers have traditionally been carried out between airport management and a negotiating committee made up of representatives of the scheduled airlines that are signatories to use agreements with the airport. In the past, negotiating committees have been an effective means of bringing the collective influence of the airlines to bear on airport management.

The nature of negotiations at some airports has changed radically since deregulation. Under regulation, the major carriers—though competitors— had reasonably similar interests and needs. They did not really compete on the basis of price, and the regulatory process guaranteed that no member of the community could surprise the others with sudden changes in operating strategy. The carriers' representatives were a small group of people who sat on the same side of the negotiating table at many different airports. Carriers generally worked with one another in an atmosphere of cooperation and presented a common position in negotiating with the management of an individual airport.

Since deregulation, however, the environment has been characterized by competition rather than cooperation. Carriers might radically alter their routes, service levels, or prices on very short notice. They are reluctant to share information about their plans for fear of giving an advantage to a competitor. These factors make group negotiations more difficult. Some airport proprietors have complained that in this competitive atmosphere, carriers no longer give adequate advance warning of changes that might directly affect the operation of the airport.

The days when most major airports are dominated by a few large airlines with long-term agreements might be passing away. One reason is the proliferation of air carriers since deregulation. The wide variation in aircraft size and performance, number of passengers, and markets served means that different classes of carriers require somewhat different facilities. Commuter carriers, with their smaller aircraft, usually do not need the same gate and apron facilities as major carriers. While there were commuters before deregulation, they are coming to constitute a larger portion of users at many airports. Other new entrants, including "no-frills" carriers, might also have different needs from those of conventional air carriers—for example, they might want more frequent gate access, but less baggage handling. These minority carriers might come to wield more power in negotiating with the airport for what they need and might challenge major carriers for a voice in investment decisions at an airport.

Airport-concessionaire relations

Services such as restaurants, book stores, gift shops, parking facilities, car rental companies, and hotels are often operated under concession agreements or management contracts with the airport. These agreements vary greatly, but in the typi-

Hotel above the terminal building at Miami International Airport.

cal *concession agreement*, the airport extends to a firm the privilege of conducting business on airport property in exchange for payment of a minimum annual fee or a percentage of the revenues, whichever is greater. Some airports prefer to retain a larger share of revenues for themselves and employ an alternative arrangement called a *management contract*, under which a firm is hired to operate a particular service on behalf of the airport. The gross revenues are collected by the airport management, which pays the firm for operating expenses plus either a flat management fee or a percentage of revenues.

Revenues from concessions are very important to an airport. At some, concessionaires and their customers yield more revenue to the airport than airline fees and leases, resulting—in effect—in cross-subsidy of air carriers by nonaviation service concessions.

Parking and automobile rentals are typically large and important concessions at airports. Despite growth in the use of buses and other high-occupancy vehicles, the continued importance of parking and car rental revenues is indicative of the relationship between the airport and the automobile.

At a number of airports, the airport operator's share of parking and car rental fees (after concession or management fees are paid) represents the largest revenue source from the terminal area—and in some cases, larger than revenue from air carrier landing fees. At many locations, the parking and car rental firms operating on the airport are complemented by (or are in competition with) similar services operating off the airport.

Another important type of concessionaire is the FBO, who provides services for airport users lacking facilities of their own, primarily general aviation. Typically, the FBO sells fuel and operates facilities for aircraft service, repair, and maintenance. The FBO might also handle the leasing of hangars and rental of short-term aircraft parking facilities. Agreements between airports and FBOs vary. In some cases, the FBO constructs and develops his own facilities on airport property; in other cases the FBO manages facilities belonging to the airport. FBOs also provide service to some commuter and startup carriers, especially those that have just entered a particular market and have not yet established (or have chosen not to set up) their own ground operations. The presence of an FBO capable of servicing small transport aircraft can sometimes be instrumental in a new carrier's decision to serve a particular airport.

In addition to concessionaires, some airport authorities serve as landlord to other tenants such as industrial parks, freight forwarders, and warehouses, all of which can provide significant revenue. These firms might lease space from the airport operator, or they might build their own facilities on the airport property.

Airport-general aviation relations

The relationship between airport operators and general aviation is seldom governed by the complex of use agreements and leases that characterize relationships with air carriers or concessionaires.

General aviation (GA) is a diverse group. At any given airport, the GA aircraft will be owned and operated by a variety of individuals and organizations for a number of personal, business, or instructional purposes. Because of the variety of ownership and the diversity of aircraft type and use, long-term agreements between the airport and GA users are not customary. GA users often lease airport facilities, especially storage space such as hangars and tiedowns, but the relationship is usually that of landlord and tenant. There are instances where owners and operators of GA aircraft assume direct responsibility for capital development of an airport, but this is not common, even at airports where general aviation is a majority user.

General aviation aircraft such as the Cessna Skywagon shown here are flown for business and pleasure purposes.

It must be remembered that while GA activities make up about half of the aircraft operations at FAA-towered airports, the average utilization of each aircraft is much lower than that of commercial aircraft. There are approximately 210,000 GA aircraft, compared to approximately 5,000 commercial aircraft. Most GA aircraft spend most of the time parked on the ground. Only a small number—usually those operated by large corporations—are used as intensively as commercial aircraft.

Thus, at the airport, the chief needs of GA are parking and storage space, along with facilities for fuel, maintenance, and repair. While an airliner might occupy a gate for an hour to load passengers and fuel, a GA user might need to park an aircraft for a day or a week while the passenger conducts business in town. At the user's home base, long-term storage facilities are needed, and the aircraft owner might own or lease a hangar or tiedown spot. In most parts of the country, the chief airport capacity problem for GA is a shortage of parking and storage space at popular airports. At some airports in the Southwest and in California, waiting lists for GA parking spaces are several years long.

Some airport operators deal directly with their general aviation customers. The airport management might operate a GA terminal, collect landing fees, and lease tiedowns or hangars to users. At some airports, condominium hangars are available for sale to individual users. A corporation with an aircraft fleet commonly owns hangar space at their base airport. Often, however, at least some of this responsibility is delegated to the FBO, who thus stands as a proxy for the airport operator in negotiating with the individual aircraft owners for use of airport facilities and collecting fees.

Liability insurance

Airports and their tenants have the same general type and degree of liability exposure as the operator of most public premises. People sustain injuries and damage their clothing when they fall over obstructions or trip over concealed obstacles, and their automobiles are damaged when struck by airport service vehicles on the airport premises. Claims from such accidents can be for large amounts, but claims stemming from aircraft accidents have even greater catastrophe potential. The occupants of aircraft might be killed or severely injured and expensive aircraft damaged or destroyed, not to mention injury to other persons or other types of property at or near an airport. Liability in such instances can stem from a defect in the surface of the runway, from the failure of airport management to mark obstructions properly, or failure to send out the necessary warnings and to close the airport when it is not in usable condition.

Airports and their tenants are liable for all such damage as is caused by their failure to exercise reasonable care. The principal areas in which litigation arises can be summarized under three main headings:

1. Aircraft Operations. Liability to tenants and the general public arising

out of aircraft accidents, fueling, maintenance and servicing, and rescue efforts.

2. Premises Operations. Liability to tenants and the general public arising out of automobile and other vehicle accidents, elevators and escalators, police and security enforcement, tripping and falling, contractual obligations, airport construction, work performed by independent contractors, and special events such as airshows.

3. Sale of Products. Liability to tenants and the general public arising out of maintenance and servicing, fueling, and food and beverage services.

Airport operators require that all tenants purchase their own insurance as appropriate for their particular circumstances and with certain minimum limits of liability. Generally, the airport operator is included as an additional insured under the tenant's insurance coverage; however, this does not relieve the airport operator from securing their own liability protection under a separate policy. The comprehensive coverage and limits of liability needed by most major airports far exceed what is required by the average tenant.

Airport liability coverage

The basic *airport premises liability policy* is designed to protect the airport operator for losses arising out of legal liability for all activities carried on at the airport. Coverage can be written for bodily injury and property damage. A number of exclusions apply to the basic policy, and consequently the insuring agreements must be amended to add certain exposures. By endorsement, the basic contract can be extended to pick up any contractual liability the airport might assume under various agreements with fuel suppliers, railroads, and so forth. Elevator liability and liability arising out of construction work performed by independent contractors might also be covered. The basic policy can also be extended to provide coverage for the airport that sponsors an airshow or some other special event.

For those airports engaged in the sale of products or services, the premises liability policy can provide coverage for the airport's products liability exposure. Aircraft accidents arising out of contaminated fuel originally stored in airport fuel storage tanks or even food poisoning from an airport restaurant would be examples.

Aircraft damaged while in the care, custody, or control of the airport for storage or safekeeping can be covered by extending the premises liability policy to provide hangarkeepers coverage.

The growth of aviation and airports during the past 25 years has increased the industry's exposure to liability claims. Airports invest thousands of dollars in purchasing adequate insurance coverage and limits of liability to protect their multimillion dollar assets. The courts have consistently held airport operators responsible for the safety of aircraft and the public as well as for the issuance of proper warning of hazards. In many cases, municipalities have not been immune, with courts determining that the operation of an airport is a proprietary or corporate function rather than a government responsibility.

Aircraft noise

Aviation noise is a fact of life at today's airports and a major—perhaps *the* major—constraint on airport expansion and development. Citizens living around airports have complained that aviation noise is annoying, disturbs sleep, interferes with conversation, and generally distracts from the enjoyable use of property. There is increasing evidence that high exposure to noise has adverse psychological and physiological effects. People repeatedly exposed to loud noises might exhibit high stress levels, nervous tension, and inability to concentrate.

Conflicts between airports and their neighbors have occurred since the early days of aviation, but airport noise became a more serious issue with the introduction of commercial jet aircraft in the 1960s. FAA estimates that the land area affected by aviation noise increased about sevenfold between 1960 and 1970. Even with this increase, the actual number of people affected by aviation noise is relatively small.

New aircraft are much quieter than earlier jets, and the noise levels at the busiest large airports have been reduced to the point that community opposition has abated in some instances. Certain cities have been able to secure community agreement to proceed with airport expansion projects, including new runways. Expansion of terminal buildings, which implies an increase in air traffic, has also been accepted in other cities. On the other hand, noise levels threaten to increase as jet traffic is introduced at secondary airports in some metropolitan areas where the surrounding communities are pressing for curfews and other airport use restrictions.

An airliner approaches Washington National Airport from the south. The Crystal City office and hotel complex in Arlington, Virginia, forms a backdrop.

Another trend that might intensify the noise issue is continuation of residential encroachment around airports. As more people come to live in noise impact areas, the opportunities for annoyance increase. Equally important, the public has become more sensitive to the issue, and it has become highly politicized. Airport neighbors have sued airports for mental anguish as well as the reduced property values related to noise exposure. Airport operators have begun to adopt noise abatement and mitigation measures so as to reduce their liability and protect themselves in legal proceedings. The noise issue has been instrumental in slowing or stopping several airport expansion programs.

Federal responsibilities

FAA's role is defined in a 1968 amendment to the Federal Aviation Act of 1958. The amendment charges the FAA administrator to "prescribe and amend such rules and regulations as he may find necessary to provide for the control and abatement of aircraft noise and the sonic boom."

The federal government pursues a program of aircraft noise control in cooperation with the aviation community. Much of the program is aimed at reducing noise at the source, through the use of quieter aircraft engines. The FAA adopted *Part 36 Certificated Airplane Noise Levels*, of the Federal Aviation Regulations in 1969, establishing noise certification standards for new design turbojet and transport category aircraft. In 1976, the Federal Aviation Regulations were amended, to provide U.S. operators until January 1, 1985, to quiet or retire the noisiest (Stage 1) aircraft. In 1977, the Federal Aviation Regulations were again amended, defining three "stage" levels to categorize aircraft noise emissions and requiring aircraft certificated after March 3, 1977, to meet the more demanding Stage 3 requirement.

The federal program to encourage the use of quieter aircraft has been effective. The retirement of early model four-engine aircraft provided tremendous benefits, lowering the residential population exposed to incompatibly high noise levels from an estimated 7 million people in 1974 to 3.2 million people in 1985. Improvement since 1985 has proceeded at a slower pace as Stage 2 aircraft are gradually replaced by quieter Stage 3 models.

The reduction of aircraft noise at the source, by using quieter aircraft, is supplemented by an ambitious program to encourage compatible land uses in areas around airports. *Part 150 Airport Land-Use Compatibility Planning*, of the Federal Aviation Regulations, adopted in January 1985, establishes the system for measuring aviation noise in the community and provides information about the land uses that are normally compatible with various levels of noise exposure.

Part 150 encourages airport operators to develop *noise exposure maps* and *noise compatibility programs*. The noise exposure maps identify land use incompatibilities and are useful in discouraging any further incompatible development. Once the FAA determines that the noise exposure maps have been prepared in accordance with Part 150, the airport operator may submit a noise compatibility program, coordinated with affected parties, outlining measures to improve airport land use compatibility.

As of July 1990, 200 airports were participating in the Part 150 program, 119 had noise exposure maps in compliance with program requirements, and 76 had airport noise compatibility programs approved by FAA.

An FAA-approved Part 150 noise compatibility program clears the way for airports to obtain federal aid for noise abatement projects. A substantial amount of federal aid is available for preparing and implementing noise compatibility programs, with 10 percent of the annual Airport Improvement Program funds being reserved for this purpose. Large scale projects have been undertaken in a number of major cities, including Atlanta, Baltimore, San Francisco, Seattle, and St. Louis, to relocate households or soundproof dwellings. Approximately $288 million has been spent at those five locations to relocate an estimated 11,000 people and soundproof the residences of an estimated 3,400 people. These projects represent about 40 percent of the $728 million in federal aid granted for airport noise compatibility since 1982.

Further significant improvements are assured by the *Aircraft Noise and Capacity Act of 1990*, which requires the establishment of a national aviation noise policy, including a general prohibition against the operation of Stage 2 aircraft of more than 75,000 pounds after December 31, 1999. In addition to the phaseout of Stage 2 aircraft, the act requires the establishment of a national program for reviewing airport noise and access restrictions. It is estimated that the phaseout of Stage 2 aircraft will reduce the population exposed to high noise levels to approximately 1.1 million people, a tremendous improvement over the situation in 1974 when 7 million people were affected.

Measurement of noise

There are several methods for measuring aircraft noise and its effect on a community. The level of sound can be measured objectively, but noise—unwanted sound—is a very subjective matter, both because the human ear is more sensitive to some frequencies than others and because the degree of annoyance associated with a noise can be influenced by psychological factors such as the hearer's attitude or the type of activity in which engaged. Techniques have been developed to measure single events measured in units such as dBA (A-weighted sound level in decibels) or EPNdB (effective perceived noise decibels). These measure the level of noise in objective terms, giving extra weight to those sound frequencies that are most annoying to the human ear.

In some cases, annoyance is due not only to intensity of a single event, but to the cumulative effects of exposure to noise throughout the day. Methods to measure this effect objectively include aggregating single event measures to give a cumulative noise profile by means of such techniques as the noise exposure forecast (NEF), the community noise equivalent level (CNEL), and the day-night average sound level (Ldn). FAA uses EPNdB to measure single event aircraft noise as part of its aircraft certification process. FAA has established dBA as the single event unit and the Ldn system as the standard measure of cumulative noise exposure to be used by airports in the preparation of noise abatement studies.

FAA has suggested, but not mandated, guidelines for determining land uses that are compatible with a given Ldn level. Ideally, residential uses should be located in areas below 65 Ldn. In the high noise impact areas (Ldn 80 to 85 or more), FAA suggests that parking, transportation facilities, mining and extraction, and similar activities are the most compatible.

Noise and land uses

The problem of aviation noise is intimately connected with the question of land use because one of the most effective insulators against annoying sound is distance. If possible, an airport should be surrounded by a noise buffer area of vacant or forested land, and the private property near the high noise impact area (under approach and departure paths and near aeronautical surfaces) should be used for activities that are less sensitive to noise: agriculture, highway interchanges, manufacturing, and other activities where a high level of ambient noise does not detract from performance. Unfortunately, many airports are surrounded by buildings devoted to incompatible activities: residences, schools, and auditoriums.

Zoning and land use planning are responsibilities of local governments. In many cases these governments have been unable or unwilling to provide mutual protection for airports and residential development. Land is a scarce resource in urban areas, and where there is great demand for housing and shopping centers, underutilized land around airports becomes extremely valuable. Even where local governments have enacted zoning ordinances to prevent encroachment, developers have been able to gain waivers. The tax revenues generated by the higher land uses might seem more important to city governments than the long-range need to protect the airport and the residential areas from one another. In some cases, local governments trying to enforce zoning rules have had them overturned when developers contested them in court.

At least part of the problem is ineffective intergovernmental cooperation. Few airports are located entirely within the borders of the municipality that owns and operates the facility. Surrounding municipalities might have conflicting practices, priorities, and philosophies of government, and each has separate zoning authority. For instance, St. Louis-Lambert Airport is surrounded by 29 municipalities, and Dallas-Fort Worth by 10. A municipality that owns an airport perceives advantages and disadvantages, and it must weigh the economic benefits of the airport against the problems of noise. A municipality that merely borders on an airport might see only disadvantages. Further, because the airport operator has sole liability for damage due to airport noise, some surrounding municipalities have felt little need to enforce zoning rules when complaints will not be directed to them but to the municipality that owns and operates the airport.

Even where sound intergovernmental agreements on zoning have been developed, time can erode them. When Dallas-Fort Worth airport was being planned and built, the surrounding municipalities developed agreements on zoning that were viewed as models of intergovernmental cooperation and coordination. Over the intervening years there have been changes in local government, in priorities, and in the local economy. There is now encroaching development such that Dallas-Fort Worth now has noise problems, despite its huge 17,600-acre size.

Local noise abatement programs

While aircraft are the source of noise at airports, aircraft operators are not liable for damage caused by noise. The courts have determined that the sole legal liability for aircraft noise rests with the airport operator. The federal government, by law and administrative action, has preempted control of aircraft in flight. Because the federal government is immune from suit (without its consent) and because the aircraft operate under federal regulation, litigants with complaints about aircraft noise have no recourse but to the airport operator. Courts have consistently held that the airport proprietor has the authority to control the location, orientation, and size of the airport and from that authority flows the liability for the consequences of its operation, including the responsibility to protect citizens from residual noise. Litigants have used various approaches in suing airports and have collected damages on the grounds of trespass, nuisance, and inverse condemnation.

Balancing their extensive exposure to liability claims, airport operators have some authority—albeit limited—to control the use of their airports in order to reduce noise. Basically, any restriction of operations at the airport must be nondiscriminatory. Further, no airport may impose a restriction that unduly burdens interstate commerce. The definition of "undue burden" is not precise, and restrictions at individual airports must be reviewed on a case-by-case basis. Restrictions must be meaningful and reasonable; a restriction adopted to reduce noise should actually have the effect of reducing noise. Finally, local restrictions must not interfere with safety or the federal prerogative to control aircraft in the navigable airspace.

Under FAR Part 150, airport operators can undertake noise compatibility studies to determine the extent and nature of the noise problem at a given airport. They can develop noise exposure maps indicating the contours within which noise exposure is greater than a permissible level. They can identify the noncompatible land uses within those contours and develop a plan for mitigating present problems and preventing future ones. Unfortunately, the airport operator's ability to prevent future problems is usually very limited. Unless the airport actually owns the land in question, the authority to make sure it is reserved for a compatible use is usually in the hands of a municipal zoning commission.

Many of these noise abatement programs allowed under current legislation are eligible for federal aid:

1. Takeoff and landing procedures to abate noise and preferential runway use to avoid noise-sensitive areas (which must be developed in cooperation with and approved by FAA).
2. Construction of sound barriers and soundproofing of buildings.
3. Acquisition of land and interests therein, such as easements, air rights, and development rights to ensure uses compatible with airport operation.
4. Complete or partial curfews.
5. Denial of airport use to aircraft types or classes not meeting federal noise standards.
6. Capacity limitations based on the relative noisiness of different types of aircraft.
7. Differential landing fees based on FAA-certificated noise levels or on time of arrival and departure.

FAA provides assistance to airport operators and air carriers in establishing or modifying flight paths to avoid noise-sensitive areas. In some cases, aircraft can be directed to use only certain runways, to stay above minimum altitudes, or to approach and depart over lakes, bays, rivers, or industrial areas rather than residential areas. Procedures might be developed to scatter the noise over several communities through some "equitable" rotation program. These noise abatement procedures might have a negative effect on airport capacity. They might require circuitous routing of aircraft or use of a runway configuration that is less than optimum with respect to capacity.

Restrictions on airport access or on the number of operations have an even more deleterious effect on airport capacity. One form of restriction is the night curfew, which effectively shuts down the airport during certain hours. Only a few airports have officially instituted curfews. One such is Washington National Airport, which has a curfew based on FAA-certificated noise standards. Aircraft with noise ratings more than 72 dBA on takeoff or 85 dBA on approach cannot use the airport between 10 p.m. and 7 a.m. This eliminates nearly all jet operations. Some other airports have reached informal agreements with carriers to refrain from operations after a certain hour, and some, like Cleveland, impose a curfew by not supplying jet fuel at night.

Air carriers are concerned about the spread of curfews as a noise abatement tool because they can play havoc with airline scheduling and reduce the capacity of the entire national airport system. Imposition of curfews at even two or three major airports on the East and West Coast could reduce the "scheduling window" for transcontinental flights to only four or five hours daily (FIG. 14-1) and would

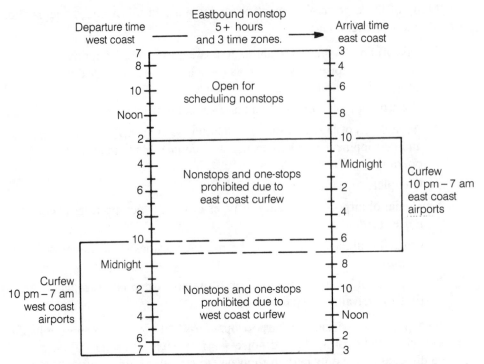

Fig. 14-1. *Effects of curfews on scheduling transcontinental service.* Federal Aviation Administration

also affect flights within each region. Curfews are especially threatening to air cargo operators, whose business is typically conducted at night. Some see widespread imposition of curfews as a burden on interstate commerce, and hence unconstitutional.

Other types of airport access restrictions—excluding certain aircraft types, instituting special fees for noncomplying aircraft, or establishing hourly limits based on a "noise budget"—are subject to the legal tests of nondiscrimination and reasonableness. For example, the ban on jet aircraft instituted at Santa Monica airport was struck down by the court in 1979 because many new technology jet aircraft that would have been banned by such a rule are quieter than the propeller-driven aircraft that would have been allowed to operate. A later ordinance by the city, banning operations by aircraft with a single-event noise rating of 76 dBA, was upheld. The court rejected the argument that enforcement of a local standard violates federal preemption. On the other hand, a federal court in 1983 struck down the curfew-quota system in effect at Westchester County airport in New York. Under that system, an average of only six aircraft with noise ratings above 76 dBA were permitted to land between the hours of midnight and 6:30 a.m.

Both air carriers and airframe manufacturers have objected to the proliferation of local noise standards and noise-based quota systems. Boeing, for example, has pointed out that airlines are already in the process of replacing or re-engining their noisier aircraft in response to FAA regulations. This replacement will require a large capital outlay on the part of carriers—capital that will have to be generated largely by continued operation of the aircraft they already have. If airports adopt local noise standards more stringent than FAA's, carriers will have to accelerate their fleet replacement programs in order to continue serving those markets. According to Boeing's estimates, such acceleration would be beyond the financial means of many airlines.

Federal funds are available to assist airport operators in soundproofing buildings or buying noise-impacted land. Usually, these are extremely expensive remedial measures, but a number of airports have been forced to undertake them. St. Louis Lambert Airport expects to spend about $50 million over the next 20 years under its Environs Plan. The airport has soundproofed some buildings and returned them to public use. In other cases, it has purchased land and resold it for more compatible use. In some cases, the land was "sterilized," that is, the buildings were torn down and the land left vacant as a noise buffer zone.

Key terms

concession agreement
management contract
airport premises liability policy
FAR Part 136 Certificated Airplane Noise Levels
FAR Part 150 Airport-Land Use Compatibility Planning
noise exposure maps
noise compatibility programs
Aircraft Noise and Capacity Act of 1990

Review questions

1. How have airport-airline relations concerning use agreements changed since deregulation?
   In the past, a joint airline negotiating committee would meet with airport management to discuss facility requirements and fees. Why is this practice changing?

2. What is a management contract? How does this arrangement differ from a typical concession agreement?
   Revenues from concessions are generally a minor portion of total revenue because of the incidental nature of their business on an airport. Do you agree? Why?
   What is the primary need of GA aircraft based at an airport?

3. What are some of the liability exposures a typical airport is subjected to in the course of conducting business?

Litigation primarily arises from three areas. Give some examples under each area.

Describe the coverages available under the airport premises liability policy.

4. Discuss the FAA's role in the control and abatement of aircraft noise. How is noise measured?

What land use around the airport is compatible with aircraft operations?

How have zoning and multigovernmental units around the airport exacerbated the problem of noise?

5. List the noise abatement programs eligible for federal aid. Explain some of the restrictions imposed on aircraft operations which are designed to reduce the problem of noise. Distinguish between noise exposure maps and noise compatibility programs. What is the primary purpose of the Aircraft Noise and Capacity Act of 1990?

Suggested readings

FAR Part 36 Certificated Airplane Noise Levels.

FAR Part 150 Airport-Land Use Compatibility Planning.

Wells, Alexander T. *Introduction to Aviation Insurance*. Krieger Publishing Company: Melbourne, Florida, 1985.

Aircraft Noise and Capacity Act of 1990.

Glossary

This glossary includes all key terms appearing at the ends of the chapters, as well as many other terms used in the text and others of significance in airport planning and management. The definitions are meant to be brief and straightforward rather than technically precise and all inclusive.

abandoned airport An airport permanently closed to aircraft operations which may be marked in accordance with current FAA standards for marking and lighting of deceptive, closed, and hazardous area on airports.

access/egress As used in the passenger handling system, the link that includes all of the ground transportation facilities, vehicles, and other modal transfer facilities required to move the passenger to and from the airport.

access/processing interface As used in the passenger handling system, the link in which the passenger makes the transition from the vehicular mode of transportation to pedestrian movement into the passenger processing activities.

access taxiway A taxiway that provides access to a particular location or area.

active based aircraft Aircraft that have a current Airworthiness Certificate and are based at an airport.

actual runway length The length of full-width usable runway from end to end of full-strength pavement where those runways are paved.

administrative building A building or buildings accommodating airport administration activity and public facilities for itinerant and local flying, usually associated with general aviation fixed-based operations.

administrative management A method of controlling airport access by setting quotas on passenger enplanements or on the number and type of aircraft operations that will be accommodated during a specific period.

advisory circular (AC) A series of external FAA publications consisting of all non-regulatory material of a policy, guidance, and informational nature.

aiming marker   A distinctive mark placed on the runway to serve as a point for judging and establishing a glide angle for landing aircraft. It is usually 1,000 feet from the landing threshold.

air carrier   A person who undertakes directly by lease, or other arrangement, to engage in air transportation. (FAR Part 1)

air carrier airport   An airport (or runway) designated by design and/or use for air carrier operations.

air carrier—certificated route   An air carrier holding a Certificate of Public Convenience and Necessity issued by the Civil Aeronautics Board to conduct scheduled services over specified routes and a limited amount of nonscheduled operations.

air carrier—commuter   An air taxi operator which: (1) performs at least five round trips per week between two or more points and publishes flight schedules which specify the times, days of the week, and places between which such flights are performed; or (2) transports mail by air pursuant to a current contract with the U.S. Postal Service.

Air Commerce Act of 1926   Designed to promote the development of and stabilize commercial aviation. Included the first licensing of aircraft, pilots, and mechanics and established the first rules and regulations for operating aircraft in the airway system.

air marker   An alphanumeric or graphic symbol on ground or building surfaces designed to give guidance to pilots in flight.

air navigation facility (NAVAID)   Any facility used as, available for use as, or designed for use as an aid to air navigation, including landing areas, lights, any apparatus or equipment for disseminating weather information, for signaling, for radio direction-finding, or for radio or other electronic communication, and any other structure or mechanism having a similar purpose for guiding and controlling flight in the air or the landing or takeoff of aircraft.

aircraft   A device that is used or intended to be used for flight in the air. (FAR Part 1)

aircraft capacity   The rate of aircraft movements on the runway/taxiway system which results in a given level of delay.

aircraft mix   The types of categories of aircraft which are to be accommodated at the airport.

Aircraft Noise and Capacity Act of 1990   Establishes a national aviation noise policy, including a general prohibition against the operation of Stage 2 aircraft of more than 75,000 pounds after December 31, 1999.

aircraft operations   The airborne movement of aircraft in controlled or noncontrolled airport terminal areas and about given en route fixes or at other points where counts can be made. There are two types of operations—*local* and *itinerant*.

(1) Local operations are performed by aircraft which:
   (a) Operate in the local traffic pattern or within sight of the airport.
   (b) Are known to be departing for, or arriving from, flight in local practice areas within a 20-mile radius of the airport.
   (c) Execute simulated instrument approaches or low passes at the airport.

(2) Itinerant operations are all aircraft operations other than local operations.

aircraft tiedown   Positions on the ground surface that are available for securing aircraft.

Airline Deregulation Act of 1978   Marked the beginning of the end of economic regulation of the certificated air carriers by the CAB. The Act called for the gradual phase-out of the CAB with its termination on December 31, 1984. All remaining essential functions were transferred to DOT and other agencies.

airport   An area of land or water that is used or intended to be used for the landing and takeoff of aircraft, and includes its buildings and facilities, if any. (FAR Part 1)

airport access plans   Proposed routing of airport access to the central business district and to points of connection with existing or planned ground transportation arteries.

airport accounting   Involves the accumulation, communication, and interpretation of economic data relating to the financial position of an airport and the results of its operations for decision-making purposes.

Airport and Airway Development Act Amendments of 1976   Extended the 1970 Act for five years and included a number of amendments including the types of airport development projects eligible for ADAP funding, increased the federal share for ADAP and PGP grants, and initiated a number of studies concerning the National Airport System Plan (NASP).

Airport and Airway Development Act of 1970   A federal aid to airports program administered by the FAA for the ten-year period ending in 1980. Over $4.1 billion was invested in the airport system during this period.

Airport and Airway Improvement Act of 1982   Reestablished the operation of the Airport and Airway Trust Fund with a slightly revised schedule of user taxes.

Airport and Airway Revenue Act of 1970   Created an airport and airway trust fund to generate revenues for airport aid. Taxes included an 8 percent surcharge on domestic passenger fares, a $3 surcharge on international passenger tickets, a 7 cents surcharge on fuel, a 5 percent surcharge on airfreight waybills, and an annual registration fee of $25 on all civil aircraft.

Airport and Airway Safety and Capacity Expansion Act of 1987   Extended the Airport and Airway Improvement Act for five years. Also provided that 10 percent of funding be available for disadvantaged small businesses.

airport authority   Similar to a port authority but with the single purpose of setting policy and management direction for airports within its jurisdiction.

airport beacon   A visual navigation aid displaying alternating white and green flashes to indicate a lighted airport or white flashes only for an unlighted airport.

airport configuration   The relative layout of component parts of an airport such as the runway-taxiway-terminal arrangement.

Airport Development Aid Program (ADAP)   A federal aid to airports program established under the Airport and Airway Development Act of 1970 for the development of airport facilities.

airport director   Sometimes referred to as airport manager or supervisor, the person responsible for the overall day-to-day operation of the airport.

airport elevation   The highest point of an airport's usable runways measured in feet from mean sea level.

airport geographical position   The designated geographical center of the airport (latitude and longitude) which is used as a reference point for the designation of airspace regulations.

airport identification beacon   Coded lighted beacon used to indicate the location of an airport where the airport beacon is more than 5,000 feet from the landing area.

airport imaginary surfaces Imaginary surfaces established at an airport for obstruction determination purposes and consisting of primary, approach-departure, horizontal, vertical, conical, and transitional surfaces.

Airport Improvement Program (AIP) A federal aid to airports program similar to ADAP covering the period from 1983 to 1987.

airport layout The major portion of the airport layout plan drawing including existing and ultimate airport development and land uses drawn to scale.

airport layout plan A plan for an airport showing boundaries and proposed additions to all areas owned or controlled by the sponsor for airport purposes, the location and nature of existing and proposed airport facilities and structures, and the location on the airport of existing and proposed nonaviation areas and improvements thereon.

airport layout plan drawing Includes the airport layout, location map, vicinity map, basic data table, and wind information.

airport master plan Presents the planner's conception of the ultimate development of a specific airport. It presents the research and logic from which the plan was evolved and displays the plan in a graphic and written report.

airport of entry *See* international airport.

airport premises liability policy Designed to protect the airport operator for losses arising out of legal liability for all activities carried on at the airport.

airport requirements First phase of the airport master plan which specifies new or expanded facilities that will be needed during the planning period. This involves cataloging existing facilities and forecasting future traffic demand. The planner compares the capacity of existing facilities with future demand, identifying where demand will exceed capacity, and what new facilities will be necessary.

airport safety self-inspection Provides a safety inspection checklist primarily designed for GA airports. (Advisory Circular 150/5200-18)

airport sponsor A public agency or tax-supported organization such as an airport authority, that is authorized to own and operate the airport, to obtain property interests, to obtain funds, and to be legally, financially, and otherwise able to meet all applicable requirements of current laws and regulations.

airport surface detection equipment (ASDE) Radar equipment specifically designed to detect all principal features on the surface of an airport, including aircraft vehicular traffic, and to present the entire picture on a radar indicator console in the control tower.

airport surveillance radar (ASR) Radar providing position of aircraft by azimuth and range data. It does not provide elevation data. It is designed for range coverage up to 60 nautical miles and is used by terminal area air traffic control.

airport system planning Airport plans as part of a system that includes national, regional, state, and local transportation planning.

airport traffic area Unless otherwise specifically designated in FAR Part 93, that airspace within a horizontal radius of 5 statute miles from the geographical center of any airport at which a control tower is operating, extending from the surface up to, but not including, an altitude of 3,000 feet above the elevation of the airport. (FAR Part 1)

airport traffic control service Air traffic control service provided by an airport traffic control tower or aircraft operating on the movement area and in the vicinity of an airport.

airport traffic control tower (ATCT) A central operations facility in the terminal air traffic control system, consisting of a tower cab structure, including an associated IFR room if radar equipped, using air/ground communications and/or radar, visual signaling and other devices, to provide safe and expeditious movement of terminal air traffic.

airport-to-airport distance The great-circle distance, measured in statute miles, between airports as listed in the Civil Aeronautics Board's official airline route and mileage manual.

airport closed to the public An airport not available to the public without permission from the owner.

airport open to the public An airport open to the public without prior permission and without restrictions within the physical capacities of available facilities.

airport use agreement Legal contracts for the air carriers' use of the airport and leases for use of terminal facilities.

air route Navigable airspace between two points which is identifiable.

air route surveillance radar (ARSR) A radar facility remotely connected to an air route traffic control center used to detect and display the azimuth and range of en route aircraft operating between terminal areas, enabling an ATC controller to provide air traffic service in the air route traffic control system.

air route traffic control center (ARTCC) A facility established to provide air traffic control service to aircraft operating on an IFR flight plan within controlled airspace and principally during the en route phase of flight.

airside facilities The airfield on which aircraft operations are carried out, including runways and taxiways.

airspace Space in the air above the surface of the earth or a particular portion of such space, usually defined by the boundaries of an area on the surface projected upward.

airspace capacity Includes the proximity of airports to one another, the relationship of runway alignments, and the nature of operations (IFR or VFR) in the area.

air taxi aircraft Aircraft operated by the holder of an Air Taxi Operating Certificate, which authorizes the carriage of passengers, mail or cargo for revenue in accordance with FAR Parts 135 and 121.

air taxi operator An operator providing either scheduled or unscheduled air taxi service or mail service.

air traffic Aircraft operating in the air or on an airport surface, exclusive of loading ramps and parking areas. (FAR Part 1)

air traffic clearance An authorization by air traffic control, for the purpose of preventing collision between known aircraft, for an aircraft to proceed under specified traffic conditions within controlled airspace (FAR Part 1)

air traffic control (ATC) A service operated by appropriate authority to promote the safe, orderly, and expeditious flow of air traffic. (FAR Part 1)

air traffic control beacon interrogator (ATCBI) That part of the ATCRBS system located on the ground that interrogates the airborne transponder and receives the reply.

air traffic control radar beacon system (ATCRBS) A radar system in which the object to be detected is fitted with cooperative equipment in the form of a radio receiver/transmitter (transponder). Radio pulses transmitted from the searching transmitter/receiver (interrogator) site are received in the cooperative equipment and used to trigger a distinctive transmission from the transponder. This latter transmission rather than a reflected signal is then received back at the transmitter/receiver site.

air transportation   Interstate, overseas, or foreign air transportation, or the transportation of mail by aircraft. (FAR Part 1)

airway   A path through the navigable airspace designated by appropriate authority within which air traffic service is provided.

Airways Modernization Act of 1957   Passed by Congress in response to several serious aircraft accidents and the coming of jet equipment, it was designed to provide for the development and modernization of the national system of navigation and traffic control facilities. Expiration was planned for June 30, 1960.

alphanumeric display   Use of letters of the alphabet and numerals to show altitude, beacon code, and other information about a target on a radar display.

alternate airport   An airport at which an aircraft may land if a landing at the intended airport becomes inadvisable. (FAR Part 1)

approach and clear zone layout   A graphic presentation to scale of the imaginary surfaces defined in FAR Part 77.

approach area   The defined area the dimensions of which are measured horizontally beyond the threshold over which the landing and takeoff operations are made.

approach clearance   Authorization issued by air traffic control to the pilot of an aircraft for an approach for landing under Instrument Flight Rules.

approach control facility   A terminal air traffic control facility (TRACON, CST, RAPCON, RATCF, tower, etc.) providing approach control service.

approach control service   Air traffic control service provided by an approach control facility for arriving and departing VFR/IFR aircraft and, on occasion, tower en route control service.

approach fix   The fix from or over which final approach (IFR) to an airport is executed.

approach gate   That point on the final approach course which is one mile from the approach fix on the side away from the airport or five miles from the landing threshold, whichever is farther from the landing threshold.

approach light beacon   An aeronautical beacon placed on the extended centerline of a runway at a fixed distance from the threshold.

approach light contact height   The height on the glide path of an instrument landing system from which a pilot making an approach can expect to see the high-intensity approach lights.

approach lighting system (ALS)   An airport lighting facility that provides visual guidance to landing aircraft by radiating light beams in a directional pattern by which the pilot aligns the aircraft with the extended centerline of the runway on his final approach and landing.

approach path   A specific flight course laid out in the vicinity of an airport and designed to bring aircraft in to safe landings; usually delineated by suitable navigational aids.

approach sequence   The order in which aircraft are positioned while awaiting approach clearance or while on approach.

approach slope ratio   The ratio of horizontal to vertical distance indicating the degree of inclination of the approach surface.

approach surface   An imaginary surface longitudinally centered on the extended centerline of the runway, beginning at the end of the primary surface and rising outward and upward to a specified height above the established airport elevation.

appropriation by activity   A form of budget where appropriate expenses are planned according to major work area or activity with no further detailed breakdown.

apron   A defined area, on a land airport, intended to accommodate aircraft for purposes of loading or unloading passengers or cargo, refueling, parking, or maintenance.

assistant director—finance and administration   Responsible for overall matters concerning finance, personnel, purchasing, facilities management and office management.

assistant director—maintenance   Responsible for planning, coordinating, directing, and reviewing the maintenance of buildings, facilities, vehicles, and utilities.

assistant director—operations   Responsible for all airside and landside operations including security and crash, fire, and rescue operations.

assistant director—planning and engineering   Provides technical assistance to all airport organizations, and ensures the engineering integrity of construction, alteration, and installation programs.

ATC data transfer and display equipment   Equipment for ATC facilities intended to provide a symbolic display of the data necessary for the control function by automatic means and providing for certain computation, storage, and recall of display data.

ATC Systems Command Center (ATCSCC)   A facility responsible for the operation of four distinct but integrated functions: Central Flow Control Function (CFCF), Central Altitude Reservations Function (CARF), Airport Reservation Position, and the Air Traffic Service Contingency Command Post (ATSCCP).

automated radar terminal systems (ARTS)   Computer-aided radar display subsystems capable of associating alphanumeric data with radar returns. Systems of varying functional capability, determined by the type of automation equipment and software, are denoted by a number/letter suffix following the name abbreviation.

automated weather observing system (AWOS)   Gathers weather data from unmanned sensors, automatically formulates weather reports, and distributes them to airport control towers.

automatic terminal information service (ATIS)   The continuous broadcast of recorded noncontrol information in selected high-activity terminal areas. Its purpose is to improve controller effectiveness and to relieve frequency congestion by automating the repetitive transmission of essential but routine information.

Aviation Safety and Noise Abatement Act of 1979   Provides assistance to airport operators to prepare and carry out noise compatibility programs. Authorizes the FAA to help airport operators develop noise abatement programs and makes them eligible for grants under ADAP.

avigation easement   A grant of a property interest in land over which a right of unobstructed flight in the airspace is established.

balanced runway concept   A runway length design concept wherein length of prepared runway is such that the accelerate-stop distance is equal to the takeoff distance for the aircraft for which the runway is designed.

based aircraft   The total number of active general aviation aircraft which use or may be expected to use an airport as a "home base."

basic data table   Shown on the airport layout plan drawing, it includes the airport elevation, runway identification and gradient, percent of wind coverage by principal runway, ILS runway when designated, normal or mean maximum daily temperature of the hottest month, pavement strength of each runway, and plan for obstruction removal, relocation of facilities.

basic runway length Runway length resulting when actual length is corrected to mean sea level, standard atmospheric, and no gradient conditions.

basic transport airport (or runway) An airport (or runway) that accommodates turbojet-powered aircraft up to 60,000 pounds gross weight.

basic utility (BU) airport Accommodates most single-engine and many of the small twin-engine aircraft.

blast fence A barrier that is used to divert or dissipate jet or propeller blast.

blast pad A specially prepared surface placed adjacent to the ends of runways to eliminate the erosive effect of the high wind forces produced by airplanes at the beginning of their takeoff rolls.

bleed-off taxiway A taxiway used as an exit from a runway to another runway, apron, or other aircraft operating area.

bond ratings A system used by major investor services (such as Moody's and Standard & Poor's) to grade bonds according to investment quality.

boundary markers Markers indicating the boundary of the surface usable for landing and takeoff of aircraft.

break-even need The annual revenue amount required to cover cost of capital investment and costs of administration, operation, and maintenance.

budgets The planned dollar amounts needed to operate and maintain the airport during a definite period of time such as a year. There are capital budgets for major capital expenditures (such as runway resurfacing) and operating budgets to meet daily expenses.

building area An area on an airport to be used, considered, or intended to be used, for airport buildings or other airport facilities or rights-of-way, together with all airport buildings and facilities located thereon.

building restriction line A line shown on the airport layout plan beyond which airport buildings must not be positioned in order to limit their proximity to aircraft movement areas.

buildings and facilities chief Responsible for assuring that buildings are adequately maintained with a minimum of cost.

Bureau of Air Commerce Established in 1934 as a separately constituted bureau of the Department of Commerce to promote and regulate aeronautics. The bureau consisted of two divisions, the division of air navigation and the division of air regulation.

busy-hour operations The total number of aircraft operations expected to occur at an airport at its busiest hour, computed by averaging two adjacent busiest hours of a typically high activity day.

capacity The ability of an airport to handle a given volume of traffic (demand). It is a limit that cannot be exceeded without incurring an operational penalty.

category II operation With respect to the operation of aircraft, means a straight-in ILS approach to the runway of an airport under a category II ILS instrument approach procedure issued by the Administrator or other appropriate authority. (FAR Part I)

causal models Highly sophisticated mathematical models that are developed and tested using historical data. The model is built on a statistical relationship between the forecasted (dependent) variable and one or more explanatory (independent) variables.

central flow control function (CFCF) A function of the ATC Systems Command Center (ATCSCC) responsible for ensuring maximum efficient use of airspace by maintaining a dynamic hour-by-hour assessment of the ATC system conditions, including weather, staffing, outages, traffic demand, and system capacity. Using this real-time system status, the CFCF may initiate flow control actions including major rerouting of traffic on a system basis, approve or disapprove intercenter restrictions or other actions deemed necessary to provide efficient flow of traffic and minimize delays.

centralized passenger processing Facilities for ticketing, baggage check-in, security, customs, and immigration all done in one building and used for processing all passengers using the building.

certificated route air carrier One of a class of air carriers holding Certificates of Public Convenience and Necessity issued by the Civil Aeronautics Board. These carriers are authorized to perform scheduled air transportation over specified routes and a limited amount of nonscheduled operations.

chief accountant Responsible for financial planning, budgeting, accounting, payroll, and auditing.

chief—airside operations Responsible for all airfield operations.

chief—landside operations Responsible for all landside operations.

chief purchasing agent Directs the procurement of materials and services to support the airport; prepares, negotiates, interprets, and administers contracts with vendors.

Civil Aeronautics Act of 1938 Created one administrative agency responsible for the regulation of aviation and air transportation. Under reorganization in 1940, two separate agencies were created: the *Civil Aeronautics Board*, primarily concerned with economic regulation of the air carriers; and the *Civil Aeronautics Administration*, responsible for the safe operation of the airway system.

Civil Aeronautics Administration (CAA) Forerunner to the FAA, responsible for supervising the construction, maintenance, and operation of the airway system including enforcement of safety regulations.

Civil Aeronautics Board (CAB) Responsible for the economic regulation of the certificated air carriers during the period from 1940 to 1985.

civil airport user categories As used by airport planners, refers to the four major types of airports; certificated air carrier, commuter, general aviation, and military.

clear air turbulence (CAT) Turbulence encountered in air where no clouds are present; more popularly applied to high-level turbulence associated with wind shear; often encountered in the vicinity of the jet stream.

clear zone Areas constituting the innermost portions of the runway approach areas as defined in FAR Part 77.

closed airport An airport temporarily closed to aircraft operations for maintenance, construction, or some other purpose while the operator is still in business.

closed field marking Panels placed in the center of the segmented circle, or in the center of the field, in the form of a cross which will signify that the field is closed to all traffic.

closed runway marking Panels placed on the ends of the runway and at regular intervals in the form of a cross, signifying that a runway is closed to all traffic.

commercial service airports Public-use commercial airports receiving scheduled passenger service and enplaning at least 2,500 passengers annually.

compensatory approach A financial management approach under which the airport operator assumes the major financial risk of running the airport and charges the airlines fees and rental rates set so as to recover the actual costs of the facilities and services that they use.

computerized aircraft manifest Produces aircraft load sheets, passenger manifests, and automatic telex reservations.

computerized baggage sorting equipment A new technique to sort baggage through the use of machine-readable tags.

computerized ticket systems Provide passengers advance reservation and sales, preassignment of seats, and automatic tagging of baggage.

concession agreement An agreement between the airport and a concession regarding the conduct of business on airport property.

concourse A passageway for passengers and public between the principal terminal building waiting area and the fingers and/or aircraft landing positions.

conical surface A surface extending from the periphery of the horizontal surface outward and upward at a slope of 20 to 1 for the horizontal distances and to the elevations above the airport elevation as prescribed by FAR Part 77.

controlled airspace Airspace designated as a continental control area, control area, control zone, terminal control area, or transition area, within which some or all aircraft may be subject to air traffic control. (FAR Part 1)

controlling obstruction The highest obstruction relative to a prescribed plane within a specific area.

control zone Airspace extending upward from the surface of the earth which may include one or more airports and is normally a circular area of five statute miles in radius with extensions where necessary to include instrument approach and departure paths.

converging runways Runways whose extended centerlines meet at a point beyond the runways themselves.

crash, fire, and rescue chief Develops procedures and implements crash, fire, and disaster plans.

criteria for design and development Specific performance measures used by airport planners in designing terminal building space requirements.

criteria for inclusion in the NPIAS The principal criteria are: 1) that the airport has (or is forecast to have within five years) at least 10 based aircraft (or engines); 2) that it be at least a 30-minute drive from the nearest existing or proposed airport currently in the NPIAS; and 3) that there is an eligible sponsor willing to undertake ownership and development of the airport.

crosswind A wind blowing across the line of flight of an aircraft.

crosswind component A wind component that is at a right angle to the longitudinal axis of the runway or the flight path of the aircraft.

crosswind leg A flight path at right angles to the landing runway off its upwind leg.

crosswind runway   A runway additional to the primary runway to provide for wind coverage not adequately provided by the primary runway.

curbside check-in   Designed to speed passenger movement by separating baggage-handling from other ticket counter and gate activities and thereby disencumbering those locations, allowing baggage to be consolidated and moved to aircraft more directly.

customs accelerated passenger inspection service (CAPIS)   The system employed at most airports of entry today which provides separate immigration and customs checkpoints.

daylight beacon operation   Operation of an airport rotating beacon during the hours of daylight means that the reported ground visibility in the control zone is less than three miles and/or the reported ceiling is less than 1,000 feet and that the ATC clearance is required for landing, takeoffs, and flight in the traffic pattern.

debt service coverage   The requirement that the airport's revenue, net of operating and maintenance expenses, be equal to a specified percentage in excess of the annual debt service (principal and interest payments) for revenue bond issues.

decentralized passenger processing   The passenger handling facilities are provided in smaller units and repeated in one or more buildings.

decibel (dB)   A unit of noise level representing a relative quantity. This reference value is a sound pressure of 20 micronewtons per square meter.

decision height (DH)   With respect to the operation of aircraft, means the height at which a decision must be made, during the ILS or PAR instrument approach, to either continue the approach or to execute a missed approach. (FAR Part 1)

defaults   Refers to the frequency with which a given type of enterprise has defaulted on a bond issue.

defederalization   Refers to a proposal to withdraw assistance for major air carrier airports.

demand management   A method of controlling airport access by promoting more effective or economically efficient use of existing facilities. The two most prevalent methods are differential pricing and auctioning of landing rights.

Department of Transportation (DOT)   Established in 1966 to promote coordination of existing federal programs and to act as a focal point for future research and development efforts in transportation.

depreciable investment   The annual cost of capital invested in plant and equipment.

Development of Landing Areas for National Defense (DLAND)   A program approved by Congress in 1940 which appropriated $40 million to be spent by the CAA for 250 airports necessary for the national defense.

directional marker   An airway marker located on the ground used to give visual direction to an aircraft; consists of an arrow indicating true north and arrows indicating names and states of the nearest town.

discrete address beacon system (DABS)   A sophisticated air traffic control surveillance system capable of interrogating each airborne DABS transponder in an "all-call" mode or with a discrete address signal encoded for each specific aircraft operating in the system. The data acquired upon response from each transponder are then processed to provide range, azimuth, altitude, and identity of each aircraft in the system on an individual basis but in sequence on a programmed interro-schedule. Since aircraft are addressed individually in DABS, the surveillance system automatically provides a natural vehicle for a data link between ground and aircraft which can be used for ATC control purposes including the proposed intermittent positive control (IPC) concepts.

displaced threshold A threshold that is located at a point on the runway other than the beginning.

downwind leg A flight path in the traffic pattern parallel to the landing runway in the direction opposite to landing. It extends to the intersection of the base leg.

dynamic hydroplaning A condition where landing gear tires ride up on a cushioning film of water on the runway surfaces.

effective perceived noise level (EPNL) Time-integrated perceived noise level calculated with adjustments for irregularities in the sound spectrum, such as that caused by discrete-frequency components (tone-correction). The unit of effective perceived noise level is the decibel, with identifying prefix for clarification, EPNdB.

effective runway length (a) Effective runway length for takeoff means the distance from the end of the runway at which the takeoff is started to the point at which the obstruction clearance plane associated with the other end of the runway intersects the runway centerline. (b) Effective runway length for landing means the distance from the point at which the obstruction clearance plane associated with the approach end of the runway intersects the centerline of the runway to the far end thereof. (FAR Part 121)

enplaned passengers The total number of revenue passengers boarding aircraft, including originating, stopover, and transfer passengers, in scheduled and nonscheduled services.

enplaning air cargo Includes the total tonnage of priority, nonpriority, and foreign mail, express and freight (property other than baggage accompanying passengers) departing on aircraft at an airport, including originations, stopover, and transfer cargo.

en route air traffic control service Air traffic control service provided aircraft on an IFR flight plan, generally by centers, when these aircraft are operating between departure and destination terminal areas.

en route flight advisory service (EFAS) A specialized system providing near real-time weather service to pilots in flight.

entrance taxiway A taxiway that provides entrance for aircraft to the takeoff end of the runway.

essential air service Guarantees air carrier service to selected small cities and provides subsidies (through 1988) if needed so as to prevent these cities from losing service.

executive aircraft operator A corporation, company, or individual which operates owned or leased aircraft, flown by pilot(s) whose primary duties involve pilotage of aircraft, as a means of transportation or personnel or cargo in the conduct of company business.

exit taxiway A taxiway used as an exit from a runway to another runway, apron or other aircraft operating area.

FAA high-density rule Quotas imposed at selected airports based on estimated limits of the air traffic control (ATC) system and airport runway capacity.

FAA Office of Systems Engineering Management (OSEM) A delay monitoring system that uses data from the Department of Transportation an operational times actually experienced by air carrier flights. Delay is measured by OSEM as the difference between an arbitrary standard flight time and the actual time reported for each flight.

facilities chief   Establishes criteria and procedures for the administration of all airport property. Responsible for inventory control of all equipment and facilities.

fan noise   General term for the noise generated within the fan stage of a turbofan engine; includes both discrete frequencies and random noise.

FAR Part 77   Contains obstruction requirements at or near airports.

FAR Part 107, Airport Security   Prescribes security rules for airport operators serving certificated air carriers.

FAR Part 136, Certificated Airport Noise Levels   Establishes noise certification standards for new design turbojet and transport category aircraft.

FAR Part 150, Airport-Land Use Compatibility Planning   Designed to assist airport operators in determining the extent and nature of the noise problem at a given airport.

Federal Airport Act of 1946   A federal aid to airports program administered by the CAA (later the FAA) to give the United States a comprehensive system of airports. Over $1.2 billion in airport development aid funds were disbursed by the Federal Government during its 24-year history.

Federal Aviation Act of 1958   Created the Federal Aviation Agency (FAA) with an administrator responsible to the President. The law retained the CAB as an independent agency and transferred the safety-rule-making powers to the FAA along with the functions of the CAA and the Airways Modernization Board.

Federal Aviation Administration (FAA)   Created by the act that established the Department of Transportation. Assumed all of the responsibilities of the former Federal Aviation Agency.

Federal Aviation Agency (FAA)   Established in 1958 to regulate, promote, and develop air commerce in a safe manner. FAA was also given the responsibility of operating the airway system and consolidating all research and development of air navigation facilities.

federal government-operated airports   Two commercial airports serving the District of Columbia and surrounding area which are managed by the FAA. They are Washington National and Dulles International.

final approach area(s)   Areas of defined dimensions protected for aircraft executing instrument approaches.

final approach (IFR)   The flight path of an aircraft which is inbound to the airport on an approved final instrument approach course, beginning at the final approach fix or point and extending to the airport or the point where circling for landing or missed approach is executed.

final approach (VFR)   A flight path, in the traffic pattern, of a landing aircraft in the direction of landing along the extended runway centerline from the base leg to the runway.

final controller   That controller providing final approach guidance utilizing radar equipment.

financial plan   An economic evaluation of the entire master plan development including revenues and expenditures.

finger   A roofed structure, with or without sidewalls, extending from the main terminal building or its concourse to the aircraft loading positions.

flareout   That portion of a landing maneuver in which the rate of descent is reduced to lessen the impact of landing.

flexible pavement A pavement structure consisting of a bituminous surface course, a base course, and in most cases, a subbase course.

flight advisory service Advice and information provided by a facility to assist pilots in the safe conduct of flight and aircraft movement.

flight advisory weather service (FAWS) Flight advisory and aviation forecast service provided by the National Weather Service.

flight interface As used in the passenger handling system, the link between the passenger processing activities and the flight.

flight plan Specified information relating to the intended flight of an aircraft, which is filed orally or in writing with air traffic control. (FAR Part 1)

flight service station (FSS) A central operations facility in the national flight advisory system utilizing data interchange facilities for the collection and dissemination of NOTAMS, weather, administrative data; and providing preflight and inflight advisory service, and other services to pilots, via air/ground communication facilities.

flight time The time from the moment the aircraft first moves under its own power for the purpose of flight until the moment it comes to rest at the next point of landing ("block-to-block" time). (FAR Part 1)

flow control Restriction applied by ATC to the flow of air traffic to keep elements of the common system, such as airports or airways, from becoming saturated.

fuel flowage fees Fees levied by the airport operator per gallon of aviation gasoline and jet fuel sold at the airport.

gate arrival A centralized terminal building layout that is aimed at reducing the walking distance by bringing the automobile as close as possible to the aircraft.

gate position A designated space or position on an apron for an aircraft to remain parked while loading or unloading passengers and cargo.

general aviation That portion of civil aviation which encompasses all facets of aviation except air carriers holding a certificate of convenience and necessity from the Civil Aeronautics Board, and large aircraft commercial operators.

general aviation airports Those airports with fewer than 2,500 annual enplaned passengers and those used exclusively by private and business aircraft not providing common-carrier passenger service.

general aviation itinerant operations Takeoffs and landings of civil aircraft (exclusive of air carrier) operating on other than local flights.

general concept evaluation A set of general considerations that an airport planner uses to evaluate and select among alternative concepts in a preliminary fashion prior to any detailed design and development.

general obligation bonds Bonds that are issued by states, municipalities, and other general-purpose governments and backed by the full faith, credit, and taxing power of the issuing government agency.

general utility (GU) airport Accommodates all general aviation aircraft.

glideslope transmitter An ILS navigation facility in the terminal area electronic navigation system, providing vertical guidance for aircraft during approach and landing by radiating a directional pattern of VHF radio waves modulated by two signals which, when received with equal intensity, are displayed by compatible airborne equipment as an "on-path" indication.

ground access capacity   Existing and planned highway and mass transit systems in the area of the airport.

ground controlled approach (GCA)   A radar landing system operated from the ground by air traffic control personnel transmitting instructions to the pilot by radio. Approach may be conducted with surveillance radar only or with both surveillance and precision approach radar.

grounds chief   Responsible for assuring that the grounds are maintained in good repair and that the landscape is adequately maintained.

guidance light facility (GDL)   A lighting facility in the terminal area navigation system located in the vicinity of an airport consisting of one or more high intensity lights to guide a pilot into the takeoff or approach corridor, away from populated areas for safety and noise abatement.

handoff   Passing of control of an aircraft from one controller to another.

heliport   An area of land, water, or structure used or intended to be used for the landing and takeoff of helicopters. (FAR Part 1)

high-intensity light   A runway or threshold light whose main beam provides a minimum intensity of 12,000 candlepower in white light through a vertical angle of 3 degrees and a horizontal angle of 6 degrees.

holding areas   Run-up areas located at or very near the ends of runways for pilots to make final checks and await final clearance for takeoff.

holding bay   An area where aircraft can be held, or bypassed, to facilitate efficient ground traffic movement.

horizontal surface   A specified portion of a horizontal plane located 150 feet above the established airport elevation which establishes the height above which an object is determined to be an obstruction to air navigation.

hubs   A city or a standard metropolitan statistical area requiring aviation services and classified by each community's percentage of the total enplaned passengers in scheduled service of certain domestic certificated route air carriers.

hydroplaning   The condition in which moving aircraft tires are separated from a pavement surface by a water or liquid rubber film, or by steam resulting in a derogation of mechanical braking effectiveness.

IFR airport   An airport with an authorized instrument approach procedure.

IFR conditions   Weather conditions below the minimum for flight under visual flight rules. (FAR Part 1)

ILS Category I   An ILS which provides acceptable guidance information from the coverage limits of the ILS to the point at which the localizer course line intersects the glide path at a height of 100 feet above the horizontal plane containing the runway threshold. A Category I ILS supports landing minima as low as 200 ft. HAT and 1800 RVR.

ILS Category II   An ILS which provides acceptable guidance information from the coverage limits of the ILS to the point at which the localizer course line intersects the glide path at a height of 50 feet above the horizontal plane containing the runway threshold. A Category II ILS supports landing minima as low as 100 feet HAT and 1200 RVR.

ILS Category III   An ILS which provides acceptable guidance information from the coverage limits of the ILS with no decision height specified above the horizontal plane containing the runway threshold. *See* ILS-CAT III A-B-C operations.

ILS-CAT III A operation   Operation, which no decision height limitation, to and along the surface of the runway with a runway visual range not less than 700 feet.

ILS-CAT III B operation   Operation, with no decision height limitation, to and along the surface of the runway without reliance on external visual reference; and, subsequently, taxiing with external visual reference with a runway visual range not less than 150 feet.

ILS-CAT III C operation   Operation, with no decision height limitation, to and along the surface of the runway and taxiways without reliance on external visual reference.

inactive airport   An airport where all flying activities have ceased yet has remained in an acceptable state of repair for civil use and is identifiable from the air as an airport.

inner marker (IM)   An ILS navigational facility in the terminal area navigation system located between the middle marker and the end of the ILS runway, transmitting a 75 megahertz fan-shaped radiation pattern modulated at 3000 Hz, keyed at six dots per second and received by compatible airborne equipment indicating to the pilot, both aurally and visually, that he is directly over the facility at an altitude of 100 feet on his final ILS approach, providing he is on the glide path.

in-runway lighting   A lighting system consisting of flush or semiflush lights placed in the runway pavement in specified patterns.

instrument approach   An approach to an airport, with intent to land, by an aircraft flying in accordance with an IFR flight plan, when the visibility is less than 3 miles and/or when the ceiling is at or below the minimum initial altitude.

instrument approach runway   A runway served by electronic aid providing at least directional guidance adequate for a straight-in approach.

instrument flight rules (IFR)   FAR rules that govern the procedures for conducting instrument flight. (FAR Part 91)

instrument landing system (ILS)   A system which provides in the aircraft, the lateral, longitudinal, and vertical guidance necessary for a landing.

instrument meteorological conditions (IMC)   Meteorological conditions expressed in terms of visibility, distance from cloud, and ceiling less than the minima specified for visual meteorological conditions.

instrument runway   A runway equipped with electronic and visual navigation aids and for which a straight-in (precision or non-precision) approach procedure has been approved or is planned.

integrated airport system planning   As defined in the Airport and Airway Improvement Act of 1982, "the initial as well as continuing development for planning purposes of information and guidance to determine the extent, type, nature, location, and timing of airport development needed in a specific area to establish a viable, balanced, and integrated system of public use airports."

international airport   (1) An airport of entry which has been designated by the Secretary of Treasury or Commissioner of Customs as an international airport for customs service. (2) A landing rights airport at which specific permission to land must be obtained from customs authorities in advance of contemplated use. (3) Airports designated under the Convention of International Civil Aviation as an airport for use by international commercial air transport and/or international general aviation. (4) As pertaining to ICAO facilitation, any airport designated by the Contracting State in whose territory it is situated as an airport of entry and departure for international air traffic, where the formalities incident to customs, immigration, public health, animal and plant quarantine and similar procedures are carried out.

intersecting runways Two or more runways which cross or meet within their lengths.

itinerant operations All aircraft arrivals and departures other than local operations.

jet noise The noise generated externally to a jet engine in the turbulent jet exhaust.

joint automated weather observation system (JAWOS) Automatically gathers local weather data and distributes it to other air traffic control facilities and to the National Weather Service.

joint-use airport An airport owned by the military, a public body, or both, where an agreement exists for joint civil-military fixed-based aviation operations.

judgmental forecasts Forecasts based on intuition and subjective evaluations by an individual who is closely acquainted with the factors related to the variable being forecast.

Kelly Act of 1925 Authorized the Postmaster General to enter into contracts with private persons or companies for the transportation of the mail by air.

landing area Any locality, either on land or water, including airports, heliports and STOLports, which is used or intended to be used for the landing and takeoff or surface maneuvering of aircraft, whether or not facilities are provided for the shelter, servicing, or repair of aircraft, or for receiving or discharging of passengers or cargo.

landing rights airport *See* international airport.

landing roll The distance from the point of touchdown to the point where the aircraft can be brought to a stop, or exit the runway.

landing strip A term formerly used to designate: (1) the graded area upon which the runway was symmetrically located and, (2) the graded area suitable for the takeoff and landing of airplanes where a paved runway was not provided.

landing strip lighting Lines or rows of lights located along the edges of the designated landing and takeoff path within the strip. *See* landing strip.

landside operations Those parts of the airport designed to serve passengers including the terminal buildings, vehicular circular drive, and parking facilities.

land use plan Shows on-airport land uses as developed by the airport sponsor under the master plan effort and off-airport land uses as developed by surrounding communities.

large aircraft Aircraft of more than 12,500 pounds maximum certificated takeoff weight. (FAR Part 1)

lead-in light facility (LDIN) A facility in the terminal area navigation system providing special light guidance to aircraft in approach patterns or landing procedures. Facility configuration consists of any number of flashers so located as to visually guide an aircraft through an approach corridor, bypassing high density residential, commercial, or obstruction areas.

lighted airport An airport where runway and associated obstruction lighting is available from sunset to sunrise or during periods of reduced visibility or on request of the pilot.

linear or curvilinear terminal A type of simple terminal layout that is repeated in a linear extension to provide additional apron frontage, more gates, and more room within the terminal for passenger processing.

line-item budget The most detailed form of budget and used quite extensively at the large commercial airports. Budgets are established for each item and often adjusted to take into consideration changes in volume of activity.

localizer beacon An ILS navigation facility in the terminal area electronic navigation system, providing horizontal guidance to the runway centerline for aircraft during approach and landing by radiating a directional pattern of VHF radio waves modulated by two signals which, when received with with equal intensity, are displayed by compatible airborne equipment as an "on-course" indication, and when received in unequal intensity are displayed as an "off-course" indication.

local operations As pertaining to air traffic operations, aircraft operating in the local traffic pattern or within sight of the tower; aircraft known to be departing for, or arriving from, flight in local practice areas located within a 20-mile radius of the control tower; aircraft executing simulated instrument approaches or low passes at the airport.

local traffic Aircraft operating in the local traffic pattern or within sight of the tower, or aircraft known to be departing for or arriving from flight in local practice areas, or aircraft executing simulated instrument approaches at the airport.

local VFR flight plan Specific information provided to air traffic service units, relative to the intended flight of an aircraft under visual flight rules within a specific local area.

location map Shown on the airport layout plan drawing, it depicts the airport, cities, railroads, major highways, and roads within 20 to 50 miles of the airport.

low-intensity light A runway or threshold light from which the light distribution through 360 degrees of azimuth and a selected 6 degrees in the vertical is not less than 10 candlepower in white light.

low level wind shear alert system (LLWSAS) Provides the air traffic control tower with information on wind conditions near the runway. It consists of an array of anemometers that read wind velocity and direction around the airport and signal the sudden changes that indicate wind shear.

lump-sum appropriation The simplest form of budget and generally only used at small GA airports. There are no specific restrictions as to how the money should be spent.

majority-in-interest clauses Found in some airport use agreements which give the airlines accounting for a majority of traffic at an airport the opportunity to review and approve or veto capital projects that would entail significant increases in the rates and fees they pay for the use of airport facilities.

management contract An agreement under which a firm is hired to operate a particular service on behalf of the airport.

manager of community relations Responsible for all public relations activities including the development of advertising and publicity concerning the airport.

marking On airports, a pattern of contrasting colors placed on the pavement, turf, or other usable surface by paint or other means to provide specific information to aircraft pilots and sometimes to operators of ground vehicles, on the movement areas.

metering Regulating the arrival time of aircraft in the terminal area so as not to exceed a given acceptance rate.

microwave landing systems (MLS) An instrument approach and landing system operating in the microwave frequencies (5.0−5.25 GHz/15.4−15.7 GHz) that provides precision guidance in azimuth, elevation, and distance measurement.

middle marker (MM) An ILS navigation facility in the terminal area navigation system located approximately 3,500 feet from the runway edge on the extended centerline, transmitting a 75-MHz fan-shaped radiation pattern, modulated at 1,300 Hz, keyed alternately dot and dash, and received by compatible airborne equipment, indicating to the pilot both aurally and visually, that he is passing over the facility.

mobile lounge or transporter Used to transport passengers to and from the terminal building to aircraft parked on the apron.

mode S data link A proposed addition to the ATCRBS transponder that will permit direct, automatic exchange of digitally encoded information between the ground controller and individual aircraft.

moving target detection An electronic device which will permit radar scope presentation only from targets which are in motion. A partial remedy for ground clutter.

multiplier effect Revenues generated by the airport are channeled throughout the community.

municipally operated airport An airport owned by a city and run as a department of the city, with policy direction by the city council and, in some cases, by a separate airport commission or advisory board.

National Airport System Plan (NASP) A plan specifying in terms of general location and type of development the projects considered by the Administrator to be necessary to provide a system of public airports adequate to anticipate and meet the needs of civil aeronautics. Replaced by the NPIAS. *See* criteria for inclusion in NPIAS.

national airspace command center (NASCOM) Receives daily reports from controllers at about 60 major airports containing information on the number of delays and judgments by controllers about the primary and secondary causes.

National Airspace Review (NAR) A 42-month study by the FAA and the aviation industry started in October 1981 to identify and implement changes to promote greater efficiency and simplify the ATC system.

National Environmental Policy Act of 1969 Requires the preparation of detailed environmental statements for all major federal airport development actions significantly affecting the quality of the environment.

NPIAS Levels of Need The NPIAS relates the airport system improvements to three levels of need: Level I—maintain the airport system in its current condition; Level II—bring the system up to current design standards; and Level III—expand the system.

National Plan of Integrated Airport Systems (NPIAS) The Airport and Airway Improvement Act of 1982 required the FAA to develop the NPIAS by September 1984. The legislation called the identification of national airport system needs including development costs in the short and long run.

national system of airports The inventory of selected civil airports that are highly correlated with those aviation demands most consistent with the national interest.

National Transportation Safety Board (NTSB) Created by the act which established the Department of Transportation to determine the cause of transportation accidents and review on appeal the suspension or revocation of any certificates or licenses issued by the Secretary of Transportation.

navaid Any facility used in, available for use in, or designated for use in aid of air navigation, including lights, any apparatus or equipment for disseminating weather information, for signaling, for radio direction finding, or for radio or other electronic communication, and any other structure or mechanism having a similar purpose for guiding or controlling flight in the air or the landing or takeoff of aircraft.

navigable airspace   Airspace at and above the minimum flight altitudes prescribed in the FARs, including airspace needed for safe takeoff and landing. (FAR Part 1)

new federalism   Refers to a proposal to turn increased responsibility for decisions on airport funding and programming over to state aviation agencies and departments of transportation.

noise compatibility programs   Outlines measures to improve airport land use compatibility.

noise exposure maps   Identify land use incompatibilities and are useful in discouraging any further incompatible development.

noise level   For airborne sound, the same as *sound level*, unless otherwise specified.

nondepreciable investment items   Those assets such as the cost of land acquisition which have a permanent value even if the airport site is converted to other uses.

noninstrument runway   A runway intended for the operation of aircraft using visual approach procedures. See *visual runway*.

nonprecision approach procedure   A standard instrument approach procedure in which no electronic glideslope is provided. (FAR Part 1)

nonprecision instrument runway   A runway having an existing instrument approach procedure utilizing air navigation facilities with only horizontal guidance for which a straight-in nonprecision instrument approach procedure has been approved.

Notice to Airmen (NOTAM)   A notice containing information (not known sufficiently in advance to publicize by other means) concerning the establishment, condition, or change in any component (facility, service, or procedure) of, or hazard in the National Airspace System, the timely knowledge of which is essential to personnel concerned with flight operations.

objective of the Airport Master Plan   To provide guidelines for future development of the airport which will satisfy aviation demand and be compatible with the environment, community development, other modes of transportation, and other airports.

obstruction light   A light, or one of a group of lights, usually red, mounted on a surface structure or natural terrain to warn pilots of the presence of a flight hazard; either an incandescent lamp with a red globe or a strobe light.

obstruction marking/lighting   Distinctive marking and lighting to provide a uniform means for indicating the presence of obstructions.

Office of Management and Budget Circular A-95   Prior to July 1982, required that designated regional agencies review airport projects before federal grants were given.

O'Hare Agreement   An agreement established in the 1950s between the City of Chicago and the airlines that established a precedent in revenue bond financing which pledged the airlines to meet any shortfall in income needed to pay off the principal and interest on the bonds.

one-stop clearance   A new inspection system used at some airports of entry which combines immigration and customs functions at a single station.

open-V runways   Two intersecting runways whose extended centerlines intersect beyond their respective thresholds.

operating statement   Records an airport's revenues and expenses over a particular time period (quarterly and annually).

operational activity forecasts   Includes forecasts of operations by major user categories (air carrier, commuter, general aviation, and military).

organization chart   Shows the formal authority relationships between superiors and subordinates at various levels, as well as the formal channels of communication within the organization.

outer fix   A fix in the destination terminal area, other than the approach fix, to which aircraft are normally cleared by an air route traffic control center or an approach control facility, and from which aircraft are cleared to the approach fix or final approach course.

outer marker (OM)   An ILS navigation facility in the terminal area navigation system located 4 to 7 miles from the runway edge on the extended centerline transmitting a 75-MHz fan-shaped radiation pattern, modulated at 400 Hz, keyed at two dashes per second, and received by compatible airborne equipment indicating to the pilot, both aurally and visually, that he is passing over the facility and can begin his final approach.

overlay   A pavement structure constructed on top of an existing pavement to increase bearing strength or to improve surface properties.

overrun   To run off the end of the runway after touching down on the runway.

overrun area   In military aviation exclusively, that area beyond the end of the designated runway with a stabilized surface of the same width as the runway and centered on the extended runway centerline.

parallel runways   Two or more runways at the same airport whose centerlines are parallel.

parallel taxiways   Two taxiways which are parallel to one another which allow traffic to move simultaneously in different directions at busy airports.

parking apron   An apron intended to accommodate parked aircraft.

passenger handling system   A series of links or processes which a passenger goes through in transferring from one mode of transportation to another.

passenger movers   Designed to speed passenger movement through the terminal. Includes buses, mobile lounges, moving sidewalks, and automated guideway systems.

passenger processing   As used in the passenger handling system, the link that accomplishes the major processing activities required to prepare the passenger for using air transportation.

pavement grooving   The mechanical serration of a pavement surface to provide escape paths for water and slush, to promote improved aircraft mechanical braking effectiveness.

pavement structure   The combination of runway base and subbase courses and surface course which transmits the traffic load to the subgrade.

pavement subgrade   The upper part of the soil, natural or constructed, which supports the loads transmitted by the runway pavement structure.

pavement surface course   The top course of a pavement, usually Portland cement concrete or bituminous concrete, which supports the traffic load.

performance measurement system (PMS)   Similar to NASCOM, which receives reports of delays at about 20 airports.

personnel manager   Responsible for administering the airport personnel program.

pier finger   A type of terminal layout evolving in the 1950s when gate concourses (fingers) were added to simple terminal buildings.

Planning Grant Program (PGP)   A federal aid to airports program established under the Airport and Airway Development Act of 1970 for approved airport planning and development project costs.

port authorities   Legally chartered institutions with the status of public corporations that operate a variety of publicly owned facilities, such as harbors, airports, toll roads, and bridges.

practical capacity   The number of operations (takeoffs and landings) that can be accommodated with no more than a given amount of delay, usually expressed in terms of maximum acceptable average delay.

precision approach   A standard instrument approach using a precision approach procedure. *See* precision approach procedure.

precision approach procedure   A standard instrument approach procedure in which an electronic glideslope is provided, such as ILS and PAR. (FAR Part 1)

precision approach radar (PAR)   A radar facility in the terminal air traffic control system used to detect and display with a high degree of accuracy, azimuth, range, and elevation of an aircraft on the final approach to a runway, enabling the air traffic control specialist to provide advisory service to the pilot.

precision approach runway   *See* precision instrument runway.

precision instrument runway   A runway having an existing instrument approach procedure utilizing an instrument landing system (ILS) or a precision approach radar (PAR). It also means a runway for which a precision approach system is planned and is so indicated by an FAA approved airport layout plan; a military service approved military airport layout plan; any other FAA planning document, or military service military airport planning document. (FAR Part 77)

primary airports   Public-use commercial airports enplaning at least 0.01 percent of all passengers enplaned annually at U.S. airports.

primary radar   *See* search radar.

primary surface   A rectangular surface longitudinally centered about a runway. Its width is a variable dimension and it usually extends 200 feet beyond each end of the runway. The elevation of any point on this surface coincided with the elevation of its nearest point on the runway centerline or extended runway centerline.

primary taxiway system   Taxiways that provide aircraft access from runways to apron the service areas.

public airport   An airport for public use, publicly owned and under control of a public agency.

public relations   The management function which attempts to create goodwill for an organization and its products, services, or ideals, with groups of people which can affect its present and future welfare.

public-use airport   An airport open to the public without prior permission and without restrictions within the physical capacities of available facilities.

quadradar   Ground radar equipment named for its four presentations: (1) surveillance; (2) airport surface detection; (3) height finding; and (4) precision approach.

radar (radio detection and ranging)   A device which, by measuring the time interval between transmission and reception of radio pulses and correlating the angular orientation of the radiated antenna beam or beams in azimuth and/or elevation, provides information on range, azimuth, and/or elevation of objects in the path of the transmitted pulses.

radar approach control (RAPCON)   A joint-use air traffic control facility, located at a U.S. Air Force Base, utilizing surveillance and precision approach radar equipment in conjunction with air/ground communication equipment, providing for the safe and expeditious movement of air traffic within the controlled airspace of that facility.

radar beacon system　A radar system in which the object to be detected is fitted with cooperative equipment in the form of a radio receiver/transmitter (transponder). Radio pulses transmitted from the searching transmitter/receiver (interrogator) site are received in the cooperative equipment and used to trigger a distinctive transmission from the transponder. This latter transmission rather than a reflected signal, is then received back at the transmitter/receiver site.

ramp　A defined area, on a land airport, intended to accommodate aircraft for purposes of loading or unloading passengers or cargo, refueling, parking, or maintenance.

red-green clearance　An inspection procedure used at some airports of entry where travelers who do not have goods to declare are separated from those who do, with only the latter passing through a secondary inspection station.

regional airport planning　Air transportation planning for the region as a whole including all airports in the region, both large and small.

reliever airports　A subset of general aviation airports which have the function of relieving congestion at primary commercial airports and providing more access for general aviation to the overall community.

relocated threshold　An area preceding the runway arrows unusable for takeoff or landing.

residual-cost approach　The airlines collectively assume significant financial risk by agreeing to pay any costs of running the airport that are not allocated to other users or covered by non-airline sources of revenue.

revenue bonds　Bonds which are payable solely from the revenues derived from the operation of a facility which was constructed or acquired with the proceeds of the bonds.

rigid pavement　A pavement structure consisting of Portland cement concrete that may or may not include a sub-base course.

rotorcraft　A heavier-than-air aircraft that depends principally for its support in flight on the lift generated by one or more rotors. (FAR Part 1)

runway　A defined rectangular area on a land airport prepared for the landing and takeoff run of aircraft along its length.

runway alignment indicator light (RAIL)　This airport lighting facility in the terminal area consists of five or more sequenced flashing lights installed on the extended centerline of the runway. The maximum spacing between lights is 200 feet, extending out from 1,600 feet to 3,000 feet from the runway threshold. Even when collocated with MALS, RAIL will be identified as a separate facility.

runway bearing　The magnetic or true bearing of the runway centerline as measured from magnetic or true north.

runway capacity　The number of aircraft operations which can be accommodated by a runway without undue delay to aircraft. Undue delays are when delays to departures average four minutes during the normal peak two-hour period of the day.

runway centerline lighting system　The runway centerline lighting system consists of single lights installed at uniform intervals along the runway centerline so as to provide a continuous lighting reference from threshold to threshold.

runway clear zone　An area at ground level whose perimeter conforms to the runway's innermost approach surface projected vertically. It begins at the end of the primary surface and it terminates directly below the point or points where the approach surface reaches a height of 50 feet above the elevation of the runway end.

runway configuration   Layout or design of a runway or runways, where operations on the particular runway or runways being used at a given time are mutually dependent. A large airport can have two or more runway configurations operating simultaneously.

runway configuration management   A software program that has been under development at Chicago O'Hare since 1980 that will assist controllers in establishing the most efficient combination of arrival and departure runways for given conditions of weather and demand.

runway contamination   Deposition or presence of dirt, grease, rubber, or other materials on runway surfaces which adversely affect normal aircraft operation or which chemically attack the pavement surface.

runway direction number   A whole number to the nearest one tenth of the magnetic bearing of the runway and measured in degrees clockwise from magnetic north.

runway end identification lights (REIL)   An airport lighting facility in the terminal area navigation system consisting of one flashing white high intensity light installed at each approach end corner of a runway and directed toward the approach zone, which enables the pilot to identify the threshold of a usable runway.

runway environment   The runway threshold or approach lighting aids or other markings identifiable with the runway.

runway gradient (effective)   The average gradient consisting of the difference in elevation of the two ends of the runway divided by the runway length may be used provided that no intervening point on the runway profile lies more than 5 feet above or below a straight line joining the two ends of the runway. In excess of 5 feet, the runway profile will be segmented and aircraft data will be applied for each segment separately.

runway grooving   One-quarter inch grooves spaced approximately one-and-one-quarter inch apart made in the runway surface designed to provide better drainage, furnish escape routes for water under the tire footprint to prevent hydroplaning.

runway length—landing   The measure length from the threshold to the end of the runway.

runway length—physical   The actual measured length of the runway.

runway length—takeoff   The measured length from where the takeoff is designated to begin to the end of the runway.

runway lights   Lights having a prescribed angle of emission used to define the lateral limits of a runway. Runway light intensity may be controllable or preset. Lights are uniformly spaced at intervals of approximately 200 feet.

runway markings   (1) Basic marking—markings on runways used for operations under visual flight rules, consisting of centerline marking and runway direction numbers, and if required, letters. (2) Instrument marking—markings on runways served by nonvisual navigation aids and intended for landings under instrument weather conditions, consisting of basic marking plus threshold marking. (3) All-weather marking—markings on runways served by nonvisual precision approach aids and on runways having special operational requirements, consisting of instrument markings plus landing zone marking and side strips.

runway occupancy time (ROT)   The time an approaching aircraft crosses the threshold until it turns off the runway or from the time a departing aircraft takes the active runway until it clears the departure end.

runway orientation   The magnetic bearing of the centerline of the runway.

runway safety area   Cleared, drained, graded, and usually turfed areas abutting the edges of the usable runway and symmetrically located about the runway. It extends 200 feet beyond each runway end. The width varies according to the type of runway. (Formerly called "landing strip.")

runway strength   The assumed ability of a runway to support aircraft of a designated gross weight for each of single-wheel, dual-wheel, and dual-tandem-wheel gear types.

runway surface lighting   Also referred to as "in-runway lighting," consisting essentially of touchdown zone (narrow gauge) lights, runway centerline lights, and exit taxiway turnoff lights, installed in the pavement.

runway threshold marking   Markings so placed as to indicate the longitudinal limits of that portion of the runway usable for landing.

runway visibility   Visibility determined by a transmissometer associated with the instrument runway(s) or by an observer stationed at the approach end of the runway.

runway visual range (RVR)   An instrumentally derived value that represents the horizontal distance a pilot can see down the runway from the approach end; it is based on the sighting of either high intensity runway lights or on the visual contrast of other targets whichever yields the greater visual range.

satellite terminals   A type of terminal layout in which all passenger processing is done in a single terminal which is connected by concourses to one or more satellite structures. The satellite generally has a common waiting room which serves a number of gate positions.

scheduled service   Transport service operated over routes based on published flight schedules, including extra sections and related nonrevenue flights.

search radar   A radar system in which a minute portion of a radio pulse transmitted from a site is reflected off an object and then received back at that site.

secondary radar   *See* radar beacon system.

secondary runway   A runway which provides additional wind coverage or capacity to expedite traffic handling.

secondary taxiway system   Taxiways that provide aircraft access from runways to hangars and tiedown areas not commonly associated with itinerant and service areas.

security chief   Enforces interior security, traffic, and safety rules and regulations and participates in law enforcement activities at the airport.

segmented circle   A basic marking device used to aid pilots in locating airports, and which provides a central location for such indicators and signal devices as may be required.

self-liquidating general obligation bonds   Like general obligation bonds, these bonds are backed by the full faith, credit, and taxing power of the issuing government body; however, there is adequate cash flow from the operation of the facility to cover the debt service and other costs of operation that the debt is not legally considered as part of the community's debt limitation.

semiflush light   A light mounted in pavement capable of rollover by aircraft.

sequencing   Specifying the exact order in which aircraft will take off or land.

short takeoff and landing (STOL) aircraft   An aircraft which, at some weight within its approved range of STOL operating weight, is capable of operating from a STOL runway in compliance with the applicable STOL characteristics, airworthiness, operations, noise, and pollution standards.

shoulder As pertaining to airports, an area adjacent to the edge of a paved surface so prepared to provide a transition between the pavement and the adjacent surface for aircraft running off the pavement, for drainage and sometimes for blast protection.

simple terminal A type of gate arrival terminal layout that consists of a common waiting and ticketing area with several exits onto a small aircraft parking apron.

single runway An airport having one runway.

site selection Second phase of the airport master plan which evaluates airspace, environmental factors, community growth, airport ground access, availability of utilities, land costs, and site development costs.

slot A block of time allocated to an airport user to perform an aircraft operation (takeoff or landing).

small aircraft Aircraft of 12,500 pounds or less maximum certificated takeoff weight. (FAR Part 1)

spacing Establishing and maintaining the appropriate interval between successive aircraft, as dictated by considerations of safety, uniformity of traffic flow, and efficiencies of runway use.

spalling Fractured edges in and around the joint area of concrete due to the tremendous pressures generated during expansion and contraction of the slabs.

standard air carrier delay reporting system (SDRS) Contains reports from American, Eastern, and United Airlines regarding delays on their entire systems and at 32 specific airports.

state aviation system plans (SASP) Plan for the development of airports within the state.

state-operated airports Airports generally managed by the state's department of transportation.

STOLport An airport specifically designed for STOL aircraft, separate from conventional airport facilities.

straight-in approach (IFR) An instrument approach wherein final approach is commenced without first having executed a procedure turn. (Not necessarily completed with a straight-in landing.)

straight-in approach (VFR) Entry into the traffic pattern by interception of the extended runway centerline without executing any other portion of the traffic pattern.

stub taxiway A short connecting taxiway to an airport facility that serves as the only connection with the remaining airport complex.

taxiway A defined path, usually paved, over which aircraft can taxi from one part of an airport to another.

taxiway centerline lighting A system of flush or semiflush in-pavement lights indicating the taxiway centerline.

taxiway safety area A cleared, drained, and graded area, symmetrically located about the extended taxiway centerline and adjacent to the end of the taxiway safety area.

taxiway turnoff lighting Single lights installed in the pavement at uniform intervals to define the path of aircraft travel from the runway centerline to a point on the taxiway.

taxiway turnoff markings Signs or lights along the runways, taxiways, and ramp surfaces of an airport used to assist a pilot in finding his way.

technological improvements Refers to new devices and equipment as well as operational concepts and procedures designed to relieve congestion, increase capacity, or reduce delay.

terminal apron An area provided for parking and positioning of aircraft in the vicinity of the terminal building for loading and unloading.

terminal area The area used or intended to be used for such facilities as terminal and cargo buildings, gates, hangars, shops, and other service buildings; automobile parking, airport motels and restaurants, and garages and vehicle service—facilities used in connection with the airport; and entrance and service roads used by the public within the boundaries of the airport.

terminal area capacity The ability of the terminal area to accept the passengers, cargo, and aircraft that the airfield accommodates.

terminal building A building or buildings designed to accommodate the enplaning and deplaning activities of air carrier passengers.

terminal facilities The airport facilities providing services for air carrier operations which serve as a center for the transfer of passengers and baggage between surface and air transportation.

terminal finger An extension of the terminal building to provide direct access to a large number of airport terminal apron gate positions.

tetrahedron A device with four triangular sides which indicates wind direction and which may be used as a landing direction indicator.

T-hangar An aircraft hangar in which aircraft are parked alternately tail to tail, each in the T-shaped space left by the other row of aircraft or aircraft compartments.

threshold The designated beginning of the runway that is available and suitable for the landing of airplanes.

threshold crossing height (TCH) The height of the straightline extension of the visual or electronic glideslope above the runway threshold.

threshold lights Lighting arranged symmetrically about the extended centerline of the runway identifying the runway threshold. They emit a fixed green light.

throughout capacity The rate at which aircraft can be brought into or out of the airfield, without regard to any delay they might experience.

time-series analysis or trend extension The oldest and in many cases the most widely used method of forecasting air transportation demand. It consists of interpreting the historical sequence of data and applying the interpretation to the immediate future. Historical data are plotted on a graph, and a trend line is drawn.

total operations All arrivals and departures performed by military, general aviation, and air carrier aircraft.

touchdown (1) The point at which an aircraft first makes contact with the landing surface. (2) In a precision radar approach, the point on the landing surface toward which the controller issues guidance instructions.

touchdown zone The area of a runway near the approach end where airplanes normally alight.

touchdown zone lighting This system in the runway touchdown zone area presents, in plain view, two rows of transverse light bars located symmetrically about the runway centerline. The basic system extends 3,000 feet along the runway.

tower *See* airport traffic tower.

tower automated ground surveillance system (TAGS) Intended to be used in conjunction with airport surface detection equipment at major airports, it will provide, for transponder-equipped aircraft, a flight identification label alongside the position indicator on the ASDE display.

traffic management system (TMS) A new software that will perform several important functions to increase the efficiency of airport and airspace utilization.

traffic pattern The traffic flow that is prescribed for aircraft landing at, taxiing on, and taking off from an airport (FAR Part 1) The usual components of a traffic pattern are upwind leg, crosswind leg, downwind leg, base leg, and final approach.

transitional surface A surface which extends outward and upward from the sides of the primary and approach surfaces normal to the runway centerline which identifies the height limitations on an object before it becomes an obstruction to air navigation.

transition area Controlled airspace extending upward from 700 feet or more above the surface of the earth when designated in conjunction with an airport for which an instrument approach procedure has been prescribed; or from 1,200 feet or higher above the surface of the earth when designated in conjunction with airway route structures or segments. Unless otherwise limited, transition areas terminate at the base of the overlying controlled airspace.

turnaround A taxiway adjacent to the runway ends which aircraft use to change direction, hold, or bypass other aircraft.

turning radius The radius of the arc described by an aircraft in making a self-powered turn, usually given as a minimum.

turnoff taxiway A taxiway specifically designed to provide aircraft with a means to expedite clearing a runway.

typical peak-hour passenger volume (design volume) The peak hour of an average day in the peak month which is used as the hourly design volume for terminal space.

undershoot To touch down short of the point of intended landing.

unicom Frequencies authorized for aeronautical advisory services to private aircraft. Services available are advisory in nature, primarily concerning the airport services and airport utilization.

upwind leg A flight path parallel to the landing runway in the direction of landing.

utility airport (or runway) An airport (or runway) which accommodates small aircraft excluding turbojet powered aircraft.

variance The differences between actual expenses and the budgeted amount.

vehicle chief Responsible for the maintenance of all vehicles utilized by the airport.

vertical takeoff and landing (VTOL) Aircraft that have the capability of vertical takeoff and landing. VTOL aircraft are not limited to helicopters.

VFR airport An airport without an authorized or planned instrument approach procedure; also, a former airport design category indicating an airport serving small aircraft only and not designed to satisfy the requirements of instrument landing operations.

VFR tower An airport traffic control tower that does not provide approach control service.

VHF omnidirectional range (VOR) A radio transmitter facility in the navigation system radiating a VHF radio wave modulated by two signals, the relative phases of which are compared, resolved, and displayed by a compatible airborne receiver to give the pilot a direct indication of bearing relative to the facility.

vibratory (or dynamic) testing A technique used to measure the strength of the composite pavement system by subjecting it to vibratory load and measuring the amount the pavement responds or deflects under this known load.

vicinity map Shown on the airport layout plan drawing, it depicts the relationship of the airport to the city or cities, nearby airports, roads, railroads, and built-up areas.

viscous hydroplaning Occurs when a thin film of oil, dirt, or rubber particles mixes with water and prevents tires from making sure contact with the pavement.

visual approach An approach wherein an aircraft on an IFR flight plan, operating in VFR conditions under the control of a radar facility and having an air traffic control authorization, may deviate from the prescribed instrument approach procedure and proceed to the airport of destination, served by an operational control tower, by visual reference to the surface.

visual approach indicator (VASI) An airport lighting facility in the terminal area navigation system used primarily under VFR conditions. It provides vertical visual guidance to aircraft during approach and landing by radiating a directional pattern of high intensity red and white focused light beams which indicate to the pilot that he is "on path" if he sees red/white, "above path" if white/white, and "below path" if red/red.

visual flight rules (VFR) Rules that govern the procedures for conducting flight under visual conditions. (FAR Part 91)

visual meteorological conditions (VMC) Meteorological conditions expressed in terms of visibility, distance from clouds, and ceiling equal to or better than specified minima.

visual runway A runway intended solely for the operation of aircraft using visual approach procedures, with no straight-in instrument approach procedure and no instrument designation indicated on an FAA-approved airport layout plan, a military service approved military airport layout plan, or by a planning document submitted to the FAA by competent authority. (FAR Part 77)

vortex advisory system (VAS) Comprises wind sensors mounted on towers along the approach path, a central computer to process wind data and predict the strength and movement of wake turbulence, and a display to alert the controller when a hazardous condition exists.

vortices As pertaining to aircraft, circular patterns of air created by the movement of an airfoil through the atmosphere. As an airfoil moves through the atmosphere in sustained flight, an area of high pressure is created beneath it and an area of low pressure is created above it. The air flowing from the high pressure area to the low pressure area around and about the tips of the airfoil tends to roll up into two rapidly rotating vortices, cylindrical in shape. These vortices are the most predominant parts of aircraft wake turbulence and their rotational force is dependent upon the wing loading, gross weight, and speed of the generating aircraft.

wake vortex A phenomenon resulting from the passage of an aircraft through the atmosphere. It is an aerodynamic disturbance that originates at the wingtips and trails in corkscrew fashion behind the aircraft. When used by ATC it includes vortices, thrust stream turbulence, jet wash, propeller wash, and rotor wash.

wind cone A free-rotating fabric truncated cone which when subjected to air movement indicates wind direction and wind force.

wind rose A diagram for a given location showing relative frequency and velocity of wind from all compass directions.

wind shear   Variation of wind speed and wind direction with respect to a horizontal or vertical plane. Low-level shear in the terminal area is a factor in the safe and expeditious landing of aircraft.

wind tee   A T-shaped free rotating device to indicate wind direction. Sometimes capable of being secured for use as a landing direction indicator.

zero-base budget   Derives from the idea that each program or departmental budget should be prepared from the ground up or base zero. By calculating the budget from a zero base, all costs are newly developed and reviewed entirely to determine their necessity.

Zulu time (Z)   Time at the Prime Meridian in Greenwich, England.

Abbreviations

AAS	airport advisory service
AC	advisory circular
ADAP	Airport Development Aid Program
ADC	air defense command
ADF	automatic direction finder
AID	airport information desk
AIM	*Airman's Information Manual*
AIP	Airport Improvement Program
AIREP	air report
AIRMET	airmen's meteorological information
ALNOT	alert notice
ALS	approach lighting system
AMIS	aircraft movement information service
ARP	airport reference point
ARSR	air route surveillance radar
ARTCC	air route traffic control center
ARTS	automated radar terminal system
ASDE	airport surface detection equipment
ASR	airport surveillance radar
ATC	air traffic control (FAR Part I)
ATCRBS	air traffic control radar beacon system
ATCSCC	ATC systems command center
ATCT	airport traffic control tower
ATIS	automatic terminal information service
CAA	Civil Aeronautics Administration

CAB	Civil Aeronautics Board
CAT	clear-air turbulence
CFCF	central flow control function
DABS	discrete address beacon system
dB	decibel
DF	direction finder
DH	decision height
DME	distance measuring equipment
DOT	Department of Transportation
EFAS	en route flight advisory service
EPNL	effective perceived noise level
FAA	Federal Aviation Administration
FAR	Federal Aviation Regulations
FAWS	flight advisory weather service
FSS	flight service station
GCA	ground controlled approach
GDL	guidance light facility
GS	guideslope
HAT	height above touchdown
ICAO	International Civil Aviation Organization
IFR	instrument flight rules (FAR Part 91)
ILS	instrument landing system
IM	inner marker
IMC	instrument meteorological conditions
JAWOS	joint automated weather observation system
LDIN	lead-in light facility
LF	low frequency
LOC	ILS localizer
MDA	minimum descent altitude (FAR Part I)
MEA	minimum en route IFR altitude
MLS	microwave landing system
MM	middle marker
MOCA	minimum obstruction clearance altitude
MSL	mean sea level
NAFEC	National Aviation Facilities Experimental Center
NAR	National Airspace Review
NAS	National Airspace System
NASCOM	national airspace command center
NASP	National Airport System Plan
NAVAID	air navigation facility
NOTAM	notice to airmen
NPIAS	National Plan of Integrated Airport Systems

NTSB	National Transportation Safety Board
OM	outer marker
OMNI	(*See* VOR)
PAR	precision approach radar
PGP	planning grant program
PIREP	pilot report
PMS	performance measurement system
PNL	perceived noise level
RAIL	runway alignment indicator light
RAPCON or **RAPCO**	radar approach control
RATCF	radar air traffic control facility
REIL	runway end identification lights
RNAV	area navigation
ROT	runway occupancy time
RVR	runway visual range
SALS	short approach light system
SASP	state aviation system plans
SECRA	secondary radar
SFL	sequenced flashing lights
SIGMET	significant meteorological information
STOL	short takeoff and landing
TACAN	tactical air navigation
TCH	threshold crossing height
TRACON	terminal radar approach control
UHF	ultra high frequency
VAS	vortex advisory system
VASI	visual approach slope indicator
VFR	visual flight rules (FAR Part 91)
VMC	visual meteorological conditions
VOR	very high frequency omni-directional range
VTOL	vertical takeoff and land
Z	zulu time

Study guide

Chapter 1   The airport-airway system: a historical perspective

Multiple Choice   Circle the letter that corresponds to the best answer.

1. The congressional act which turned over the carriage of mail by air to private contractors was the:

   a. Air Commerce Act.
   b. Civil Aeronautics Act.
   c. Kelly Act.
   d. Federal Airport Act.

2. The primary purpose of the Air Commerce Act of 1926 was to:

   a. provide funding for the establishment, operation, and maintenance of airports.
   b. establish the Civil Aeronautics Authority.
   c. encourage the use of airplanes in world trade.
   d. stabilize and promote the development of commercial aviation.

3. The congressional act that placed all the functions of air and regulation of aviation in one agency was the:

   a. Air Commerce Act.
   b. Civil Aeronautics Act.
   c. Department of Transportation Act.
   d. Airways Modernization Act.

4. Section 303 of the Civil Aeronautics Act of 1938 authorized the expenditure of federal funds for construction of landing areas, provided:

   a. the local community funded 50 percent of the total costs.

   (b) such landing areas were reasonably necessary for use in air commerce or in the interests of national defense.

   c. the areas were within 50 miles of a major metropolitan city.

   d. consideration was given to general aviation airports as well as to air carrier airports.

5. An advisory committee, established by the Civil Aeronautics Act, reported the following recommendation to Congress in November 1944:

   a. that Congress appropriate up to $50 million annually for aid to airports.

   (b.) that a good precedent for the proportionate sharing of costs existed in the public roads program.

   c. that all sponsors of projects be required to submit contractors' names for CAA approval, to ensure compliance with civil rights legislation.

   d. that airports developed with federal aid be made available for use by United States government aircraft at reduced charges.

6. Under the Federal Airport Act of 1946:

   (a.) the federal government would pay as much as 50 percent of the cost.

   b. the federal funding assistance was based on population only.

   c. the federal funding assistance was based on land area only.

   d. the funding formula favored smaller cities.

7. Which of the following guarantees was *not* required by the administrator under the Federal Airport Act of 1946?

   a. Aerial approaches would be cleared and protected and future hazards would be prevented.

   b. All airport records would be available for inspection.

   (c.) The military services would be given preference for all facilities developed from federal aid.

   d. Proper zoning would be provided to restrict encroachment of land adjacent to the airport.

8. Which one of the following events prompted the expedient passage of the Federal Aviation Act of 1958?

   a. Mismanagement of the airport aid program by the CAA.

   (b.) A series of airplane accidents.

   c. The need to increase airport funding.

   d. None of these.

9. Which of the following was not a major responsibility of the administrator under the Federal Aviation Act of 1958?

    a. Determining the need for capital improvements at air carrier airports.
    b. Promoting the development of civil aeronautics.
    c. Regulating and control of navigable airspace in the United States.
    d. Consolidating research and development with respect to air navigation facilities.

10. The National Transportation Safety Board (NTSB) was created by the:

    a. Airways Modernization Act.
    b. Civil Aeronautics Act.
    c. Department of Transportation Act.
    d. Federal Aviation Act.

11. During its 24-year lifetime (1946-1969), the Federal Aid for Airports Program generated _____ in federal aid to airports.

    a. approximately $500 million   c. over $1 billion
    b. just under $1 billion   d. over $2 billion

12. Which of the following factors *cannot* be considered as a reason for the passage of the Airport and Airway Development Act of 1970?

    a. Tremendous growth in all segments of aviation during the 1960s.
    b. A series of major accidents involving commercial airliners.
    c. Congestion at major airports and strain on the air traffic control system.
    d. Anticipated arrival of wide-bodied jets.

13. Under ADAP:

    a. annual appropriations remained about the same as under the Federal Airport Act.
    b. the FAA was required to develop a National Airport Plan (NASP).
    c. appropriations for general aviation airports was reduced.
    d. the formula for distribution of funds was the same as under the Federal Airport Act.

14. Which of the following was *not* an amendment under the Airport and Airway Development Act of 1976?

    a. Expanded the types of airport development projects eligible for ADAP funding.

b. Established the "commuter service airport," a new air carrier airport category.

c. Increased the federal share for ADAP grants.

d. Eliminated PGP grants for all but air carrier airports.

15. The Airport and Airway Improvement Act of 1982:

a. increased taxes on avgas and jet fuel.

b. encouraged the joint use of underutilized, nonstrategic U.S. military fields.

c. authorized close to $5 billion in airport aid between 1983 and 1987.

d. included all of these.

16. Which of the following is *not* a criticism of federal policy since passage of the Airport and Airway Development Act of 1970?

a. Federal aid has distorted the airport system by favoring capital intensive solutions to managing growth.

b. Federal aid has concentrated too heavily on airside capacity such as runways and taxiways.

c. FAA interpretation of federal policy has been too broad in defining what constitutes airports of national importance.

d. Federal aid has been given on a "first come, first serve" basis instead of a rational evaluation of each proposal.

17. The Airways Modernization Act of 1957:

a. led to the formation of the Federal Aviation Administration.

b. appropriated $200 million for a three-year period.

c. repealed the Civil Aeronautics Act of 1938.

d. provided none of the above.

18. Which of the following was not a reason for passage of the act creating the Department of Transportation?

a. The need for coordination of the national transportation system.

b. To promote the development of civil aeronautics.

c. To act as a focal point for future research and development efforts in transportation.

d. None of the above.

19. The Airport and Airway Safety and Capacity Expansion Act of 1987:

a. eliminated funding for noise compatibility programs.

b. established the Airport and Airway Trust Fund to finance safety programs and expand airport capacity.

c. extended the authority for the Airport Improvement Program for five years.

d. provided assistance to the FAA to enhance security programs at primary hub airports.

20. Which of the following statements concerning NPIAS is correct?

 a. An airport must be included in this plan in order to be eligible to receive a grant under the AIP.

 b. The estimated cost from 1990 to 1999 is $10 billion.

 c. The largest portion of the proposed development is for reliever airports.

 d. The plan contemplates an inflation rate of 3 percent per year for 10 years.

21. Air travel during the 1980s:

 a. increased modestly because of a sluggish economy during the latter part of the decade.

 b. has prompted airport planners to plan a number of new airports for the 1990s and beyond.

 c. has caused congestion and delay at many of the nation's largest airports.

 d. has focused attention on the need to expand terminal facilities but not necessarily runway capacity because the latter should be adequate through the year 2020.

True/False Circle T if the statement is true; circle F if it is false.

T F 1. Early airmail service in the United States was established by the Post Office Department.

T F 2. The Air Commerce Act of 1926 prohibited the federal government from giving direct financial aid to airports.

T F 3. The Bureau of Air Commerce was established shortly after passage of the Air Commerce Act.

T F 4. The first financial aid to airports from the federal government came during the great depression.

T F 5. Under DLAND, monies were spent by the CAA for airport development but only with the approval of the Secretaries of War, Commerce, and the Navy.

(T)   F   6. Many of the new airports constructed during WWII were planned to be useful to civil aviation in the postwar period.

T   (F)   7. Under the Federal Airport Act of 1946, 50 percent of any congressional appropriation was placed in a discretionary fund to be used by the Civil Aeronautics Administrator.

(T)   F   8. In order to receive aid under the Federal Airport Act of 1946, the airport had to be in the National Airport Plan.

T   (F)   9. The purpose of the Airways Modernization Act of 1957 was to provide additional emergency funding for airports planning to accommodate jet aircraft.

(T)   F   10. The administrator of the Federal Aviation Agency reported directly to the president.

T   (F)   11. Edward P. Curtis was appointed the first administrator of the Federal Aviation Agency.

(T)   F   12. The Department of Transportation was established to promote the coordination of federal programs and to serve as a focal point for research and development efforts in transportation.

(T)   F   13. The administrator of the FAA now reports to the Secretary of Transportation.

(T)   F   14. The Airport and Airway Trust Fund was modeled after the Highway Trust Fund.

T   (F)   15. Revenues for the trust fund created by the Airway Revenue Act of 1970 were generated soley by a tax on domestic passenger fares.

(T)   F   16. The major weaknesses of the Federal Airport Act were the inadequacy of resources provided under it and the nature of the formula for distributing those resources.

T   (F)   17. The provision for planning grants was similar under FAAP and ADAP.

(T)   F   18. Funding for the first five years under ADAP exceeded the entire 24-year history under FAAP.

T (F) 19. Under the Airport and Airway Development Act Amendments of 1976, the federal share for ADAP grants was increased from 50 percent to 66.7 percent.

T (F) 20. Deregulation has had a profound effect on the air carriers but actually very little effect on the airport system and airport management.

(T) F 21. The Aviation Safety and Noise Abatement Act provided assistance to airport operators to prepare and carry out noise compatibility programs.

T (F) 22. The basic philosophy of AIP is quite different from ADAP in that the former was intended to support a national system of integrated airports, whereas the latter recognized the independence of individual airports.

(T) F 23. The newly created CAB assumed the functions of the former Air Safety Board by 1940.

(T) F 24. Many airports constructed for the military during World War II were turned over to civil authorities after the war.

T (F) 25. The primary purpose for the creation of the Department of Transportation was the development and operation of a common system of air traffic control for both military and civil aircraft.

T (F) 26. The Airport and Airway Development Act of 1970 created the NTSB.

(T) F 27. One of the major weaknesses of the Federal Airport Act was the nature of the formula for distributing funding.

T (F) 28. The NPIAS emphasizes airline-airport planning on an international level.

T (F) 29. The largest portion of proposed development funding under NPIAS is for reliever airports.

(T) F 30. The tremendous growth in air travel during the 1980s has caused a serious problem of congestion and delay.

T Ⓕ 31. Many new primary hub airports are planned during the next two decades.

Ⓣ F 32. One criticism of federal airport policy is that financial aid has favored air carrier airports while neglecting general aviation and reliever airports.

Chapter 1   Answers
Multiple Choice

1. c	7. c	13. b	19. c
2. d	8. b	14. d	20. a
3. b	9. a	15. d	21. c
4. b	10. c	16. d	
5. b	11. c	17. d	
6. a	12. b	18. b	

True/False

1. T	9. F	17. F	25. F
2. T	10. T	18. T	26. F
3. F	11. F	19. F	27. T
4. T	12. T	20. F	28. F
5. T	13. T	21. T	29. F
6. T	14. T	22. F	30. T
7. F	15. F	23. T	31. F
8. T	16. T	24. T	32. T

Chapter 2   The airport system
Multiple Choice   Circle the letter that corresponds to the best answer.

1. Primary airports enplane at least _____ percent of all passengers enplaned annually at U.S. airports.

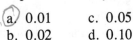
    a. 0.01   c. 0.05
    b. 0.02   d. 0.10

2. Those airports enplaning fewer than 2,500 passengers or used exclusively by private and business aircraft are classified as:

    a. commercial service.   c. general aviation.
    b. feeder service.   d. reliever.

3. The leading airport in the United States in terms of passenger enplanements is:

   a. Atlanta Hartsfield.   c. Dallas/Fort Worth.
   b. Chicago O'Hare.   d. New York (JFK).

4. The leading airport in the United States in terms of cargo tons enplaned is:

   a. Atlanta Hartsfield.   c. Dallas/Fort Worth.
   b. Chicago O'Hare.   d. New York (JFK).

5. The principal function of GA airports is to:

   a. provide isolated communities with a link to other population centers.
   b. serve as reliever airports.
   c. provide facilities for privately owned aircraft used for business and personal flying.
   d. serve as military facilities in the event of a national emergency.

6. Airports stimulate economic growth through a multiplier effect. This means:

   a. airports attract industry.
   b. aviation dollars are channeled throughout the community.
   c. employment at the airport increases.
   d. real estate values increase.

7. Federal policy regarding financial aid has been criticized for all of the following reasons, *except*:

   a. encouraging airport operators to overbuild.
   b. facilities have been more expensive than needed to accomplish their intended function.
   c. Federal aid has distorted investment decisions and led airport operators to build not necessarily what they need but what the government is willing to help pay for.
   d. traffic projections have been too low to warrant such capital expenditures.

8. Which of the following is *not* an argument in favor of defederalization?

   a. Large airports are capable of financing their own development.
   b. It would free large airports from many legal and administrative requirements involved in accepting federal assistance.

(c.) Defederalization would adversely affect smaller airports who would be cut off from necessary funding.

d. The government could reduce the overall cost of the aid program.

9. All of the following are objections to the concept of new federalism, *except*:

(a) state agencies are in a better position to determine local airport needs.
b. state agencies vary in strength.
c. it would create an additional layer of bureaucracy.
d. problems could arise involving interstate or multistate cooperation.

10. Which of the following statements regarding noise is *not* true?

a. The problem is related to land use planning.
b. Intergovernmental cooperation is often needed in solving the problem.
(c.) Recent technological advances in airframe and jet engine design have virtually eliminated the problem in certain areas.
d. Noise is an important constraint on the expansion of airports in many areas.

11. The NPIAS has been criticized on three principal points. They include all of the following, *except*:

(a.) not enough privately owned airports are included.
b. it is not really a plan.
c. many of the airports included are not truly of national interest.
d. it deals strictly with the development needs of individual airports.

12. The following organization represents 150 U.S. and 70 foreign air carrier airports enplaning 75 percent of the free-world air passengers:

a. AIA.   c. ATA.
(b.) AOCI.   d. AAAE.

13. There are approximately _____ airports included in the NPIAS.

a. 5,600   c. 1,400
(b.) 3,300   d. 390

14. The total number of landing areas in the U.S. _____ each year, and the number that are open to the public is _____.

a. decreases, increasing   c. decreases, decreasing
b. increases, increasing   (d.) increases, decreasing

15. The FAA classified airports in four major categories. They are:

    a. Commercial service, hub, reliever, and general aviation.
    b. Private, commercial, reliever, and joint use.
    c. Commercial service, primary, reliever, and general aviation.
    d. Primary, commerical service, joint use, and general aviation.

16. Which of the following statements concerning general aviation is not correct?

    a. GA includes 98 percent of all registered civil aircraft.
    b. Most of the aircraft activity at commercial service airpots is general aviation.
    c. GA airports represent four of the top five airports in the U.S. in terms of total aircraft operations.
    d. GA airports serve many functions for a wide variety of aircraft.

17. A reliever airport must be located in a SMSA with a population of at least:

    a. 250,000.   c. 750,000.
    b. 500,000.   d. 1,000,000.

18. Takeoff and landing slots:

    a. are controlled by the FAA.
    b. represent one of the most significant barriers to entry in the airline business today.
    c. are controlled by the airport authorities.
    d. can be sold by the air carriers but the proceeds go into the federal treasury.

True/False   Circle T if the statement is true, circle F if it is false.

T   F   1. As of June 30, 1990 there were over 20,000 airports on record with the FAA.

T   F   2. Roughly one-half of the world's airports are in the United States.

T   F   3. Virtually all airports in the continental United States are included in the NPIAS.

T   F   4. Of the total number of airports eligible to receive federal aid, most are classified as relievers.

T   F   5. The top 20 airports in the United States account for almost two-thirds of all passenger enplanements.

T   F   6. A hub is a metropolitan area served by more than one primary airport.

T   F   7. A large share of activity at commercial service airports is general aviation.

T   F   8. Over the years, where forecasted traffic demand has exceeded capacity, federal policy has generally been to provide capital aid to build new facilities.

T   F   9. FAA projections of future traffic demand indicate that there could be severe airside congestion at a number of major airports over the next 20 years.

T   F   10. Most critics of federal funding policy argue that the government has not done enough in providing financial assistance.

T   F   11. Opponents of defederalization claim that it would lead to subsidy of smaller airports by larger ones.

T   F   12. In general, the major airlines are in favor of defederalization.

T   F   13. New federalism refers to the concept of increased responsibility for decisions on airport funding being given to the Department of Transportation.

T   F   14. Long-term use agreements between air carriers and airports seem to be on the increase because of the instability of the deregulated environment.

T   F   15. An operating slot is a block of time allocated to an airport user to perform an aircraft operation.

T   F   16. New entrant airlines tend to favor operating slots.

T   F   17. The imposition of local noise standards often adds to confusion because standards vary between localities.

T   F   18. Many of the national aviation organizations are located in Washington, D.C., and serve as a lobbying group.

(T)   F   19. Only approximately one-third of the civil landing areas in the United States are open to the public.

T   (F)   20. The federal government owns and operates five airports.

(T)   F   21. The NASP was replaced in 1986 by the NPIAS.

(T)   F   22. Primary airports are defined as those commercial service airports having 10,000 or more enplanements.

(T)   F   23. International passengers represent over 50 percent of the passengers going through JFK International Airport.

T   (F)   24. Approximately 60 percent of the GA airport fleet are single-engine piston aircraft.

T   (F)   25. An itinerant operation originates and terminates at the same airport.

(T)   F   26. Reliever airports now account for most of the aircraft landings and takeoffs in major metropolitan areas.

T   (F)   27. The Airport Operators Council International (AOCI) represents over 1,000 airport managers at 650 airports.

Fill-in   Complete the following sentences:

1. List four ways in which an airport serves the local economy:

   a. _____

   b. _____

   c. _____

   d. _____

2. Indicate the national aviation organization based on the following descriptions:

   a. Represents the nation's
       certificated air carriers   _____

   b. Represents over 1,000
       airport managers   _____

    c. Represents manufacturers
       of GA aircraft and
       components   _____

    d. Represents departments
       of transportation and
       state aviation
       departments   _____

    e. Represents corporate
       aircraft operators   _____

Chapter 2   Answers

Multiple choice

1.	a	7.	d	13.	b
2.	c	8.	c	14.	d
3.	b	9.	a	15.	c
4.	d	10.	c	16.	c
5.	c	11.	a	17.	a
6.	b	12.	b	18.	b

True/False

1.	F	8.	T	15.	T	22.	T
2.	T	9.	T	16.	F	23.	T
3.	F	10.	F	17.	T	24.	F
4.	F	11.	T	18.	T	25.	F
5.	T	12.	F	19.	T	26.	T
6.	T	13.	F	20.	F	27.	F
7.	T	14.	F	21.	T		

Fill-in

1. a. a transportation link   c. stimulating economical growth
   b. attracting industry   d. influencing real estate values

2. a. Air Transport Association (ATA)
   b. American Association of Airport Executives (AAAE)
   c. General Aviation Manufacturers Association (GAMA)
   d. National Association of State Aviation Officials (NASAO)
   e. National Business Aircraft Association (NBAA)

Chapter 3 Airport system planning

Multiple Choice Circle the letter that corresponds to the *best* answer.

1. Which of the following statements regarding the NPIAS is *not* correct?

   a. It was required under the Airport and Airway Development Act of 1970.
   b. It establishes priorities and proposes levels of funding.
   c. It is only updated periodically by the FAA.
   d. Projected costs of airport needs are included under five categories.

2. Which of the following projects would be eligible for federal aid?

   a. Land acquisition   c. Parking areas
   b. Construction of hangars   d. Revenue-producing terminal areas

3. The NPIAS relates airport system improvements to _____ level(s) of need.

   a. 1   c. 3
   b. 2   d. 4

4. Which of the following is *not* a criteria for inclusion in the NPIAS?

   a. Airport must have (or forecast to have within five years) at least 10 based aircraft.
   b. Airport must serve a SMSA with a population of 500,000.
   c. Airport must be at least a 30-minute drive from the nearest existing or proposed airport currently in NPIAS.
   d. Airport must have an eligible sponsor.

5. Regional airport planning was assisted by:

   a. the Airport and Airway Development Act of 1970.
   b. the Airport and Airway Improvement Act of 1982.
   c. the establishment of SASPs.
   d. Office of Management and Budget Circular A-95.

6. Which of the following statements is correct concerning state airport planning?

   a. Airport planning at the state level is very similar to planning on the local and regional level.
   b. Before 1970, very few states conducted extensive or systematic airport planning.
   c. SASPs are very similar to one another because of federal guidelines.
   d. Funding generally presents very little problem at the state level.

7. The National Plan of Integrated Airport Systems (NPIAS) calls for:

    a. federal control of all public-use airports.
    b. integrated airport system planning at the national level.
    c. coordination of all airports within a state.
    d. integrated airport system planning at all levels.

8. The need for an airport, or expansion of an existing one, generally begins with:

    a. federal determination.   c. regional impact studies.
    b. state sponsorship.   d. local initiative.

9. Which of the following is *not* an objective of the airport master plan?

    a. To provide a graphic presentation of the ultimate development of the airport.
    b. To establish a schedule of priorities and phasing for the various improvements proposed in the plan.
    c. To present backup information and data.
    d. None of these—all are objectives.

10. In developing an airport master plan:

    a. consultants are generally only used by smaller airports which do not have the expertise in house.
    b. community organizations, environmental groups, and the general public should be excluded at the early stages.
    c. effective coordination between members of the planning teams is critical to the success of the plan.
    d. only airport users and area-wide planning agencies should be brought into the process.

11. All of the following are levels of need under the NPIAS, except:

    a. maintain the airport system in its current condition.
    b. bring the system up to current design standards.
    c. improve the system by utilizing the latest technology.
    d. expand the system.

12. Federal and State airport planning suffer from all of the following factors, except:

    a. the lack of common goals.
    b. the difference in expertise.

c. the state plans contain many more airports than the NPIAS.

d. the lack of coordination.

True/False Circle T if the statement is true, F if it is false.

T (F) 1. Airport system planning is basically the same as airport master planning.

(T) F 2. The NPIAS generally overstates the amount that will actually be spent on airport improvements.

T (F) 3. Inclusion in the NPIAS generally infers a federal agreement to fund a project and a local commitment to carry it out.

(T) F 4. The three-level system of needs under NPIAS is a move towards prioritizing different types of projects.

(T) F 5. The NPIAS has been criticized for being more of a "wish list" than a planning document.

(T) F 6. Regional airport planning seeks to overcome the rivalries and the jurisdictional overlaps of the various local agencies.

T (F) 7. Allocation of traffic between airports serving a particular area is a relatively easy process because of federal control.

(T) F 8. Some states participate in airport planning for major metropolitan areas, although most leave this responsibility to local officials.

(T) F 9. The Airport and Airway Improvement Act of 1982 called for integrated airport system planning.

(T) F 10. An airport master plan presents the planner's conception of the ultimate development of a specific airport.

(T) F 11. A public agency is required in order to qualify for federal airport aid.

T (F) 12. Larger airports very rarely use consultants in developing their master plan.

T   (F)   13. Present airport planning at the local, regional, state, and federal levels is very well coordinated and integrated.

(T)   F   14. SASPs vary greatly in scope, detail, expertise, and planning philosophy.

(T)   F   15. The ground transportation system providing access to the airport can affect airport congestion, delay, and cost of airport operation.

T   (F)   16. Airport planning at the state level involves issues that are very similar to those at the local level.

T   (F)   17. Airport development begins with FAA initiative by demonstrating how the local airport fits into the national system plan.

T   (F)   18. Airport planning is generally removed from the political process.

Chapter 3   Answers
Multiple Choice

1. a	5. d	9. d
2. a	6. b	10. c
3. c	7. d	11. c
4. b	8. d	12. b

True/False

1. F	7. F	13. F
2. T	8. T	14. T
3. F	9. T	15. T
4. T	10. T	16. F
5. T	11. T	17. F
6. T	12. F	18. F

Chapter 4   Airport requirements and site selection
Multiple Choice   Circle the letter that corresponds to the best answer:

1. The first phase of the airport master plan includes:

a. site selection. c. airport layout.
(b.) airport requirements. d. financial planning.

2. Which of the following is *not* included in the inventory of existing airport facilities?

   a. Historical review of airports and facilities.
   b. Airport related land use.
   c. Forecasts of aviation demand.
   d. Socioeconomic factors.

3. An area's demography, disposable personal income per capita, and competitive position are all part of:

   a. community values.
   b. demand/capacity analysis.
   c. socioeconomic factors.
   d. forecasting.

4. Which of the following statements regarding socioeconomic factors is *not* correct?

   a. A community's population, size, and economic character affect its air traffic generating potential.
   b. An airport's competitive position refers to its ability to compete with alternate modes of transportation.
   c. Demography refers to the geographic distribution and distances between populations and commerce within the area the airport serves.
   d. Disposable personal income per capita refers to the purchasing power available to residents in any period of time.

5. The forecasting technique that projects (extrapolates) historical trends is called:

   a. time series.
   b. causal models.
   c. judgmental.
   d. logistic.

6. Which of the following statements concerning judgmental forecasts is *not* correct?

   a. They are particularly good when used in conjunction with causal models or time-series analysis.
   b. They are more accurate than time-series analysis.
   c. They are often difficult to defend.
   d. They are educated guesses.

7. The four major civil airport user categories are:

   a. air carrier, air taxi operators, business aviation, and military.
   b. air carrier, commuters, general aviation, and ultralights.

    c. air carrier, general aviation, military, and special uses.

    d. air carrier, commuters, general aviation, and military.

8. In forecasting enplaning air cargo, planners:

    a. review national air cargo forecasts prepared by airlines and governmental agencies.

    b. consider the growth of airmail.

    c. estimate air cargo lift potential and the impact of new cargo aircraft.

    d. all of the above.

9. Itinerant operations:

    a. include local operations.

    b. are all aircraft arrivals and departures other than local operations.

    c. include all general aviation operations.

    d. are all air carrier training flights within a 20-mile radius of the airport.

10. Based aircraft includes:

    a. all active general aviation aircraft that use or might be expected to use an airport as home base.

    b. all active and inactive aircraft normally hangared or tied down at the airport.

    c. all air carrier and general aviation aircraft parked at the airport for 30 days during an annual period.

    d. none of these.

11. Busy-hour operations generally include the busiest hour during the:

    a. busiest day of an average month.

    b. average day of the busiest month.

    c. busiest day of the two busiest months.

    d. average day of the two busiest months.

12. The annual publication *Aviation Forecasts* is prepared by the:

    a. Aerospace Industries Association.

    b. Air Transport Association.

    c. Federal Aviation Administration.

    d. General Aviation Manufacturers Association.

13. Assessment of facility requirements is included in the:

    a. inventories stage.   c. demand/capacity analysis.

b. forecasting stage.   d. site selection.

14. Improvements to airline and general aviation apron areas would be considered under:

    a. airfield capacity analysis.
    b. terminal area capacity analysis.
    c. airspace capacity analysis.
    d. ground access capacity analysis.

15. Which of the following acts requires the preparation of detailed environmental statements for all major federal airport development?

    a. FAA Act of 1958.
    b. Land Use Act of 1969.
    c. FAA Order 5335.2.
    d. National Environmental Policy Act of 1969.

16. One of the most effective means of reducing the problem of noise is through:

    a. technological advances.
    b. restricting use of the airport.
    c. stiff penalties to violators of noise codes.
    d. proper land use planning.

17. Which of the following would *not* be considered in an environmental impact statement?

    a. Meteorological conditions.
    b. Scenic beauty.
    c. Breeding, nesting, or feeding habits of wildlife.
    d. Moving a significant number of people.

18. The Federal Aviation Regulation entitled Notice of Construction, Alteration, Activation, and Deactivation of Airports is Part:

    a. 77.   c. 153.
    b. 151.   d. 157.

19. Runway clear zones refer to:

    a. the first 200 feet of runway.
    b. part of the approach area.
    c. the area between the end of the runway and the approach area.
    d. a horizontal plane 150 feet above the airport elevation.

20. Which of the following factors is *not* a major consideration in selecting an airport site?

    a. Airspace analysis.   c. Connecting hub for air carriers.
    b. Convenience to population.   d. Availability of utilities.

21. Public hearings enable the airport sponsor to do all of the following, except:

    a. identify local business and commercial reliance on air transportation.
    b. to emphasize benefits and downplay costs.
    c. identify the local airport's role in state, regional, and national airport plans.
    d. cite examples of nearby communities that have benefited from an airport.

22. Which of the following would not be a significant operational activity forecast?

    a. aircraft operations during the night   c. busy-hour operations
    b. based aircraft   d. aircraft mix

23. The most useful forecast of aircraft mix would include:

    a. based and nonbased aircraft
    b. general aviation and air carrier aircraft
    c. seating capacity groups for air carrier aircraft.
    d. fixed wing and rotary aircraft.

24. The most serious environmental problem to overcome in the development of an airport is:

    a. aircraft noise.   c. water pollution.
    b. natural environmental values.   d. all of the above.

25. The proximity of airports to one another, the relationship of runway alignments, and the nature of operations (IFR or VFR) are important considerations in assessing:

    a. airfield capacity.   c. ground access capacity.
    b. airspace capacity.   d. demand analysis.

26. From the FAA's standpoint, a major consideration in the site selection process is:

    a. convenience to population.   c. airspace analysis.
    b. meteorological conditions.   d. expansion potential.

True/False   Circle T if the statement is true, F if it is false.

T   (F)   1. The airport requirements phase of the airport master plan includes an in-depth analysis of alternative sites.

(T)   F   2. The principal determinant of future airport system requirements is the amount of aeronautical activity that will be generated in the metropolitan area.

T   (F)   3. Demography refers to the purchase power available to residents in any period of time, and therefore, a good indicator of average living standards and financial ability to travel.

(T)   F   4. Political factors can influence the volume of traffic at an airport.

(T)   F   5. The Airport and Airway Development Act of 1970 required that airport sponsors must hold public hearings for various major airport projects.

(T)   F   6. Poor airport-community relations can influence the ability to implement an airport master plan.

T   (F)   7. A judgmental forecast is developed by finding variables that explain, statistically, the changes in the variable to be forecast.

(T)   F   8. Forecasts of aviation demand form the basis for facilities planning.

T   (F)   9. Enplaning air cargo includes baggage accompanying passengers.

(T)   F   10. In forecasting enplaning passengers, originations, stopover, and transfer passengers are generally identified separately.

(T)   F   11. General aviation aircraft movements can be either itinerant or local operations.

(T)   F   12. General aviation operations forecasts at air carrier and general aviation control tower airports are generally developed from historical growth trends.

(T)   F   13. Aircraft mix refers to the types of categories of aircraft which are to be accommodated at the airport.

T   *F*   14. The demand/capacity analysis is critical because it provides a final review of the need to expand facilities and the cost of these improvements.

T   *F*   15. Airspace capacity analysis includes the rate of aircraft movements on the runway/taxiway system.

T   *F*   16. Improvements in design of engines used on the newer aircraft such as the Boeing 757 and 767 have virtually eliminated the problem of noise.

T   *F*   17. Normally, airport planners will consider locations for airport development near wildlife and waterfowl refuges because of the wide open spaces.

T   F   18. The Department of Transportation Act requires responsible federal action in assuring the protection of natural environmental values.

T   *F*   19. The initial investigation of airport sites is generally the responsibility of the FAA.

T   F   20. The FAA requires that the airport owner has an adequate property interest in the clear zone area.

T   F   21. Public hearings enable the airport sponsor to explain how the airport master plan will accommodate potential local environmental problems.

T   F   22. Judgmental forecasts are educated guesses.

T   *F*   23. Military operations are normally considered in forecasting busy-hour operations.

T   F   24. The forecasting technique that uses time as the independent variable is trend extension.

T   F   25. Aircraft noise is probably the worst environmental problem to overcome in the development of an airport.

T   F   26. One method of forecasting a metropolitan area's air cargo is calculating a percentage ratio of the area's cargo to the national total and projecting a future trend.

T   (F)   27. Airport site selection is generally a nonpolitical process in order to avoid controversy.

T   (F)   28. One of the problems with the Airport and Airway Development Act of 1970 and subsequent legislation is that there is no funding available to acquire land for future airport development.

Fill-in Complete the following.

1. List the five major types of operational activity forecasts considered necessary to determine future facility requirements.

     a. _____

     b. _____

     c. _____

     d. _____

     e. _____

2. A capacity analysis includes four distinct elements. They are:

     a. _____

     b. _____

     c. _____

     d. _____

3. An environmental impact statement that accompanies an airport master plan must demonstrate that the proposed development will not (list five factors):

     a. _____

     b. _____

     c. _____

     d. _____

     e. _____

4. The major factors that require careful analysis in the final evaluation of airport sites include (list five factors):

a. _____

b. _____

c. _____

d. _____

e. _____

Chapter 4   Answers

Multiple Choice

1.	b	8.	d	15.	d	22.	a
2.	c	9.	b	16.	d	23.	c
3.	c	10.	a	17.	a	24.	a
4.	c	11.	b	18.	d	25.	b
5.	a	12.	c	19.	b	26.	c
6.	b	13.	c	20.	c		
7.	d	14.	b	21.	b		

True/False

1.	F	8.	T	15.	F	22.	T
2.	T	9.	F	16.	F	23.	F
3.	F	10.	T	17.	F	24.	T
4.	T	11.	T	18.	T	25.	T
5.	T	12.	T	19.	F	26.	T
6.	T	13.	T	20.	T	27.	F
7.	F	14.	F	21.	T	28.	F

Fill-in

1. a. enplaning passengers   d. based aircraft
   b. enplaning air cargo   e. busy-hour operations
   c. aircraft operations

2. a. airfield capacity   c. airspace capacity
   b. terminal area capacity   d. ground access capacity

3. a. noticeably affect the ambient noise level for a significant number of people
   b. displace significant numbers of people.

 c. have a significant aesthetic or visual effect.
 d. divide or disrupt an established community.
 e. have any effect on areas of unique interest or scenic beauty.
Other answers may include: destroy or derogate from important recreational areas; substantially alter the pattern of behavior for a species; interfere with important wildlife breeding, nesting, or feeding grounds; significantly increase air or water polution; adversely affect the water table of an area.

4. a. airspace analysis.   d. availability of utilities.
 b. surrounding obstructions.   e. meterological conditions.
 c. expansion.
 Other answers may include: economy of construction; convenience to population; noise; cost comparisons of alternate sites.

Chapter 5 Airport layout and land use plans

Multiple Choice Circle the letter that corresponds to the best answer:

1. A vicinity map, basic data table, and wind information are all part of the:

 a. land use plan.   c. airport layout plan drawing.
 b. approach layout plan.   d. airport components.

2. Which of the following components is *not* generally considered part of the landside facilities?

 a. Loading and storage area for air cargo.
 b. Baggage handling facilities.
 c. Apron and gate areas.
 d. Car rental facilities.

3. The capacity of two intersecting runways can be increased:

 a. the farther the intersection is from the takeoff and landing threshold.
 b. if the intersection bisects the runways.
 c. the closer the intersection is to the takeoff and landing threshold.
 d. if the intersection forms a right angle.

4. Which of the following statements concerning runways is correct?

 a. Intersecting runways generally yield higher capacities than open-V runways.
 b. There are two types of parallel runways: close and far.
 c. The FAA includes over 40 different layouts in an advisory circular.
 d. The primary runway should be oriented as closely as possible to the direction of the prevailing winds.

5. A runway having an instrument approach procedure using air navigation facilities with only horizontal guidance is classified:

   a. visual.
   (b.) nonprecision instrument.
   c. precision instrument.
   d. all weather.

6. Markings common to all runways include:

   a. centerlines and threshold markings.
   b. centerlines and side stripes.
   c. designator and touchdown zone markers.
   (d.) designator and holding indications.

7. Which of the following statements concerning taxiways is *not* correct?

   (a.) Parallel one-way taxiways are often found at busy airports so that they can be used as holding areas.
   b. Exit and entrance taxiways are normally constructed at right angles to the runway.
   c. When possible, taxiways are planned so as not to cross an active runway.
   d. At busy airports, blue-edge lights mark the sides of the taxiway.

8. Apron areas located at various points off taxiways for temporary storage of aircraft are called:

   a. holding areas.
   (b.) holding bays.
   c. parallel taxiways.
   d. none of these.

9. The most frequently used parking position at major airports is:

   a. angled nose-in.
   b. angled nose-out.
   (c.) nose-in.
   d. parallel.

10. The approach and clear zone layout includes:

   a. prominent airport facilities.
   b. pavement strength of each runway.
   (c.) areas under the imaginary surfaces.
   d. a wind rose.

11. A surface longitudinally centered on the extended runway centerline and extending outward and upward from each end of the primary surface is called the _____ surface.

   a. horizontal
   b. conical
   (c.) approach
   d. transitional

12. Which of the following land uses would be most compatible within the airport boundaries?

    a. Electronics firm engaged in research and development.
    b. Wheat farm.
    c. City dump.
    d. Public warehouses.

13. Land use zoning has several shortcomings. Which of the following is *not* a shortcoming?

    a. It is not retroactive.
    b. It is not enforceable.
    c. A conflict between several political jurisdictions.
    d. The locality may want to increase the tax base by encouraging growth of companies whose facilities conflict with appropriate airport land use.

14. Which of the following is probably the least desirable approach to land use planning around an airport?

    a. Subdivision regulations for future building.
    b. Insulation requirements as part of existing building codes.
    c. Relocation of residences.
    d. Getting the air carriers to change traffic patterns.

15. The _____ provides a graphic presentation to scale of existing and proposed airport facilities and land uses.

    a. location map   c. phase drawing
    b. airside and landside plan   d. airport layout plan

16. Which of the following statements concerning open-V runways is correct?

    a. When there is little or no wind, both runways can be used simultaneously.
    b. When the operations are toward the V, the hourly capacity is increased.
    c. The capacity of open-V runways greatly depends upon the distance at the far end of the V.
    d. The capacity of open-V runways increases if the aircraft mix is similar, regardless of the wind direction.

17. Lights that illuminate in sequence to guide the pilot's eyes towards the runway centerline are:

    a. touchdown zone lights.   c. VASIs.
    b. threshold lights.   d. none of the above.

18. The airport layout plan report includes:

    a. areas under the imaginary surfaces.
    b. a plan for obstruction removal and relocation of facilities.
    c. basis for runway orientation if not aligned for maximum wind coverage.
    d. all of the above.

19. Tall smokestacks, television and radio transmission towers, and garbage dumps would all be shown in the:

    a. airport layout plan report.   c. airside components layout.
    b. airport layout plan drawing.   d. approach and clear zone layout.

20. The transitional surfaces:

    a. are longitudinally centered 200 feet beyond the end of the primary surface.
    b. are vertical planes extending 150 feet above the established airport elevation.
    c. extend outward and upward from the periphery of the horizontal surface.
    d. extend outward and upward at right angles to the runway centerline.

True/False   Circle T if the statement is true, F if it is false.

T   F   1. The basic data table on the airport layout plan drawing includes the percent of wind coverage by principal runway and temperatures during the hottest month.

T   F   2. A wind rose is always included in the airport layout plan drawing with the runway orientation superimposed.

T   F   3. The terms landside and airside of an airport refer to the apron/gate areas and runway/taxiways respectively.

T   F   4. The capacity of intersecting runways greatly depends upon the location of the intersection and how runways are operated.

T   F   5. Far parallel runways are spaced a minimum of 3,500 feet apart.

T   F   6. When there is little or no wind, open-V runways can be used simultaneously.

(T) F 7. Runways, other than utility, should be oriented so planes may land at least 95 percent of the time with crosswind components not exceeding 15 mph (13 knots).

(T) F 8. A visual runway is intended solely for the operation of aircraft using visual approach procedures.

T (F) 9. A displaced threshold is another name for relocated threshold.

(T) F 10. The ILS has been the standard approach and landing system in the U.S. since the early 1940s.

T (F) 11. Run-up areas are commonly referred to as holding bays.

T (F) 12. Angled nose-in aircraft parking requires the smallest gate area per aircraft.

T (F) 13. Obstruction clearance requirements at or near airports are contained in FAR Part 177.

(T) F 14. The conical surface extends outward and upward from the periphery of the horizontal surface at a slope of 20 to 1 for a horizontal distance of 4,000 feet.

(T) F 15. Large airports with a great deal of land—in excess of what is needed for aeronautical purposes—may be used for other uses.

T (F) 16. Water contamination is the biggest objection voiced by people in areas near an airport.

(T) F 17. The airport layout includes approach and clear zone outlines.

T (F) 18. The greater the aircraft mix utilizing a single runway, the higher the PANCAP and PHOCAP.

(T) F 19. From a planning standpoint, a single-direction runway configuration can achieve greater capacity and ease air traffic control.

(T) F 20. An analysis of the prevailing wind is essential in planning runways.

Ⓣ   F   21. Temporarily closed runways have a cross at both ends, whereas permanently closed runways have crosses at intervals along the length of the runways.

T   Ⓕ   22. Touchdown zone lights mark an undershoot zone 1,000 feet long in which approaching aircraft should not land.

Ⓣ   F   23. The Microwave Landing System (MLS) is actually cheaper than the ILS to install at airports.

T   Ⓕ   24. Land use zoning around an airport is a relatively easy approach to controlling the noise problem.

T   Ⓕ   25. Subdivision regulations means relocating residences that do not meet local building codes.

Fill-in   Complete the following sentences.

1. List the four basic runway configurations.

   a. _____

   b. _____

   c. _____

   d. _____

2. The airport layout plan drawing includes:

   a. _____

   b. _____

   c. _____

   d. _____

   e. _____

Chapter 5   Answers
Multiple Choice

1. c	4. d	7. a	10. c
2. c	5. b	8. b	11. c
3. c	6. d	9. c	12. d

13.	b	15.	d	17.	d	19.	d
14.	c	16.	a	18.	c	20.	d

True/False

1.	T	8.	T	15.	T	22.	F
2.	T	9.	F	16.	F	23.	T
3.	F	10.	T	17.	T	24.	F
4.	T	11.	F	18.	F	25.	F
5.	F	12.	F	19.	T		
6.	T	13.	F	20.	T		
7.	T	14.	T	21.	T		

Fill-in

1. a. single runways   c. open-V runways
   b. parallel runways   d. intersecting runways

2. a. airport layout   d. basic data table
   b. location map   e. wind information
   c. vicinity map

Chapter 6   Terminal area and airport access plans

Multiple Choice   Circle the letter that corresponds to the best answer.

1. Public transportation to and from the airport and parking for the public, airline employees and rental cars must be taken into consideration by airport planners under which of the following terminal area factors?

   a. Passengers.   c. Airport operations.
   b. Passenger vehicles.   d. Safety.

2. Information for terminal requirements is obtained from all of the following sources *except*:

   a. air carriers.   c. airport concessionaires.
   b. airport management.   d. environmental groups.

3. Which of the following is an advantage of the centralized passenger processing terminal?

   a. Facilitates control of passenger-transfers and security.
   b. Minimizes walking distances.
   c. Optimizes the level of service/convenience for passengers.
   d. Accommodates expansion.

4. Which of the following is a disadvantage of the decentralized passenger processing terminal?

    a. Creates vehicular congestion at curbside.
    b. Maximizes walking distances.
    c. Necessitates decentralization of personnel.
    d. Limits expansion.

5. Which of the following statements concerning the linear terminal concept is *not* true?

    a. The more sophisticated linear terminals often feature a two-level structure.
    b. The linear concept provides close-in public parking.
    c. The linear concept requires long concourses.
    d. Linear terminals can be expanded with almost no interference to passenger processing or aircraft operations.

6. Aircraft gates are located at the end of a long concourse in the case of _____ terminals.

    a. linear   c. simple
    b. pier finger   d. satellite

7. People mover systems are commonly found in which of the following terminals?

    a. Linear.   c. Simple.
    b. Pier finger.   d. Satellite.

8. The mobile lounge or transporter concept:

    a. is sometimes called the remote aircraft parking concept.
    b. has good expansion capability.
    c. improves aircraft maneuvering capability.
    d. all of these.

9. Which of the following links or processes in the passenger-handling system includes the vehicular circular drive, sidewalks, and bus stops?

    a. Access/egress.   c. Passenger processing.
    b. Access/processing interface.   d. Flight interface.

10. The flight interface link in the passenger handling system includes:

    a. the vehicular circular drive.
    b. ticketing and baggage check-in counters.
    c. gate lounges and counters.
    d. baggage claim area.

11. The access/egress link in the passenger handling system includes all of the following *except*:

    a. highways.
    b. vehicular circular drive.
    c. rail and metropolitan train service.
    d. V/STOL facilities.

12. Hospitality/VIP lounges are facilities normally provided for:

    a. airport operations and management.
    b. airlines.
    c. government agencies
    d. visitors.

13. International passengers:

    a. tend to check in early.
    b. are generally familiar with the airport.
    c. frequently arrive alone.
    d. generally do not utilize the concessions to a great degree.

14. Processing costs per passenger, occupancy levels for lounges and corridors, and estimated revenues from concessionaires are all a part of:

    a. general concept evaluation.
    b. specific design and development criteria.
    c. the passenger handling system.
    d. airport access plans.

15. The design volume is generally based on:

    a. average hour, peak day, average month.
    b. peak hour, average day, average month.
    c. average hour, peak day, peak month.
    d. peak hour, average day, peak month.

16. The first step in determining space requirements is:

    a. determining the type of passengers.
    b. determining the passenger type by facility.
    c. forecasting the annual passenger volume.
    d. approximating the hourly volume of passengers.

17. Actual space requirements for areas within the terminal building are determined by multiplying the estimated number of passengers by:

    a. an empirical factor.   c. the aircraft operations per hour.
    b. the square footage.   d. none of these.

18. Which of the following statements regarding airport access plans is *not* correct?

    a. All modes of access are considered, including highways, rapid transit, and V/STOL aircraft.
    b. State and local highway departments play an important role.
    c. Most of the actual planning is done by airport management.
    d. The biggest problem concerning access is the peaking of traffic.

19. Rapid transit is used from the downtown area to:

    a. Phoenix Sky Harbor.   c. Dallas/Fort Worth International.
    b. Miami International.   d. Cleveland Hopkins International.

20. A separate parking facility away from the main parking area is normally provided for:

    a. people having business with airport tenants.
    b. airline employees only.
    c. airline and other airport employees.
    d. spectators.

21. Short-term parkers (three hours or less) typically represent about _____ percent of the total maximum vehicle accumulation.

    a. 10   c. 40
    b. 20   d. 50

22. Airport planners consider a number of terminal area factors in designing a terminal area concept. They include considerations affecting passengers, passenger vehicles, airport operations, aircraft, and:

    a. expansion capabilities.   c. safety.
    b. capital investment.   d. all of the above.

23. An advantage of the centralized passenger processing terminal is:

    a. optimizaton of the level of service/convenience for passengers.
    b. the simplified vehicular and pedestrian information system.
    c. the dispersion of vehicular circulation for curbside drop-off and parking.
    d. the shorter walking distances.

24. The pier finger terminal:

    a. evolved in the 1970s.
    b. provides common areas for processing passengers.
    c. limits the possibility for expansion.
    d. often features a two-level structure.

25. The baggage claim area is part of the:

    a. flight interface.   c. passenger processing link.
    b. access/egress link.   d. access/processing interface.

26. A *general* concept evaluation criteria for space requirements include:

    a. compatibility with ground access systems.
    b. processing costs per passenger.
    c. walking distances for various types of passengers.
    d. operating and maintenance expenses.

27. The type of passenger is broadly classified as domestic, international, or transfer. A further breakdown by type might include all of the following, except:

    a. with or without checked baggage.
    b. business or pleasure.
    c. mode of access to or egress from the airport.
    d. scheduled, charter, or general aviation flight.

28. One of the biggest problems involving airport road access is the fact that:

    a. airport management is more concerned with airside problems.
    b. there is a bias on the part of federal authorities towards rapid transit.
    c. state and local authorities are generally uncooperative.
    d. airport travel tends to peak in the same morning and afternoon periods as does urban and suburban auto traffic.

True/False   Circle T if the statement is true, F if it is false.

T   F   1. The entrance and service roads used by the public within the boundaries of the airport are considered a part of the terminal area.

T   F   2. Developing the terminal area concept is generally the sole responsibility of airport management.

T   F   3. A big disadvantage of the centralized passenger processing terminal is the fact that it generates vehicular congestion at curbside.

T   F   4. The linear or curvilinear terminal concept is merely an extension of the simple terminal concept.

T   F   5. The pier finger terminal concept evolved in the 1950s to shorten the walking distance for passengers.

T   F   6. Satellite terminal gates are usually served by a common hold room rather than individual hold rooms.

T   F   7. It is relatively easy to expand satellite terminals.

T   F   8. At most airports the design of the terminal building has evolved over time and not in the pure forms discussed in this chapter.

T   F   9. Dallas/Fort Worth Airport was planned as a major connecting hub.

T   F   10. Airport planners today tend to favor flexible terminal building designs that can be modified to meet changing conditions.

T   F   11. Passengers are processed in the access/processing interface link of the passenger handling system.

T   F   12. Facilities for government agencies are always housed in the terminal building.

T   F   13. A terminal building is designed around the needs and wants of airlines.

T   F   14. The short-haul business traveler generally arrives at the terminal shortly before departure, frequently alone, with little baggage, and does not frequent the concessions as long as the leisure passenger.

T   F   15. When a domestic arrival passenger transfers to an international departure, he must go to the airline ticket counter for a passport verification before proceeding to the international gate.

(T) F 16. The question of how many levels a terminal building should have depends primarily on the volume of passengers.

(T) F 17. The general concept evaluation of space requirements is preliminary in nature.

T (F) 18. The type of passenger is first classified as arriving or departing.

(T) F 19. A great deal of the passenger delay in the terminal building can be attributable to the baggage flow.

T (F) 20. Airport access plans are really not a part of the master planning process because they involve other governmental units.

T (F) 21. One of the most important factors affecting the air traveler is availability and location of concessionaires.

T (F) 22. An advantage of the decentralized passenger processing terminal is the lower operating and maintenance costs.

(T) F 23. The linear terminal concept does not lend itself to common facilities such as waiting rooms.

(T) F 24. Although the pier finger concept has afforded one of the most economical means of adding gate positions, its capability for expansion is limited.

(T) F 25. Walking distances are held to a minimum with the mobile lounge concept.

T (F) 26. On balance, most planners agree that the satellite terminal concept is the best.

T (F) 27. Domestic short-haul travelers tend to utilize the concessions and other facilities to a great degree.

(T) F 28. One of the most important specific design and development criteria is construction costs.

(T) F 29. Multiplying the estimated number of passengers using each facility with an empirical factor is a step in determining space requirements.

T   Ⓕ   30. Road construction from the airport boundary to the parking area is largely the responsibility of state and local highway departments.

Fill-in   Complete the following.

1. The four terminal building design concepts are:

 a. _____

 b. _____

 c. _____

 d. _____

2. The passenger-handling system includes four links or processes. They are:

 a. _____

 b. _____

 c. _____

 d. _____

3. Passengers can be divided into three primary groups. They are:

 a. _____

 b. _____

 c. _____

4. List eight objectives that are sought by planners in planning terminal building space requirements from the standpoint of passengers and air carriers.

 a. _____

 b. _____

 c. _____

 d. _____

 e. _____

 f. _____

g. _____

h. _____

Chapter 6   Answers
Multiple Choice

1.	b	7.	d	13.	a	19.	d	25.	c
2.	d	8.	d	14.	b	20.	c	26.	a
3.	a	9.	b	15.	d	21.	b	27.	b
4.	c	10.	c	16.	c	22.	d	28.	d
5.	c	11.	b	17.	a	23.	b		
6.	d	12.	b	18.	c	24.	c		

True/False

1.	T	7.	F	13.	F	19.	T	25.	T
2.	F	8.	T	14.	T	20.	F	26.	F
3.	T	9.	F	15.	T	21.	F	27.	F
4.	T	10.	T	16.	T	22.	F	28.	T
5.	F	11.	F	17.	T	23.	T	29.	T
6.	T	12.	F	18.	F	24.	T	30.	F

Fill-in

1. a. gate arrival   c. satellite
   b. pier finger   d. transporter

2. a. access/egress   c. processing
   b. access/processing interface   d. flight interface

3. a. domestic
   b. international
   c. transfer

4. a. minimization of delays in processing
   b. minimization of walking distance
   c. protection from the elements—weather and noise
   d. simplification of orientation and provision of comfort and convenience
   e. minimization of operating costs per passenger handled
   f. maximization of capacity per dollar invested
   g. minimization of delays in operations
   h. provision for sufficient capacity to handle expected demand

Chapter 7   Financial planning

Multiple Choice   Circle the letter that corresponds to the best answer:

1. The fourth phase of the airport master plan is the:

    a. site evaluation.   c. terminal building plan.
    b. financial plan.   d. airport access plan.

2. Break-even need refers to the revenues required to cover:

    a. capital investment only.
    b. operating expenses only.
    c. capital investment and operating expenses.
    d. terminal building expenses.

3. Nondepreciable investment items include all of the following *except*:

    a. land acquisition.   c. excavation and fill operations.
    b. multilevel parking garage. d. road relocations.

4. Which of the following is *not* a depreciable investment?

    a. People-mover system.   c. Loading bridges.
    b. Cargo building.   d. Excavation and fill operations.

5. Which of the following facilities would most likely be financed by private interests?

    a. Public parking area.   c. Gate and ramp areas.
    b. Airline terminal buildings. d. Airport hotel.

6. Concession rental rates are based on a minimum rental payment and/or a percentage of the concessionaire's:

    a. gross revenue.   c. net income.
    b. gross income.   d. salary expenses.

7. The most commonly used method for charging rentals such as cargo buildings, hangars, and airline leased areas is a rate per:

    a. square foot per year.   c. number of employees utilizing the facility.
    b. square yard per year.   d. passengers enplaned.

8. General obligation bonds:

    a. are issued at lower interest rates than other types of bonds.
    b. are used quite extensively to finance hangars, fuel distribution systems and hotels.

   c. have become increasingly popular in financing large airport expansion projects.

   d. do not require voter approval.

9. The distinguishing feature between self-liquidating general obligation bonds and general obligation bonds is the fact that the former:

   a. do not require voter approval.

   b. normally do not include the debt as part of the community's debt limitation.

   c. can be issued at lower interest rates.

   d. are primarily used to finance privately owned facilities.

10. The most commonly used method of financing capital improvements at large airports today is:

   a. general obligation bonds.

   b. self-liquidating general obligation bonds.

   c. revenue bonds.

   d. private financing.

11. Airport hotels are normally financed by:

   a. general obligation bonds.

   b. self-liquidating general obligation bonds.

   c. revenue bonds.

   d. private financing.

12. The first airport revenue bond was used to buy:

   a. LaGuardia Airport.

   b. Chicago O'Hare Airport.

   c. Miami International Airport.

   d. San Francisco International Airport.

13. The O'Hare agreement:

   a. committed the city of Chicago to raise taxes to finance O'Hare International Airport.

   b. provided that the airlines would make up the difference if the airport income fell short of the total needed to pay off the principal and interest on bonds.

   c. provided that Cook County would make up the difference if the airport income fell short of the total needed to pay off the principal and interest on bonds.

   d. committed the airlines to set aside a separate trust fund to meet unforeseen expenses.

14. The predominant source of funding capital projects at GA airports is:

   a. general obligation bonds.

   b. federal grants.

   c. revenue bonds.

   d. private financing.

15. Which of the following would be considered a medium grade bond?

 a. AA   c. A—
 b. Aa   d. BBB

16. Credit analysts at the major investor services rate an airport revenue bond according to all of the following factors *except*:

 a. financial performance of the airport.
 b. size of the city.
 c. the strength of passenger demand.
 d. use agreements with the airlines serving the airport.

17. Revenue from taxi cabs, buses, and hotel vans would fall under:

 a. airline terminal buildings.   c. commercial facilities.
 b. public parking areas.   d. none of these.

18. _____ require taxpayer approval but are not considered part of the community's debt limitation.

 a. General obligation bonds
 b. Self-liquidating general obligation bonds
 c. Revenue bonds
 d. State grants for airport construction

19. Credit analysts at the major investor services rate an airport revenue bond according to a variety of factors, including all of the following, except:

 a. financial performance of the airport.
 b. passenger demand.
 c. number of air carriers and based GA aircraft.
 d. use agreements with the air carriers.

20. Revenue bonds:

 a. typically pay lower interest rates than general obligation bonds.
 b. are offered for sale competitively or under a negotiated sale.
 c. are not affected by general economic conditions.
 d. all of the above.

True/False Circle T if the statement is true, F if it is false.

T F   1. An economic evaluation of the airport master plan is only of secondary importance because the primary objective is to develop a design concept.

T (F) 2. Land acquisition is a depreciable investment expense.

(T) F 3. Public parking is usually operated on a concessionaire basis.

(T) F 4. Revenues from concessionaires and ground transportation services are usually based on a percentage of gross income.

(T) F 5. General obligation bonds usually are offered at a lower interest rate than revenue bonds.

T (F) 6. Financing airport improvements by private sources, such as the air carriers, FBOs, and concessionaires, is rarely done because of the easy availability of other sources.

T (F) 7. Recently airport authorities have relied more heavily on general obligation bonds than revenue bonds to finance capital needs.

(T) F 8. Self-liquidating general obligation bonds are backed by a governmental body.

T (F) 9. The debt service on revenue bonds is payable solely from taxes collected from the community.

(T) F 10. Revenue bond financing for airport improvements has become the most common financing method.

(T) F 11. Revenue bonds are usually issued for longer yearly terms than general obligation bonds.

(T) F 12. The role of bond financing in overall investment varies greatly according to an airport's size and type of traffic served.

(T) F 13. Debt financing plays a smaller role at GA airports.

(T) F 14. A medium grade bond means that rating firms see the investment as carrying a measure of speculative risk.

(T) F 15. Investor services today place greater emphasis on local economic strength than on airport use agreements in evaluating bond offerings.

T (F) 16. On the average, larger airports pay higher interest payments to bondholders than smaller airports.

T   (F)   17. Investors are particularly cautious about airport bond offerings because of the number of defaults which have affected their credit rating.

(T)   F   18. Basically, the goal of an overall economic analysis is to determine if revenues will equal or exceed the break-even need.

T   (F)   19. General obligation bonds generally pay a higher interest rate than self-liquidating general obligation bonds.

T   (F)   20. GA airports account for approximately 40 percent of the total airport bond sales.

T   (F)   21. The number of based GA aircraft at a commercial airport is a major factor in rating an airport revenue bond.

(T)   F   22. General market conditions represent the most important determinant of interest costs on airport revenue bonds.

Fill-in   Complete the following.

1. List five airport revenue-producing areas.

   a. _____

   b. _____

   c. _____

   d. _____

   e. _____

2. List five methods of airport financing.

   a. _____

   b. _____

   c. _____

   d. _____

   e. _____

Chapter 7 Answers
Multiple Choice

1.	b	6.	b	11.	d	16.	b
2.	c	7.	a	12.	c	17.	a
3.	b	8.	a	13.	b	18.	b
4.	d	9.	b	14.	b	19.	c
5.	d	10.	c	15.	d	20.	b

True/False

1.	F	7.	F	13.	T	19.	F
2.	F	8.	T	14.	T	20.	F
3.	T	9.	F	15.	T	21.	F
4.	T	10.	T	16.	F	22.	T
5.	T	11.	T	17.	F		
6.	F	12.	T	18.	T		

Fill-in

1. a. landing area
   b. aircraft aprons and parking areas
   c. airline terminal buildings
   d. public parking areas
   e. cargo buildings

   Other answers could include: aviation fuel, hangars, commercial facilities, other usable areas.

2. a. general obligation bonds
   b. self-liquidating general obligation bonds
   c. revenue bonds
   d. private financing
   e. federal and state grants

Chapter 8 Airport capacity and delay

Multiple Choice   Circle the letter that corresponds to the best answer.

1. Throughput capacity is the:

   a. number of aircraft operations that can be accommodated with no more than a given amount of delay.
   b. number of passengers that can be handled within the terminal building at any given time.
   c. rate at which aircraft can be brought into or out of the airfield, without regard to any delay they might experience.
   d. level of operations that results in not more than four minutes average delay per aircraft.

2. Which of the following categories of factors affecting capacity and delay would close proximity of two or more airports fall into?

   a. Airfield characteristics.   c. Air traffic control.
   (b.) Airspace characteristics.   d. Demand characteristics.

3. The rules governing aircraft separation, runway occupancy, and spacing of arrivals and departures would fall under which of the following categories of factors affecting capacity and delay?

   a. Airfield characteristics.   (c.) Air traffic control.
   b. Airspace characteristics.   d. Demand characteristics.

4. Which of the following delay measurement systems depends upon reports from air traffic controllers?

   (a.) NASCOM.   c. OSEM.
   b. SDRS.   d. CBO.

5. Which of the following is a problem with delay measurement and reporting systems?

   a. Some are based on controller reports, and the quality and completeness of reporting vary considerably with controller workload.
   b. Delays might be incurred en route and not be attributable to conditions at the airport.
   c. Most airline schedules into and out of busy airports have a built-in allowance for delay.
   (d.) All of the above.

6. NASCOM data during the late 1980s indicate that close to 80 percent of all delays were due to:

   a. equipment failure.   (c.) weather.
   b. labor problems.   d. airport construction.

7. Which of the following is *not* an administrative management approach to reducing delay?

   a. Diversion of traffic.   c. Quotas.
   (b.) Slot auctions.   d. Rehubbing.

8. Which of the following is a demand management approach to reducing delay?

   (a.) Differential pricing.   c. Diversion of traffic.
   b. Restriction of access by aircraft type.   d. Quotas.

9. Diversion of air traffic is:

   a. a relatively easy solution to the problem of delay.
   b. not a practical solution in the case of major hub cities.
   c. only possible where there are adequate reliever airports.
   d. probably the best solution to the problem of delay.

10. Which of the following is *not* a reason why air carriers are reluctant to divert traffic to alternate airports serving the same city?

   a. Sensitivity to public preferences.
   b. Lack of personnel.
   c. Scheduling problems.
   d. Additional expense of setting up duplicate ground services.

11. Restriction of access by aircraft type means:

   a. diverting GA aircraft to reliever airports.
   b. only allowing aircraft of certain size or performance characteristics into the airport.
   c. restricting the number of a particular type of aircraft into the airport.
   d. limiting the number of air carriers using the airport.

12. Quotas mean:

   a. a limit on the number of operations per hour.
   b. a limit on the number of passenger enplanements per year.
   c. a designated number of air carriers serving an airport.
   d. the same as operational slots.

13. At airports where the quota system is in force:

   a. GA slots are generally distributed through a reservation system.
   b. air carrier slots are generally distributed through a reservation system.
   c. GA and air carrier slots are allocated by negotiation.
   d. scheduling committees determine all slot allocations.

14. Some air carriers, especially those with a high proportion of interconnecting flights, might voluntarily move some operations to underutilized airports located some distance from the congested airport. This is called:

   a. the high density rule.
   b. restriction of access by aircraft type.
   c. rehubbing.
   d. diversion of traffic.

15. Basically, the demand management approach to reducing delay depends upon the:

    a. FAA.   c. price mechanism.
    b. assigning of quotas.   d. air carriers.

16. Peak hour surcharges:

    a. would probably not be passed on to passengers in the form of higher fares because of competitive reasons.
    b. are relatively easy to determine.
    c. would impose less of a burden on commuters and new entrants.
    d. would reduce anticipated air carrier delay costs.

17. One airport which has used differential pricing policies for a number of years is:

    a. Chicago O'Hare.   c. Frankfurt Main.
    b. London Heathrow.   d. Atlanta Hartsfield.

18. Which of the following is *not* a problem regarding slot auctions?

    a. Who should organize the auction?
    b. Who should receive the proceeds of the auction?
    c. Which airports should initiate the slot auctions?
    d. Do the slots become the property of the air carriers once they have become auctioned?

19. Slot auctions:

    a. would probably impose an unfair burden on international carriers.
    b. are easier to allocate in a deregulated environment.
    c. are particularly popular with new entrants.
    d. would be best determined by the FAA.

20. Demand management approaches to reducing delay:

    a. are unquestionably the best.
    b. have become easier to initiate since deregulation.
    c. have become more difficult to initiate since deregulation.
    d. should be strictly handled by the FAA to avoid conflicts.

21. A condition where demand approaches or exceeds capacity is called:

    a. practical capacity.   c. congestion.
    b. throughput capacity.   d. delay.

22. Some delay is unavoidable due to:

    a. weather conditions.
    b. the fact that it might be too expensive to eliminate.
    c. the randomness of demand for service.
    d. all of the above.

23. Balanced use of large airports means:

    a. diverting GA traffic to reliever airports.
    b. commercial airpots in several metropolitan areas are not used in a balanced manner.
    c. restricting the use of large airports to large transport aircraft.
    d. smoothing out the peaks in demand.

24. Which of the following statements concerning the administrative management approach is correct?

    a. Virtually all GA aircraft can be diverted to reliever airports.
    b. Diverting air carrier traffic to alternate airports is a simple and inexpensive approach to increasing capacity.
    c. When aircraft are of similar size, speed, and operating characteristics, runway acceptance rate is greater.
    d. Since 1986, slots are considered the property of the airport authority.

25. Peak hour charges:

    a. would probably affect GA aircraft operators more than the air carriers.
    b. would cause the air carriers to change schedule patterns.
    c. would be relatively easy to determine.
    d. would be easy to implement.

26. Critics of the current slot sale rule argue that:

    a. funds should go to the airports.
    b. the process gives an advantage to incumbent airlines.
    c. there should be slot auctions at all airports.
    d. the slots should be evenly divided among the major air carriers, regionals, and general aviation operators.

True/False   Circle T if the statement is true, F if it is false.

T   F   1. Capacity refers to the ability of an airport to handle a given volume of traffic (demand).

T   F   2. Practical annual capacity (PANCAP) is the level of operations which results in not more than four minutes average delay per aircraft in the normal peak two-hour operating period.

T   F   3. Practical capacity is always less than throughput capacity.

T   F   4. Some delay is unavoidable and some other, although avoidable, might be too expensive to eliminate.

T   F   5. The rules and procedures of air traffic control, intended primarily to assure safety of flight, are basic determinants of airfield capacity and delay.

T   F   6. Noise-abatement procedures generally have little effect on capacity and delay.

T   F   7. Visual meteorological conditions (VMC) refers to atmospheric conditions which do not permit one aircraft from seeing another and safe separation must be assured solely by ATC rules and procedures.

T   F   8. Differences in speed and size between successive aircraft in the arrival stream allows air traffic controllers to decrease separation.

T   F   9. NASCOM and PMS are based on controller reports, and the quality and completeness of reporting vary considerably with controller workload.

T   F   10. Chronic delay is limited to a very few specific times and places, and one of the principal causes is peaking of traffic flow.

T   F   11. There is no valid reason why all GA traffic could not be diverted from busy air carrier airports to reliever airports.

T   F   12. The system of reliever airports in the United States has developed with the planning and coordination of larger airports.

T   F   13. Diverting air carrier traffic to alternate airports is one of the best solutions to the problems of capacity and delay.

T   F   14. At airports covered by the FAA high density rule, all slots are allocated to the air carriers.

T   F   15. If air carrier and commuter representatives fail to reach an agreement regarding slot allocations, the FAA reserves the right to allocate slots.

T   F   16. Rehubbing has played a significant role in reducing delays at major airports in recent years.

T   F   17. Increasing landing fees is probably the best solution to restricting air carrier use of airports.

T   F   18. Much of the traffic moved away from peak hours by higher landing fees would probably be GA.

T   F   19. GA users often contend that differential pricing is discriminatory.

T   F   20. Slot auctions allow peak-hour access only to those users willing to pay a market-determining price.

T   F   21. As demand approaches the limit of throughput capacity, delays increase sharply, and theoretically, become infinite when demand equals or exceeds throughput capacity.

T   F   22. The capacity of an airfield is relatively constant over time.

T   F   23. Airfield characteristics refers to the interdependence of approach and departure paths for nearby airports.

T   F   24. For most airports, it is the combined effect of weather, runway configuration, and ATC rules and procedures that results in the most severe loss of capacity and delay.

T   F   25. Most airline schedules, especially for flights into and out of busy airports, have a built-in allowance for delay.

T   F   26. GA slots are generally distributed through a reservation system.

T   F   27. Landing fees make up a large percent of operating cost, and consequently, increases would have a significant effect on demand during peak periods.

T   F   28. A major problem with the concept of peak-hour surcharges is how to determine the level of surcharge.

T   F   29. The impact of slots extends far beyond the few airports where they are imposed.

T   F   30. Some critics argue that regulations restricting airport access are unconstitutional.

Fill-in Complete the following.

1. List five administrative management approaches to reducing delay.

   a. _____

   b. _____

   c. _____

   d. _____

   e. _____

2. List two demand management approaches to reducing delay.

   a. _____

   b. _____

Chapter 8 Answers

Multiple Choice

1. c	8. a	15. c	22. d
2. b	9. c	16. d	23. b
3. c	10. b	17. b	24. c
4. a	11. b	18. c	25. a
5. d	12. a	19. a	26. b
6. c	13. a	20. c	
7. b	14. c	21. c	

True/False

1. T	9. T	17. F	25. T
2. T	10. T	18. T	26. T
3. T	11. F	19. T	27. F
4. T	12. F	20. T	28. T
5. T	13. F	21. T	29. T
6. F	14. F	22. F	30. T
7. F	15. T	23. F	
8. F	16. F	24. T	

Fill-in

1. a. diversion of traffic
   b. balanced use of large airports
   c. restriction of access by aircraft type
   d. quotas
   e. rehubbing

2. a. differential pricing
   b. slot auctions or sales

Chapter 9   Airside technological improvements

Multiple Choice   Circle the letter that corresponds to the best answer:

1. Which of the following is *not* a new technology that could improve aircraft guidance, surveillance, and control?

   a. ILS.
   b. MLS.
   c. Surveillance radar.
   d. Automated traffic management systems.

2. The microwave landing system (MLS):

   a. provides guidance by radio beams that define a straight line path to the runway at a fixed slope.
   b. permits aircraft to fly any of several approach angles.
   c. will have very little or no effect on capacity.
   d. cannot provide guidance for the aircraft during a missed approach.

3. Which of the following statements is correct?

   a. ILS and MLS cannot be colocated and operated simultaneously.
   b. The U.S. is committed to retaining ILS service at international gateway airports until 2000.
   c. The phaseout of ILS systems is scheduled to be completed by 1995.
   d. None of these are correct.

4. The automated radar terminal system (ARTS III):

   a. is a form of search radar which displays precipitation and weather fronts.
   b. is the least sophisticated equipment being developed.
   c. detects, tracks, and predicts the position of aircraft.
   d. includes an improvement called moving target detection.

5. Regulating the arrival time of aircraft in the terminal area so as not to exceed a given acceptance rate is called:

   a. metering.
   b. sequencing.
   c. spacing.
   d. traffic flow.

6. The new traffic management system (TMS):

   a. is an advanced radar system designed to overcome the problems of ground clutter.
   b. is a set of procedures governing the use of terminal airspace and airport runways.
   c. is designed to eliminate wake vortex.
   (d.) is a software package designed to increase the efficiency of airport and airspace utilization.

7. Improved airspace procedures call for all of the following, *except*:

   a. reduced lateral separation.
   b. reduced longitudinal separation on final approach.
   c. separate short runways for small aircraft.
   (d.) separate airports for GA aircraft.

8. Separate short runways:

   a. cost about the same as a longer runway when considering engineering and construction costs.
   (b.) have little advantage if the traffic mix is reasonably uniform.
   c. provide about as much flexibility as a longer runway.
   d. would have little effect on capacity.

9. The vortex advisory system (VAS) is a (an):

   a. guidance, surveillance, and control technology.
   (b.) weather related technology.
   c. airport surface utilization technology.
   d. noise control and abatement technology.

10. An aerodynamic disturbance that originates at the wingtips and trails in corkscrew fashion behind the aircraft is called:

    a. microbursts.   (c.) wake vortex.
    b. instrument meteorological conditions.   d. wind shear.

11. The low level wind shear alert system (LLWSAS) is a (an):

    a. automated weather observing system.
    (b.) array of anemometers that read wind velocity and direction around the airport.
    c. advanced Doppler radar system.
    d. federal study designed to provide a better understanding of wind shear.

12. Which of the following is *not* an approach to curtailing noise?

    a. Operational restrictions.
    b. Reducing compressor and turbine noise.
    c. FAR Part 91.
    d. Streamlining the fuselage.

13. Airport surface detection equipment (ASDE) is designed to:

    a. assist controllers in locating and monitoring the movement of aircraft and ground equipment on runways and taxiways.
    b. measure runway occupancy time.
    c. relieve aircraft congestion at the gates.
    d. improve taxiway marking and lighting.

14. The tower automated ground surveillance system (TAGS) is intended for use in conjunction with:

    a. ASDE.   c. ARTS III.
    b. MLS.   d. ASR-9.

15. Runway occupancy time (ROT) can be improved by:

    a. lengthening runways.
    b. improving the placement of taxiways.
    c. allowing more aircraft on the active runway at one time.
    d. all of these.

16. Proponents of the microwave landing system (MLS) argue that it is:

    a. more reliable and less susceptible to electromagnetic interference than the ILS.
    b. relatively easy to install.
    c. more flexible because it allows alternate approach paths.
    d. all of the above.

17. The least sophisitcated radar display equipment is:

    a. ARTS II.   c. ARTS IIIA.
    b. ARTS III.   d. TPX-42.

18. Which of the following problems affecting primary radar and display equipment is considered the most severe?

    a. maintenance   c. weather masking
    b. ground clutter   d. false targets generated by flocks of birds

19. Spacing air traffic means:

    a. regulating the arrival time of aircraft in the terminal area so as not to exceed a given acceptance rate.

    b. establishing and maintaining the appropriate interval between successive aircraft.

    c. specifying the exact order in which aircraft take off and land.

    d. determining the runway acceptance rate.

20. An operational solution to the wake vortex problem on closely spaced parallel runways entail all of the following additional conditions, except:

    a. wind monitors must be set up along the approach path.

    b. the upwind runway must have a high-angle glideslope.

    c. small aircraft must use the downwind runway of the closely spaced pair.

    d. there must be a steady crosswind.

21. The FAA is considering all of the following changes in airspace procedures under IMC, except:

    a. reduced lateral separation for converging and dependent parallel runways.

    b. reduced longitudinal separation on final approach.

    c. reduced runway occupancy time.

    d. separate short runways for small aircraft.

22. The FAA is developing a number of systems intended to provide better and more timely weather information. They include all of the following, except:

    a. AWOS.   c. VASI.

    b. JAWOS.   d. NEXRAD.

23. Which of the following research efforts are primarily designed for exit taxiways?

    a. improved lighting and signing

    b. pavement sensors

    c. surface treatments to improve traction

    d. clearer airport maps for pilots

True/False   Circle T if the statement is true, F if it is false.

T   F   1. The runway utilization rate under IMC could come closer to that attainable under VMC if aircraft could follow multiple approach paths.

T   F   2. The primary motive for the FAA in seeking to develop and deploy the MLS is not the potential capacity benefits but its operational advantages.

T   F   3. The air traffic control radar beacon system (ATCRBS) displays only replies from aircraft equipped with transponders.

T   F   4. The ASR-9 system will allow controllers to assess the severity of storms and also detect small aircraft without transponders.

T   F   5. Runway configuration management is primarily designed to alleviate the problem of noise.

T   F   6. The TMS and AERA are relatively inexpensive programs to implement and are expected to be in service by the early 1990's.

T   F   7. Many airspace users feel that revisions of the existing instrument flight procedures are needed.

T   F   8. The National Airspace Review (NAR) was designed to study the problem of wind shear.

T   F   9. Current ATC procedures allow approaches to triple parallel runways only during VMC.

T   F   10. Current procedures require longitudinal (intrail) separation of one nautical mile between aircraft conducting instrument approaches to the same runway.

T   F   11. One disadvantage of separate short runways is the fact that they do not provide as much operational flexibility as a full-length additional air carrier runway.

T   F   12. Wind shear is basically the same as wake vortex.

T   F   13. The vortex advisory system (VAS) has proven to be an extremely successful technology.

T   F   14. Implementation of the automated weather observing system (AWOS) is scheduled for the 1990s.

T   F   15. FAR Part 91 sets the timetable for meeting the noise requirements under FAR Part 36.

T   F   16. It has been estimated that the phasing out of aircraft with low bypass engines will reduce noise significantly.

T   F   17. Current ATC rules allow two aircraft to occupy the active runway under certain conditions.

T   F   18. The MLS can be installed on runways where ILS is not possible.

T   F   19. A big advantage of MLS is its capability to provide nonconflicting routes into closely situated airports where approach or departure paths may mutually interfere and limit capacity utilization.

T   F   20. ARTS III does not track aircraft or predict their position and is used at airports with low to medium levels of activity.

T   F   21. ASR-9 radars will provide more reliable and accurate surveillance information.

T   F   22. FAA studies suggest that the diagonal spacing requirements for IFR operation on dependent parallel runways could be reduced.

T   F   23. Independent instrument approaches to parallel runways separated by at least 4,300 feet are presently authorized when aircraft are turned onto the approach path, they must be separated vertically by at least one mile or laterally by 5 nmi from aircraft turning on approach to the other runway.

T   F   24. The current practice in air traffic control is to organize aircraft by type of aircraft.

T   F   25. NEXRAD will provide minute by minute observations needed to detect small localized downbursts of rain that produce wind shear.

T   F   26. Airport operators prefer operational restrictions as an approach to reducing noise.

T   F   27. ASDE-3 will be able to identify aircraft and surface vehicles under all weather conditions.

Chapter 9   Answers

Multiple Choice

1.	a	7.	d	13.	a	19.	b
2.	b	8.	b	14.	a	20.	c
3.	b	9.	b	15.	b	21.	c
4.	c	10.	c	16.	d	22.	c
5.	a	11.	b	17.	d	23.	a
6.	d	12.	c	18.	c		

True/False

1.	T	8.	F	15.	T	22.	T
2.	T	9.	T	16.	T	23.	F
3.	T	10.	F	17.	F	24.	F
4.	T	11.	T	18.	T	25.	F
5.	F	12.	F	19.	T	26.	F
6.	F	13.	F	20.	F	27.	F
7.	T	14.	F	21.	T		

Chapter 10   Landside technological improvements

Multiple Choice   Circle the letter that corresponds to the best answer.

1. Which of the following statements concerning buses and mobile lounges is *not* true?

   a. They add to airside surface traffic.
   b. They are labor-intensive.
   c. They are relatively inexpensive to operate.
   d. They are less practical than automated guideway systems for longer distances and large volumes of traffic.

2. Computerized ticket systems are primarily designed to speed up which of the following ticket counter functions?

   a. Flight information.   c. Baggage check-in.
   b. Ticket transactions.   d. All of these.

3. One of the simplest and most widely applied methods to expedite baggage handling is:

   a. to discourage passengers from checking in luggage.
   b. curbside check-in.
   c. hotel check-in.
   d. to encourage carry-on luggage.

4. Computerized baggage sorting equipment:

    a. distributes luggage with machine-readable tags.
    b. allows passengers to check and claim luggage either in the terminal or at remote locations on or off the airport.
    c. assists in passenger security screening.
    d. is designed to eliminate carry-on luggage.

5. Which of the following statements is correct?

    a. New aircraft contain smaller overhead storage bins in order to have more cabin room.
    b. The chief drawback of X-ray machines as screening devices is their limited capacity to detect explosives and other volatile substances.
    c. CAPIS is an accelerated passenger inspection service where travelers who do not have goods to declare are separated from those who do.
    d. The U.S. Department of State is now issuing passports at the airport if travelers have the proper identification.

6. Landside capital improvements sponsored by FAA are limited to:

    a. terminal buildings.   c. guideways and walkways only.
    b. on-airport roadways only.   d. answers b and c.

7. Which of the following would be the easiest and least expensive changes to alleviate congestion at the terminal curb front?

    a. Construct bypass lanes.
    b. Establish remote park and ride facilities.
    c. Construct passenger underpass.
    d. Strictly enforce the parking restrictions.

8. Most airline passengers arrive at the airport by:

    a. limousine.   c. shuttle bus.
    b. private passenger auto. d. taxi.

9. Which of the following airport ground access methods would be the most expensive to develop and operate?

    a. Shuttle bus service.   c. Rail rapid transit system.
    b. Limousine service.   d. All of these.

10. Which of the following is *not* a problem of rail transit systems to airports in the United States?

a. Few passengers want to travel between the airport and the central business district.

b. Public resistance to building a system to serve airport users exclusively.

c. It's more time consuming for passengers than other surface modes of transportation.

d. Passengers encumbered by baggage find rail transit inconvenient.

11. The value of new technology as a solution to the problem of capacity and delay can be measured by a number of factors. Which of the following is a direct benefit?

    a. higher efficiency   c. improved reliablity
    b. greater safety   d. greater convenience

12. Moving sidewalks:

    a. are the best solution for very long walking distances.
    b. increase passenger movement time significantly.
    c. are costly to operate and maintain.
    d. can be fitted with accelerating devices to permit greater line speeds.

13. Ticket dispensing machines:

    a. will eliminate ticketing at airport terminals.
    b. have caused travel agent ticket sales to decline.
    c. are now used by most air carriers.
    d. none of the above.

14. Which of the following statements is correct?

    a. Most larger airports combine immigration and customs facilities.
    b. New security equipment has actually speeded up passenger flow through the terminal.
    c. Computerized baggage sorting equipment is now employed at most of the larger airports.
    d. Computerized ticket systems available today offer passengers advance reservations and sales, preassignment of seats, and automatic tagging of baggage.

15. Funding for on-airport roadways is sponsored by the:

    a. FAA.   c. UMTA.
    b. FHWA.   d. state and local authorities.

16. Bypass lanes on the vehicular circular drive:

    a. greatly improve safety.
    b. segregate foot and vehicular traffic.
    c. reduce curbfront congestion.
    d. all of the above.

17. Which of the following statements concerning rail transit to the airport is correct?

    a. The capital cost per passenger is relatively low.
    b. The public might object because other parts of the metropolitan area might need service more than airport users.
    c. Passengers find the service convenient when carrying several pieces of luggage.
    d. Many business travelers would use the service between the central business district and the airport.

18. Which of the following airport ground access modes of transportation frequently suffers low patronage and infrequent service?

    a. rail   c. bus
    b. taxi   d. all of the above

True/False   Circle T if the statement is true, F if it is false.

T   F   1. The influence of the terminal and other landside facilities on the functional requirements and performance of airside facilities is significant compared with the inverse effect that the airside exerts on the landside facilities.

T   F   2. Landside technological improvements are of great concern to the FAA and other governmental policymakers.

T   F   3. Passenger movers are best suited to servicing those locations and intraterminal trips where there is a great fluctuation in demand.

T   F   4. For longer distances or where the volume of traffic is large, automated guideway systems are more practical than buses or mobile lounges.

T   F   5. The computerized aircraft manifest is designed to provide passengers with preassignment of seats and automatic tagging of baggage.

T   F   6. The entry of mass-marketing firms such as Sears and Ticketron, along with the growth in the number of tickets written by travel agents, might greatly reduce the need for ticketing at airport terminals.

T   F   7. A new inspection service called "One Stop" combines immigration and customs functions at a single station.

T   F   8. It is estimated that more than 90 percent of all airline passenger trips to and from airports are by private automobile or taxi.

T   F   9. In general, the solution to landside access problems does not appear to be management techniques, but the application of new technology.

T   F   10. Rapid rail transit offers the best solution to the problem of airport ground access in the 1990s.

T   F   11. The popularity of the remote airline terminal concept has risen in recent years.

T   F   12. Moving sidewalks are relatively inexpensive and easy to maintain.

T   F   13. Automated guideway systems are only cost-effective at very large airports.

T   F   14. At many airports, automobile traffic is a principal source of landside congestion and delay.

T   F   15. Passengers generally do not object to remote parking and ride facilities as long as the fees are lower than airport parking facilities.

T   F   16. Pedestrian overpasses and underpasses improve safety but have little effect on vehicular traffic flow at the terminal curbfront.

T   F   17. Bus and airline limousine service has greatly reduced the problem of excessive auto traffic at the terminal.

T   F   18. Helicopter shuttle service between the airport and city center offers a viable solution to the auto congestion problem at many large airports.

Chapter 10   Answers
Multiple Choice:

1. c	6. d	11. a	16. c
2. b	7. d	12. c	17. b
3. b	8. b	13. d	18. c
4. a	9. c	14. d	
5. b	10. c	15. a	

True/False:

1. F	6. T	11. F	16. F
2. F	7. T	12. F	17. F
3. T	8. T	13. T	18. F
4. T	9. F	14. T	
5. F	10. F	15. F	

Chapter 11   Financial management

Multiple Choice   Circle the letter that corresponds to the best answer.

1. Airfield area revenues come from all of the following sources, *except*:

   a. landing fees.
   b. FBO fuel flowage fees.
   c. aircraft parking charges.
   d. airline ground equipment rentals.

2. Revenue from auto parking and ground transportation services would be included under:

   a. terminal area concessions.
   b. other leased areas.
   c. other operating revenue.
   d. nonoperating revenue.

3. Nonoperating revenue is generated from:

   a. food and beverage concessions.
   b. aircraft parking charges.
   c. grants-in-aid.
   d. governmental units.

4. Service on airport equipment such as cars and trucks falls under which of the following expense areas?

   a. Airfield area.
   b. Terminal area.
   c. Hangars and cargo facilities.
   d. General and administrative expenses.

5. Nonoperating expenses include:

   a. maintenance on employee parking lot.
   b. interest payments on outstanding debt.
   c. concession improvements.
   d. utilities.

6. The most detailed budget which establishes numerical codes for each capital and expense item is called:

   a. the line-item budget.　　　c. appropriation by activity.
   b. zero-base budget.　　　　　d. lump-sum appropriation.

7. The zero-base budget:

   a. builds on the base of a previous period.
   b. is the most flexible form of budget.
   c. is the most detailed form of budgeting.
   d. is prepared from the ground up.

8. When the airport operator assumes the major financial risk of running the airport and charges the airline's fees and rental rates set to recover the actual costs, this is called the:

   a. residual-cost approach.　　　c. majority-in-interest.
   b. net income approach.　　　　d. compensatory approach.

9. Airports using the residual-cost approach:

   a. tend to retain considerably larger percentages of their gross revenues.
   b. are guaranteed that the airport will always break even.
   c. generate total revenues which are not constrained to the amount needed to break even.
   d. cannot retain earnings for use in capital projects.

10. Which of the following statements is *not* correct?

    a. At residual-cost airports, the landing fee for airlines is typically the item that balances the budget.
    b. General aviation landing fees vary greatly from airport to airport, ranging from charges similar to the air carriers to none at all.
    c. Most landing fees are assessed on the basis of certificated takeoff weight.
    d. At compensatory airports, airline landing fees are based on calculation of the average actual costs of airfield facilities used by the airlines.

11. Terminal concession contracts with restaurants, snack bars, and gift shops normally guarantee the airport operator an annual minimum payment or a specified percentage of the concessionaire's:

    a. gross revenue.　　　c. net revenue.
    b. gross income.　　　 d. net income.

12. Terminal rental rates for square footage leased by the air carriers is determined by all of the following methods, *except*:

    a. actual cost of the facilities used.   c. carrier profitability.
    b. market value.   d. negotiation.

13. Terminal rental rates for the airlines:

    a. differ according to the type of space leased (ticket counters, baggage claim areas).
    b. are typically adjusted annually at compensatory airports.
    c. differ according to whether the space is leased on an exclusive, preferential, or joint-use basis.
    d. all of these.

14. Which of the following statements is correct?

    a. Smaller airports typically have a more diversified revenue base than larger commercial airports.
    b. Terminal concessions typically generate a greater percentage of total operating revenue as passenger enplanements increase.
    c. Airport public parking facilities typically generate a small percent of overall terminal area revenue.
    d. Airport restaurants and snack bars typically generate the largest single source of nonairline revenue in the terminal area.

15. Which of the following is a trend in airport financial management since deregulation?

    a. Longer terms for airport use agreements and nonairline leases.
    b. A movement away from compensatory forms of financial management.
    c. Diversification of revenues.
    d. Greater reliance on use agreements than the local air travel market.

16. A grant-in-aid from the state for a runway expansion program would be considered:

    a. airfield area revenue.   c. landing area fees.
    b. other operating revenue.   d. nonoperating revenue.

17. Expenses associated with maintaining the airport employee parking lot would be included under:

    a. terminal area.
    b. other buildings and grounds.

    c. nonoperating expenses.

    d. general and administrative expenses.

18. Which of the following statements is not correct?

    a. A majority of the nation's large commercial airports have some form of residual-cost approach to financial management.

    b. Debt service coverage means that the airport's revenue, net of operating, and maintenance expenses must be equal to a specified percentage in excess of the annual debt service for revenue bond issues.

    c. Air carriers at a compensatory airport provide a guarantee that fees and rents will enable the airport to meet its annual operating and debt service requirements.

    d. Most airports have a number of different cost centers whether or not the residual-cost or compensatory-approach to financial management is utilized.

19. Majority-in-interest clauses:

    a. provide protection for airlines that have assumed financial risk under a residual-cost agreement.

    b. are fairly standardized.

    c. do not apply to compensatory-cost airports.

    d. all of the above.

20. Residual-cost airports:

    a. typically have shorter term use agreements than do compensatory airports.

    b. generally have use agreements with terms of 20 or more years.

    c. lack the built-in security afforded compensatory airports.

    d. generally do not offer majority-in-interest clauses to the airlines.

21. Most landing fees are assessed on the basis of certificated:

    a. gross takeoff weight.   c. gross empty weight.

    b. gross landing weight.   d. passenger capacity.

22. The largest source of revenue from the terminal area at large commercial airports is:

    a. restaurants and fast food stands.   c. display advertising.

    b. news and book stores.   d. auto parking facilities.

True/False Circle T if the statement is true, F if it is false.

T   F   1. The airport operating statement records assets, liabilities, and net worth at a particular time.

T   F   2. Revenue from freight forwarders, fixed base operators, governmental units and businesses in the airport industrial area would be included in other operating revenue.

T   F   3. Revenue from display advertising would be included under terminal area concessions.

T   F   4. Operating expenses, unlike revenues, are very similar when comparing airports.

T   F   5. Some airports compute depreciation on the full value of facilities including that portion built with federal and other aid.

T   F   6. Plans precede budgets.

T   F   7. Under the appropriation by activity budget, there are no specific restrictions as to how the money should be spent.

T   F   8. Under the zero-base budget, managers are forced to look at a program in its entirety rather than as an expense add-on to an existing budget.

T   F   9. In drawing up a budget, the first step normally involves an estimate of revenues from all sources for the coming year.

T   F   10. An airport using a compensatory approach lacks the built-in security afforded by the airlines' guarantee that the airport will break even every year.

T   F   11. Most airport capital improvement programs are undertaken without consultation with the air carriers because of their transient nature since deregulation.

T   F   12. Majority-in-interest clauses give the airlines accounting for a majority of traffic at an airport the opportunity to review and approve or veto capital projects.

T   F   13. Compensatory approach airports typically have longer term use agreements than do residual-cost airports.

T   F   14. Many small GA airports do not generate sufficient revenue to cover their operating costs, much less capital investment.

T   F   15. The pricing of facilities and services for airlines and other aeronautical users is generally on a market pricing basis.

T   F   16. Because most GA aircraft are relatively light, they pay very low landing fees at most commercial airports.

T   F   17. Some airports impose peak-hour surcharges on commercial airlines to help ease congestion problems.

T   F   18. Terminal space may be assigned to individual airlines on a preferential or joint-use basis but never on an exclusive basis.

T   F   19. The method of calculating rental rates for other leased areas on an airport is fairly standard.

T   F   20. Airport public parking facilities generally provide the largest single source of nonairline revenue in the terminal area.

T   F   21. Airline deregulation has had a tremendous effect on the air carriers but actually very little on airport management.

T   F   22. Many airports have shortened the terms of nonairline leases and contracts with concessionaires since deregulation.

T   F   23. Many commercial airports are now seeking to increase and diversify their revenues by a variety of strategies.

T   F   24. In general, the compensatory approach becomes attractive as airports develop strong markets and thus increase their revenue-generating potential.

T   F   25. Revenue from outside terminal concessions such as the auto parking lot is included under other operating revenue.

T   F   26. Interest payments on revenue bonds is a nonoperating expense.

T   F   27. The difference between actual expenses and the budgeted amount is called net profit.

T   F   28. The airport use agreement is a legal contract between the airport and an air carrier regarding landing rights.

T   F   29. Under the residual-cost approach to financial management, the airlines collectively assume the risk of assuring that the airport will break even.

T   F   30. Market pricing of concessions and other nonairline sources of revenue is a feature of both residual-cost and compensatory airports.

T   F   31. Terminal concession contracts are often bid competitively, and they range in term from month-to-month agreements to contracts of 10 to 15 years.

T   F   32. On average, terminal concessions account for at least one-half of total operating revenues at large and medium commercial airports.

Fill-in   Complete the following sentences.

1. Airport operating revenues fall into five major groupings. They are:

    a. _____

    b. _____

    c. _____

    d. _____

    e. _____

2. Airport operating expenses fall into four major groupings. They are:

    a. _____

    b. _____

    c. _____

    d. _____

Chapter 11   Answers
Multiple Choice

1.	d	4.	a	7.	d	10.	c
2.	a	5.	b	8.	d	11.	a
3.	c	6.	a	9.	b	12.	c

13.	d	16.	d	19.	a	22.	d
14.	b	17.	b	20.	b		
15.	c	18.	c	21.	b		

True/False

1.	F	9.	T	17.	F	25.	F
2.	F	10.	T	18.	F	26.	T
3.	T	11.	F	19.	F	27.	F
4.	F	12.	T	20.	T	28.	F
5.	T	13.	F	21.	F	29.	T
6.	T	14.	T	22.	T	30.	T
7.	F	15.	F	23.	T	31.	T
8.	T	16.	T	24.	T	32.	F

Fill-in

1. a. airfield area
   b. terminal area
   c. airline leased areas
   d. other leased areas
   e. other operating revenue

2. a. airfield area
   b. terminal area
   c. hangars, cargo, other buildings and grounds
   d. general and administrative expenses

Chapter 12 Organization and administration

Multiple Choice Circle the letter that corresponds to the *best* answer.

1. Which of the following is *not* a reason why there has been a gradual transition from city and county controlled airports to airport authorities?

   a. Many airports have outgrown the political jurisdiction whose responsibility the airport entails.
   b. The ability to specialize on airport matters.
   c. The ability to hire a greater number of employees.
   d. Less political impact on the business of running the airport.

2. The federal government owns and operates which of the following airports?

   a. Baltimore Friendship
   b. Dulles International
   c. Atlanta Hartsfield
   d. none of these

3. Which of the following is *not* a purpose of an organization chart?

   a. Gives brief job descriptions.
   b. Shows formal authority relationships.

    c. Provides a framework within which management functions are carried out.

    d. Shows employees their position in the organization relative to others.

4. Inventory control and negotiation of tenant leases would be the responsibility of:

    a. Operations.   c. Planning and engineering.

    b. Maintenance.   d. Finance and administration.

5. The assistant director-operations is responsible for:

    a. all construction plans to determine technical integrity.

    b. receiving and analyzing all public complaints.

    c. investigating violations of airport regulations.

    d. inspection of maintenance work for compliance with plans, specifications and applicable laws.

6. Which of the following is *not* a function of the crash, fire and rescue chief?

    a. Inspecting and testing all types of fixed fire prevention and extinguishing equipment.

    b. Securing gates and locks and watching buildings and facilities for indications of fire, dangerous conditions, unauthorized entry, and vandalism.

    c. Inspecting all facilities for fire and/or safety hazards.

    d. Developing procedures and implementing major disaster plans.

7. The grounds chief is responsible for:

    a. developing an approved maintenance schedule for all buildings.

    b. inspecting and testing all types of fixed fire prevention and extinguishing equipment.

    c. providing information to the public regarding locations and operations of the airport.

    d. developing approved schedules for maintaining all airport surface areas.

8. The best educational preparation for a career in airport management would include courses in:

    a. pilot training.   c. aviation management.

    b. aeronautical engineering.   d. maintenance technology.

9. Airport managers should have:

   a. as a minimum, a commercial pilot's license.
   b. good communicative and public relations skills.
   c. an accounting background.
   d. experience in a technical field.

10. Which of the following statements concerning public relations is *not* correct?

   a. Every airport and every company and interest on the airport has public relations, whether or not it does anything about them.
   b. Public relations is primarily used to respond to a negative situation.
   c. Airport public relations goes beyond press relations and publicity.
   d. Public goodwill is the greatest asset that can be enjoyed by any airport.

11. The air carriers and FBOs located on the airport would be members of the:

   a. external business public.   c. internal business public.
   b. external general public.   d. internal employee public.

12. The external general public would include:

   a. the local hotel association.
   b. a homeowner's group concerned with aircraft noise.
   c. a local flying club based at the airport.
   d. a restaurant chain with a facility at the airport.

13. An airport owned by a city and run as a separate department with policy direction by the city council or an airport commission is a (an):

   a. airport authority.   c. municipally operated airport.
   b. port authority.   d. advisory board.

14. A typical commercial airport would be organized into four functional areas. They include:

   a. Finance and administration; security, operations; and maintenance.
   b. Planning and engineering; community relations; finance; and maintenance.
   c. Operations; planning and engineering; maintenance; and finance and administration.
   d. Operations; administration; finance; and crash, fire, and rescue.

15. The individual most directly responsible for enforcing regulations applicable to aircraft traffic on the airport is the:

    a. airport director.   c. security chief.
    b. assistant director-operations.   d. grounds chief.

16. The chief-landside operations:

    a. coordinates all parking facility activities.
    b. negotiates leases with tenants.
    c. is responsible for all airport guides and information booths.
    d. secures gates and locks and watches buildings including the terminal area for indications of fire, dangerous conditions, unauthorized entry, and vandalism.

17. An airport manager's primary duty is:

    a. maintaining good relations with airport employees, tenants, air carriers, governmental authorities, and the community.
    b. maximizing profits through effective budgeting and cost control.
    c. the safe and efficient operation of the airport.
    d. all of the above.

18. An individual who passes the intensive program offered through the American Association of Airport Executives (AAAE) may use the initials _____ after his or her name.

    a. Accredited Manager of Airports (AMA)
    b. Master of Business Administration-Airports (MBA-A)
    c. Approved Airport Administrator (AAA)
    d. Accredited Airport Executive (AAE)

19. One of the most important and challenging aspects of an airport manager's job is:

    a. budgeting and cost control.
    b. keeping abreast of the latest advances in aviation technology.
    c. public relations.
    d. securing new air carriers to use the airport.

20. A basic principle underlying the public relations process includes:

    a. responding to negative situations.
    b. the interest of every company on the airport.
    c. mostly good publicity.
    d. none of the above.

21. Airlines, FBOs, and other aviation related business are considered the:

   a. internal business public.   c. internal employee public.
   b. external business public.   d. external general public.

True/False Circle T if the statement is true, F if it is false.

T   F   1. Port authorities and airport authorities have the power to issue their own debt, in the form of revenue bonds, to finance capital projects.

T   F   2. Since the early 1950s there has been a gradual transition from airport and port authorities to city and county controlled airports.

T   F   3. The larger the airport, the greater the specialization of tasks and the greater the departmentalization.

T   F   4. The facilities chief would normally report to the assistant director-operations.

T   F   5. The manager of community relations reports directly to the airport director because of the importance of this position.

T   F   6. The chief-landside operations assigns gate and parking spaces to all aircrafts.

T   F   7. The security chief provides information to the public regarding locations and operations of the airport.

T   F   8. Basically, the job of an airport manager is very similar regardless of the size of the airport.

T   F   9. The airport manager's primary duty is the safe and efficient operation of the airport.

T   F   10. In order to qualify for the A.A.E. designation, an individual must have a minimum of three years work experience in airport management.

T   F   11. A large percentage of the flying public has very little opinion of airports, either positive or negative.

T   F   12. A group of environmentalists concerned with an airport expansion program which may affect the nesting habits of an endangered bird would be an example of an external general public.

T   F   13. Gaining citizen participation and support in airport planning and hearings is part of the public relations effort.

T   F   14. Answering general and environmental complaints on an individual basis is rarely done because of the time involved.

T   F   15. The predominant form of airport ownership and operation is an airport authority.

T   F   16. One big advantage of the port authority or airport authority form of ownership and operation is better management procedures by the airport administration.

T   F   17. Most state operated commercial airports are found in Alaska.

T   F   18. The responsibility for security would normally fall under the authority of the assistant director of operations.

T   F   19. Noise level studies involving the surrounding area would normally be the responsibility of the planning and engineering staff.

T   F   20. Airport management is similar to the management of any large public enterprise in terms of hours and working conditions.

T   F   21. Airport managers are normally political appointees with little or no background in the administration of airports.

T   F   22. Airport public relations is basically good press relations and publicity.

T   F   23. Local citizens often do not understand airport problems, and consequently, they should only be apprised of particular concerns such as noise.

Chapter 12   Answers
Multiple Choice

1. c	3. a	5. c	7. d
2. d	4. d	6. b	8. c

9.	b	13.	c	17.	c	21.	a
10.	b	14.	c	18.	d		
11.	c	15.	b	19.	c		
12.	b	16.	a	20.	b		

True/False

1.	T	7.	T	13.	T	19.	F
2.	F	8.	F	14.	F	20.	F
3.	T	9.	T	15.	F	21.	F
4.	F	10.	T	16.	F	22.	F
5.	F	11.	F	17.	T	23.	F
6.	F	12.	T	18.	T		

Chapter 13   Airport operations

Multiple Choice   Circle the letter that corresponds to the best answer.

1. Asphalt paving:

   a. resists deterioration from oil or fuel spillage better than concrete.
   b. loses its elasticity after years of use.
   c. is more expensive to install than concrete.
   d. requires less maintenance in the long run.

2. Which of the following statements regarding concrete runways and taxiways is *not* true?

   a. Concrete has a higher load bearing capacity than asphalt.
   b. Concrete resists deterioration from oil or fuel spillage better than asphalt.
   c. Concrete paving requires no visible joints or seams.
   d. Concrete expands and contracts with temperature change.

3. Potholes are usually caused by:

   a. concrete shrinkage.   c. excessive weight.
   b. lack of expansion space.   d. moisture seepage.

4. The most effective and economical method of reducing hydroplaning on the runway pavement surface is:

   a. vibratory testing.   c. grooving.
   b. spalling.   d. sandblasting.

5. The removal of rubber deposits and other contaminants from runway surfaces includes:

    a. high pressure water.   c. high velocity impact techniques.
    b. chemical solvents.   d. all of these.

6. The first step in a snow removal program is:

    a. a listing of the personnel and organizations responsible for the snow removal program.
    b. training of personnel.
    c. a brief statement of the purpose of the plan.
    d. standards and procedures to be followed.

7. Snow removal operations normally are started on the:

    a. active runways.   c. taxiways.
    b. inactive runways.   d. ramp areas.

8. Snow blowers are primarily used:

    a. to clean up the residue left on the surface of the runway.
    b. for removal of hazardous snow accumulations such as windrows and snow banks.
    c. to move the snow to the pavement edges.
    d. to clear ramp area.

9. Which of the following statements concerning snow brushes is *not* correct?

    a. They can be used year-round.
    b. They are used as the initial attack machine.
    c. They have the slowest operating speed of the three basic types of snow removal equipment.
    d. Brushes are available with either steel or synthetic bristles.

10. A clearly marked yellow center line is part of the _____ safety inspection of a typical GA airport.

    a. fueling facilities   c. taxiway
    b. runway   d. ramp/apron area

11. A sign indicating "No unauthorized vehicles allowed" would be most appropriately located:

    a. near the runway.   c. on the ramp/apron area.
    b. along the taxiway.   d. in the parking lot.

12. Which of the following techniques used to eliminate a large number of birds would be least appropriate?

    a. Elimination of food sources.   c. Noise makers.
    b. Elimination of habitat.   d. Firearms.

13. FAR, Part 139 indicates that the first CFR vehicle must be able to reach the midpoint of the farthest runway from its assigned post within _____ minutes from the time the alarm is sounded.

    a. 3   c. 6
    b. 5   d. 10

14. Which of the following statements concerning cooling agents is *not* true?

    a. Dry powder is most effective on localized fires in wheels or tires.
    b. Foam must be applied in large quantities to be effective.
    c. Water is only effective for fires in electrical apparatus.
    d. Foam is produced by mixing water, air, and a concentrate with suitable agitation.

15. FAA's interest in aviation security under Part 107:

    a. covers the entire airport.
    b. is limited to security as it affects or could affect safety in flight.
    c. covers the airside of the airport only.
    d. is limited to terminal operations.

16. A thin film of oil, dirt, or rubber particles mixed with water preventing tires from making contact with pavement is called:

    a. spalling.   c. viscous hydroplaing.
    b. dynamic hydroplaning.   d. vibratory conditioning.

17. Which of the following statements concerning snow removal operations is correct?

    a. Snow removal operations normally are started on the taxiways and ramp areas because they take more time than the runways.
    b. Snow removal is generally geared to the operational limitations of the most critical aircraft using the airport.
    c. Large jet aircraft have a takeoff limitatoin of one inch of heavy wet snow or slush.
    d. All of the above statements are correct.

18. Snow removal normally begins:

    a. as soon as there are traces of precipitation on the runways.
    b. after one-half inch of snow of medium moisture content appears on the active runway.
    c. after the airport has been closed and all traffic advisories have been issued.
    d. during off-peak periods during daylight hours.

19. A reminder sign denoting USE YOUR CHECKLIST would most likely be found at which of the following airport safety self-inspection areas?

    a. ramp/apron   c. runways
    b. taxiways   d. fueling facilities

20. Aircraft fires are different than conventional building fires because:

    a. of the speed with which they develop.
    b. of the intense heat and smoke that is generated.
    c. of the wide area that might be involved.
    d. all of the above.

21. Which of the following statements concerning CFR personnel is correct?

    a. Women are generally discouraged from applying for positions because of the physical requirements of the job.
    b. Quite often personnel and equipment are used to fight off-airport fires.
    c. Many airport CFR personnel may never become involved in a full-scale aircraft crash that demands utilization of all training skills.
    d. CFR personnel concentrate on the aircraft accident and do not need emergency medical training because paramedics are available.

22. The FAA requires that an airport security program include the following elements, except a (an):

    a. listing of each air operations area.
    b. identification of those areas with little or no protection against unauthorized access.
    c. listing of all tenants on the airport and confirmation that each has been advised of the security program.
    d. plan for upgrading the security for air operations areas with a time schedule for each improvement project.

True/False   Circle T if the statement is true, F if it is false.

T   F   1. The first concrete runways appeared in the United States during World War I.

T   F   2. Jet fuel spills cause more harm to runways and taxiways than gasoline.

T   F   3. Moisture is the primary enemy of asphalt runways.

T   F   4. Spalling is a condition where landing gear tires ride up on a cushioning film of water on the runway surfaces.

T   F   5. One of the most effective nondestructive pavement testing techniques is vibratory (or dynamic) testing.

T   F   6. Chemical solvents can be used to remove contaminants from cement but not asphalt runways.

T   F   7. The ATA sponsors an annual international aviation snow symposium.

T   F   8. Snow removal is generally geared to the operational limitations of the most critical aircraft using the airport.

T   F   9. Large jet aircraft have a takeoff limitation of one-half inch of heavy wet snow or slush.

T   F   10. Most snow removal is accomplished by using chemical methods.

T   F   11. Rubber blades used on snow plows have a shorter life than steel blades but cost considerably less.

T   F   12. Snow brushes are primarily used to clean up the residue left on the surface by the plow or the blower.

T   F   13. Snow removal from the ramp areas normally begins as soon as there are traces of precipitation.

T   F   14. Ice presents a greater hazard to aircraft operations than snow.

T   F   15. Fueling facilities are normally located away from the aircraft parking area.

T   F   16. Many airport managers call upon the expertise of a botanist to help analyze bird problems at their location.

T   F   17. Chemical poisoning of nuisance birds is generally not allowed by the Environmental Protection Agency.

T   F   18. Most airport CFR facilities are based on the quick delivery of foam extinguishing agents to the scene of a crash.

T   F   19. Passenger carry-on luggage is generally only checked in the case of international flights because of the threat of terrorism.

T   F   20. The security staff is trained to recognize the "profile" of a typical hijacker.

T   F   21. Concrete parking ramps are generally preferred over asphalt.

T   F   22. The high-pressure water method of removing rubber deposits and other contaminants from the runway may be used during all temperature conditions and seasons except during rain, in standing water, slush, snow, or ice.

T   F   23. Some airports use personnel and equipment from the Streets and Sanitation Department during snow removal operations.

T   F   24. Protection of the public is a major responsibility of airport management but is not emphasized in the *FAA Airport Certification Program Handbook*.

T   F   25. The FAA airport safety self-inspection recommends that all airport buildings be numbered.

T   F   26. Chemical poisoning is considered the best method of eliminating large concentrations of birds on airport property.

T   F   27. Applying a good blanket of foam and keeping it intact is a primary objective of any CFR training program.

T   F   28. FAR Part 107 requires that the airport operator must implement a master security plan in a time frame approved by the FAA and also requires persons and vehicles allowed in the air operations areas to be suitably identified.

T   F   29. At most airports, bonded stores for duty-free goods and surveillance cages for valuable cargo reduce all but organized pilferage and theft during delivery or loading.

Fill-in Complete the following sentence.

1. Seven obvious indications of potential runway problems are:

a. _____

b. _____

c. _____

d. _____

e. _____

f. _____

g. _____

Chapter 13 Answers

Multiple Choice

1.	b	7.	a	13.	a	19.	b
2.	c	8.	b	14.	c	20.	d
3.	d	9.	b	15.	b	21.	c
4.	c	10.	c	16.	c	22.	c
5.	d	11.	c	17.	b		
6.	c	12.	d	18.	a		

True/False

1.	F	9.	T	17.	T	25.	T
2.	T	10.	F	18.	T	26.	F
3.	T	11.	F	19.	F	27.	T
4.	F	12.	T	20.	T	28.	T
5.	T	13.	F	21.	T	29.	T
6.	F	14.	T	22.	F		
7.	F	15.	T	23.	T		
8.	T	16.	F	24.	F		

Fill-in

1. a. ponding of water on or near runways and taxiways
    b. build-up of soil or heavy turf at pavement edges, preventing water runoff
    c. clogged or overgrown ditches
    d. erosion of soil at runway edges
    e. open or silted-in joints
    f. surface cracking or crumbling
    g. undulating or bumpy surfaces

Chapter 14   Airport relations with tenants and the public

Multiple Choice   Circle the letter that corresponds to the best answer.

1. Which of the following statements concerning airport-airline relations since deregulation is *not* correct?

    a. Short-term use agreements and leases are becoming more common.
    b. The nature of negotiations at some airports has changed radically.
    c. Most major airports are now dominated by a few large air carriers.
    d. Commuter carriers, with their smaller aircraft, usually do not need the same gate and apron facilities as major carriers.

2. An agreement in which a firm is hired to operate a particular service on behalf of the airport is called a:

    a. use agreement.   c. negotiated contract.
    b. concession agreement.   d. management contract.

3. The relationship between airport operators and the general aviation community is:

    a. similar to the relationship with air carriers only.
    b. similar to the relationship with concessionaires only.
    c. quite different from the relationship with air carriers and concessionaires.
    d. differs considerably between major airports.

4. An airport may be held liable for loss or damage to property or injury to persons arising out of:

    a. neglect in properly marking obstructions.   c. the sale of products.
    b. failure to send out NOTAMS.   d. all of these.

5. The basic airport premises policy is designed to protect the airport operator for losses:

a. to buildings caused by fire.
b. arising out of legal liability.
c. arising out of the sale of products.
d. to aircraft in the care, custody or control of the airport.

6. FAR Part 36, Certificated Airplane Noise Levels:

   a. establishes noise standards for newly manufactured aircraft engines.
   b. establishes criteria for aircraft operating procedures designed to reduce noise.
   c. establishes standards for measuring noise.
   d. establishes standards for developing a local noise abatement program.

7. Which land use would be most compatible with a high-noise noise impact area?

   a. light manufacturing
   b. schools
   c. civic auditorium
   d. high-rise apartments

8. Which of the following statements is *not* true?

   a. Few airports are located entirely within the borders of the municipality that owns and operates the facility.
   b. Time can erode intergovernmental agreements regarding zoning.
   c. Airport operators have a great deal of authority to control the use of their airports in order to reduce noise.
   d. While aircraft are the source of noise at airports, aircraft operators are not liable for damage caused by noise.

9. Which of the following noise abatement programs would *not* be eligible for federal aid?

   a. Construction of sound barriers and sound-proofing of buildings.
   b. Subsidy to air carriers for the purchase of quieter engines.
   c. Acquisition of land as a buffer zone.
   d. None of these is eligible for federal aid.

10. Which of the following operating restrictions designed to reduce noise is *not* practical?

    a. Not allowing aircraft with a noise rating above 72 dbA to take off between 10 p.m. and 7 a.m.
    b. Eliminating all jet fuel sales after a certain hour.
    c. Instituting special fees for aircraft operated after a certain hour.
    d. Requiring aircraft operators to initiate short takeoff procedures.

11. Which of the following statements concerning airport-airline relations since deregulation is correct?

    a. Air carriers can change their routes, service levels, and prices on short notice.
    b. Long-term agreements between airports and air carriers have become more important because of the increased competition.
    c. Growth in the number of commuters and regionals serving commercial airports.
    d. a and c are correct statements.

12. FBOs:

    a. can provide service to some commuter and startup carriers.
    b. frequently lease hangars and rent short-term aircraft parking facilities.
    c. often construct and develop their own facilities on airport property.
    d. all of the above.

13. GA aircraft:

    a. are used more intensively than commercial aircraft.
    b. require longer term parking facilities.
    c. operations represent less than 10 percent of total operations at FAA-towered airports.
    d. owners quite frequently negotiate fee schedules and use of airport facilities directly with the airport authority.

14. Aircraft damaged while in the care, custody, or control of the airport for storage or safekeeping can be covered under:

    a. contractual liability coverage.
    b. airport premises liability coverage.
    c. hangarkeepers liability coverage.
    d. products liability coverage.

15. The most frequent airport liability claims arise out of:

    a. aircraft operations.   c. sale of products.
    b. premises operations.   d. contractual obligations.

16. Aircraft noise:

    a. became a more serious problem during the 1950s.
    b. actually affects a relatively small number of people.
    c. has become a greater problem with each passing decade.
    d. is a lesser problem than other environmental issues.

17. The noisiest aircraft are defined in the FARs as Stage:

    a. 1.   c. 3.
    b. 2.   d. 4.

18. FAR Part 150, Airport Land-Use Compatibility:

    a. established a system for measuring aviation noise in a community.
    b. encourages airport operators to develop Noise Exposure Maps.
    c. clears the way for airports to obtain federal aid for noise abatement projects.
    d. all of the above.

19. _____ calls for the phaseout of Stage 2 aircraft by the end of 1999.

    a. FAR Part 36 Certificated Airplane Noise levels
    b. The Noise Compatibility Program
    c. FAR Part 150 Airport Land-Use Compatibility Planning
    d. The Aircraft Noise and Capacity Act

20. Ideally, residential areas should be located in places below _____ day-night average sound level (Ldn).

    a. 29   c. 65
    b. 35   d. 85

21. The courts have ruled that the legal liability for aircraft noise rests with the:

    a. air carriers.   c. airport operator.
    b. local governmental authorities. d. federal government.

True/False   Circle T if the statement is true, F if it is false.

T   F   1. Long-term agreements between airports and major airlines are becoming more common because of the long-lived nature of the investments involved.

T   F   2. A management contract is one in which the airport extends to a firm the privilege of conducting business at the airport.

T   F   3. At a number of major airports, fees from parking and car rentals represent the largest source of revenue.

T   F   4. The presence of an FBO capable of servicing small transport aircraft can sometimes be instrumental in a new carrier's decision to serve a particular airport.

T   F   5. The chief need of GA aircraft owners at an airport is parking and storage space.

T   F   6. Airport operators require that all tenants purchase their own insurance as appropriate for their particular circumstances and with certain minimum limits of liability.

T   F   7. Muncipalities are normally immune from legal liability because of their governmental status.

T   F   8. The actual number of people affected by aviation noise is large and has been growing rapidly in recent years.

T   F   9. FAA has suggested, but not mandated, guidelines for determining land uses that are compatible with a given noise level.

T   F   10. Zoning and land use planning are primarily the responsibility of local governments.

T   F   11. Any restriction of operations at an airport to reduce noise must be nondiscriminatory.

T   F   12. The air carriers have been receptive to the establishment of hourly takeoff and landing limits based on a noise budget.

T   F   13. Federal funds are available to assist airport operators in sound-proofing buildings or buying noise-impact land.

T   F   14. The imposition of curfews as a noise abatement tool has little effect on airline scheduling because most curfews are at night.

T   F   15. The nature of negotiations between airports and airlines has changed radically since deregulation.

T   F   16. A concession agreement is a form of management contract.

T   F   17. Parking and automobile rentals as a source of revenue are declining relative to airport buses and limousine service.

T   F   18. Long-term agreements between the airport and GA users are similar to agreements with the air carriers.

T   F   19. The basic airport premises liability policy covers sponsorship of an air show.

T   F   20. In most cases, municipalities, as governmental units, are immune from liability actions.

T   F   21. The noise issue has been instrumental in slowing or stopping some airport expansion.

T   F   22. Noise exposure maps identify land use incompatibilities and are useful in discouraging further development.

T   F   23. An FAA-approved Noise Compatibility Program is needed to obtain federal aid for noise abatement projects.

T   F   24. Zoning and land use planning present the fewest problems in addressng noise compatibility.

T   F   25. The FAA has generally been reluctant to assist airport operators and air carriers in establishing or modifying flight paths to avoid noise-sensitive areas.

T   F   26. If airports adopt local noise standards more stringent than the FAA's, carriers will have to accelerate their fleet replacement programs in order to continue serving those markets.

Chapter 14 Answers

Multiple Choice

1. c	7. a	13. b	19. d
2. d	8. c	14. c	20. c
3. c	9. b	15. b	21. c
4. d	10. d	16. b	
5. b	11. d	17. a	
6. a	12. d	18. d	

True/False

1. F	3. T	5. T	7. F
2. F	4. T	6. T	8. F

9.	T	14.	F	19.	F	24.	F
10.	T	15.	T	20.	F	25.	F
11.	T	16.	F	21.	T	26.	T
12.	F	17.	F	22.	T		
13.	T	18.	F	23.	T		

Index

A

abbreviations, 397-399
access, airport access, 139, 167-171, 433-441
  access/egress facilities, passenger-handling systems, 153
  access/processing interface, passenger-handling systems, 153-154
  passenger-handling systems, 153-154
  segments of airport-access, 168-169
  study-guide questions, 433-441
  technological improvements, 259-264
  vehicle parking areas, 169, 171
accidents, 14
accountants and accounting (*see* airport accounting)
administrative management to reduce delays (*see* delay-management)
advanced en route automation (AERA), 226
Aeronautics Branch of Department of Commerce established, 8
Aerospace Industries Association (AIA), 55
Air Commerce Act of 1926, 31, 7
Air Line Pilots Association (ALPA), 55
air pollution (*see* environmental concerns)
air traffic control, 225-227
  advanced en route automation (AERA), 226
  capacity and delay factors, 195, 212
  metering, 225
  Mode S data links, 226
  radar beacon system (ATCRBS), 223-224
  runway configuration management, 226
  separation, 225
  separation, lateral separation reduction, 228-231
  separation, longitudinal separation reduction, 231-232
  sequencing, 225
  small-aircraft-only runways, 232-233
  spacing aircraft, 225
  traffic management systems (TMS), 226-227
air traffic control radar beacon system (ATCRBS), 223-224
Air Transport Association (ATA), 56
air travel history and development, 3-33, 401-407
  current estimates, revenues, passengers, 26-27, 38-39, 59

air-carrier capacity, forecasting airport needs, 88
aircraft operations capacity, forecasting airport needs, 90-92
Aircraft Owners and Pilots Association (AOPA), 55
airfield capacity, requirements/site selection, 95
Airline Deregulation Act of 1978 (*see* deregulation)
airline-airport relations, 350-353
airmail service, 5, 7
  Contract Air Mail Act of 1925 (Kelly Act), 7
airport accounting, 272-276
  accountants, organization and administration, 298-299
  chief accountant's role, organization and administration, 298-299
  depreciation, 276
  leased areas, revenues, 274
  nonoperating expenses, 276
  nonoperating revenues, 275
  operating expenses, 275-276
  operating revenues, 274-275
Airport and Airway Development Act of 1970, 16-23, 26, 29, 86
  Airport Development Aid Program (ADAP), 17-20, 47, 49, 64, 74
  Amendments of 1976, 20-22
  grant programs, 32, 17
  National Airport System Plan (NASP), 18
  Planning Grant Program (PGP), 17
  user charge/trust-fund approach, 17
Airport and Airway Improvement Act of 1982, 23-25, 44, 50
Airport and Airway Safety and Capacity Expansion Act of 1987, 24
airport authorities, organization and administration, 295
airport capacity and delays (*see* capacity management; delay management)
Airport Development Aid Program (ADAP), 17-20, 26, 47, 49, 64, 74
airport director's role, organization and administration, 297-298
Airport Improvement Program (AIP), 23, 26, 29, 30, 44, 48, 49, 50, 64
airport management careers, 306-313
  duties and responsibilities, 307-308
  education and training, 308-309
  public relations, 309-313
airport operations, 317-348, 479-486
  bird hazards, 332-333
  buildings and facilities for airport-operations, 156

  crash, fire and rescue equipment and personnel, 333-338
  ground-support equipment, 341-346
  pavement maintenance, 318-324
  safety inspection program, 329-332
  security services, 338-341
  snow removal, 324-329
  study-guide questions, 479-486
Airport Operators Council International (AOCI), 55
airport premises liability insurance, 357-358
airport relations (*see* public relations)
airport surface detection equipment (ASDE), 241-242
airport system planning, 35-60, 415-418
  activity, services, investment in airports, 38-39
  ADAP, 47, 49
  Airport Improvement Program (AIP), 44, 48, 49, 50, 64
  air travel, current estimates, 38-39, 59
  Airport and Airway Improvement Act of 1982, 50, 75
  Alaska, 41
  basic utility (BU) airports, 43
  civil vs. military airports, 37-38
  classification of airports, 40-44
  commercial service airports, 40
  current issues in airport-system development, 47-54
  defederalization of airports, 49-51
  delay, access problems, 48-49
  deregulation of airlines, 51-53
  economic impact of airports on local economies, 44-47
  environmental concerns (*see also* noise abatement), 53-54
  federal policy and strategy, 47-51
  funding issues, 49
  general aviation airports, 42-43
  general utility (GU) airports, 43
  hub airports, 41
  information sources for airports, 54-59
  international airports, 41-42
  itinerant operations, 43-44
  joint-use airports, 37-38
  landing areas, U.S., 39
  local operations, 43
  management issues, 51-53
  military vs. civil airports, 37-38
  NASP, 40
  noise abatement, 53-54

airport system planning (*cont.*)
  NPIAS, 36, 37, 40, 54
  organizations and associations, 54-59
  ownership of airports, 36-37
  planning issues, 54
  primary airports, 40
  private airports, 38
  reliever airports, 43-44
  scheduled-services airports, 40
  size of present-day airport system, 36-37
  slots, slot allocations, 52-53
  study guide questions, 415-418
airport use agreements, 278-279
airports, history and development, 3-33, 401-407
airside facilities, 113-114, 137
airspace capacity, requirements/site selection, 95
airspace-use technology (*see also* air traffic control; radar), 227-223
  convergent runways, 228
  dependent parallel runways, 228-229
  independent parallel runways, 230
  instrument meteorological conditions (IMC), 227
  lateral separation reduction, 228-231
  longitudinal separation reduction, 231-232
  National Airspace Review (NAR), 227
  small-aircraft-only runways, 232-233
  triple parallel runways, 230-231
  visual meteorological conditions (VMC), 227
Airways Modernization Act of 1957, 14-15
Alaskan airport system, 41
American Association of Airport Executives (AAAE), 56
approach zone requirements, 130-132
apron and gate facility technological improvements, 244-245
Army Air Corps, World War II, 10
assistant director's role, organization and administration, 298, 300, 303
automated radar terminal system (ARTS II), 224
Aviation Distributors and Manufacturers Association (ADMA), 56
Aviation Safety and Noise Abatement Act of 1979, 23, 32
Aviation/Space Writers Association (AWA), 56

B

baggage handling
  automation systems, 256
  ground-support equipment, 341-346
  terminal building facilities design, 166-167

balanced-use concept to reduce delays, 201-202
based-aircraft capacity, forecasting airport needs, 92
basic data table, layout of airport, 112
basic utility (BU) airports, 43
bird hazards, 332-333
bonds, financial planning, 179
  defaults, 185
  general-obligation bonds, 179
  interest costs, 184
  market for airport bonds, 181-182
  municipal bonds, 181-185
  ratings, 182-184
  revenue bonds, 180
  self-liquidating general-obligation bonds, 179-180
Boyde, Alan S., 15
break-even amounts, financial planning, 176
budgeting, financial management, 276-278
buildings and facilities chief's role, organization
  and administration, 303-304
buildings (*see* terminal building design)
Bureau of Air Commerce established, 8
busy-hour operations capacity, forecasting airport needs, 93

C

capacity management (*see also* delay management), 189-213, 447-455
  air carrier capacity needs, 88
  air traffic control, 195
  aircraft operations capacity needs, 90-92
  airfield capacity requirements, 95
  airfield characteristics, 194-195
  airspace capacity requirements, 95
  airspace characteristics, 195
  based-aircraft capacity needs, 92
  busy-hour operations capacity needs, 93
  capacity defined, 191-192
  cargo-handling capacity requirements, 90
  commuter-airline capacity needs, 88-89
  congestion, 191
  demand characteristics, 196
  demand/capacity analysis, 94-96
  enplaning-passengers capacity needs, 89-90
  factors affecting capacity, 194-196
  general-aviation capacity requirements, 89
  ground-access capacity requirements, 95
  itinerant operations capacity requirements, 91

  lack of capacity factors, 190
  local operations capacity requirements, 90-91
  meteorological conditions, 195-196
  military-use capacity requirements, 89
  practical capacities, PHOCAP and PANCAP, 192
  study-guide questions, 447-455
  terminal-area capacity requirements, 95
  throughput concepts, 191-192
careers in airport management (*see* airport management careers)
cargo hauling
  current estimates, 27-28
  forecasting airport needs, 90
causal modeling, forecasting airport needs, 87
centralized passenger processing approach, terminal building design, 144
chief accountant's role, organization and administration, 298-299
chief of airside operations' role, 301-302
chief of landside operations' role, 302
Civil Aeronautics Act of 1938, 8-9, 10
Civil Aeronautics Administration (CAA) established, 9
Civil Aeronautics Authority (CAA) established, 9
Civil Aeronautics Board (CAB) established, 9
Civil Air Patrol (CAP), 56
civil airport users, demand-forecasting, 88-89
civil vs. military airports, 37-38
classification of airports, 40-44
clear zone requirements, 99, 130-132
closed runways, 119
commercial service airports, 40
commuter-airline capacity, forecasting airport needs, 88-89
compensatory approach to financial management, 280-282
concessions and concessionaires, 285, 287
  public relations, 353-355
conflict alerts, 224
congestion, airport capacity and delays, 191
Contract Air Mail Act of 1925 (Kelly Act), 7
contracts, financial management, 290
control technology (*see* air traffic control)
convergent runways, 228
crash/fire/rescue services, 333-338
  chief's role, organization and administration, 303
  extinguishing agents, 336-338

response times, 334-336
training of personnel, 338
vehicles required, 334-336
Curtis, Edward P., 13
customs accelerated passenger inspection service (CAPIS), 258

D

data table, layout of airport, 112
debt service coverage, financial management, 279
decentralized passenger processing approach, terminal building design, 145
decision height, ILS, 122
defaults, bonds and financing, 185, 186
defederalization of airports and airways, 23, 49-51
delay management (*see also* capacity management), 189-213, 447-455
access problems, 29, 48-49
administrative management to reduce delays, 198-199
air traffic control factors, 195, 212
airfield characteristics factors, 194-195
airspace characteristics factors, 195
balanced-use concepts to reduce delays, 201
congestion, 191
delays defined, 190, 192-194
demand characteristics, 196
demand management to reduce delays, 198, 205-212
deregulation and slot allocation, 210
differential pricing schemes to reduce delays, 206
diversion of traffic, 199-201
factors affecting capacity and delay, 194-196, 210
lack of capacity factors, 190
measuring delays, 196-198
meteorological conditions, 195-196
NASCOM information, 196-198
OSEM information, 197
Performance Measurement System (PMS), 197
practical capacities, PHOCAP and PANCAP, 192
quota systems to reduce delays, 203-204
reducing delays, 198-212
rehubbing to reduce delays, 204-205
restrictions on aircraft type to reduce delays, 202
SDRS information, 197
slot auctions to reduce delays, 209-210
study-guide questions, 447-455
technological improvements to reduce delays, 251-258

throughput concepts, 191-192
demand characteristics, capacity and delay factors, 196, 212
demand management to reduce delays, 198
demand/capacity analysis, requirements/site selection, 94-96
Department of Transportation established, 1966, 15-16
dependent parallel runways, 228-229
depreciable investments, financial planning, 176-177, 276
deregulation of airlines, 22, 51-53, 60, 210
financial management affected, 289-291
design volume, terminal building design, 165
Development of Landing Areas for National Defense (DLAND), 9-10
differential pricing to reduce delays, 206-209
displaced-threshold runways, 117, 118
diverting traffic to reduce delays, 199-201
Doppler radar, 235
dual-lane runways, 116
dynamic hydroplaning, 323

E

economic impact of airports on local economies, 44-47, 59, 83-85, 103
enplaning of passengers capacity, forecasting airport needs, 89-90
environmental concerns (*see also* noise abatement), 68, 96-99
air pollution, 97
environmental-value preservation, 97
federal environmental policy, 98
National Environmental Policy Act of 1969, 96, 98-99
water pollution, 97-98, 97
estimating costs, financial planning, 175-176
expense accounting, 177, 275-276
Experimental Aircraft Association (EAA), 57
extinguishing agents, fires, 336-338

F

facilities chief's role, organization and administration, 299
FAR Part 77, obstruction clearance, 130-132
federal aid (*see* financial management; financial planning; history of air travel and airports)
Federal Airport Act of 1946, 10-12
Federal Aviation Act of 1958, 13-15
Federal Aviation Administration (FAA) established, 16

Federal Aviation Agency (FAA) established, 15
Federal Inspection Service (FIS), 258
federal policy and strategy, airport system, 47-51
financial management, 271-292, 466-473
airport accounting, 272-276
airport use agreements, 278-279
approaches to financial management at commercial airports, 278
appropriations methods, 277-278
budgeting, 276-278
compensatory approach, 280-282
concessions, terminal area concessionaires, 285, 287
contracts, 290
debt service coverage, 279
deregulation's effect on financial management, 289-291
fuel flowage fees, 284
landing fees, 286
leased areas, pricing guidelines, 287-288
majority-in-interest clauses, 282-283
operating revenues, 288-289
planning processes, 276-278
pricing of facilities and services, 283-289
residual-cost approach, 279-280, 281-282
revenue maximization, 291
study-guide questions, 466-473
term-of-use agreements, 283
variances, budgets vs. actual expenditures and revenues, 277
zero-base budgets, 278
financial planning, 173-186, 276-278, 442-447
bonds, general-obligations, 179
bonds, municipal bonds, 181-185
bonds, revenue bonds, 180
bonds, self-liquidating general-obligation bonds, 179-180
break-even amounts, 176
depreciable investments, 176-177
economic evaluations, 174-179
estimates of cost, 175-176
expenses of administration, operation, etc., 177
grants, federal and state, 180
methods of financing, 179-185
nondepreciable investments, 176
O'Hare Agreement, 181
private financing, 180
revenue potential, 177-178
study-guide questions, 442-447
fires (*see* crash/fire/rescue services)
flight interface facilities, passenger-handling systems, 155-156
Flight Safety Foundation (FSS), 57

forecasting airport needs (*see also* capacity management), 86-94
air carrier capacity, 88
aircraft mix ratios, 94
aircraft operations capacity, 90-92
aviation-demand forecasting, 88
based-aircraft capacity, 92
busy-hour operations, 93
causal models, 87
civil airport users, demand-forecasting, 88-89
commuter capacity, 88-89
enplaning of air cargo requirements, 90
enplaning of passengers requirements, 89-90
general aviation capacity, 89
itinerant operations capacity, 91
judgmental forecasting, 88
local operations capacity, 90-91
methods of forecasting, 87-88
military use, 89
operational activity forecasts, 89-94
time-series analysis, 87
trend extension, 87
fuel flowage fees, 284
fueling areas, safety inspection procedures, 331-332
funding issues (*see* financial management; financial planning)

G

gate arrival concept, terminal building design, 145-147
general aviation airports, 42-43
forecasting airport needs, 89
public relations issues, 355-356
General Aviation Manufacturers Association (GAMA), 57
general utility (GU) airports, 43
general-obligation bonds, financial planning, 179
glideslope transmitter, ILS, 122
government agency facilities, terminal area plans, 156
government funding (*see* financial management; financial planning; history of air travel and airports)
grants, federal and state, financial planning, 180
Great Depression and airport development, 8
Civil Works Administration, FERA, 8
Works Progress Administration (WPA), 8
ground control areas, 125
lineman signals, 128
ground-access capacity, requirements/site selection, 95
ground-support equipment, 341-346
grounds chief's role, organization and administration, 304

growth management, 187-268
airport-capacity and delays, 189-213
technological improvements, airside, 215-247
technological improvements, landside, 249-268
guidance technology improvements, airside, 220

H

Harding Committee, 1958, 13
Harding, William B., 13
height and hazard zoning, land-use plans, 134
Helicopter Association International (HAI), 57
heliports, 119, 120
history of air travel and airports, 3-33, 401-407
accidents, 14
Aeronautics Branch of the Department of Commerce, 8
Air Commerce Act of 1926, 7
air travel, current estimates, revenue, 26
Airline Deregulation Act of 1978, 22
airmail service, 5, 7
Airport and Airway Development Act of, 16, 23, 26, 29, 44, 86
Airport and Airway Safety and Capacity, 24
Airport Development Aid Program (ADAP, 19, 26
Airport Improvement Program (AIP), 23, 26, 29, 30, 44, 48, 49, 50, 64
Airways Modernization Act of 1957, 14
Army Air Corps expansion, World War II, 10
assessment of federal airport policies, 25
Aviation Safety and Noise Abatement Act, 23
Bureau of Air Commerce established, 8
cargo hauling, current estimates, 27-28
Civil Aeronautics act of 1938, 8-9
Civil Aeronautics Administration (CAA), 9
Civil Aeronautics Authority (CAA) established, 9
Civil Aeronautics Board (CAB) established, 9
Contract Air Mail Act of 1925 (Kelly Act), 7
criticism of federal policies, 29-31
Curtis Committee, 13
defederalization of airports, airways, 23
Department of Transportation established, 15

deregulation of airlines, 22
Development of Landing Areas for National Defense (DLAND), 9
Federal Airport Act of 1946, 10-13
Federal Aviation Act of 1958, 13-15
Federal Aviation Administration (FAA), 16
Federal Aviation Agency (FAA) established, 15
formative period, 5
Great Depression, 8
Harding Committee, 1958, 13
National Airport Plan established, 9-10
National Airport System Plan (NASP), 18
National Plan of Integrated Airport System (NPIAS), 24, 30
National Transportation Safety Board (NTSB), 16
new-airport development, 28-29
noise abatement programs, 22-23
postwar federal aid to airports, 12-16
regulation of aircraft, airways, 7-8
safety regulations, 14, 25
study-guide questions, 401-407
user charge/trust fund approach to federal funding, 17
World War II developments, 9-12
holding areas, 125, 126
holding bays, 125, 126
hub airports, 41
hydroplaning prevention, 323

I

"imaginary surfaces," obstruction clearance, 130-132
independent parallel runways, 230
information sources, airports, 54-59
instrument landing system (ILS), 120, 122-123
decision height, 122
glideslope transmitter, 122
localizer beacon, 122
microwave landing system (MLS), 122
middle marker, 122
outer marker, 122
instrument meteorological conditions (IMC), 196, 227
insurance, liability insurance, 356-358
International Air Transport Association (IATA), 57
international airports, 41-42
International Civil Airports Association (ICAA), 57
International Civil Aviation Organization (ICAO), 58
intersecting runways, 116-117
itinerant operations, 43-44
forecasting airport needs, 91

J

joint automated weather observation system (JAWOS), 235
joint-use airports, 37-38
judgmental forecasting, forecasting airport needs, 88

K

Kelly Act (Contract Air Mail Act of 1925), 7

L

land-use plans, 107-109, 132-135, 427-433
 height and hazard zoning, 134
 land use zoning, 134
 on-airport land use, 133-134
 study-guide questions, 427-433
 subdivision regulations, 134
 surround-area land use, 134
landing areas, U.S., 39
landing fees, 286
landside facilities, 113, 141
layout of airport, 107-132, 427-433
 airside facilities, 113-114
 approach zone requirements, 130-132
 basic data table, 112
 clear zone requirements, 130-132
 components of airports, 112-129
 drawing the layout, 109-112
 ground control areas, 125
 holding areas, 125, 126
 holding bays, 125, 126
 "imaginary surfaces," obstruction clearance, 130-132
 instrument landing system (ILS), 120, 122-123
 landside facilities, 113
 lighting for runways, 120-121
 location map, 112
 microwave landing system (MLS), 122
 obstruction clearance, FAR Part 77, 130-132
 parking areas, 125, 127-129
 report on the airport layout plan, 129
 runways, 115-120
 study-guide questions, 427-433
 taxiways, 124
 vicinity map, 112
 wind information, wind rose, 112
leased areas
 pricing guidelines, 287-288
 revenues, 274
liability insurance, 356-358
lighting systems, 120-121
lineman signals, 128
local-level system planning, 71-73
local operations, 43
 forecasting airport needs, 90-91
localizer beacon, ILS, 122

location map, layout of airport, 112
low level wind shear alert system (LLWSAS), 234-235

M

majority-in-interest clauses, financial management, 282-283
management (*see* airport management careers; organization and administration)
management/airport operations facilities, terminal area plans, 156
master plans, 71-73
 coordination of efforts, 72-73
 objectives and goals, 72
 planning airport system, 63
maximization of revenues, financial management, 291
meteorological conditions
 airside technology, 233-236
 capacity and delay factors, 195, 212
 Doppler radar, 235
 hydroplaning prevention, 323
 instrument meteorological conditions (IMC), 196, 227
 joint automated weather observation system (JAWOS), 235
 NEXRAD, 235
 snow and ice removal, 324-329
 visual meteorological conditions (VMC), 196, 227
 wake vortex/wake turbulence, 233-234
 water removal, surface friction, 322-324
 wind shear, 234-236
metering, 225
microwave landing system (MLS), 122, 220-223
middle marker, ILS, 122
military airports, 37-38
 forecasting airport needs, 89
mobile lounge/transporter, terminal building design, 149-150
Mode S data links, 226
moving-target detection systems, radar, 225
municipal bonds, financial planning, 181-185
municipally operated airports, organization and administration, 294-295

N

National Air Transportation Association (NATA), 58
National Airport Plan established, 9-12
National Airport System Plan (NASP), 18, 40
National Airspace Command Center (NASCOM), delay reporting, 196-198
National Airspace Review (NAR), 227

National Association of State Aviation Officials (NASAO), 58, 68
National Business Aircraft Association (NBAA), 58
National Environmental Policy Act of 1969, 96, 98-99
National Plan of Integrated Airport Systems (NPIAS), 24-25, 30, 36, 37, 40, 54, 63-66, 70-71
 criteria for airport inclusion in NPIAS, 66
 levels-of-need concept, 65
National Transportation Safety Board (NTSB) established, 16
NEXRAD, 235
noise abatement (*see also* environmental concerns), 22-23, 53-54, 68, 96-97, 102, 104, 236-240
 aircraft noise components, 236-237
 aircraft operating procedures to reduce noise, 239-240
 airframe noise reduction technology, 238-239
 engine noise reduction technology, 237-238
 Federal rules and responsibilities, 359-360
 land-uses vs. noise, 361-362
 local programs, 362-365
 public relations, 358-365
nondepreciable investments, financial planning, 176
nonoperating expenses, 276
nonprecision instrument runways, 117, 118

O

O'Hare Agreement, financial planning, 181
obstruction clearance requirements, FAR Part 77, 130-132
Office of Systems Engineering Management (FAA), OSEM, delay reporting, 197
open-v runways, 116
operating expenses, 275-276
operating revenues, 288-289
operational activity forecasts, 89-94
organization and administration, 293-315, 473-479
 airport authorities, 295
 airport director's role, 297-298
 assistant directors' role, 298, 300, 303
 buildings and facilities chief's role, 303-304
 careers in airport management, 306-313
 chief accountant's role, 298-299
 chief of airside operations' role, 301-302
 chief of landside operations' role, 302

organization and administration (*cont.*)
  chief purchasing agent's role, 299
  crash, fire, rescue chief's role, 303
  facilities chief's role, 299
  grounds chief's role, 304
  manager of community relations role, 299-300
  municipally operated airports, 294-295
  organization chart for airport management, 296
  ownership of airports, 294-296
  personnel manager's role, 298
  port authorities, 295
  security chief's role, 302-303
  state-operated airports, 296
  study-guide questions, 473-479
  transition of control, 295-296
  vehicle chief's role, 305
organization chart for airport (*see* organization and administration
organizations and associations, 54-59
outer marker, ILS, 122
ownership of airports, 36-37, 294-296

P

parallel runways, 116
parking areas, aircraft, 125, 127-129
  lineman signals, 128
  remote aircraft parking, terminal building design, 149
parking areas, vehicular, 169, 171
passenger movers, 253-254
passenger-handling systems, 153-156
  access/egress facilities, 153
  access/processing interface, 153-154
  flight interface facilities, 155-156
  ground-support equipment, 341-346
  passenger processing facilities, 154-155
pavement maintenance, 318-324
  contaminant removal techniques, 324
  grooved pavements, 323
  runway pavements, 319-320
  surface friction and water removal, runways, 322-342
  testing pavement materials, 321-322
  vibratory (dynamic) testing, 321-322
peak-hour passenger volume, terminal building design, 165
Performance Measurement System (PMS), delay reporting, 197
personnel manager's role, organization and administration, 298
pier finger design, terminal building design, 147
planning airport system, 61-76
  ADAP, 64, 74
  Airport Improvement Program (AIP), 64

Airport and Airway Improvement Act of 1982, 75
  environmental concerns, 68
  integration needed among plans and planners, 74-75
  local level planning, 71-73
  master plans, 63, 71-73
  national-level planning process, 64-66
  noise abatement, 68
  NPIAS, 63-66, 70-71
  regional planning, 63, 66-68
  state aviation system plans (SASP), 69, 75
  state-level planning, 68-70
Planning Grant Program (PGP), 17, 32
pollution (*see* environmental concerns; noise abatement)
port authorities, organization and administration, 295
precision instrument runways, 117, 118
pricing facilities and services, 283-289
  airfield area pricing, 284-285
  concessions and concessionaires, 285, 287
  differential pricing to reduce delays, 206-209
  fuel flowage fees, 284
  landing fees, 286
  leased areas, 287-288
  variation in source of operating revenues, 288, 289
primary airports, 40
private airports, 38
private financing, 180
Professional Aviation Maintenance Association (PAMA), 58
public relations, 308-313, 349-366, 486-492
  airport-airline relations, 350-353
  airport-as-landlord concepts, 350-356
  airport-general aviation relations, 355-356
  concessions and concessionaires, 353-355
  liability insurance, 356-358
  manager of community relations role, 299-300
  noise and noise abatement, 358-365
  study-guide questions, 486-492
purchasing agent's role, organization and administration, 299

Q

Quesada, Elwood R., 14
quota systems to reduce delays, 203-204

R

radar
  air traffic control radar beacon system (ATCRBS), 223-224

automated radar terminal system (ARTS II), 224
  conflict alerts, 224
  Doppler radar, 235
  moving-target detection systems, 225
  NEXRAD, 235
  primary and secondary radar, 223
  radar beacon system, 223
  search radar, 223
  surveillance radar, 223-225
  transponders, 224
Regional Airline Association (RAA), 58
regional system planning, 63, 66-68
rehubbing to reduce delays, 204-205
reliever airports, 43-44
relocated threshold runways, 117, 118
remote aircraft parking concepts, terminal building design, 149
remote satellite designs, terminal building design, 148
requirements/site selection, 79-105, 418-427
  aeronautical activity amounts, 83
  air-carrier capacity, 88
  aircraft mix ratios, 94
  aircraft operations capacity, 90-92
  airfield capacity, 95
  Airport and Airway Development Act of 1970, 86
  airspace capacity, 95
  airspace structure, existing facilities, 82
  based-aircraft capacity, 92
  busy-hour operations capacity, 93
  capacity analysis, 95
  cargo-handling capacity, 90
  clear zone requirements, 99
  community-value impact, 85
  commuter-airline capacity, 88-89
  competitive advantage considerations, 84-85
  convenience factors, 102
  cost of construction considerations, 102-103
  demand/capacity analysis, 94-96
  demographic considerations, 84
  enplaning of passengers requirements, 89-90
  environmental impact concerns, 96-99
  expansion capability, 99-100
  forecasting needs, 86-94
  general-aviation capacity, 89
  geographic considerations, 84
  ground-access capacity, 95
  historical review of existing facilities, 81-82
  inventorying existing facilities, 81-86
  itinerant operations capacity, 91
  local operations capacity, 90-91
  master plans, 103
  meteorological site conditions, 102

military-use capacity, 89
National Environmental Policy Act of 1969, 96, 98-99
Navaids, existing facilities, 82
noise abatement, 96-97, 102
operational activity forecasts, 89-94, 94-95
political considerations, 85
related-lands use, 82-83
site-selection processes, 99-103
sociological considerations, 85
socioeconomic factors, 83-85
study-guide questions, 418-427
terminal area capacity, 95
utility availability, 102
rescue (*see* crash/fire/rescue services)
residual-cost approach to financial management, 279-280, 281-282
restricted access to reduce delays, 202-203
revenue bonds, financial planning, 180
revenue potential, financial planning, 177-178
revenues
  leased-area revenues, 274-275
  maximization of revenues, 291
  nonoperating revenues, 275
  operating revenues, 274-275, 288-289
runway occupancy time (ROT), 242
runways and runway management, 115-120
  apron/gate facilities technology, 244-245
  classification of runways, 117
  close, intermediate, far runways, 116
  closed runways, 119
  configuration management, 226
  convergent runways, 228
  dependent parallel runways, 228-229
  displaced-threshold runways, 117, 118
  dual-lane runways, 116
  grooved-pavement, 323
  heliports, 119, 120
  hydroplaning prevention, 323
  independent parallel runways, 230
  instrument landing systems (ILS), 120, 122-123
  intersecting runways, 116-117
  lighting , 120-121
  longitudinal separation reduction, 231-232
  markings for runways, 117
  microwave landing system (MLS), 122, 220-223
  nonprecision instrument runways, 117, 118
  open-v runways, 116
  parallel runways, 116
  pavement maintenance, 318-324
  precision instrument runways, 117, 118

reduced lateral separation techniques, 228-231
relocated threshold runways, 117, 118
runway occupancy time (ROT), 242
safety inspection program, 329-332
single runways, 116
small-aircraft-only runways, 232-233
snow and ice removal, 324-329
surface friction, water removal, 322-324
taxiway-utilization technology, 242-244
taxiways, 124
triple parallel runways, 230-231
visual runways, 117, 118

S

safety inspection program, 329-332
safety regulations, 14, 25
satellite terminal design, terminal building design, 148-149
scheduled-services airports, 40
security services, 338-341
  customs accelerated passenger inspection service (CAPIS), 258
  Federal Inspection Service (FIS), 258
  screening passengers, 258
  security chief's role, organization and administration, 302-303
  X-ray machines, 339-341
self-liquidating general-obligation bonds, 179-180
separation of aircraft
  lateral separation reduction, 228-231
  longitudinal separation reduction, 231-232
sequencing of aircraft, 225
signals, lineman signals, 128
site selection (*see* requirements/site selection)
slot allocation, 52-53, 209-210
snow and ice removal, 324-329
space requirements for terminal area and buildings, 162-166
spacing aircraft, 225
Standard Air Carrier Delay Reporting System (SDRS), delay reporting, 197
state airport system planning, 68-70
state aviation system plans (SASP), 69
state-operated airports, organization and administration, 296
study guide, 401-492
subdivision regulations, land-use plans, 134
surveillance radar, 223-225
surveillance technology (*see also* radar), 220
  airport surface detection equip (ASDE), 241
  tower automated ground surveillance

system (TAGS), 242

T

taxiways, 124
technological improvements, airside, 242-244
technological improvements, airside, 215-247, 455-461
  advanced en route automation (AERA), 226
  airport surface detection equipment (ASDE), 241-242
  airport surface utilization, 240-245
  airport technology, 218-220
  airspace technology, 218-220
  airspace use technology, 227-223
  apron and gate facility technology, 244-245
  automated radar terminal system (ARTS II), 224
  conflict alerts, radar surveillance, 224
  control technology, 220
  Doppler radar or NEXRAD, 235
  guidance technology, 220
  joint automated weather observation system (JAWOS), 235
  low level wind shear alert system (LLWSAS), 234-235
  meteorological conditions, 233-236
  metering, 225
  microwave landing system (MLS), 220-223
  Mode S data links, 226
  moving-target detection systems, 225
  noise abatement technology, 236-240
  runway configuration management, 226
  runway occupancy time (ROT) factors, 242
  sequencing, 225
  spacing, 225
  study-guide questions, 455-461
  surveillance radar systems, 223-225
  surveillance technology, 220
  taxiway technology, 242-244
  tower automated ground surveillance system (TAGS), 242
  traffic management techniques, 225-227
  transponders, 224
  vortex advisory system (VAS), 233-234
technological improvements, landside, 249-268, 461-466
  access-improvement technology, 259-264
  airport-grounds access, 262-264
  application of technology to airport problems, 264-267
  baggage handling automation, 256
  customs accelerated passenger inspec-

technological improvements, landslide (*cont.*)
  tion service (CAPIS), 258
Federal Inspection Service (FIS), 258
passenger movers, 253-254
security screening, 258
study-guide questions, 461-466
terminal curbfront design improvements, 261-262
terminal facilities and services, 251-258
ticketing systems, computerized, 254-255
term-of-use agreements, financial management, 283
terminal area capacity, requirements/site selection, 95
terminal area plans, 139-171, 433-441
  aircraft movement through area, 144
  airport operations/management facilities, 156
  airport-operations factors in layout, 143-144
  baggage handling facilities, 166-167
  buildings, terminal design (*see* terminal building design)
  centralized passenger processing approach, 144
  decentralized passenger processing approach, 145
  domestic passenger flow, 157
  factors affecting terminal area layout, 143
  government-agency facilities, 156
  international passenger flow, 159
  passenger flow through terminal, 156-162
  passenger-handling systems (*see also* passenger-handling systems), 153-156
  passengers, flow of passengers

    through area, 143
  planning for terminal area layout, 142
  safety factors, 144
  space requirements, 162-166
  study-guide questions, 433-441
  terminal area defined, 141
  transfer-passenger flow, 159
  typical peak-hour passenger volume or design volume, 165
  vehicles, flow of vehicles through area, 143
  vertical distribution of passenger flow, 159, 161, 162
terminal building design, 144-153
  baggage handling facilities, 166-167
  buildings and facilities chief's role, 303-304
  centralized passenger processing, 144
  curbfront design improvements, 261-262
  decentralized passenger processing, 145
  gate arrival concept, 145-147
  linear or curvilinear design, 146-147
  mobile lounge or transporter design, 149-150
  over- or under-estimation of volume, 151, 153
  pier finger design, 147
  remote aircraft parking concepts, 149
  remote satellite designs, 148
  safety inspection procedures, 332
  satellite terminals, 148-149
  space requirements, 162-166
  typical peak-hour passenger volume or design volume, 165
throughput, airport capacity and delays, 191-192
ticketing systems, computerized, 254-255

time-series analysis, forecasting airport needs, 87
tower automated ground surveillance system (TAGS), 242
traffic management systems (TMS), 226-227
transponders, 224
trend extension, forecasting airport needs, 87
triple parallel runways, 230-231

V

vehicle chief's role, organization and administration, 305
vibratory (dynamic) testing of pavements, 321-322
vicinity map, layout of airport, 112
viscous hydroplaning, 323
visual meteorological conditions (VMC), 196, 227
visual runways, 117, 118
vortex advisory system (VAS), 233-234

W

wake vortex/wake turbulence, 233-234
water pollution (*see* environmental concerns)
weather (*see* meteorological conditions)
wind information, layout of airport, 112
wind shear, 234-236
World Aviation Directory, 55
World War II developments in airport, airways, 9-12
Wright brothers, 5

Z

zero-base budgets, financial management, 278
zoning regulations, land-use plans, 134